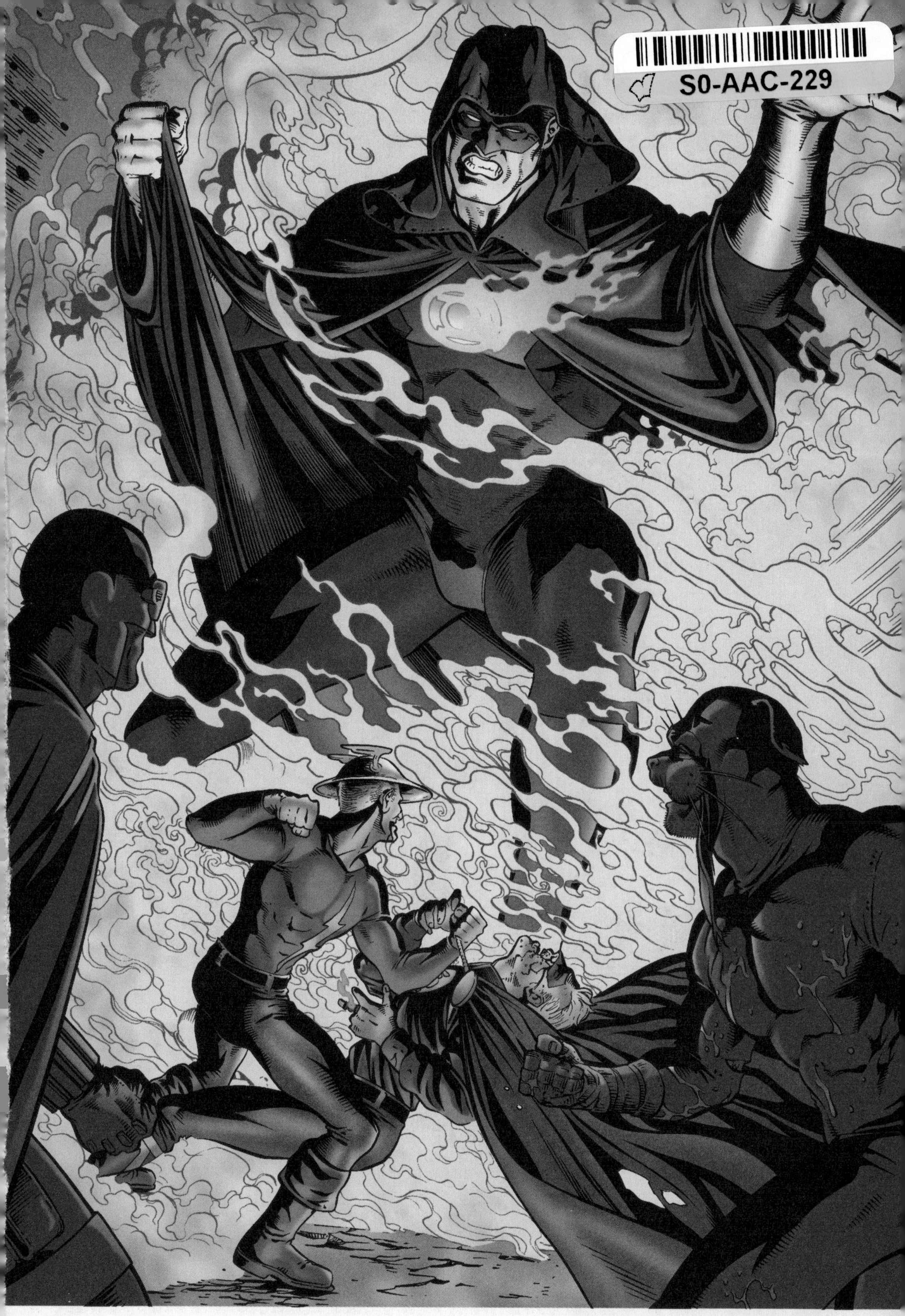



# JSA LOST

Dan DiDio VP-Executive Editor   Peter Tomasi Editor-original series   Stephen Wacker Associate Editor-original series   Robert Greenberger Senior Editor-collected edition   Robbin Brosterman Senior Art Director
Paul Levitz President & Publisher   Georg Brewer VP-Design & DC Direct Creative   Richard Bruning Senior VP-Creative Director   Patrick Caldon Senior VP-Finance & Operations   Chris Caramalis
VP-Finance   Terri Cunningham VP-Managing Editor   Stephanie Fierman Senior VP-Sales & Marketing   Alison Gill VP-Manufacturing   Rich Johnson VP-Book Trade Sales   Hank Kanalz VP-General Manager,
WildStorm   Lillian Laserson Senior VP & General Counsel   Jim Lee Editorial Director-WildStorm   Paula Lowitt Senior VP-Business & Legal Affairs   David McKillips VP-Advertising & Custom Publishing
John Nee VP-Business Development   Gregory Noveck Senior VP-Creative Affairs   Cheryl Rubin Senior VP-Brand Management   Jeff Trojan VP-Business Development, DC Direct   Bob Wayne VP-Sales

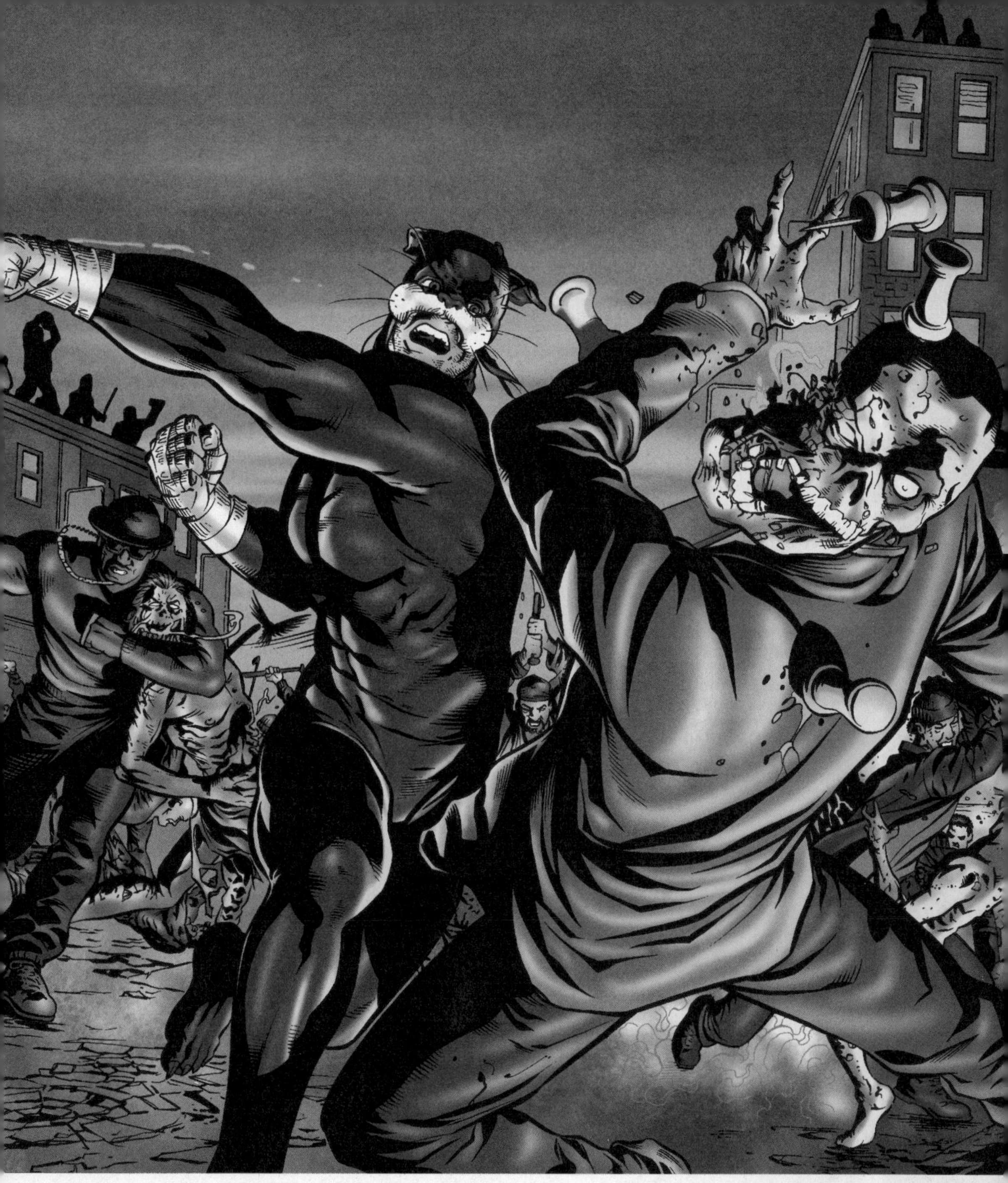

# JSA LOST

GEOFF JOHNS WRITER DAVE GIBBONS PAGES 181-199 DON KRAMER PAGES 32-50, 54-72, 76-94, 140-179 TOM MANDRAKE PAGES 29-31, 51-53, 73-75 JERRY ORDWAY PAGES 95-138 SEAN PHILLIPS PAGES 7-28 PENCILLERS KEITH CHAMPAGNE PAGES 32-50, 54-72, 76-94, 140-179 WAYNE FAUCHER PAGES 95-116 JAMES HODGKINS PAGES 181-199 TOM MANDRAKE PAGES 29-31, 51-53, 73-75 SEAN PHILLIPS PAGES 7-28 PRENTIS ROLLINS PAGES 117-138 INKERS JOHN KALISZ PAGES 140-199 HI-FI PAGES 7-138 COLORISTS JARED K. FLETCHER PAGES 7-28, 51-94 ROB LEIGH PAGES 29-50, 140-161 KEN LOPEZ 95-138, 163-199 LETTERERS ETHAN VAN SCIVER JH WILLIAMS ORIGINAL COVERS

There has always been a need for heroes. In the dawning days of World War II, America produced a generation of heroes the likes of which had never before been seen. The mightiest of them banded together to protect the innocent as the Justice Society of America. For a decade they fought the good fight, retiring from the public spotlight when their day had passed.

But now the need for heroes has never been greater. So the JSA lives once more, led by the survivors of the original team who are training a new generation of crime-fighters. Under their elders' guidance, these younger heroes not only learn how to harness their power but also come to understand who paved their way and the tremendous legacy that they have inherited.

Since its re-formation, the JSA has rediscovered old friends, fought familiar enemies, and buried some of their comrades. The team has also reestablished its roots in New York City, with their headquarters doubling as meeting place and museum open to the public.

A look at the key events since the team has regrouped:

## IN RECENT TIMES

The Spectre convinces the suicidal Michael Holt to answer a higher call and take the role of Mister Terrific (THE SPECTRE [*third series*] #54).

In the 853rd century, various heroes meet the ultimate extension of Rex Tyler, an android "Master of Time" called Hourman (JLA: ROCK OF AGES).

The Flash, Sentinel, Starman and Wildcat pay their respects to the Spectre before his human aspect, Jim Corrigan, is accepted into Heaven (THE SPECTRE [*third series*] #62).

After a visit to the 20th century (JLA ONE MILLION), the 853rd century's Hourman begins an extended stay in the present (JLA: WORLD WAR III).

No longer capable of controlling the green magic within him, Sentinel expels most of it from his body, losing his newfound youth in the process (GREEN LANTERN [*third series*] #110).

The Flash, Sentinel and Wildcat meet the new Hourman and reunite with Hippolyta to help the Justice League fight an invasion from the Fifth Dimension. In the course of the battle, they succeed in reviving the Spectre and meet J.J. Thunder, the latest master of the Thunderbolt (JLA: WORLD WAR III).

Blinded as the result of an attempt on his life, physician Pieter Cross takes the persona of Doctor Mid-Nite (DOCTOR MID-NITE).

Pat (Stripesy) Dugan's stepdaughter, Courtney Whitmore, lays claim to Sylvester Pemberton's cosmic belt and becomes the new Star-Spangled Kid, forcing Pat to accompany her in the robotic form of S.T.R.I.P.E. (STARS AND S.T.R.I.P.E. #1-3).

## JSA: JUSTICE BE DONE

In Manhattan, Albert Rothstein abandons his Nuklon persona for the new identity of Atom Smasher. Meanwhile, "Speed" Saunders's granddaughter Kendra assumes the guise of Hawkgirl in Texas.

Wesley Dodds dies after a confrontation with Mordru, the Dark Lord, and past and future members of the Justice Society gather to honor the Sandman's memory. Those in attendance become embroiled in a race to prevent Mordru from seizing the reincarnated Doctor Fate for himself. In the course of the adventure, the JSA also meets the new Hawkgirl. The new Fate proves to be a reborn Hector Hall, who is offered guidance by the spirit of Kent Nelson.

With Sandy "Sand" Hawkins as leader and financier, the Justice Society decides to formally regroup. Official members are Atom-Smasher, Black Canary, the Flash, Hawkgirl, Hourman, Sand, Sentinel, the Star-Spangled Kid and Wildcat with Starman and Hippolyta as reserves.

Sand unexpectedly discovers that his long period as a sand creature has left him with the ability to transform himself into a silicon being at will. Now capable of flowing through the surface of the planet to any locale on Earth, Sand travels to Africa for his first solo outing and defeats the Geomancer, an agent of the Council.

With Earth being overrun by the dead and an evil-tainted Spectre, the JSA joins the world's heroes in seeking a solution (DAY OF JUDGMENT #1). At the gates of Heaven, Sentinel meets the spirits of the Atom, Doctor Mid-Nite, Hourman and Mister Terrific before being turned down for help by the spirit of Jim Corrigan (#2). Hal Jordan agrees to serve as a new host for the Spectre (#3), narrowly avoiding death thanks to Doctor Fate and the JSA (#4) before assuming the cloak of the ancient spirit (#5).

## JSA: DARKNESS FALLS

The new Mister Terrific is invited to visit the revived Justice Society.

As Mister Bones, now head of the Department of Extranormal Operations, watches, a press conference formally establishes the Justice Society's return and the team clashes with Black Adam.

Corrupted by Ian Karkull, Obsidian begins to spread darkness over his native Milwaukee, progressively expanding until the entire planet has been engulfed. Doctor Mid-Nite joins the JSA in fighting the threat, but the battle ultimately comes down to a clash of father and son. Sentinel expels the darkness from Earth and defeats his son, but a weakened Obsidian flees before he can be taken into custody.

Wildcat holds off an attack on JSA headquarters by the Injustice Society, now composed of Johnny Sorrow, Blackbriar Thorn, Count Vertigo, Geomancer, the Icicle, Golden Wasp and the Tigress.

Atom-Smasher's mother is killed in a plane crash caused by Kobra. Kobra incapacitates Sand and appears to execute the JSA's leader on live television. Thanks to Mid-Nite and Terrific, Sand escapes death and Maser, a teen metahuman ally, is freed while the rest of the team apprehends Kobra.

With the survival of the timestream at stake, the entire JSA takes on Extant. Using the Worlogog, Atom-Smasher causes a wrinkle in time that permits him to rescue his mother and place Extant in her place to die. At battle's end, he decides to take a leave of absence to reassess the implications of his actions as does Doctor Fate, who hopes to locate the absent Fury. Hourman resigns from the team altogether, as does Starman.

In the wake of Hourman's resignation, the JSA learns of his involvement in several questionable activities (HOURMAN #19).

Hippolyta invites Black Canary, Hawkgirl and the Star-Spangled Kid for a training session on Paradise Island. Soon after, they join a heroine named Nemesis in her war on the Council, unaware that the evil organization is allied with the Ultra-Humanite (JSA ANNUAL #1).

## JSA: THE RETURN OF HAWKMAN

Johnny Sorrow and the Injustice Society return, now including Black Adam, Shiv, the Rival and the Thinker among their ranks. Sentinel is mortally wounded by Blackbriar Thorn, and Sorrow unleashes the King of Tears before Black Adam betrays the villain and summons the Spectre. Though the Ghostly Guardian fails, Mister Terrific conceives a plan utilizing Doctor Mid-Nite, Black Adam and the Flash that enables them to banish both Sorrow and the King of Tears from the earthly plane. Elsewhere, the Spectre heals the dying Sentinel.

Doctor Fate finds a comatose Lyta Hall in the same British Columbia hospital where he was reborn.

J.J. Thunder helps the team during the Johnny Sorrow crisis before declaring that he now wants to be known as Jakeem. Frustrated by the twelve-year-old's attitude, Mister Terrific takes satisfaction in the youthful Star-Spangled Kid's upbraiding of Thunder over his lack of respect.

The resolution of the Johnny Sorrow affair catapults Jay Garrick into the distant past, where he meets Prince Khufu, Nabu and Teth-Adam in Egypt. The trio explain how they came into possession of the Thanagarian spacecraft and present Garrick with the Claw of Horus, cryptically referring to the crucial role that it and the reincarnations of Khufu and his beloved Chay-Ara will play in the defeat of an enemy "who threatens not only the world our visitors came from, but this world as well." With the Claw in tow, the Flash returns to his own time period.

Confronted by Sand over the scars on her wrists and the other secrets of her past, Hawkgirl takes to the skies. There, she meets the angel Zauriel, who reveals that Kendra's soul has "moved on" and that Shiera Hall's spirit now inhabits her body. In denial, Hawkgirl reacts violently to the JSA's offer of support and, in the midst of her struggles, vanishes in a burst of light only to find herself teleported to Thanagar. Doctor Fate reluctantly leaves his wife's side to bring the Justice Society, including a returning Atom-Smasher, to her aid.

Hawkgirl learns that Thanagar was conquered during its reconstruction by Onimar Synn, allegedly one of the planet's mythical Seven Devils. In search of their hereditary champion, the Thanagarian resistance movement uses Kendra as an "emotional beacon" to pull Carter Hall back from the dimension prison where Katar Hol was transported. The original Hawkman is successfully freed from limbo, albeit with black hair rather than blonde.

Although Kendra resists Carter's attempts to express his love for her, Hector has an emotional reunion with his father. Charging into battle, Hawkman wears the Claw of Horus, canceling out the Nth Metal worn by the Wingmen corpses in Onimar Synn's army. Using a variation on the Nth Metal's "psychic backlash," the so-called Sineater subdues the Hawks but they escape to join the JSA in defeating his underlings, Crypt and Phade. After Synn attracts all of Thanagar's Nth Metal — including the Claw of Horus — into a humanoid body for himself, Hawkman insists that he and Kendra use their influence over the ancient glove. Urging her to "believe in our destiny, believe in us," Hawkman kisses Hawkgirl and the Sineater's body is destroyed. While admitting an attraction, Kendra pulls away, reiterating that she needs "time to sort things out."

## JSA: FAIR PLAY

Black Canary, Wildcat and Nemesis raid a Council facility in Austria and discover that the Ultra-Humanite is at large.

While dreaming, Sand receives a series of cryptic warnings from the dead members of the Justice Society.

A gladiatorial match arranged by Roulette ends with the death of the current incarnation of Firebrand, and the gambler sets her sights on the Justice Society.

Alex Montez, cousin of the late second Wildcat, Yolanda Montez, is hired to be curator of the JSA Museum.

Hawkman insists that Sand not relinquish the JSA chairmanship out of deference to Hawkman's past leadership. "There's no one I *trust* more to lead this team into the future — or to teach my son how to be a hero."

Doctor Fate's efforts to revive Lyta Hall continue to meet with failure, while Hawkman's efforts at courting Kendra are similarly fruitless. Frustrated by Carter's "expectations" of her, Kendra reaches out to Sand with a kiss that Hawkman witnesses.

Black Adam's interest in joining the JSA and alleged reformation is met with skepticism and leads to a visit from Captain Marvel, who suggests that he "deserves a second chance."

The team elects Mister Terrific as its new chairman.

## JSA: STEALING THUNDER

His mind now inhabiting the body of Johnny Thunder, the Ultra-Humanite uses his Thunderbolt to reshape the world. A ragtag band including Captain Marvel, Hourman II, Power Girl, Icicle III and the mysterious Crimson Avenger helps bring about Ultra's defeat. The team also mourns the loss of Johnny Thunder, who lives on, after a fashion, as the personification of Jakeem Thunder's Thunderbolt. Afterwards, Captain Marvel and Hourman both agree to join the Justice Society.

## JSA: ALL STARS

A being calling himself Legacy targets the surviving original members of the JSA — Flash, Green Lantern, Wildcat and Sand. To prepare them for the fight, the Spectre instructs the current JSA members to revisit their emotional pain, deal with it and prevent Legacy from using it against them.

Star changes her name to Stargirl, honoring the legacies of both the Star-Spangled Kid and the original Starman.

Legacy is revealed to be the Wizard and is defeated by the JSA. He is ultimately brought down by the Spectre when he's forced to review his own past failings, such as killing his beloved younger sister Shannon in a black magic ritual. The Spectre sends the Wizard to Purgatory to deal with his sister's spirit.

## JSA: PRINCES OF DARKNESS

The Justice Society is left reeling when Mordru displaces Doctor Fate and reveals his sinister alliance with Eclipso and Obsidian. In the midst of the crisis, Kobra escapes government custody, Black Adam and Atom Smasher quit the team and the comatose "Lyta Trevor" is revealed to be Dove II, who joins the battle alongside the JSA Reserves.

Using specialized tattoos, Alex Montez imprisons Eclipso in his body, ostensibly harnessing the villain's power as his own.

The essence of the Starheart again manifests itself as a ring, which Alan Scott again takes as his own, relinquishing his Sentinel alias and once more declaring himself Green Lantern. With renewed determination, GL purges the darkness from Obsidian and Todd Rice regains his human, sane form.

With the entire Earth literally shaking apart because of the temporary shifting of the Moon's orbit, Sand spreads himself across the planet's fault lines, easing the distress but disappearing as a consequence.

On Gemworld, Power Girl helps free the spirit of Arion, which reveals to her that she is *not* of Atlantean origin before moving on to the afterlife. Elsewhere, Mordru (who had stolen Arion's body) is defeated by Doctor Fate and imprisoned within the Rock of Eternity.

Black Adam, now accompanied by Atom Smasher, Brainwave and a mutated Northwind, locates and murders Kobra.

Jesse Chambers becomes the Justice Society's business manager. Elsewhere, most of Wildcat's nine lives are exhausted when he's repeatedly gunned down by the new Crimson Avenger, who blames him for the death of Charles Durham. And in Ithaca, Black Adam destroys the Council and recruits Nemesis to join his group.

The JSA informs Ma Hunkel that the last of the Yellow Mask Mob has died and she's free to return home. They invite her to become their new museum curator and she accepts.

## JSA: BLACK REIGN

Kent Nelson and his wife Lyta are imprisoned within the Fate amulet. With the help of all the Fates, Fury escapes to the outside world while Nabu is imprisoned within. Secretly working with the JSA, the Atom discovers that Brainwave has been under the influence of Mister Mind and expels the vile worm from his mind. In the end, the JSA acknowledges that Black Adam truly cares for the people of his homeland and agrees to allow him to rule — provided he not leave its borders. For his own missteps in the war, Hawkman is asked to leave the Justice Society.

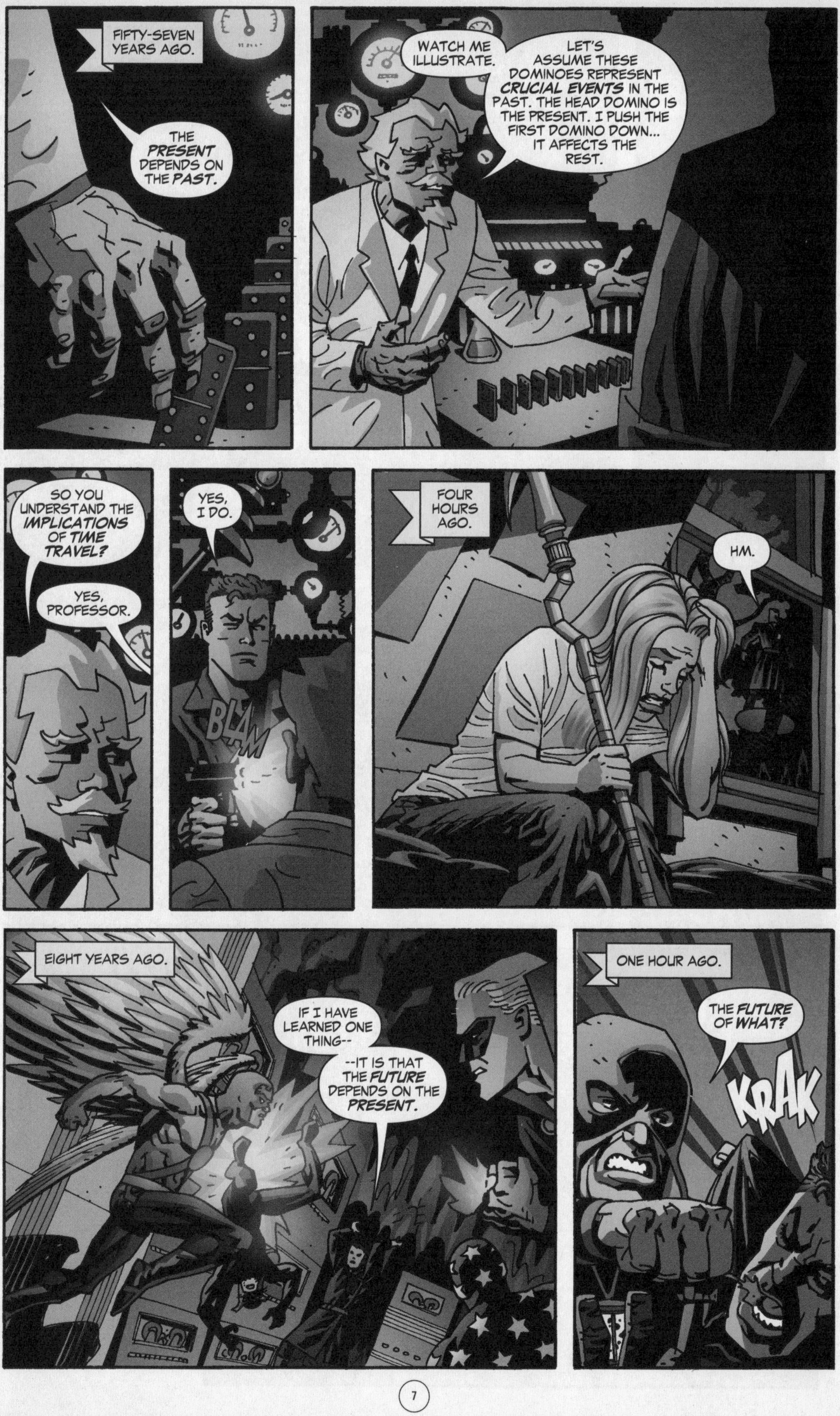
FIFTY-SEVEN YEARS AGO.
THE PRESENT DEPENDS ON THE PAST.
WATCH ME ILLUSTRATE.
LET'S ASSUME THESE DOMINOES REPRESENT CRUCIAL EVENTS IN THE PAST. THE HEAD DOMINO IS THE PRESENT. I PUSH THE FIRST DOMINO DOWN... IT AFFECTS THE REST.
SO YOU UNDERSTAND THE IMPLICATIONS OF TIME TRAVEL?
YES, PROFESSOR.
YES, I DO.
BLAM
FOUR HOURS AGO.
HM.
EIGHT YEARS AGO.
IF I HAVE LEARNED ONE THING--
--IT IS THAT THE FUTURE DEPENDS ON THE PRESENT.
ONE HOUR AGO.
THE FUTURE OF WHAT?
KRAK

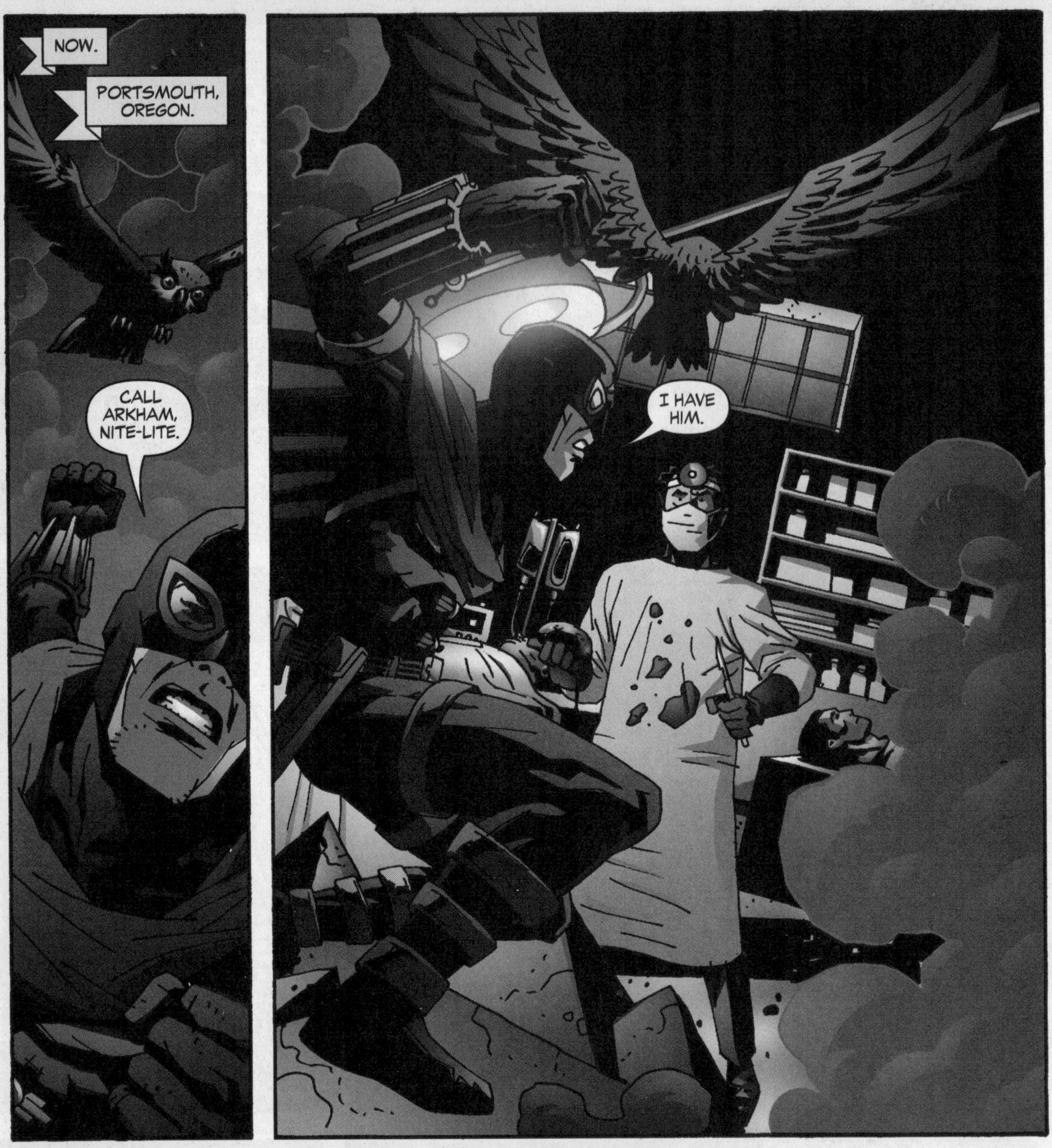
NOW.
PORTSMOUTH, OREGON.
CALL ARKHAM, NITE-LITE.
I HAVE HIM.

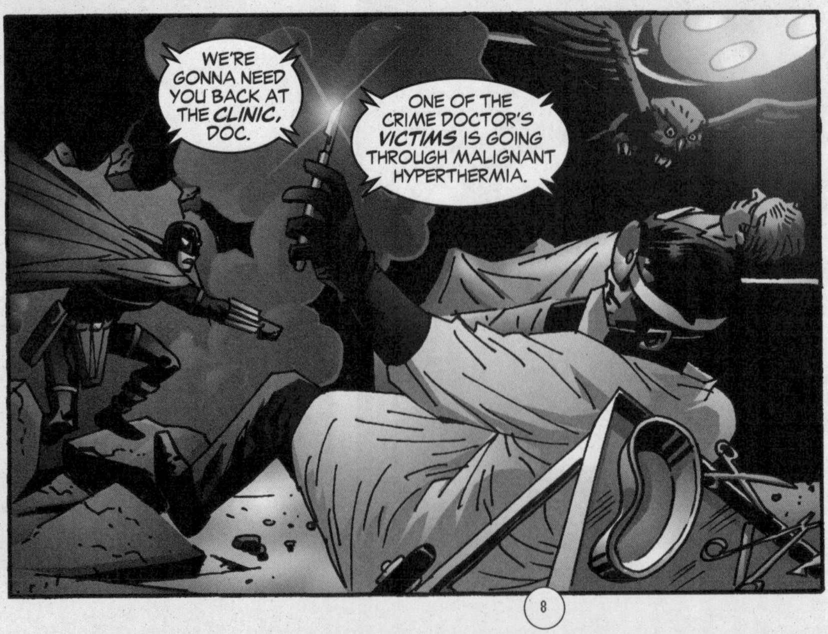
WE'RE GONNA NEED YOU BACK AT THE CLINIC, DOC.
ONE OF THE CRIME DOCTOR'S VICTIMS IS GOING THROUGH MALIGNANT HYPERTHERMIA.

# TIME AND TIME AND TIME AGAIN

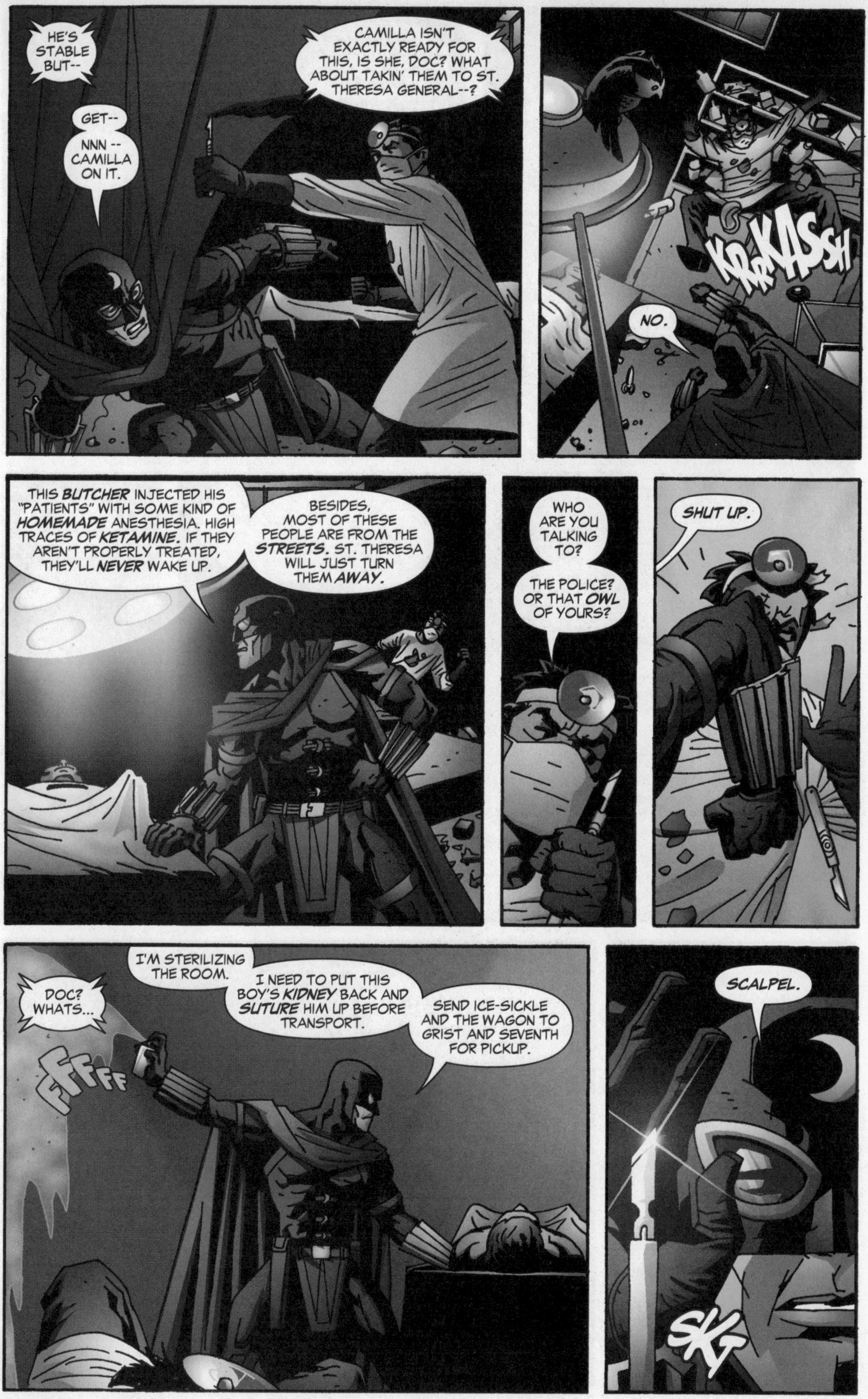
HE'S STABLE BUT--
CAMILLA ISN'T EXACTLY READY FOR THIS, IS SHE, DOC? WHAT ABOUT TAKIN' THEM TO ST. THERESA GENERAL--?
GET-- NNN -- CAMILLA ON IT.
KRRKASSH
NO.
THIS BUTCHER INJECTED HIS "PATIENTS" WITH SOME KIND OF HOMEMADE ANESTHESIA. HIGH TRACES OF KETAMINE. IF THEY AREN'T PROPERLY TREATED, THEY'LL NEVER WAKE UP.
BESIDES, MOST OF THESE PEOPLE ARE FROM THE STREETS. ST. THERESA WILL JUST TURN THEM AWAY.
WHO ARE YOU TALKING TO?
THE POLICE? OR THAT OWL OF YOURS?
SHUT UP.
DOC? WHATS...
I'M STERILIZING THE ROOM.
I NEED TO PUT THIS BOY'S KIDNEY BACK AND SUTURE HIM UP BEFORE TRANSPORT.
SEND ICE-SICKLE AND THE WAGON TO GRIST AND SEVENTH FOR PICKUP.
FFFFF
SCALPEL.
SKT

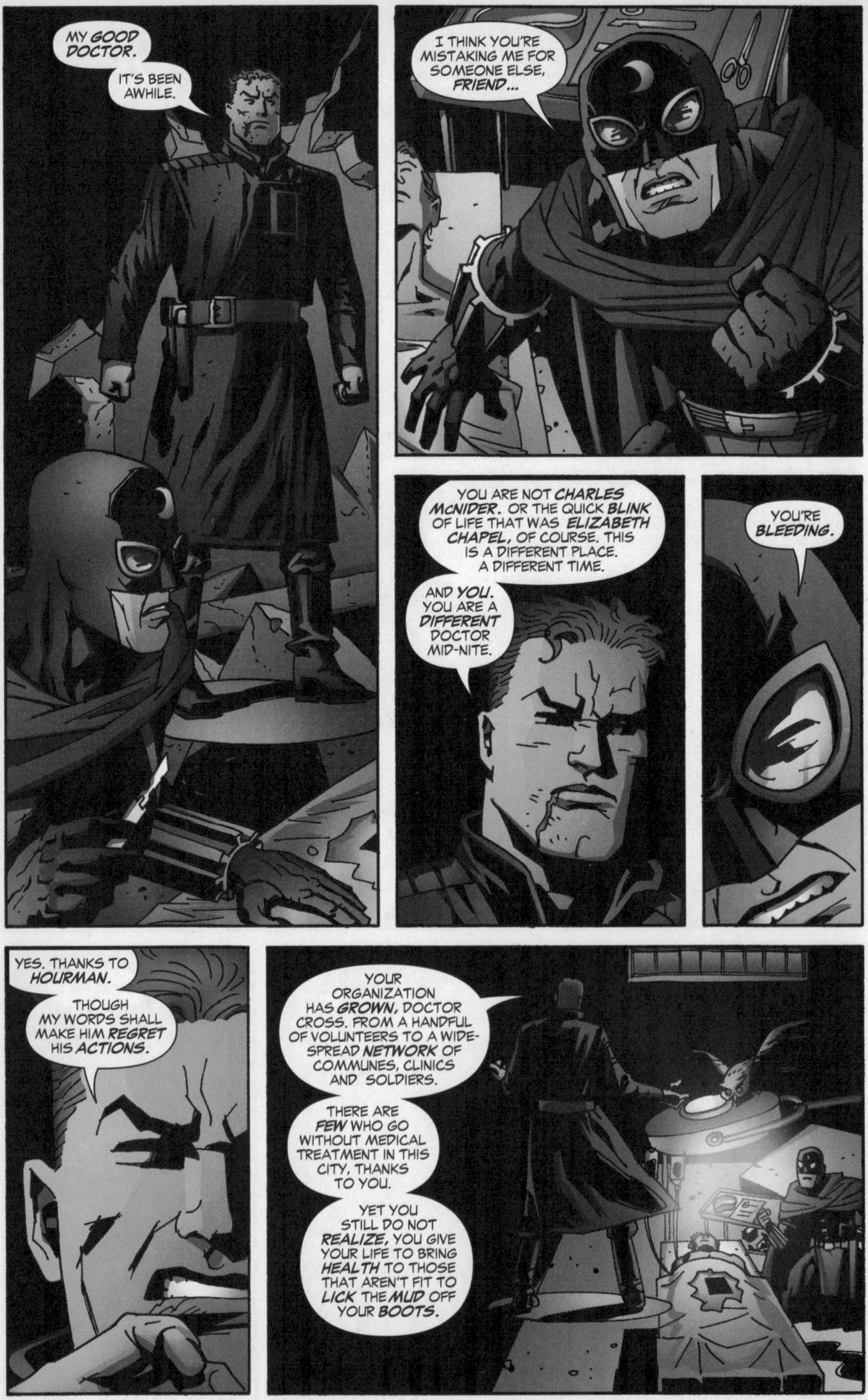
MY GOOD DOCTOR.
IT'S BEEN AWHILE.
I THINK YOU'RE MISTAKING ME FOR SOMEONE ELSE, FRIEND...
YOU ARE NOT CHARLES McNIDER. OR THE QUICK BLINK OF LIFE THAT WAS ELIZABETH CHAPEL, OF COURSE. THIS IS A DIFFERENT PLACE. A DIFFERENT TIME.
AND YOU. YOU ARE A DIFFERENT DOCTOR MID-NITE.
YOU'RE BLEEDING.
YES. THANKS TO HOURMAN.
THOUGH MY WORDS SHALL MAKE HIM REGRET HIS ACTIONS.
YOUR ORGANIZATION HAS GROWN, DOCTOR CROSS. FROM A HANDFUL OF VOLUNTEERS TO A WIDE-SPREAD NETWORK OF COMMUNES, CLINICS AND SOLDIERS.
THERE ARE FEW WHO GO WITHOUT MEDICAL TREATMENT IN THIS CITY, THANKS TO YOU.
YET YOU STILL DO NOT REALIZE, YOU GIVE YOUR LIFE TO BRING HEALTH TO THOSE THAT AREN'T FIT TO LICK THE MUD OFF YOUR BOOTS.

THE *STRONG* SURVIVE, DOCTOR CROSS. BUT THOUGH YOU *ARE* STRONG...

...YOUR *BLEEDING HEART* MAKES YOU *WEAK.*

BY THE WAY...

I AM SORRY ABOUT YOUR *PROTÉGÉ.*

E.T.A. IS *FIVE,* MID-NITE. MID-NITE...?

YES, ICE-SICKLE. I...

YOU ALL RIGHT?

I'M... FINE.

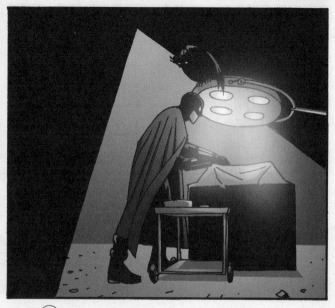

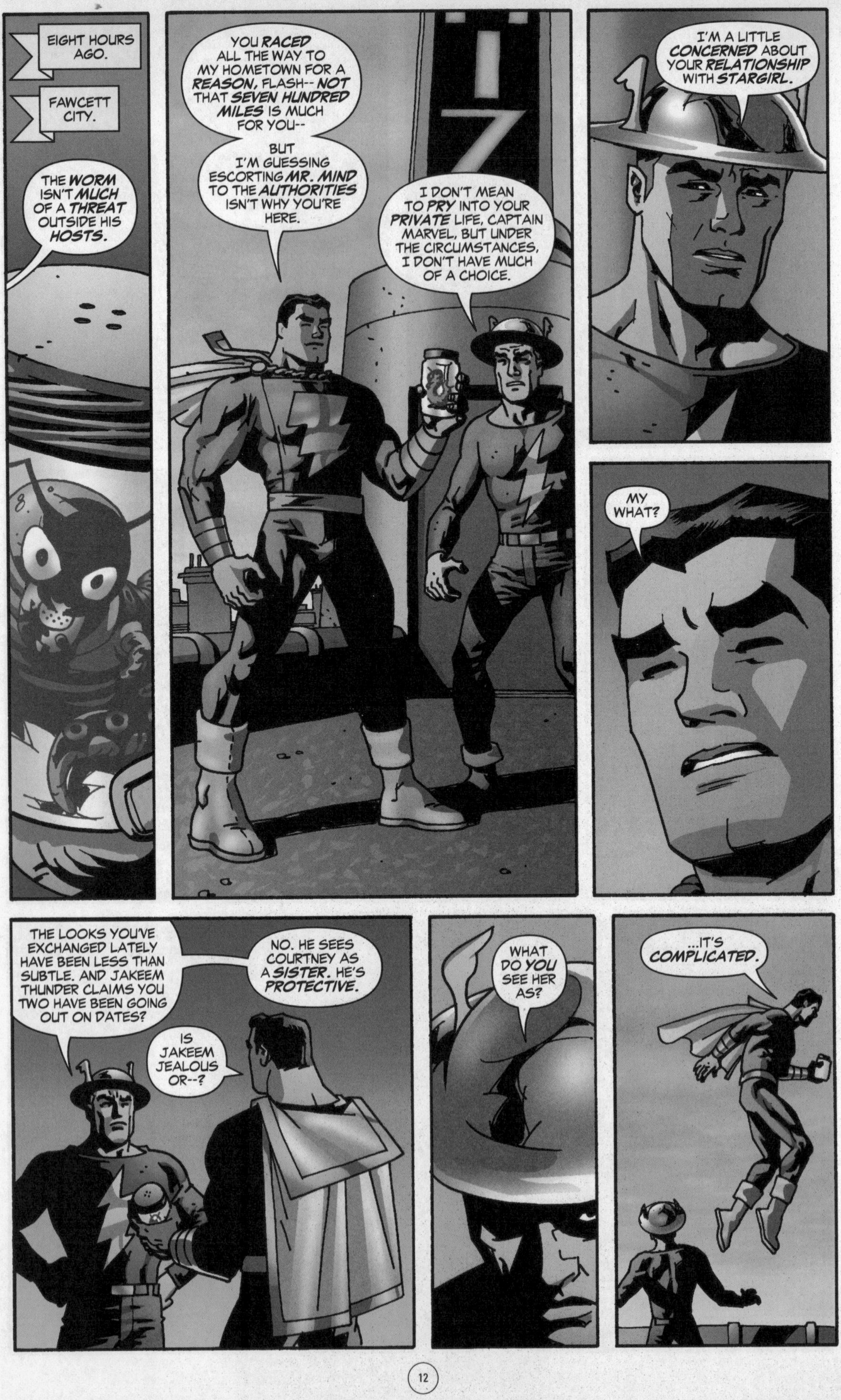
EIGHT HOURS AGO.
FAWCETT CITY.
THE WORM ISN'T MUCH OF A THREAT OUTSIDE HIS HOSTS.
YOU RACED ALL THE WAY TO MY HOMETOWN FOR A REASON, FLASH-- NOT THAT SEVEN HUNDRED MILES IS MUCH FOR YOU--
BUT I'M GUESSING ESCORTING MR. MIND TO THE AUTHORITIES ISN'T WHY YOU'RE HERE.
I DON'T MEAN TO PRY INTO YOUR PRIVATE LIFE, CAPTAIN MARVEL, BUT UNDER THE CIRCUMSTANCES, I DON'T HAVE MUCH OF A CHOICE.
I'M A LITTLE CONCERNED ABOUT YOUR RELATIONSHIP WITH STARGIRL.
MY WHAT?
THE LOOKS YOU'VE EXCHANGED LATELY HAVE BEEN LESS THAN SUBTLE. AND JAKEEM THUNDER CLAIMS YOU TWO HAVE BEEN GOING OUT ON DATES?
IS JAKEEM JEALOUS OR--?
NO. HE SEES COURTNEY AS A SISTER. HE'S PROTECTIVE.
WHAT DO YOU SEE HER AS?
...IT'S COMPLICATED.

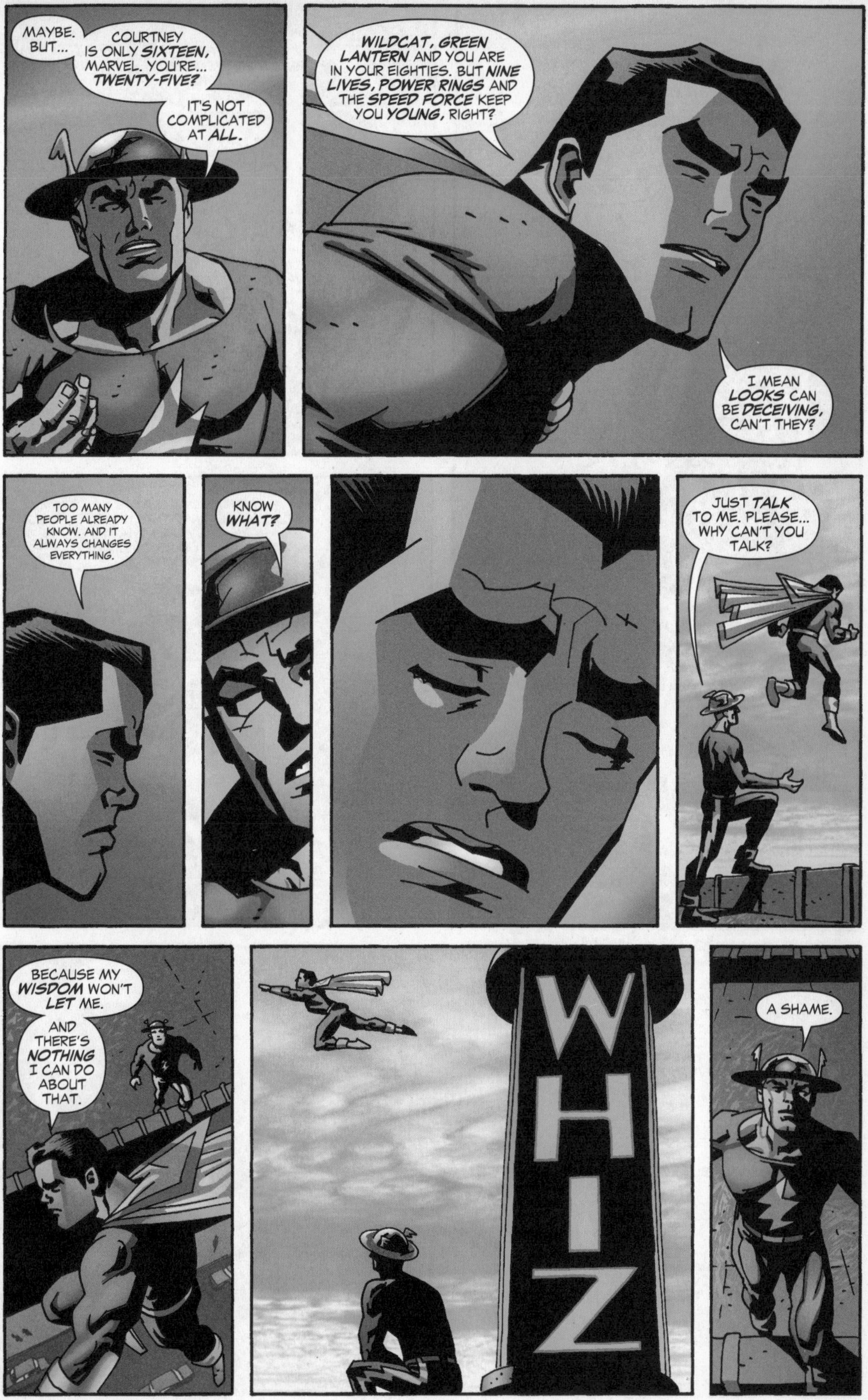

MAYBE. BUT...
COURTNEY IS ONLY SIXTEEN, MARVEL. YOU'RE... TWENTY-FIVE?
IT'S NOT COMPLICATED AT ALL.
WILDCAT, GREEN LANTERN AND YOU ARE IN YOUR EIGHTIES. BUT NINE LIVES, POWER RINGS AND THE SPEED FORCE KEEP YOU YOUNG, RIGHT?
I MEAN LOOKS CAN BE DECEIVING, CAN'T THEY?
TOO MANY PEOPLE ALREADY KNOW. AND IT ALWAYS CHANGES EVERYTHING.
KNOW WHAT?
JUST TALK TO ME. PLEASE... WHY CAN'T YOU TALK?
BECAUSE MY WISDOM WON'T LET ME.
AND THERE'S NOTHING I CAN DO ABOUT THAT.
WHIZ
A SHAME.

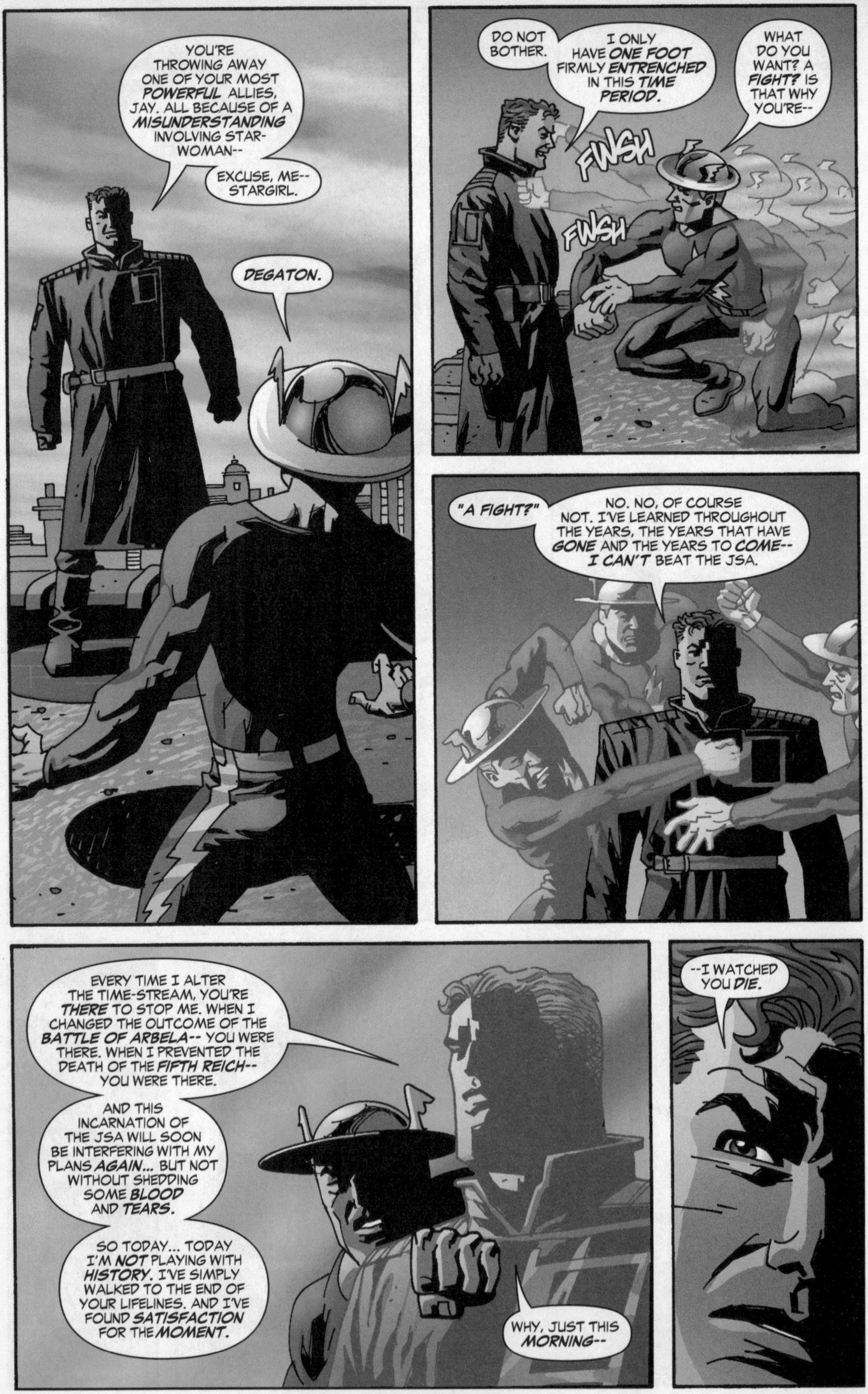
YOU'RE THROWING AWAY ONE OF YOUR MOST POWERFUL ALLIES, JAY. ALL BECAUSE OF A MISUNDERSTANDING INVOLVING STAR-WOMAN--
EXCUSE, ME-- STARGIRL.
DEGATON.
DO NOT BOTHER.
I ONLY HAVE ONE FOOT FIRMLY ENTRENCHED IN THIS TIME PERIOD.
WHAT DO YOU WANT? A FIGHT? IS THAT WHY YOU'RE--
FWSH
FWSH
"A FIGHT?"
NO. NO, OF COURSE NOT. I'VE LEARNED THROUGHOUT THE YEARS, THE YEARS THAT HAVE GONE AND THE YEARS TO COME-- I CAN'T BEAT THE JSA.
EVERY TIME I ALTER THE TIME-STREAM, YOU'RE THERE TO STOP ME. WHEN I CHANGED THE OUTCOME OF THE BATTLE OF ARBELA-- YOU WERE THERE. WHEN I PREVENTED THE DEATH OF THE FIFTH REICH-- YOU WERE THERE.
AND THIS INCARNATION OF THE JSA WILL SOON BE INTERFERING WITH MY PLANS AGAIN... BUT NOT WITHOUT SHEDDING SOME BLOOD AND TEARS.
SO TODAY... TODAY I'M NOT PLAYING WITH HISTORY. I'VE SIMPLY WALKED TO THE END OF YOUR LIFELINES. AND I'VE FOUND SATISFACTION FOR THE MOMENT.
WHY, JUST THIS MORNING--
--I WATCHED YOU DIE.

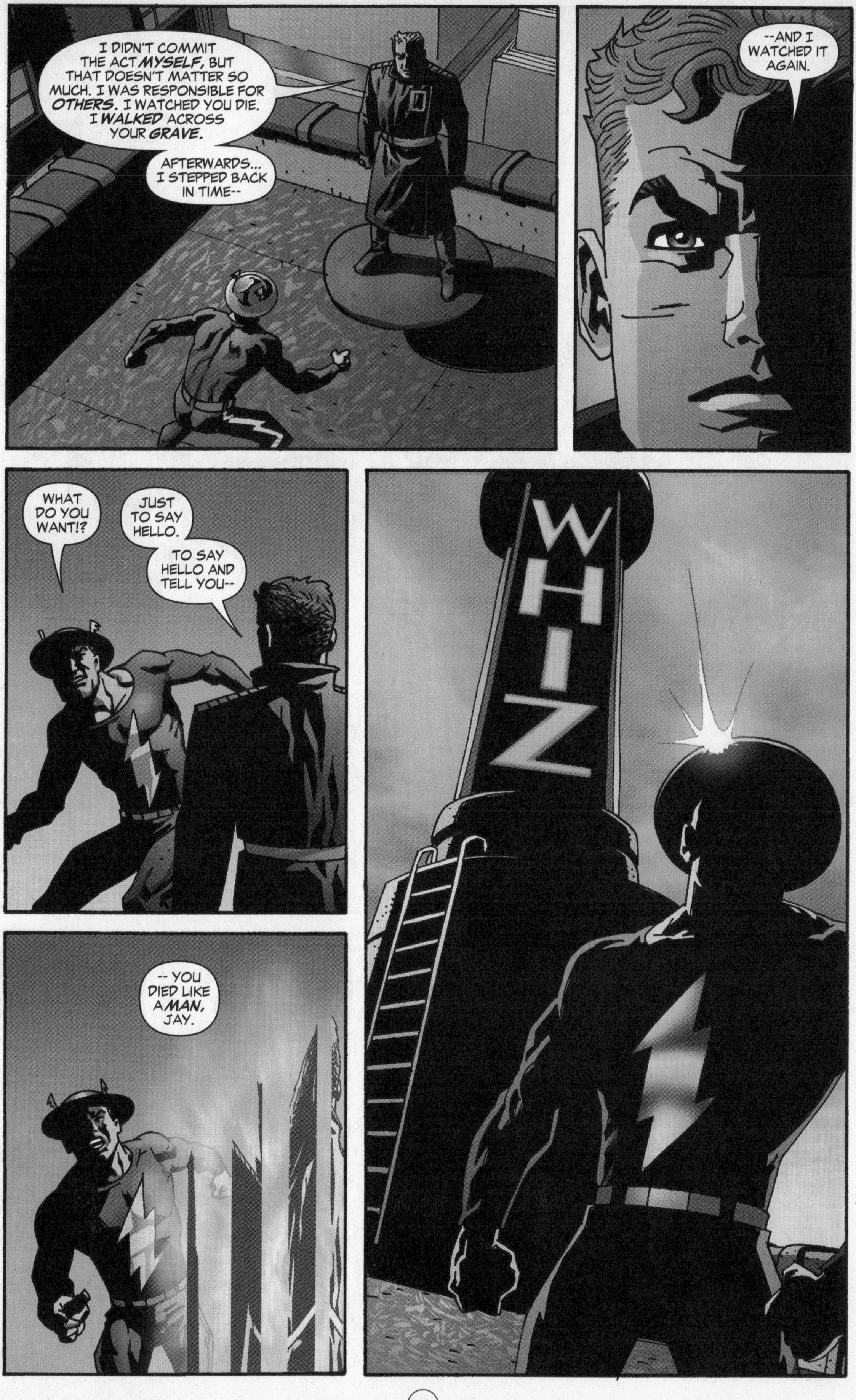
I DIDN'T COMMIT THE ACT MYSELF, BUT THAT DOESN'T MATTER SO MUCH. I WAS RESPONSIBLE FOR OTHERS. I WATCHED YOU DIE. I WALKED ACROSS YOUR GRAVE.
AFTERWARDS... I STEPPED BACK IN TIME--
--AND I WATCHED IT AGAIN.
WHAT DO YOU WANT!?
JUST TO SAY HELLO.
TO SAY HELLO AND TELL YOU--
-- YOU DIED LIKE A MAN, JAY.
WHIZ

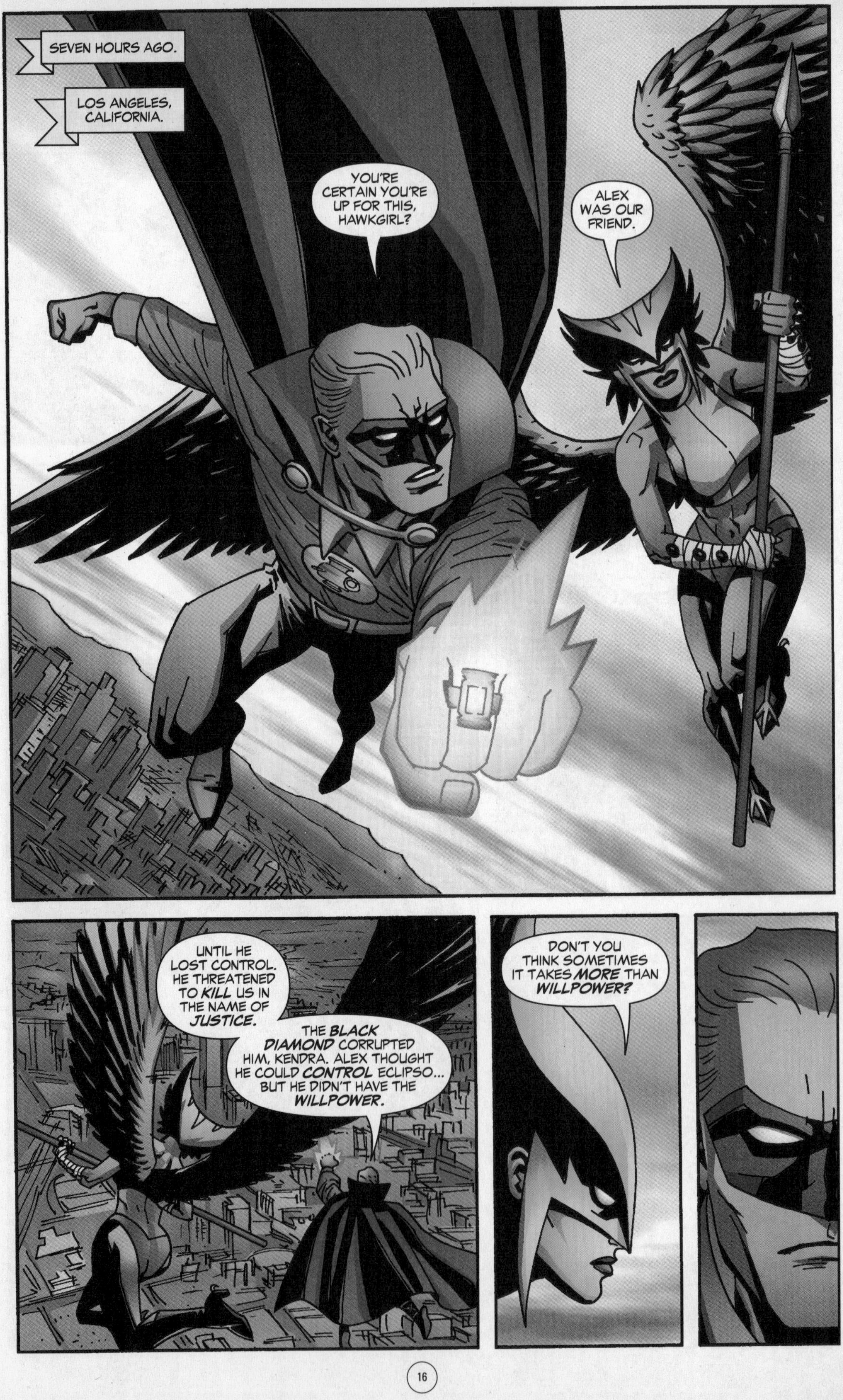
SEVEN HOURS AGO.
LOS ANGELES, CALIFORNIA.
YOU'RE CERTAIN YOU'RE UP FOR THIS, HAWKGIRL?
ALEX WAS OUR FRIEND.
UNTIL HE LOST CONTROL. HE THREATENED TO KILL US IN THE NAME OF JUSTICE.
THE BLACK DIAMOND CORRUPTED HIM, KENDRA. ALEX THOUGHT HE COULD CONTROL ECLIPSO... BUT HE DIDN'T HAVE THE WILLPOWER.
DON'T YOU THINK SOMETIMES IT TAKES MORE THAN WILLPOWER?

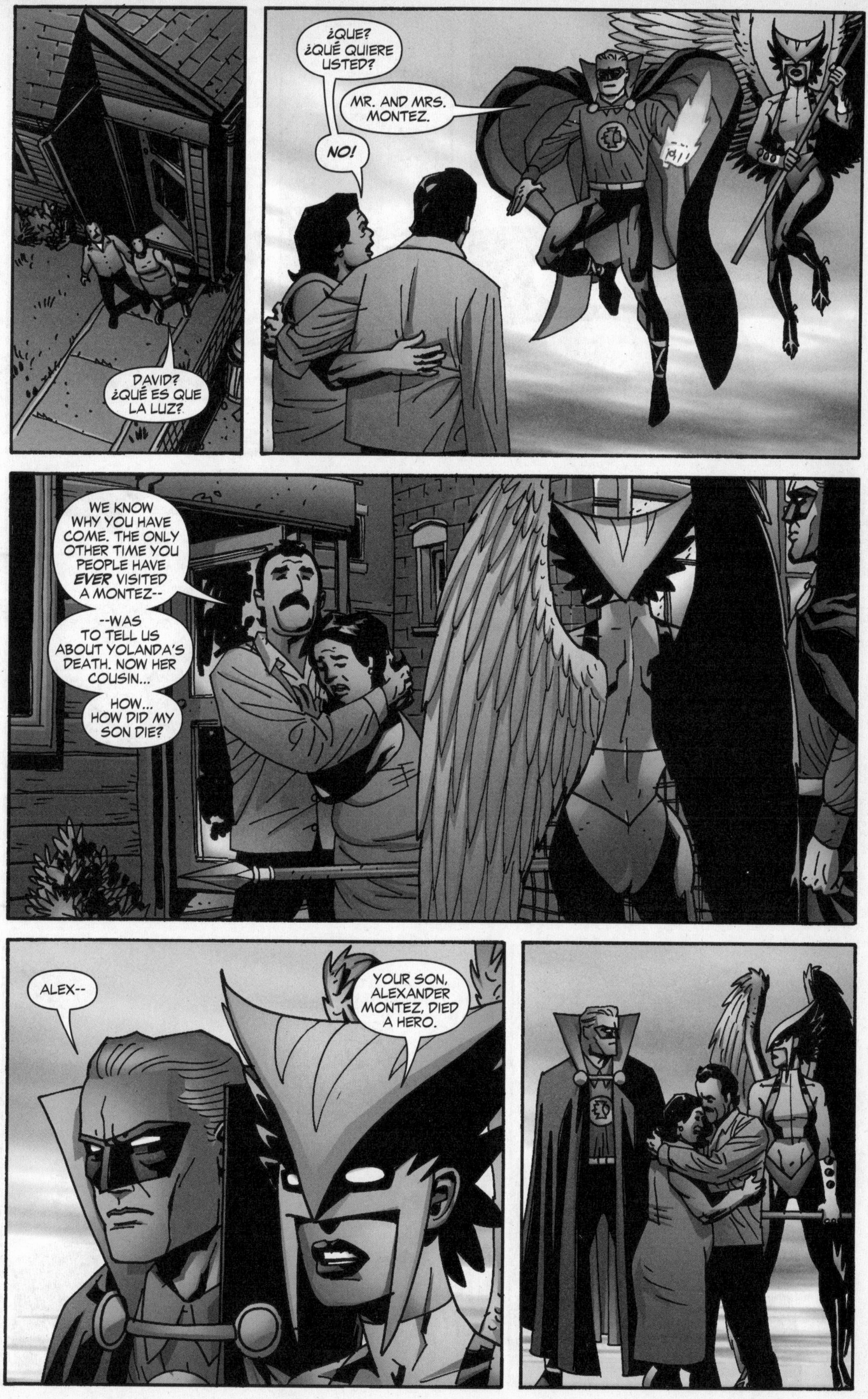
DAVID? ¿QUÉ ES QUE LA LUZ?
¿QUE? ¿QUÉ QUIERE USTED?
NO!
MR. AND MRS. MONTEZ.
WE KNOW WHY YOU HAVE COME. THE ONLY OTHER TIME YOU PEOPLE HAVE EVER VISITED A MONTEZ--
--WAS TO TELL US ABOUT YOLANDA'S DEATH. NOW HER COUSIN...
HOW... HOW DID MY SON DIE?
ALEX--
YOUR SON, ALEXANDER MONTEZ, DIED A HERO.

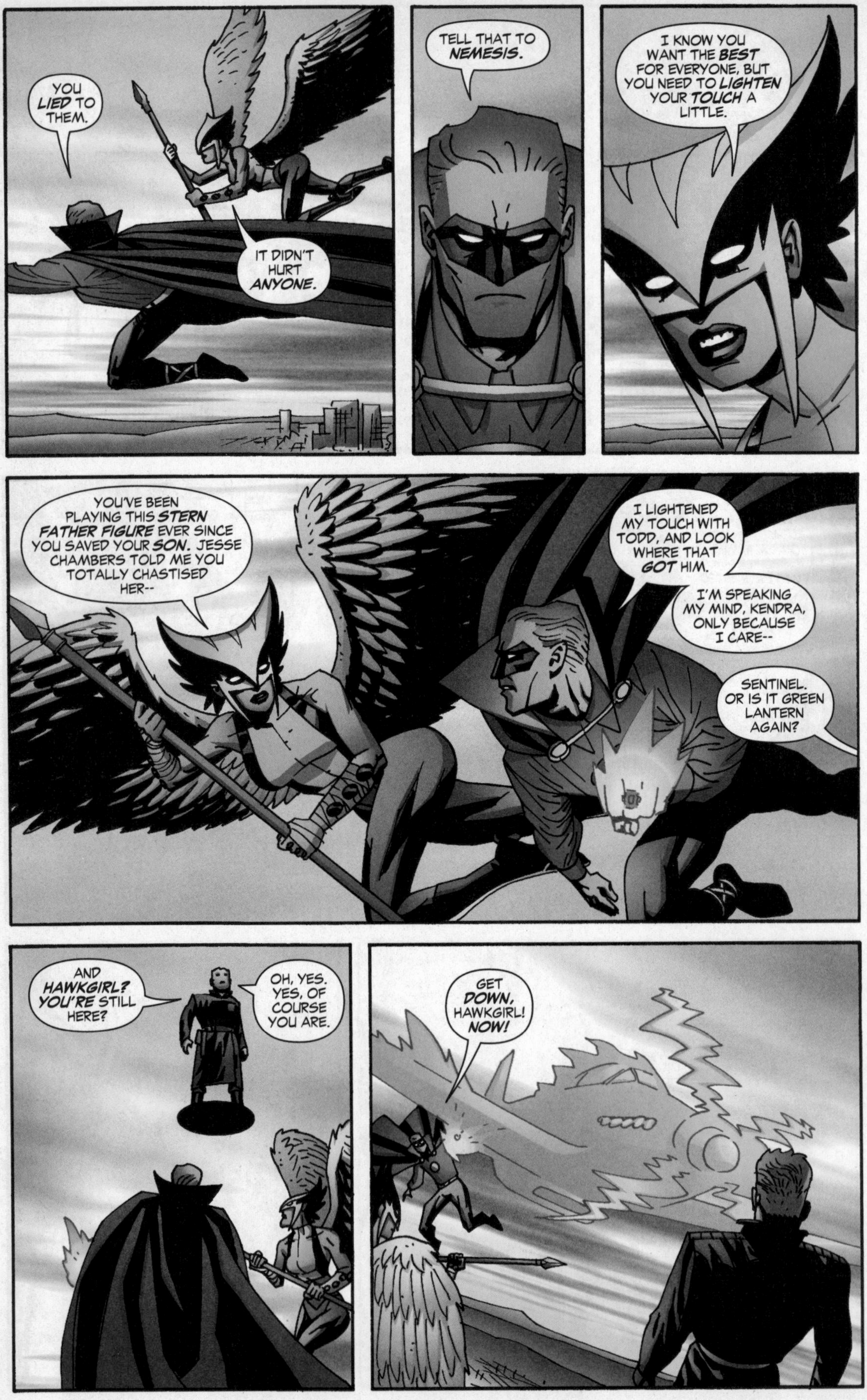
YOU LIED TO THEM.
IT DIDN'T HURT ANYONE.
TELL THAT TO NEMESIS.
I KNOW YOU WANT THE BEST FOR EVERYONE, BUT YOU NEED TO LIGHTEN YOUR TOUCH A LITTLE.
YOU'VE BEEN PLAYING THIS STERN FATHER FIGURE EVER SINCE YOU SAVED YOUR SON. JESSE CHAMBERS TOLD ME YOU TOTALLY CHASTISED HER--
I LIGHTENED MY TOUCH WITH TODD, AND LOOK WHERE THAT GOT HIM.
I'M SPEAKING MY MIND, KENDRA, ONLY BECAUSE I CARE--
SENTINEL. OR IS IT GREEN LANTERN AGAIN?
AND HAWKGIRL? YOU'RE STILL HERE?
OH, YES. YES, OF COURSE YOU ARE.
GET DOWN, HAWKGIRL! NOW!

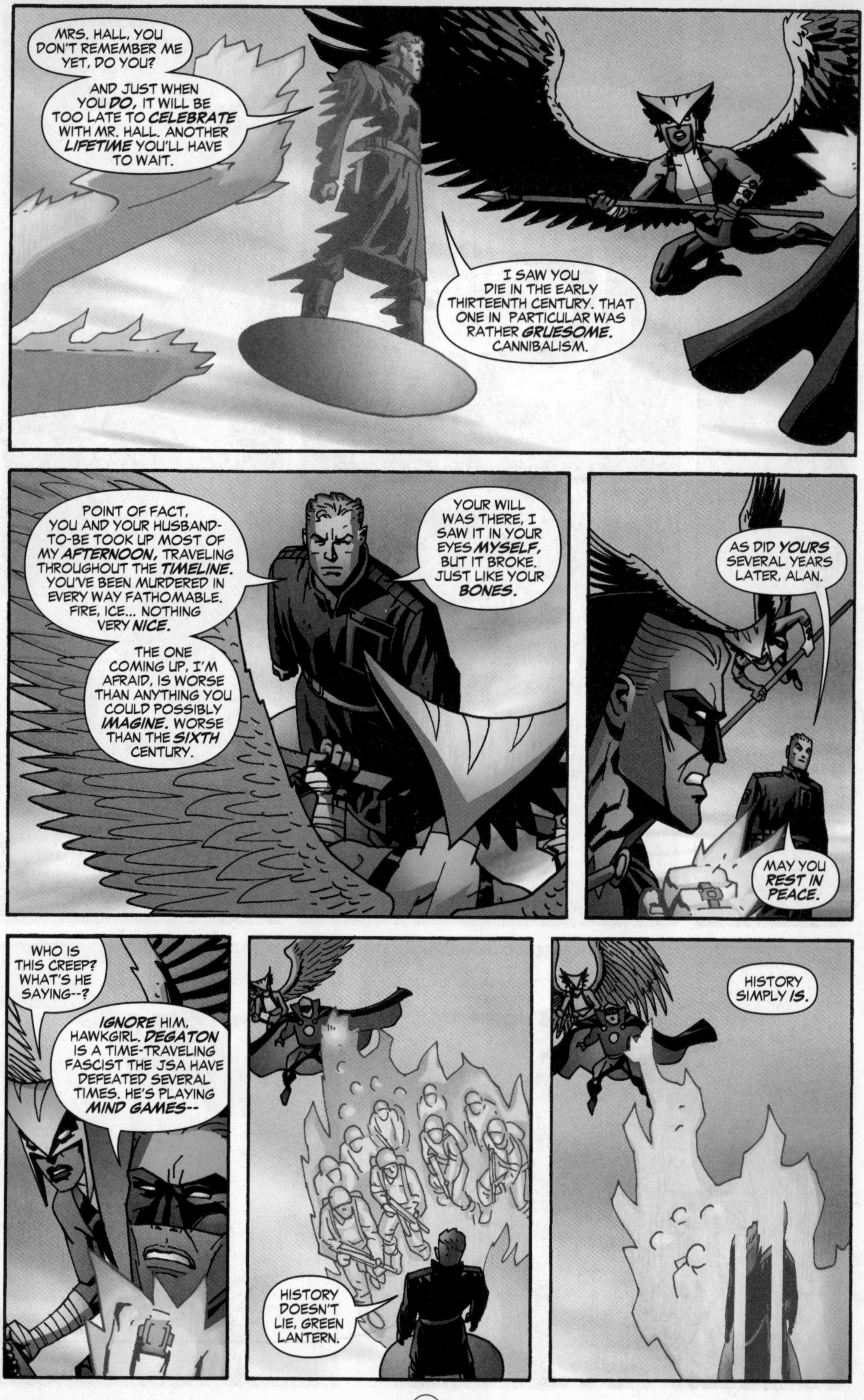

MRS. HALL, YOU DON'T REMEMBER ME YET, DO YOU?
AND JUST WHEN YOU DO, IT WILL BE TOO LATE TO CELEBRATE WITH MR. HALL. ANOTHER LIFETIME YOU'LL HAVE TO WAIT.
I SAW YOU DIE IN THE EARLY THIRTEENTH CENTURY. THAT ONE IN PARTICULAR WAS RATHER GRUESOME. CANNIBALISM.
POINT OF FACT, YOU AND YOUR HUSBAND-TO-BE TOOK UP MOST OF MY AFTERNOON, TRAVELING THROUGHOUT THE TIMELINE. YOU'VE BEEN MURDERED IN EVERY WAY FATHOMABLE. FIRE, ICE... NOTHING VERY NICE.
THE ONE COMING UP, I'M AFRAID, IS WORSE THAN ANYTHING YOU COULD POSSIBLY IMAGINE. WORSE THAN THE SIXTH CENTURY.
YOUR WILL WAS THERE, I SAW IT IN YOUR EYES MYSELF, BUT IT BROKE. JUST LIKE YOUR BONES.
AS DID YOURS SEVERAL YEARS LATER, ALAN.
MAY YOU REST IN PEACE.
WHO IS THIS CREEP? WHAT'S HE SAYING--?
IGNORE HIM, HAWKGIRL. DEGATON IS A TIME-TRAVELING FASCIST THE JSA HAVE DEFEATED SEVERAL TIMES. HE'S PLAYING MIND GAMES--
HISTORY DOESN'T LIE, GREEN LANTERN.
HISTORY SIMPLY IS.

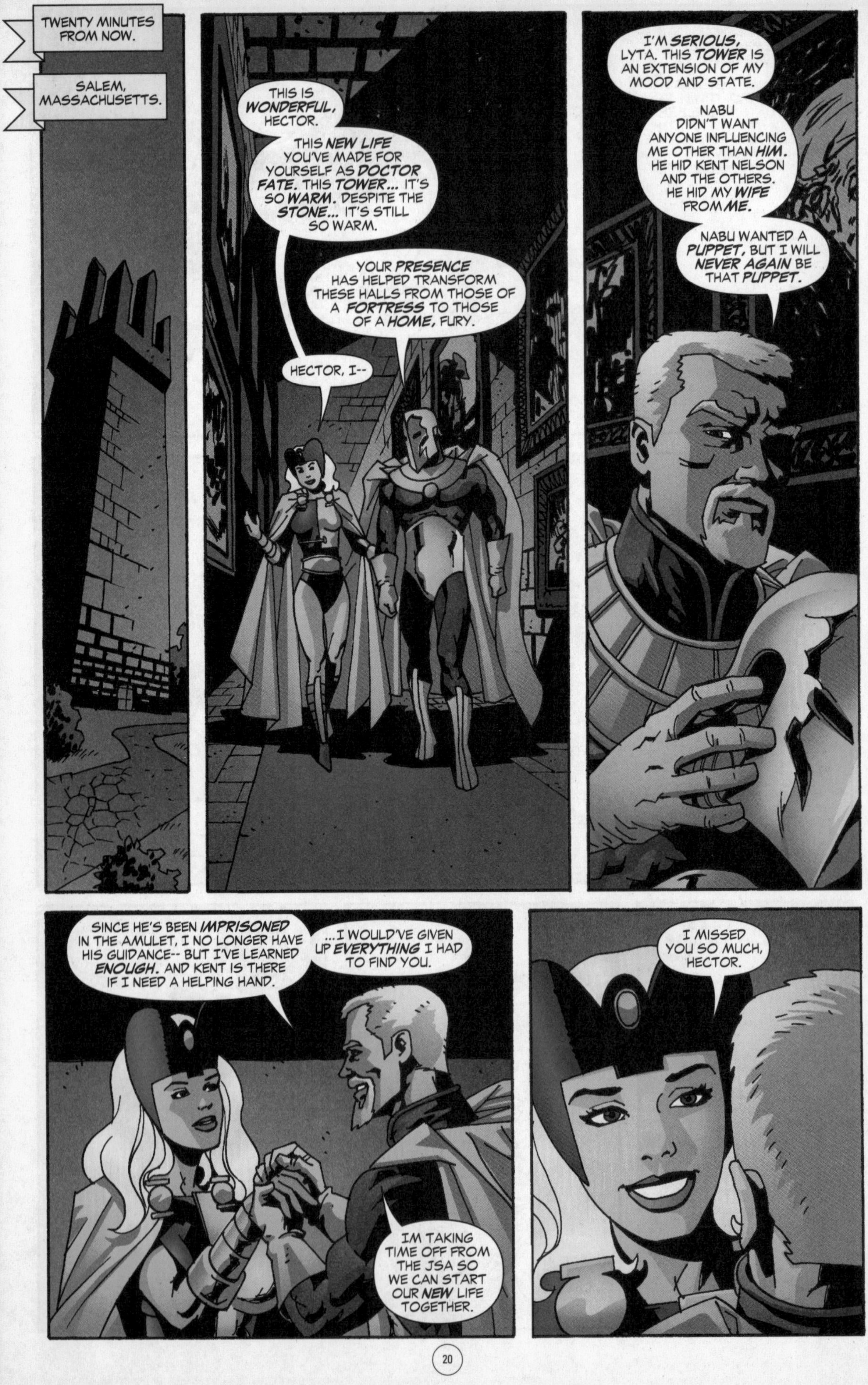
TWENTY MINUTES FROM NOW.
SALEM, MASSACHUSETTS.
THIS IS WONDERFUL, HECTOR.
THIS NEW LIFE YOU'VE MADE FOR YOURSELF AS DOCTOR FATE. THIS TOWER... IT'S SO WARM. DESPITE THE STONE... IT'S STILL SO WARM.
YOUR PRESENCE HAS HELPED TRANSFORM THESE HALLS FROM THOSE OF A FORTRESS TO THOSE OF A HOME, FURY.
HECTOR, I--
I'M SERIOUS, LYTA. THIS TOWER IS AN EXTENSION OF MY MOOD AND STATE.
NABU DIDN'T WANT ANYONE INFLUENCING ME OTHER THAN HIM. HE HID KENT NELSON AND THE OTHERS. HE HID MY WIFE FROM ME.
NABU WANTED A PUPPET, BUT I WILL NEVER AGAIN BE THAT PUPPET.
SINCE HE'S BEEN IMPRISONED IN THE AMULET, I NO LONGER HAVE HIS GUIDANCE-- BUT I'VE LEARNED ENOUGH. AND KENT IS THERE IF I NEED A HELPING HAND.
...I WOULD'VE GIVEN UP EVERYTHING I HAD TO FIND YOU.
IM TAKING TIME OFF FROM THE JSA SO WE CAN START OUR NEW LIFE TOGETHER.
I MISSED YOU SO MUCH, HECTOR.

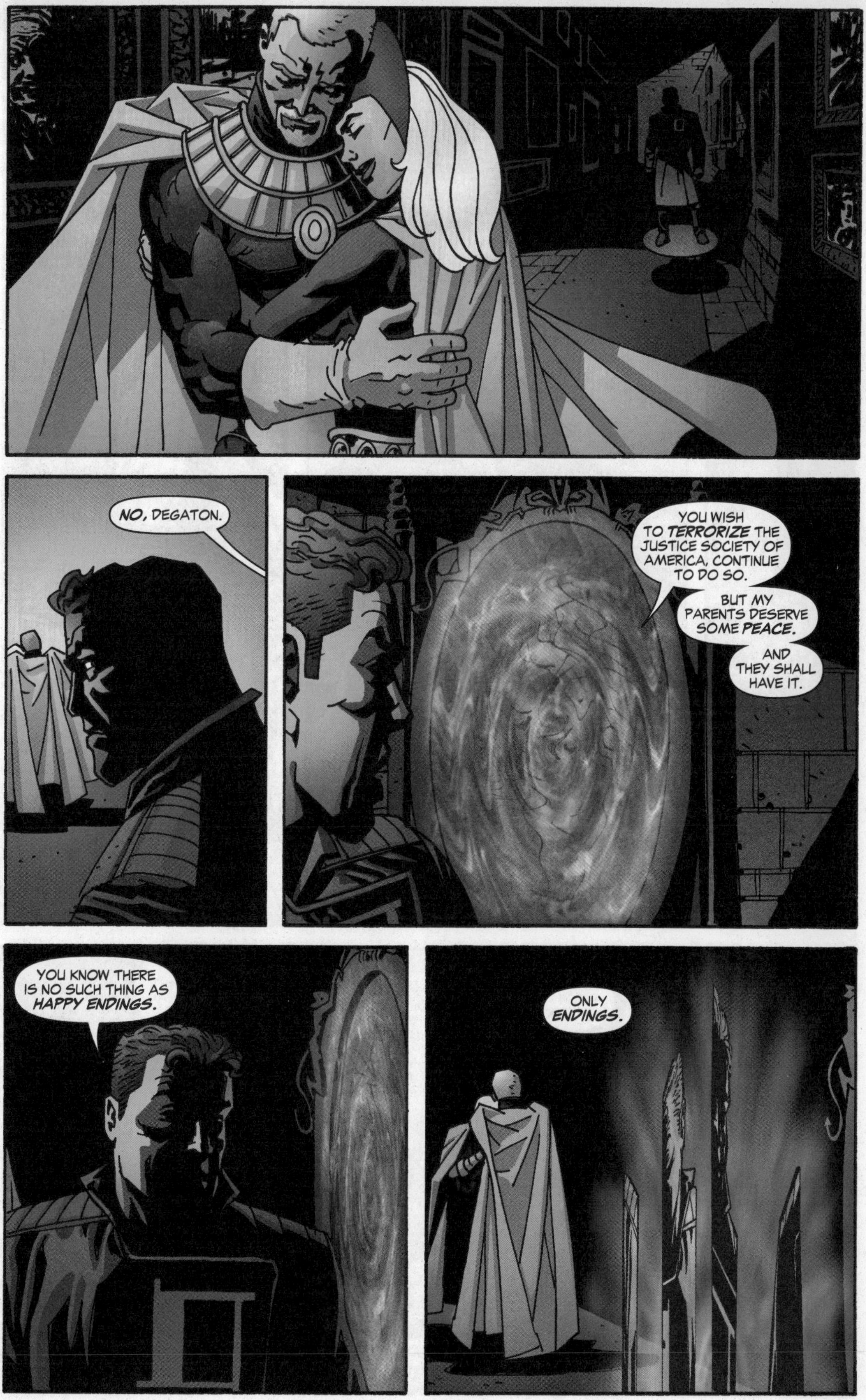

NO, DEGATON.
YOU WISH TO TERRORIZE THE JUSTICE SOCIETY OF AMERICA, CONTINUE TO DO SO.
BUT MY PARENTS DESERVE SOME PEACE.
AND THEY SHALL HAVE IT.
YOU KNOW THERE IS NO SUCH THING AS HAPPY ENDINGS.
ONLY ENDINGS.

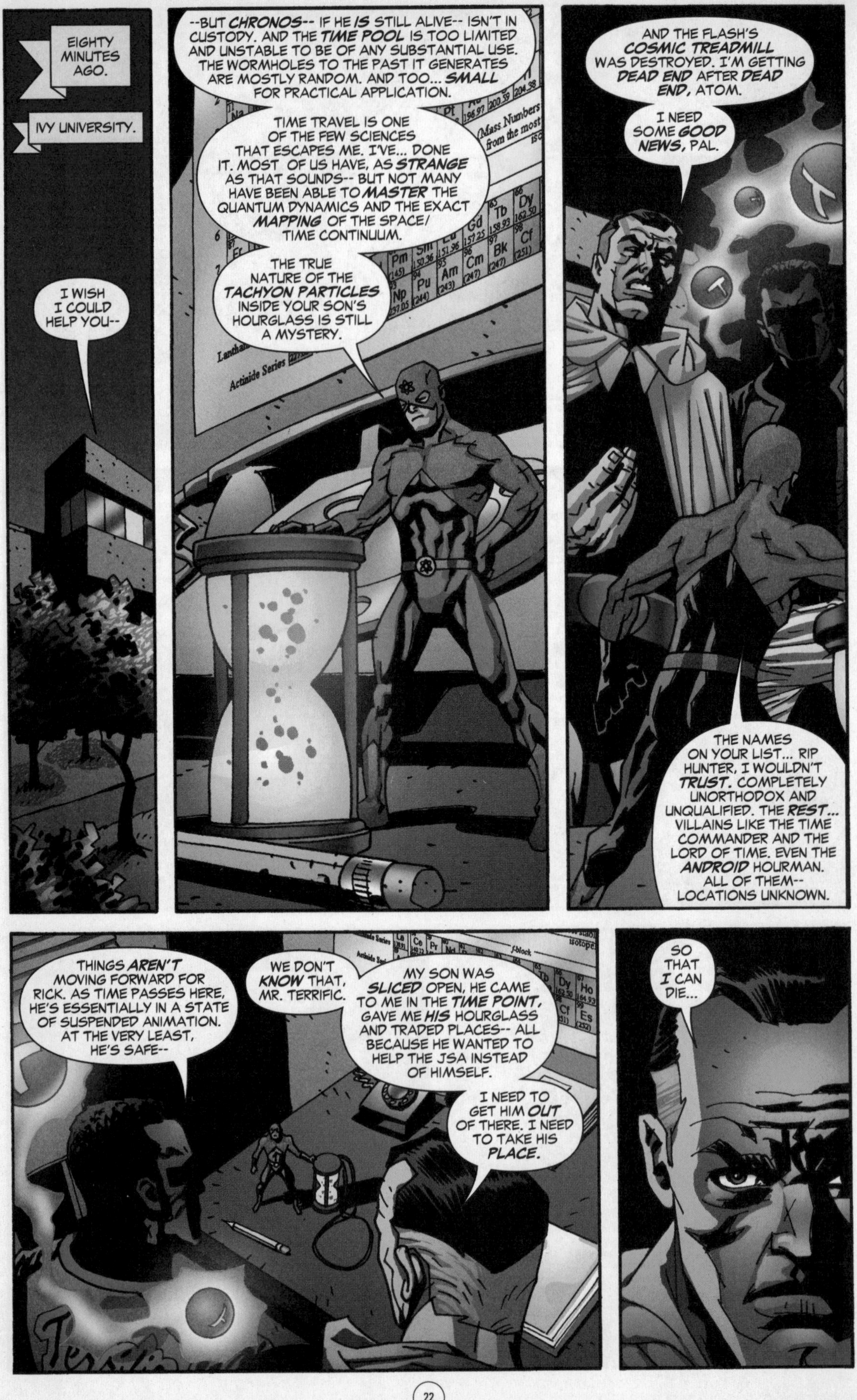
EIGHTY MINUTES AGO.
IVY UNIVERSITY.
I WISH I COULD HELP YOU--
--BUT CHRONOS-- IF HE IS STILL ALIVE-- ISN'T IN CUSTODY. AND THE TIME POOL IS TOO LIMITED AND UNSTABLE TO BE OF ANY SUBSTANTIAL USE. THE WORMHOLES TO THE PAST IT GENERATES ARE MOSTLY RANDOM. AND TOO... SMALL FOR PRACTICAL APPLICATION.
TIME TRAVEL IS ONE OF THE FEW SCIENCES THAT ESCAPES ME. I'VE... DONE IT. MOST OF US HAVE, AS STRANGE AS THAT SOUNDS-- BUT NOT MANY HAVE BEEN ABLE TO MASTER THE QUANTUM DYNAMICS AND THE EXACT MAPPING OF THE SPACE/ TIME CONTINUUM.
THE TRUE NATURE OF THE TACHYON PARTICLES INSIDE YOUR SON'S HOURGLASS IS STILL A MYSTERY.
AND THE FLASH'S COSMIC TREADMILL WAS DESTROYED. I'M GETTING DEAD END AFTER DEAD END, ATOM.
I NEED SOME GOOD NEWS, PAL.
THE NAMES ON YOUR LIST... RIP HUNTER, I WOULDN'T TRUST. COMPLETELY UNORTHODOX AND UNQUALIFIED. THE REST... VILLAINS LIKE THE TIME COMMANDER AND THE LORD OF TIME. EVEN THE ANDROID HOURMAN. ALL OF THEM-- LOCATIONS UNKNOWN.
THINGS AREN'T MOVING FORWARD FOR RICK. AS TIME PASSES HERE, HE'S ESSENTIALLY IN A STATE OF SUSPENDED ANIMATION. AT THE VERY LEAST, HE'S SAFE--
WE DON'T KNOW THAT, MR. TERRIFIC.
MY SON WAS SLICED OPEN, HE CAME TO ME IN THE TIME POINT, GAVE ME HIS HOURGLASS AND TRADED PLACES-- ALL BECAUSE HE WANTED TO HELP THE JSA INSTEAD OF HIMSELF.
I NEED TO GET HIM OUT OF THERE. I NEED TO TAKE HIS PLACE.
SO THAT I CAN DIE...

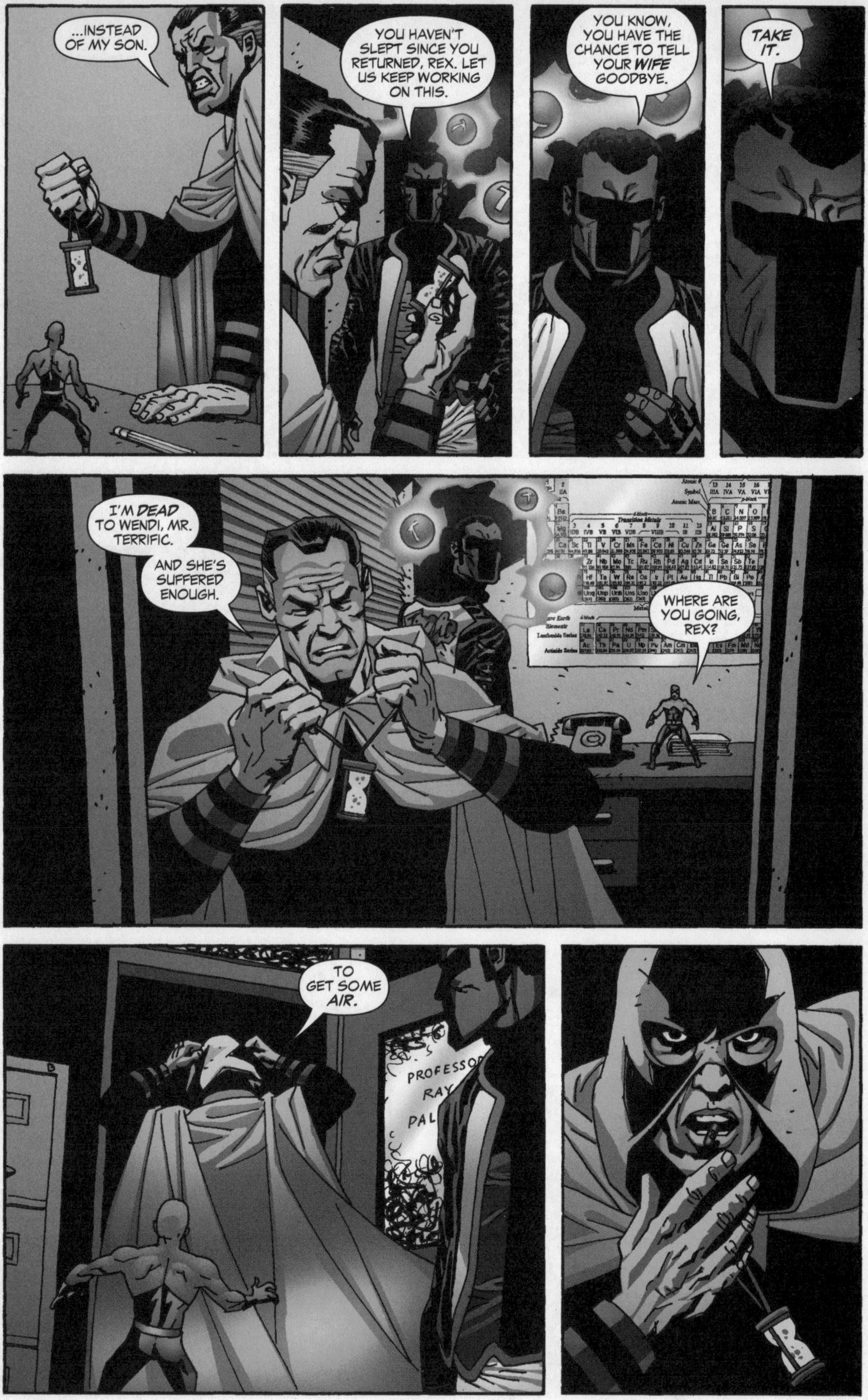
...INSTEAD OF MY SON.
YOU HAVEN'T SLEPT SINCE YOU RETURNED, REX. LET US KEEP WORKING ON THIS.
YOU KNOW, YOU HAVE THE CHANCE TO TELL YOUR *WIFE* GOODBYE.
*TAKE IT.*
I'M *DEAD* TO WENDI, MR. TERRIFIC.
AND SHE'S SUFFERED ENOUGH.
WHERE ARE YOU GOING, REX?
TO GET SOME *AIR.*
PROFESSOR RAY PAL

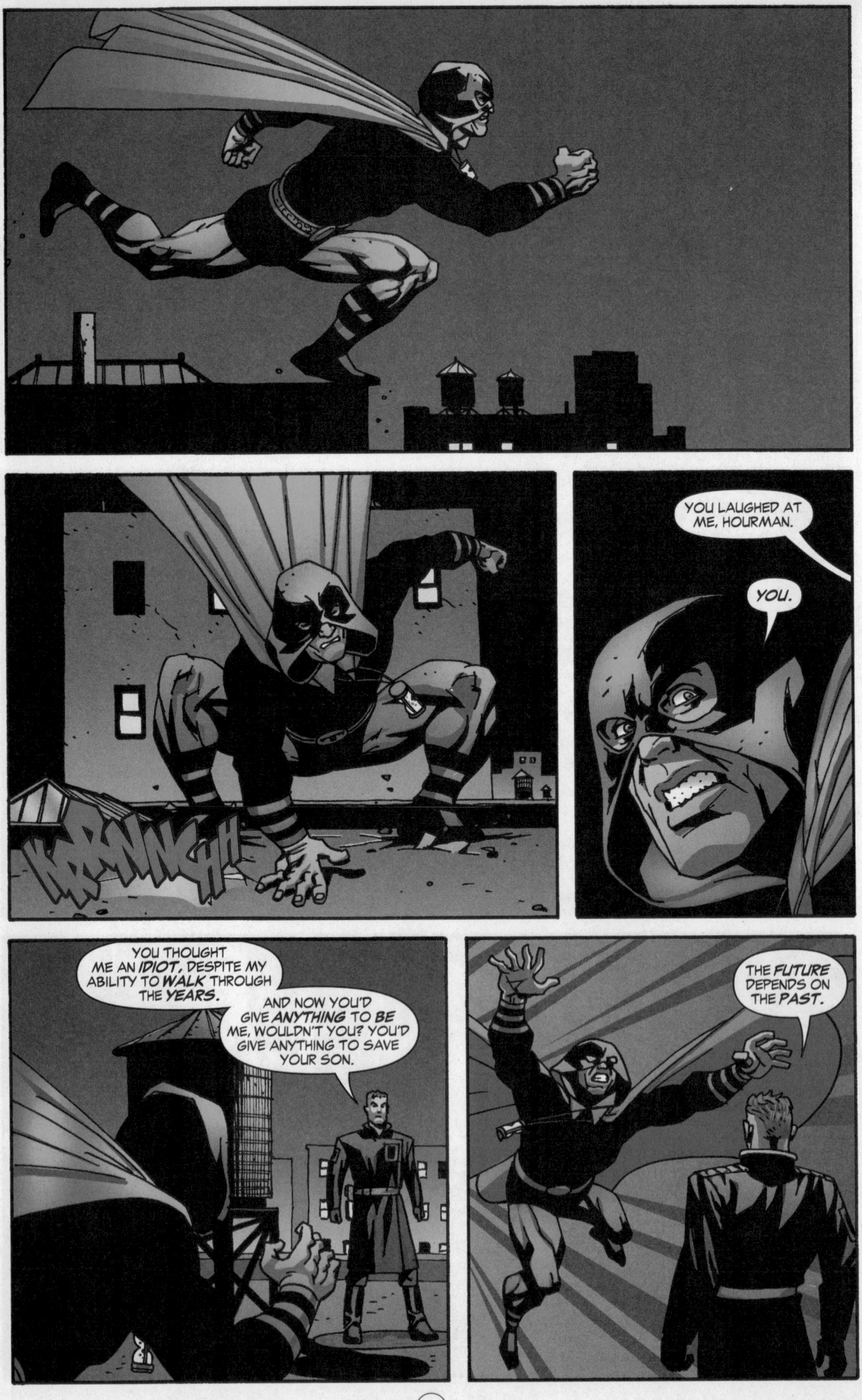
WRRNNCHH
YOU LAUGHED AT ME, HOURMAN.
YOU.
YOU THOUGHT ME AN IDIOT, DESPITE MY ABILITY TO WALK THROUGH THE YEARS.
AND NOW YOU'D GIVE ANYTHING TO BE ME, WOULDN'T YOU? YOU'D GIVE ANYTHING TO SAVE YOUR SON.
THE FUTURE DEPENDS ON THE PAST.

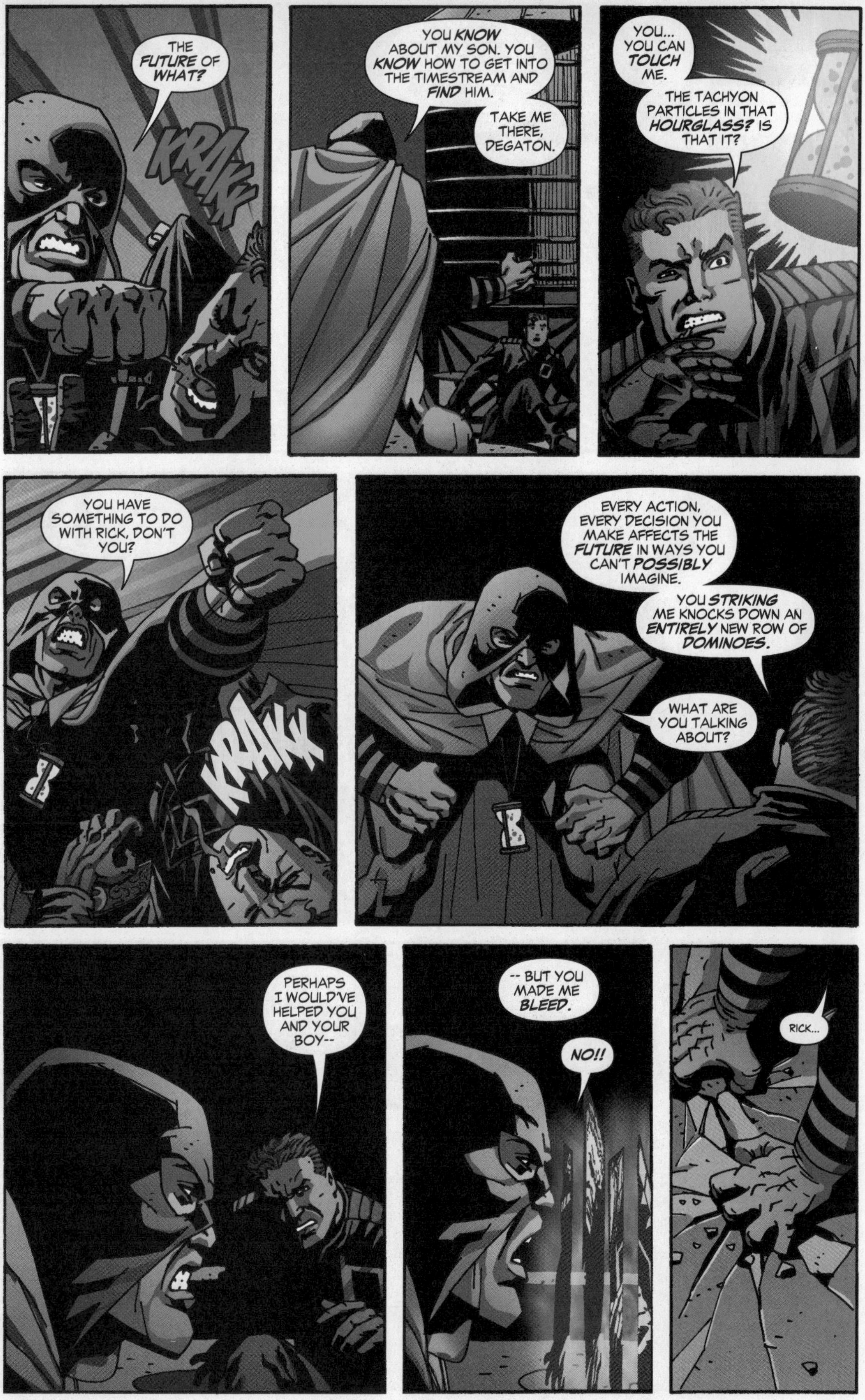
THE FUTURE OF WHAT?
KRAKK
YOU KNOW ABOUT MY SON. YOU KNOW HOW TO GET INTO THE TIMESTREAM AND FIND HIM.
TAKE ME THERE, DEGATON.
YOU... YOU CAN TOUCH ME.
THE TACHYON PARTICLES IN THAT HOURGLASS? IS THAT IT?
YOU HAVE SOMETHING TO DO WITH RICK, DON'T YOU?
KRAKK
EVERY ACTION, EVERY DECISION YOU MAKE AFFECTS THE FUTURE IN WAYS YOU CAN'T POSSIBLY IMAGINE.
YOU STRIKING ME KNOCKS DOWN AN ENTIRELY NEW ROW OF DOMINOES.
WHAT ARE YOU TALKING ABOUT?
PERHAPS I WOULD'VE HELPED YOU AND YOUR BOY--
-- BUT YOU MADE ME BLEED.
NO!!
RICK...

FOUR HOURS AGO.

BLUE VALLEY, NEBRASKA.

FIXING THE COSMIC ROD SHOULDN'T BE THAT HARD... IF I COULD ACTUALLY READ THESE BLUE-PRINTS.

PAT IS *TOTALLY* GONNA MAKE ME *EAT* MY WORDS.

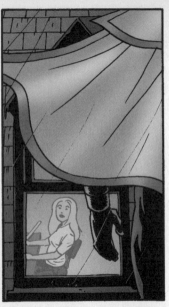

B-BILLY?

BILLY, WHAT'S GOING ON? IT'S *LATE.* AND IF MY MOM CATCHES ME WITH A *BOY* IN MY ROOM--

I...

COURTNEY, I'M LEAVING THE JUSTICE SOCIETY.

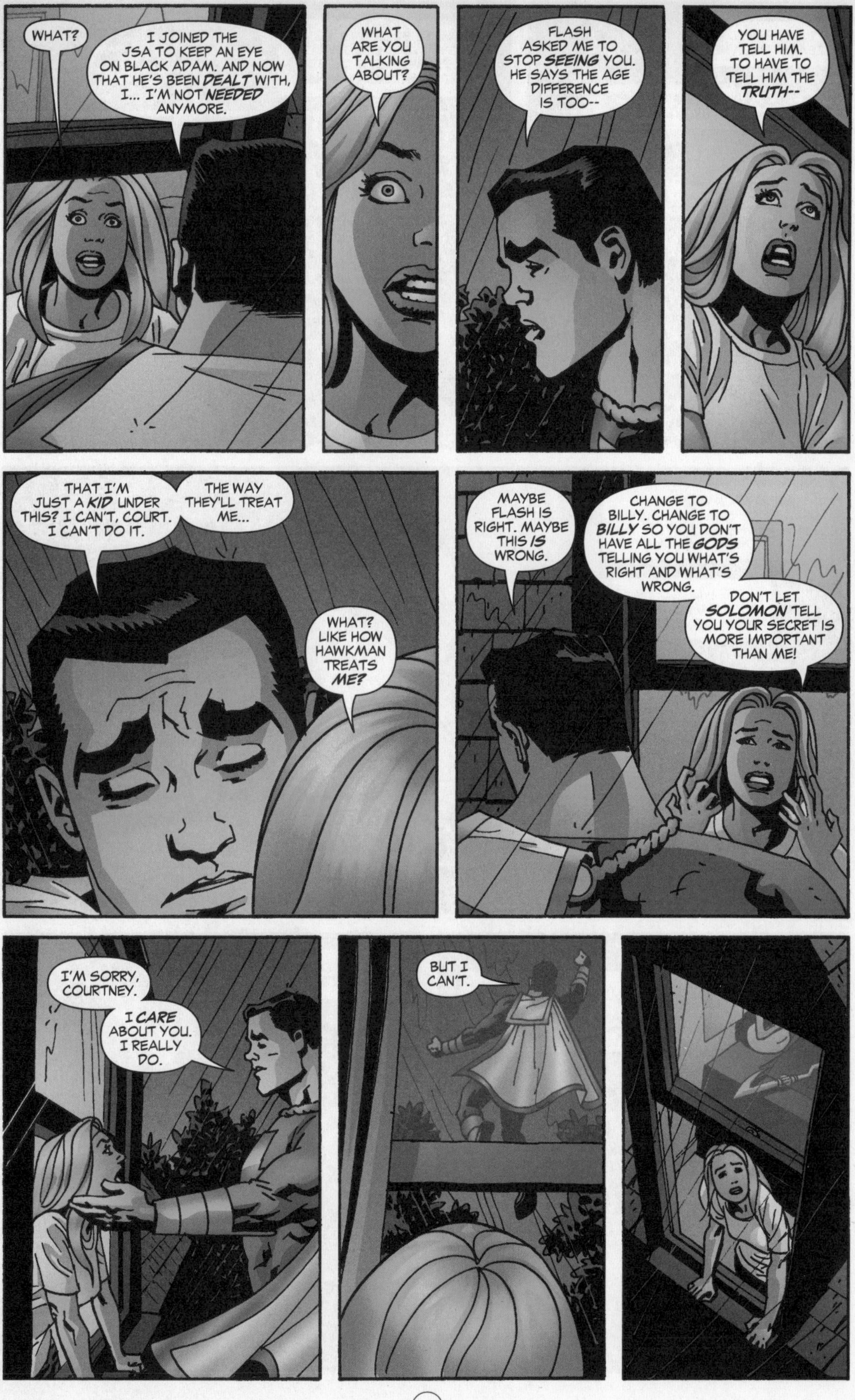
WHAT?
I JOINED THE JSA TO KEEP AN EYE ON BLACK ADAM. AND NOW THAT HE'S BEEN DEALT WITH, I... I'M NOT NEEDED ANYMORE.
WHAT ARE YOU TALKING ABOUT?
FLASH ASKED ME TO STOP SEEING YOU. HE SAYS THE AGE DIFFERENCE IS TOO--
YOU HAVE TELL HIM. TO HAVE TO TELL HIM THE TRUTH--
THAT I'M JUST A KID UNDER THIS? I CAN'T, COURT. I CAN'T DO IT.
THE WAY THEY'LL TREAT ME...
WHAT? LIKE HOW HAWKMAN TREATS ME?
MAYBE FLASH IS RIGHT. MAYBE THIS IS WRONG.
CHANGE TO BILLY. CHANGE TO BILLY SO YOU DON'T HAVE ALL THE GODS TELLING YOU WHAT'S RIGHT AND WHAT'S WRONG.
DON'T LET SOLOMON TELL YOU YOUR SECRET IS MORE IMPORTANT THAN ME!
I'M SORRY, COURTNEY.
I CARE ABOUT YOU. I REALLY DO.
BUT I CAN'T.

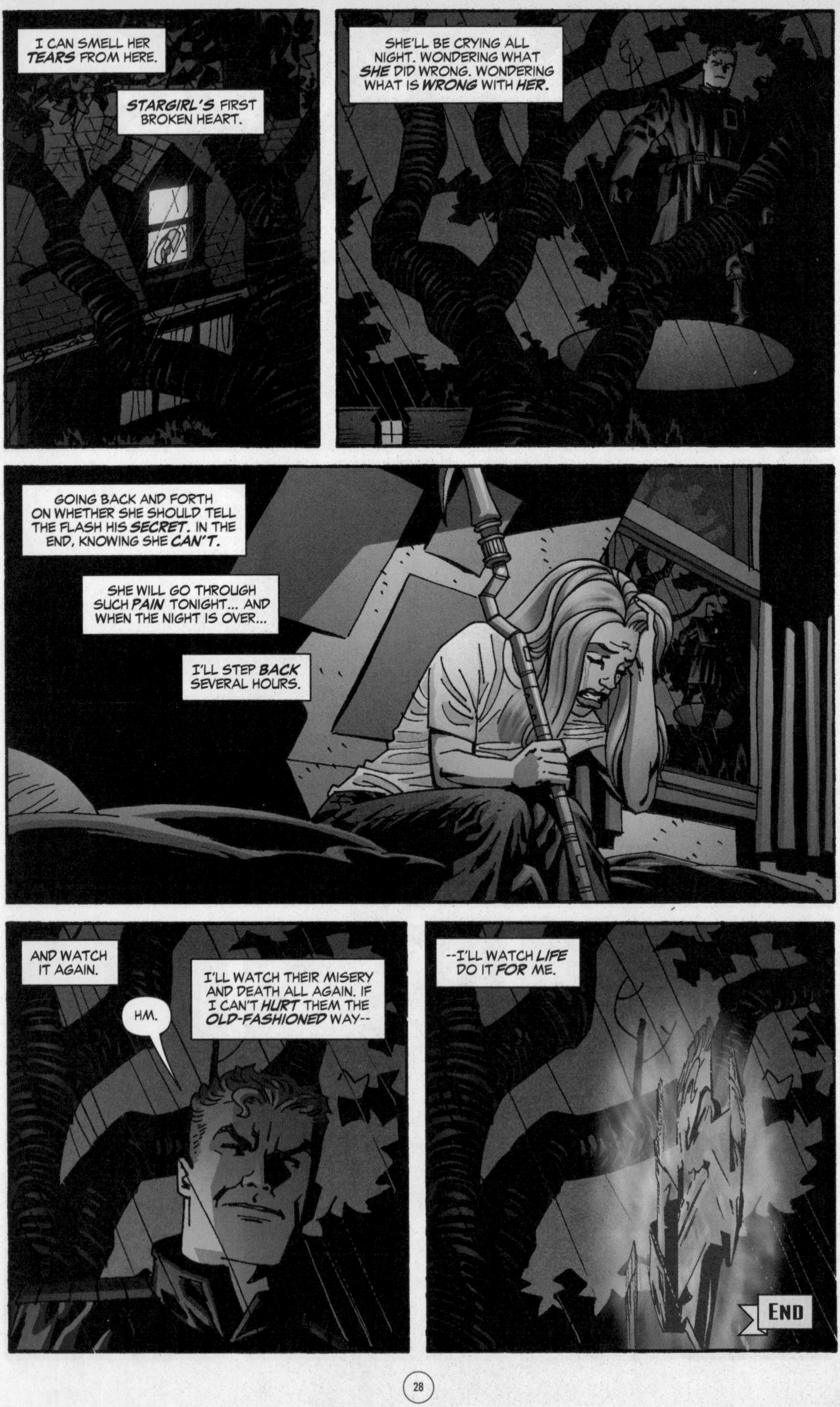
I CAN SMELL HER TEARS FROM HERE.
STARGIRL'S FIRST BROKEN HEART.
SHE'LL BE CRYING ALL NIGHT. WONDERING WHAT SHE DID WRONG. WONDERING WHAT IS WRONG WITH HER.
GOING BACK AND FORTH ON WHETHER SHE SHOULD TELL THE FLASH HIS SECRET. IN THE END, KNOWING SHE CAN'T.
SHE WILL GO THROUGH SUCH PAIN TONIGHT... AND WHEN THE NIGHT IS OVER...
I'LL STEP BACK SEVERAL HOURS.
AND WATCH IT AGAIN.
I'LL WATCH THEIR MISERY AND DEATH ALL AGAIN. IF I CAN'T HURT THEM THE OLD-FASHIONED WAY--
HM.
--I'LL WATCH LIFE DO IT FOR ME.
END

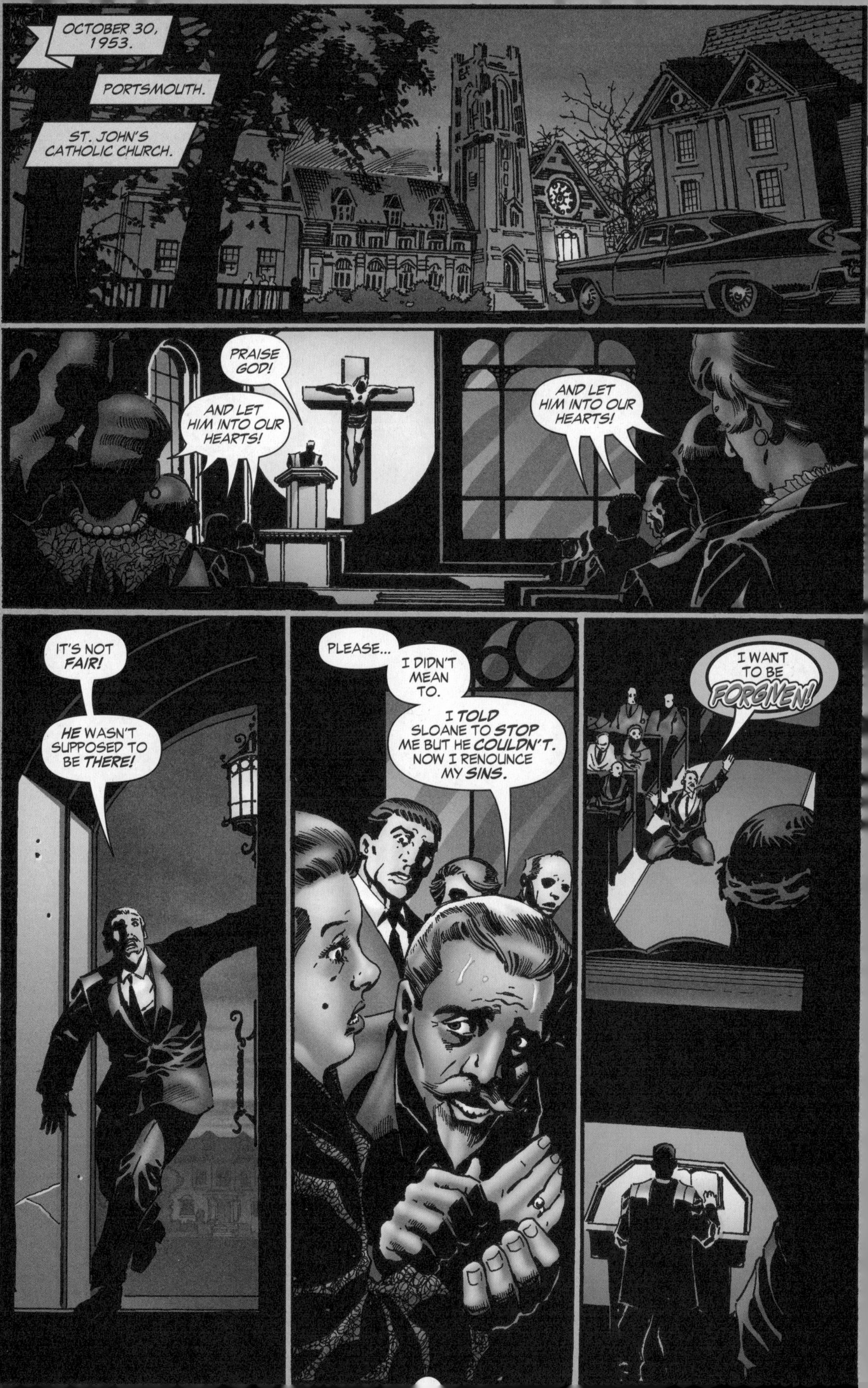

OCTOBER 30, 1953.
PORTSMOUTH.
ST. JOHN'S CATHOLIC CHURCH.
PRAISE GOD!
AND LET HIM INTO OUR HEARTS!
AND LET HIM INTO OUR HEARTS!
IT'S NOT FAIR!
HE WASN'T SUPPOSED TO BE THERE!
PLEASE...
I DIDN'T MEAN TO.
I TOLD SLOANE TO STOP ME BUT HE COULDN'T. NOW I RENOUNCE MY SINS.
I WANT TO BE FORGIVEN!

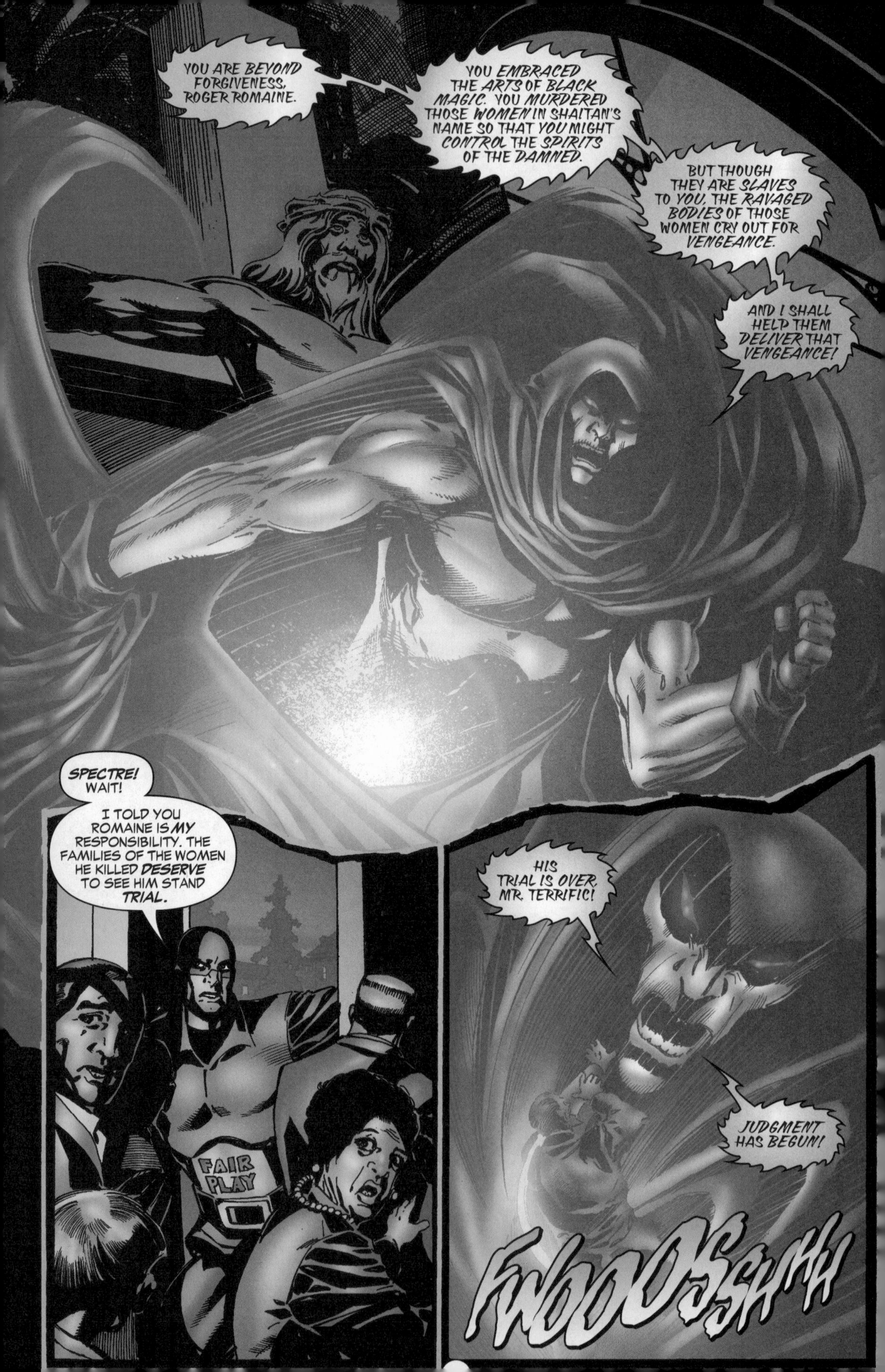

YOU ARE BEYOND FORGIVENESS, ROGER ROMAINE.
YOU EMBRACED THE ARTS OF BLACK MAGIC. YOU MURDERED THOSE WOMEN IN SHAITAN'S NAME SO THAT YOU MIGHT CONTROL THE SPIRITS OF THE DAMNED.
BUT THOUGH THEY ARE SLAVES TO YOU, THE RAVAGED BODIES OF THOSE WOMEN CRY OUT FOR VENGEANCE.
AND I SHALL HELP THEM DELIVER THAT VENGEANCE!
SPECTRE! WAIT!
I TOLD YOU ROMAINE IS MY RESPONSIBILITY. THE FAMILIES OF THE WOMEN HE KILLED DESERVE TO SEE HIM STAND TRIAL.
FAIR PLAY
HIS TRIAL IS OVER, MR. TERRIFIC!
JUDGMENT HAS BEGUN!
FWOOOSHHH

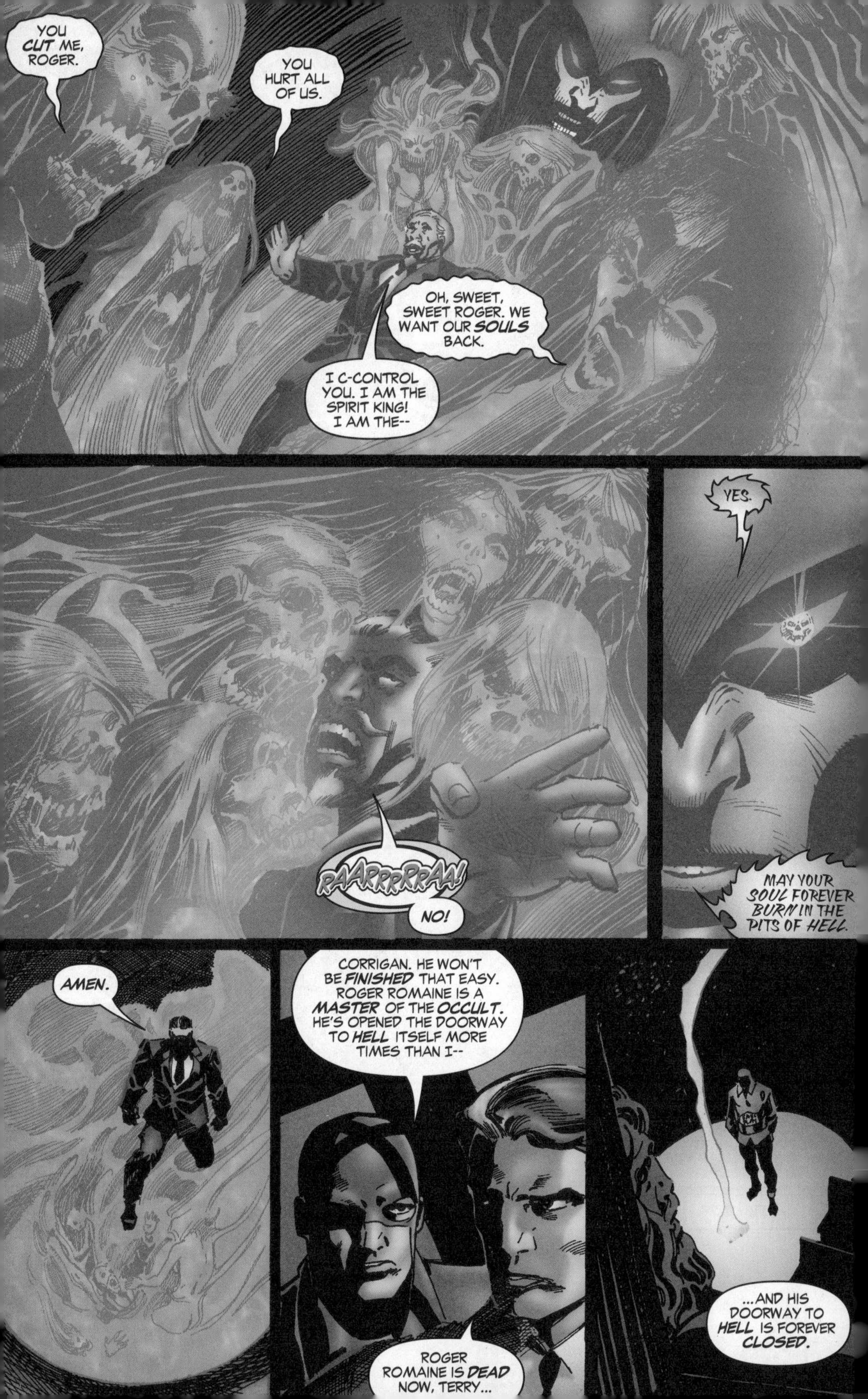

YOU CUT ME, ROGER.
YOU HURT ALL OF US.
OH, SWEET, SWEET ROGER. WE WANT OUR SOULS BACK.
I C-CONTROL YOU. I AM THE SPIRIT KING! I AM THE--
YES.
RAARRRRRAA!
NO!
MAY YOUR SOUL FOREVER BURN IN THE PITS OF HELL.
AMEN.
CORRIGAN. HE WON'T BE FINISHED THAT EASY. ROGER ROMAINE IS A MASTER OF THE OCCULT. HE'S OPENED THE DOORWAY TO HELL ITSELF MORE TIMES THAN I--
ROGER ROMAINE IS DEAD NOW, TERRY...
...AND HIS DOORWAY TO HELL IS FOREVER CLOSED.

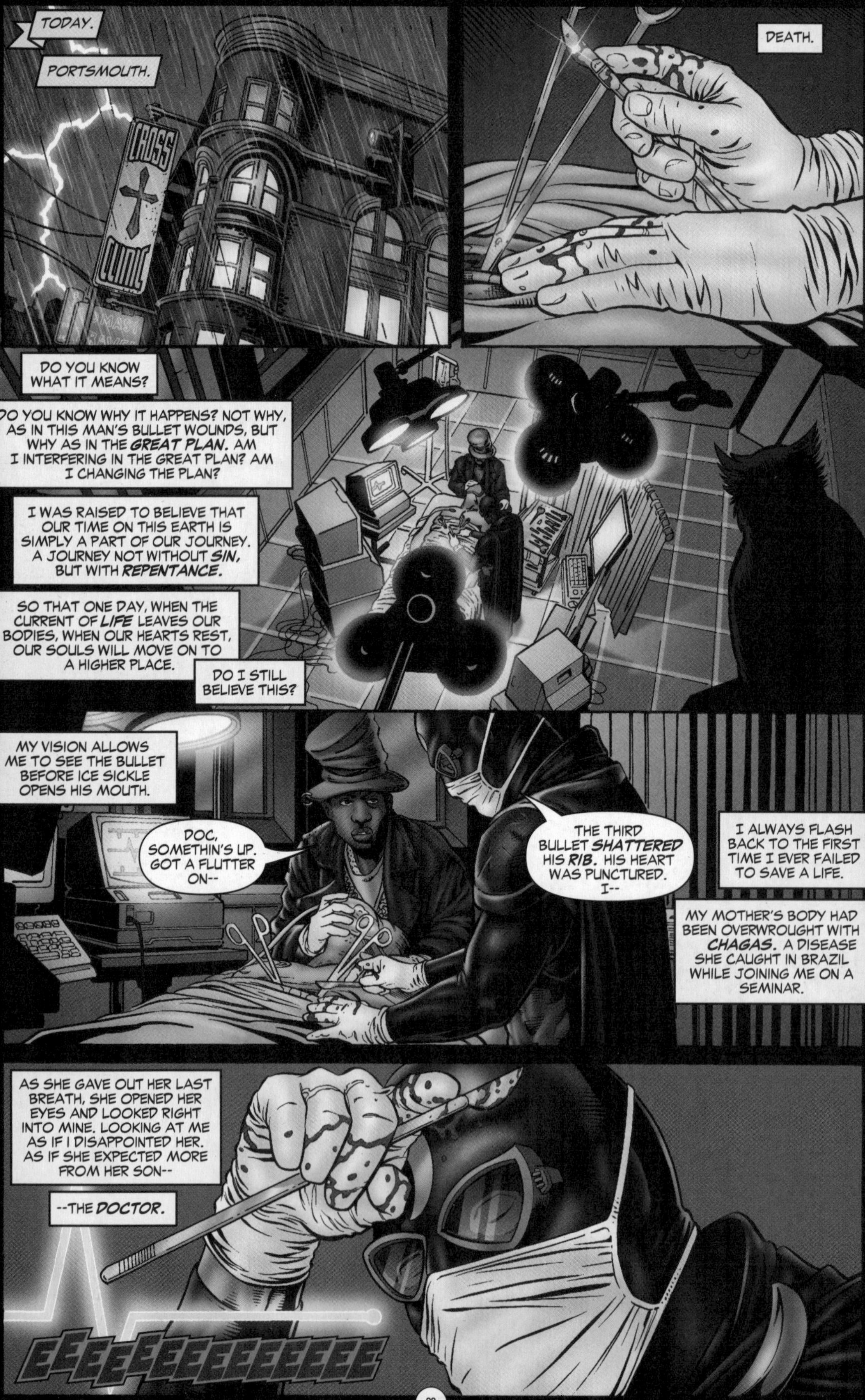
TODAY.
PORTSMOUTH.
CROSS CLINIC
DEATH.
DO YOU KNOW WHAT IT MEANS?
DO YOU KNOW WHY IT HAPPENS? NOT WHY, AS IN THIS MAN'S BULLET WOUNDS, BUT WHY AS IN THE GREAT PLAN. AM I INTERFERING IN THE GREAT PLAN? AM I CHANGING THE PLAN?
I WAS RAISED TO BELIEVE THAT OUR TIME ON THIS EARTH IS SIMPLY A PART OF OUR JOURNEY. A JOURNEY NOT WITHOUT SIN, BUT WITH REPENTANCE.
SO THAT ONE DAY, WHEN THE CURRENT OF LIFE LEAVES OUR BODIES, WHEN OUR HEARTS REST, OUR SOULS WILL MOVE ON TO A HIGHER PLACE.
DO I STILL BELIEVE THIS?
MY VISION ALLOWS ME TO SEE THE BULLET BEFORE ICE SICKLE OPENS HIS MOUTH.
DOC, SOMETHIN'S UP. GOT A FLUTTER ON--
THE THIRD BULLET SHATTERED HIS RIB. HIS HEART WAS PUNCTURED. I--
I ALWAYS FLASH BACK TO THE FIRST TIME I EVER FAILED TO SAVE A LIFE.
MY MOTHER'S BODY HAD BEEN OVERWROUGHT WITH CHAGAS. A DISEASE SHE CAUGHT IN BRAZIL WHILE JOINING ME ON A SEMINAR.
AS SHE GAVE OUT HER LAST BREATH, SHE OPENED HER EYES AND LOOKED RIGHT INTO MINE. LOOKING AT ME AS IF I DISAPPOINTED HER. AS IF SHE EXPECTED MORE FROM HER SON--
--THE DOCTOR.
EEEEEEEEEEEEEE

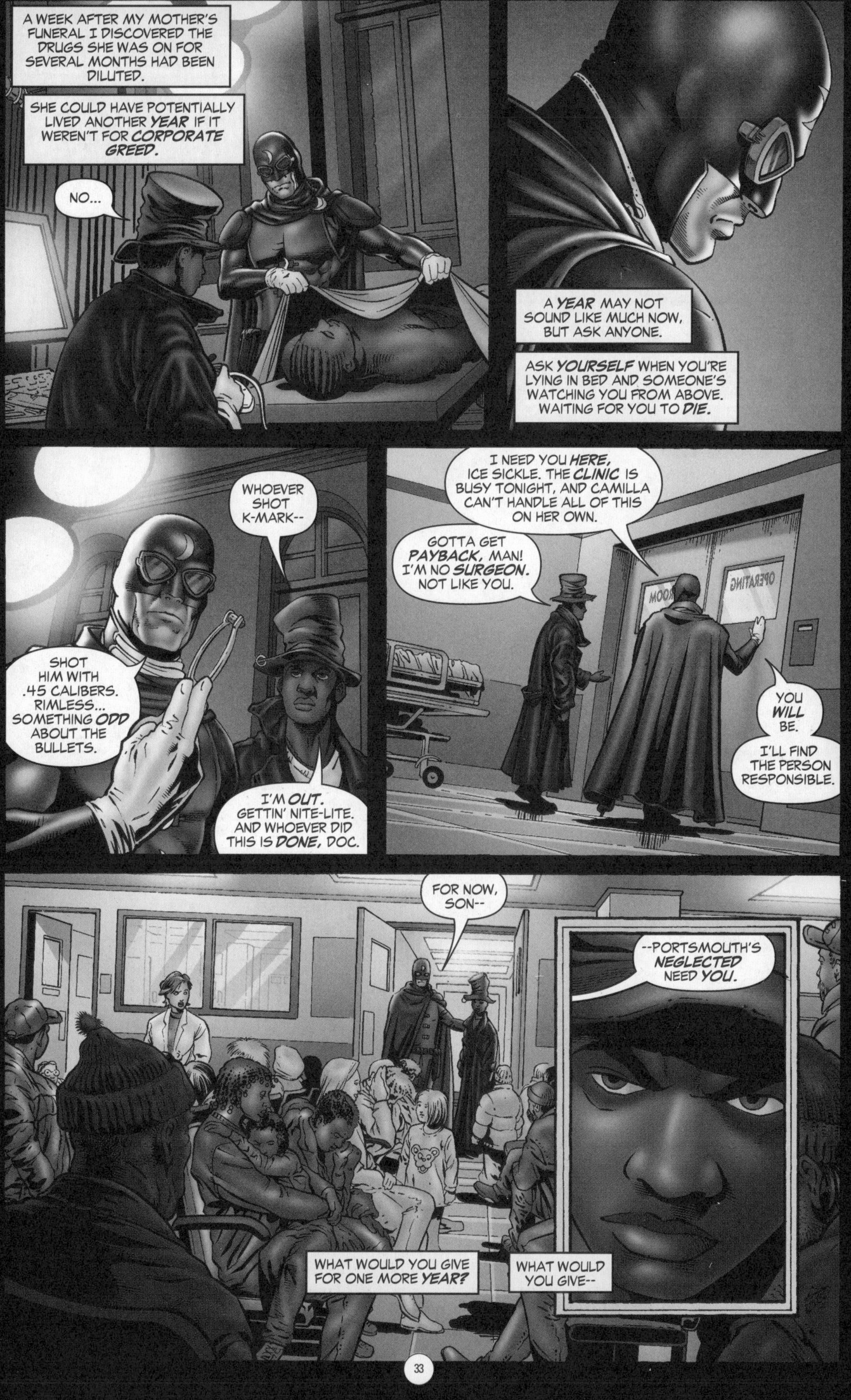
A WEEK AFTER MY MOTHER'S FUNERAL I DISCOVERED THE DRUGS SHE WAS ON FOR SEVERAL MONTHS HAD BEEN DILUTED.
SHE COULD HAVE POTENTIALLY LIVED ANOTHER YEAR IF IT WEREN'T FOR CORPORATE GREED.
NO...
A YEAR MAY NOT SOUND LIKE MUCH NOW, BUT ASK ANYONE.
ASK YOURSELF WHEN YOU'RE LYING IN BED AND SOMEONE'S WATCHING YOU FROM ABOVE. WAITING FOR YOU TO DIE.
WHOEVER SHOT K-MARK--
SHOT HIM WITH .45 CALIBERS. RIMLESS... SOMETHING ODD ABOUT THE BULLETS.
I'M OUT. GETTIN' NITE-LITE. AND WHOEVER DID THIS IS DONE, DOC.
I NEED YOU HERE, ICE SICKLE. THE CLINIC IS BUSY TONIGHT, AND CAMILLA CAN'T HANDLE ALL OF THIS ON HER OWN.
GOTTA GET PAYBACK, MAN! I'M NO SURGEON. NOT LIKE YOU.
YOU WILL BE.
I'LL FIND THE PERSON RESPONSIBLE.
FOR NOW, SON--
--PORTSMOUTH'S NEGLECTED NEED YOU.
WHAT WOULD YOU GIVE FOR ONE MORE YEAR?
WHAT WOULD YOU GIVE--

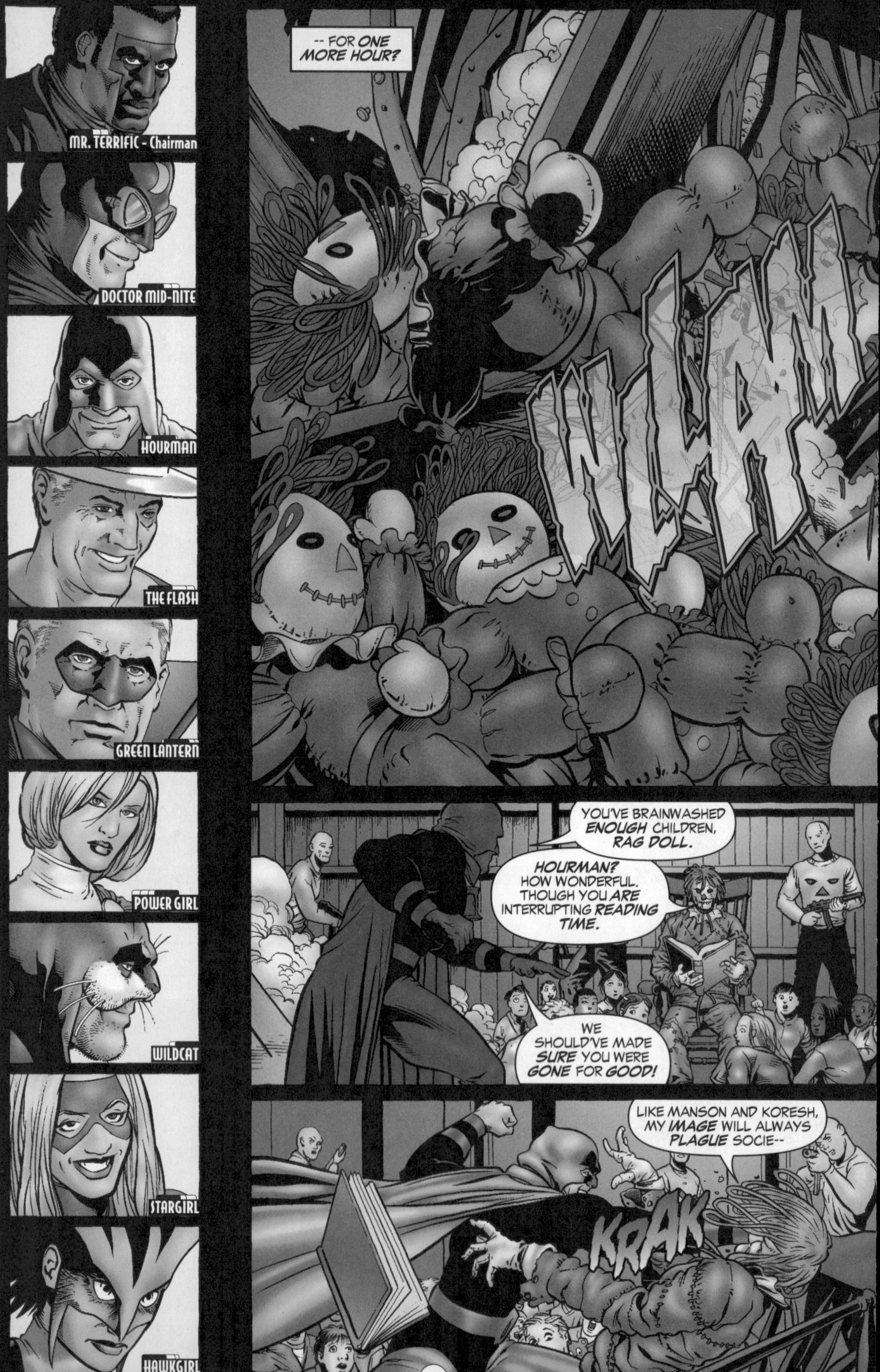
MR. TERRIFIC - Chairman
DOCTOR MID-NITE
HOURMAN
THE FLASH
GREEN LANTERN
POWER GIRL
WILDCAT
STARGIRL
HAWKGIRL
-- FOR ONE MORE HOUR?
WUMM
YOU'VE BRAINWASHED ENOUGH CHILDREN, RAG DOLL.
HOURMAN? HOW WONDERFUL. THOUGH YOU ARE INTERRUPTING READING TIME.
WE SHOULD'VE MADE SURE YOU WERE GONE FOR GOOD!
LIKE MANSON AND KORESH, MY IMAGE WILL ALWAYS PLAGUE SOCIE--
KRAK

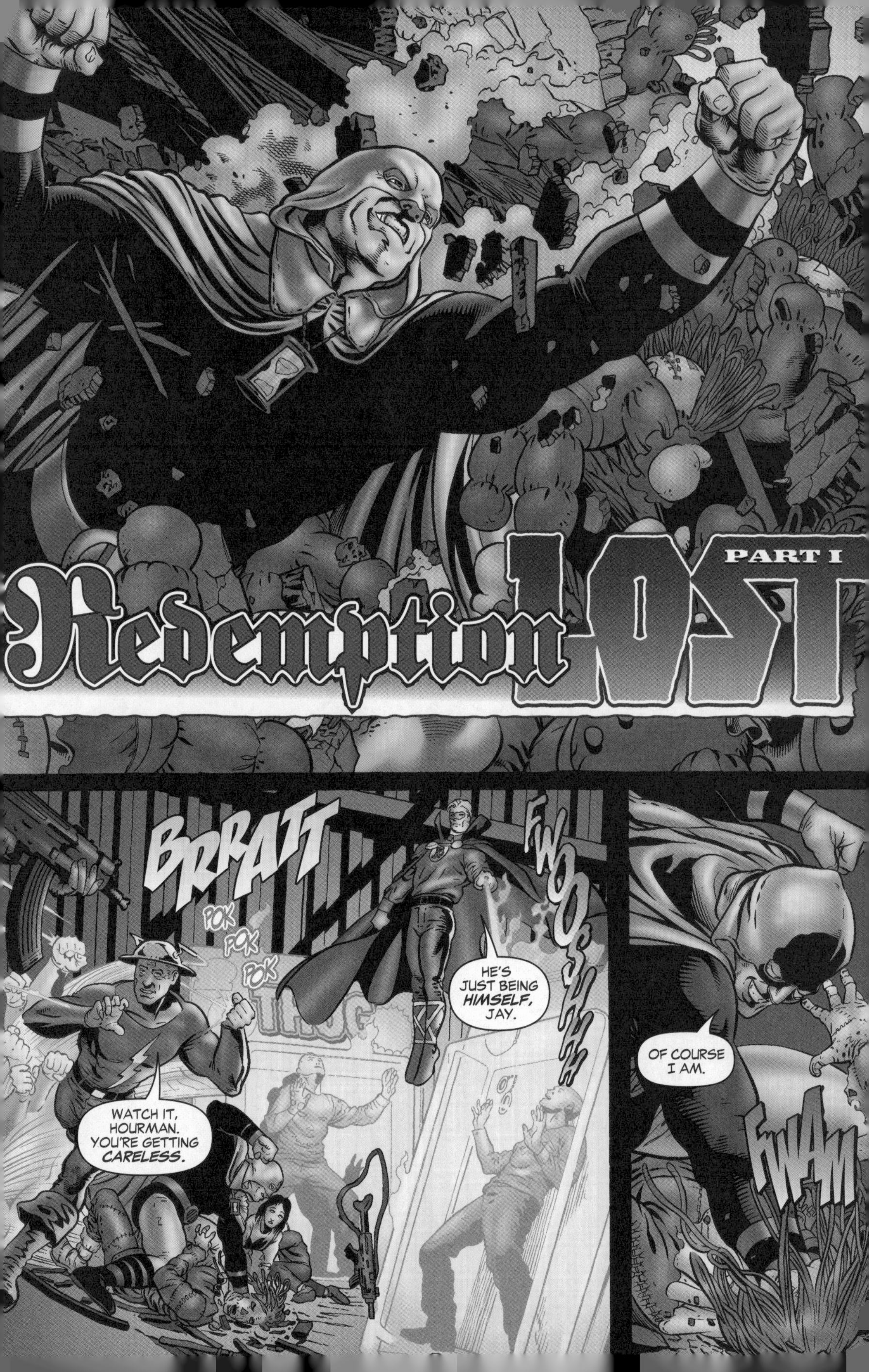
PART I
Redemption LOST
BRRATT
POK
POK
POK
WATCH IT, HOURMAN. YOU'RE GETTING CARELESS.
HE'S JUST BEING HIMSELF, JAY.
FWOOSHHH
OF COURSE I AM.
FWAM

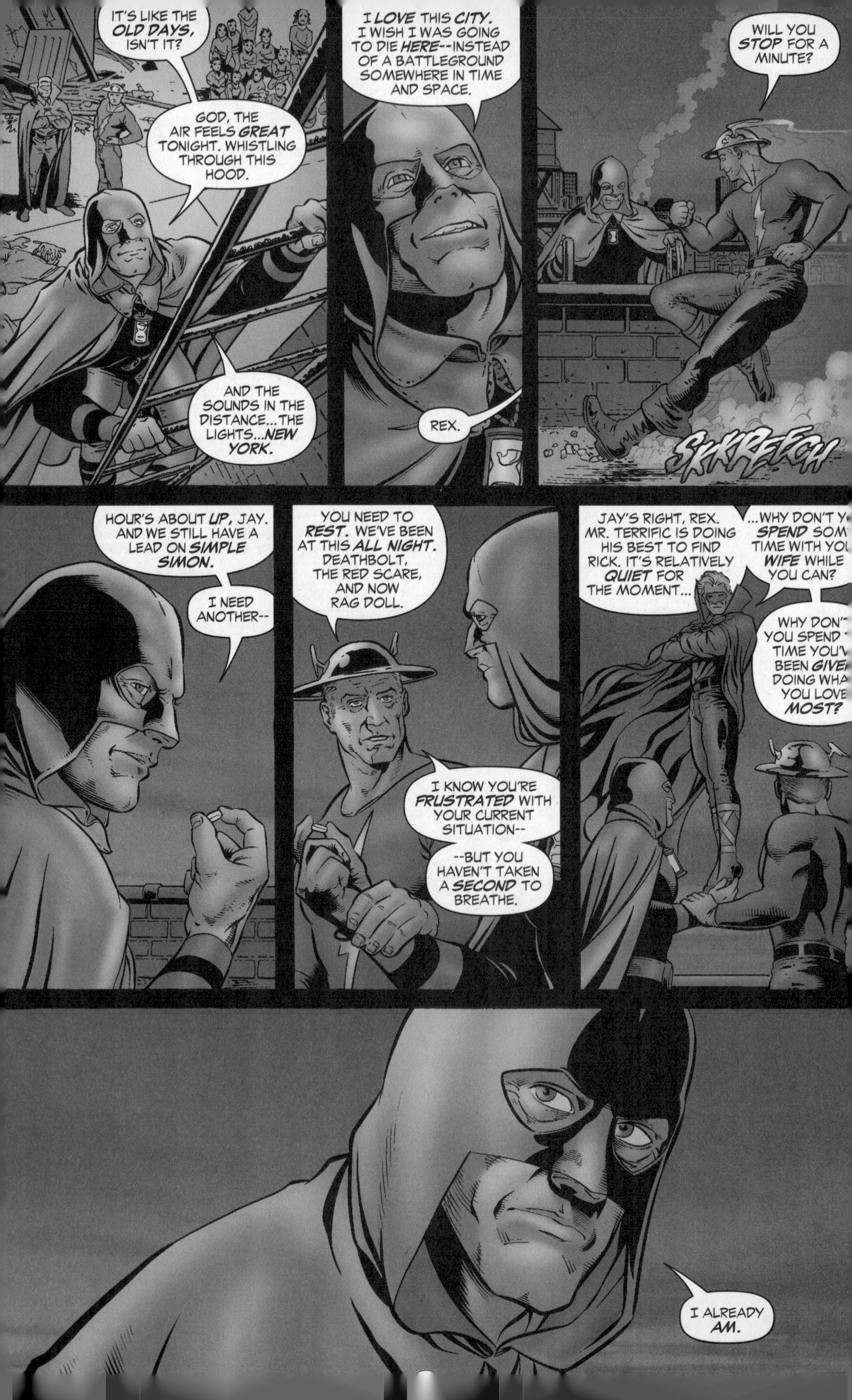
IT'S LIKE THE OLD DAYS, ISN'T IT?
GOD, THE AIR FEELS GREAT TONIGHT. WHISTLING THROUGH THIS HOOD.
AND THE SOUNDS IN THE DISTANCE...THE LIGHTS...NEW YORK.
I LOVE THIS CITY. I WISH I WAS GOING TO DIE HERE--INSTEAD OF A BATTLEGROUND SOMEWHERE IN TIME AND SPACE.
REX.
WILL YOU STOP FOR A MINUTE?
SKKREECH
HOUR'S ABOUT UP, JAY. AND WE STILL HAVE A LEAD ON SIMPLE SIMON.
I NEED ANOTHER--
YOU NEED TO REST. WE'VE BEEN AT THIS ALL NIGHT. DEATHBOLT, THE RED SCARE, AND NOW RAG DOLL.
I KNOW YOU'RE FRUSTRATED WITH YOUR CURRENT SITUATION--
--BUT YOU HAVEN'T TAKEN A SECOND TO BREATHE.
JAY'S RIGHT, REX. MR. TERRIFIC IS DOING HIS BEST TO FIND RICK. IT'S RELATIVELY QUIET FOR THE MOMENT...
...WHY DON'T Y SPEND SOM TIME WITH YOU WIFE WHILE YOU CAN?
WHY DON' YOU SPEND TIME YOU'V BEEN GIVE DOING WHA YOU LOVE MOST?
I ALREADY AM.

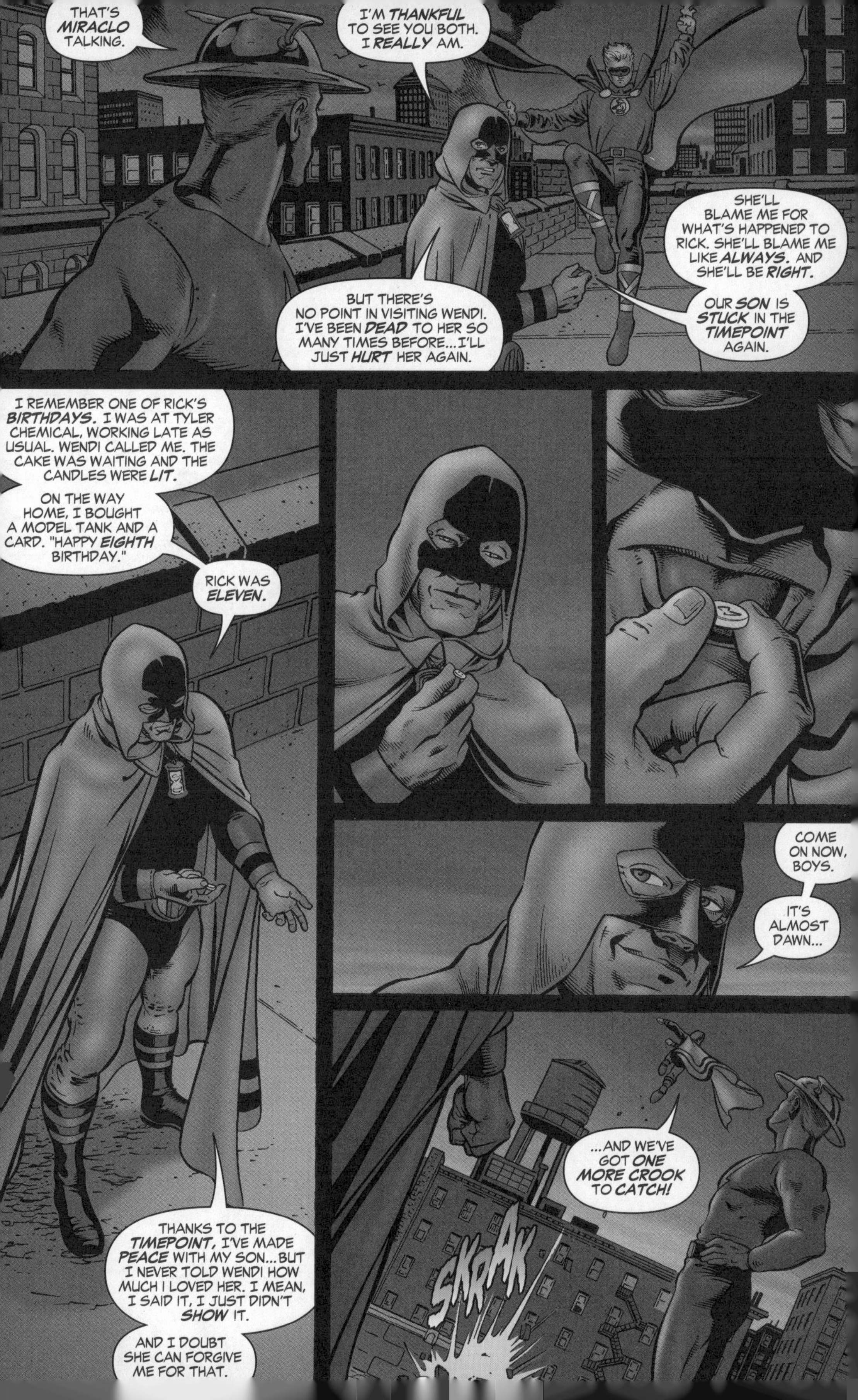
THAT'S MIRACLO TALKING.
I'M THANKFUL TO SEE YOU BOTH. I REALLY AM.
BUT THERE'S NO POINT IN VISITING WENDI. I'VE BEEN DEAD TO HER SO MANY TIMES BEFORE...I'LL JUST HURT HER AGAIN.
SHE'LL BLAME ME FOR WHAT'S HAPPENED TO RICK. SHE'LL BLAME ME LIKE ALWAYS. AND SHE'LL BE RIGHT.
OUR SON IS STUCK IN THE TIMEPOINT AGAIN.
I REMEMBER ONE OF RICK'S BIRTHDAYS. I WAS AT TYLER CHEMICAL, WORKING LATE AS USUAL. WENDI CALLED ME. THE CAKE WAS WAITING AND THE CANDLES WERE LIT.
ON THE WAY HOME, I BOUGHT A MODEL TANK AND A CARD. "HAPPY EIGHTH BIRTHDAY."
RICK WAS ELEVEN.
THANKS TO THE TIMEPOINT, I'VE MADE PEACE WITH MY SON...BUT I NEVER TOLD WENDI HOW MUCH I LOVED HER. I MEAN, I SAID IT, I JUST DIDN'T SHOW IT.
AND I DOUBT SHE CAN FORGIVE ME FOR THAT.
COME ON NOW, BOYS.
IT'S ALMOST DAWN...
...AND WE'VE GOT ONE MORE CROOK TO CATCH!
SKRAK

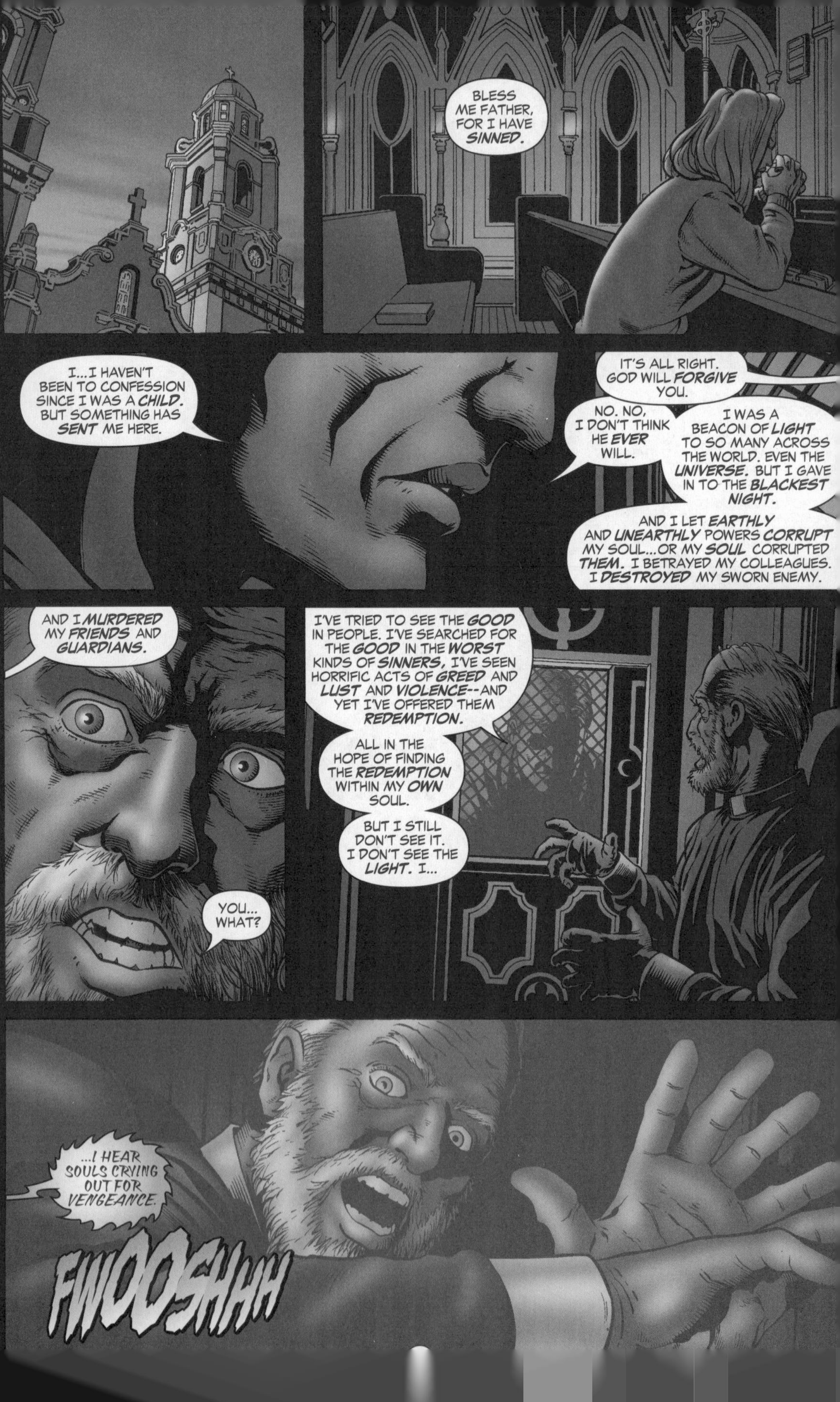
BLESS ME FATHER, FOR I HAVE SINNED.
I...I HAVEN'T BEEN TO CONFESSION SINCE I WAS A CHILD. BUT SOMETHING HAS SENT ME HERE.
IT'S ALL RIGHT. GOD WILL FORGIVE YOU.
NO. NO, I DON'T THINK HE EVER WILL.
I WAS A BEACON OF LIGHT TO SO MANY ACROSS THE WORLD. EVEN THE UNIVERSE. BUT I GAVE IN TO THE BLACKEST NIGHT.
AND I LET EARTHLY AND UNEARTHLY POWERS CORRUPT MY SOUL...OR MY SOUL CORRUPTED THEM. I BETRAYED MY COLLEAGUES. I DESTROYED MY SWORN ENEMY.
AND I MURDERED MY FRIENDS AND GUARDIANS.
I'VE TRIED TO SEE THE GOOD IN PEOPLE. I'VE SEARCHED FOR THE GOOD IN THE WORST KINDS OF SINNERS, I'VE SEEN HORRIFIC ACTS OF GREED AND LUST AND VIOLENCE--AND YET I'VE OFFERED THEM REDEMPTION.
ALL IN THE HOPE OF FINDING THE REDEMPTION WITHIN MY OWN SOUL.
BUT I STILL DON'T SEE IT. I DON'T SEE THE LIGHT. I...
YOU... WHAT?
...I HEAR SOULS CRYING OUT FOR VENGEANCE.
FWOOSHHH

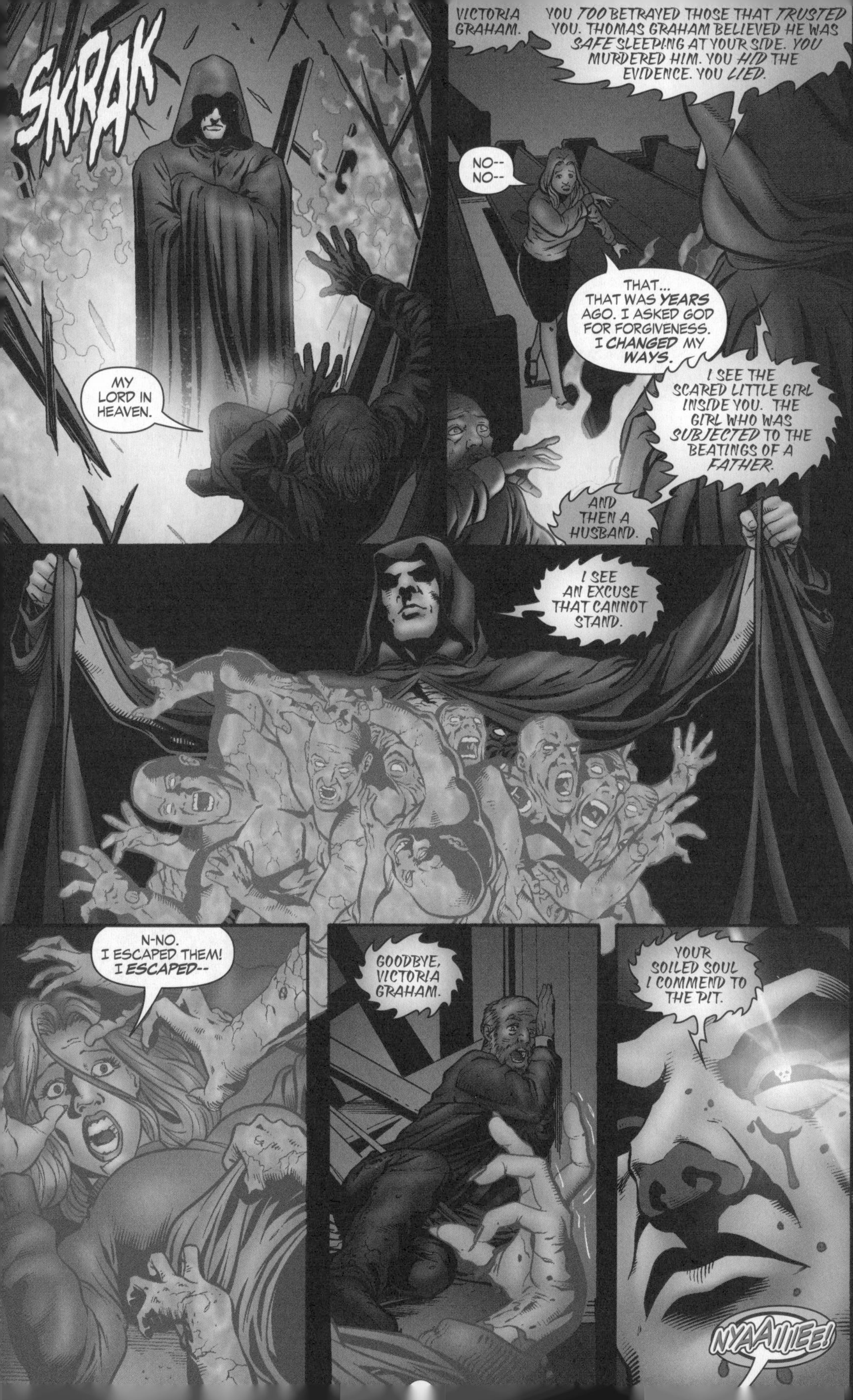
SKRAK
MY LORD IN HEAVEN.
VICTORIA GRAHAM.
YOU TOO BETRAYED THOSE THAT TRUSTED YOU. THOMAS GRAHAM BELIEVED HE WAS SAFE SLEEPING AT YOUR SIDE. YOU MURDERED HIM. YOU HID THE EVIDENCE. YOU LIED.
NO-- NO--
THAT... THAT WAS YEARS AGO. I ASKED GOD FOR FORGIVENESS. I CHANGED MY WAYS.
I SEE THE SCARED LITTLE GIRL INSIDE YOU. THE GIRL WHO WAS SUBJECTED TO THE BEATINGS OF A FATHER.
AND THEN A HUSBAND.
I SEE AN EXCUSE THAT CANNOT STAND.
N-NO. I ESCAPED THEM! I ESCAPED--
GOODBYE, VICTORIA GRAHAM.
YOUR SOILED SOUL I COMMEND TO THE PIT.
NYAAIIIEE!

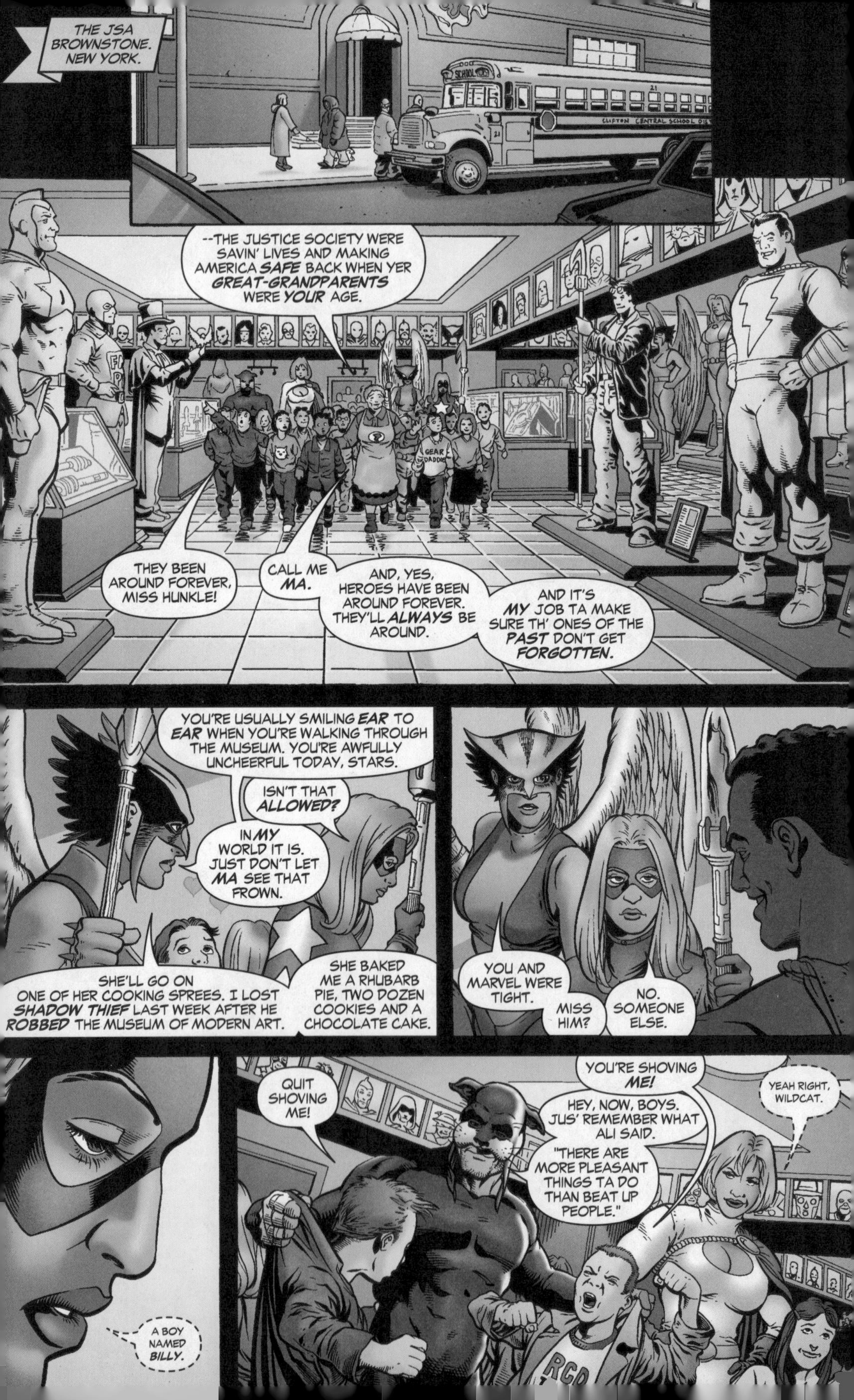

THE JSA BROWNSTONE. NEW YORK.
SCHOOL
CLIFTON CENTRAL SCHOOL DIS
--THE JUSTICE SOCIETY WERE SAVIN' LIVES AND MAKING AMERICA SAFE BACK WHEN YER GREAT-GRANDPARENTS WERE YOUR AGE.
THEY BEEN AROUND FOREVER, MISS HUNKLE!
CALL ME MA.
AND, YES, HEROES HAVE BEEN AROUND FOREVER. THEY'LL ALWAYS BE AROUND.
AND IT'S MY JOB TA MAKE SURE TH' ONES OF THE PAST DON'T GET FORGOTTEN.
YOU'RE USUALLY SMILING EAR TO EAR WHEN YOU'RE WALKING THROUGH THE MUSEUM. YOU'RE AWFULLY UNCHEERFUL TODAY, STARS.
ISN'T THAT ALLOWED?
IN MY WORLD IT IS. JUST DON'T LET MA SEE THAT FROWN.
SHE'LL GO ON ONE OF HER COOKING SPREES. I LOST SHADOW THIEF LAST WEEK AFTER HE ROBBED THE MUSEUM OF MODERN ART.
SHE BAKED ME A RHUBARB PIE, TWO DOZEN COOKIES AND A CHOCOLATE CAKE.
YOU AND MARVEL WERE TIGHT.
MISS HIM?
NO. SOMEONE ELSE.
A BOY NAMED BILLY.
QUIT SHOVING ME!
YOU'RE SHOVING ME!
HEY, NOW, BOYS. JUS' REMEMBER WHAT ALI SAID.
"THERE ARE MORE PLEASANT THINGS TA DO THAN BEAT UP PEOPLE."
YEAH RIGHT, WILDCAT.

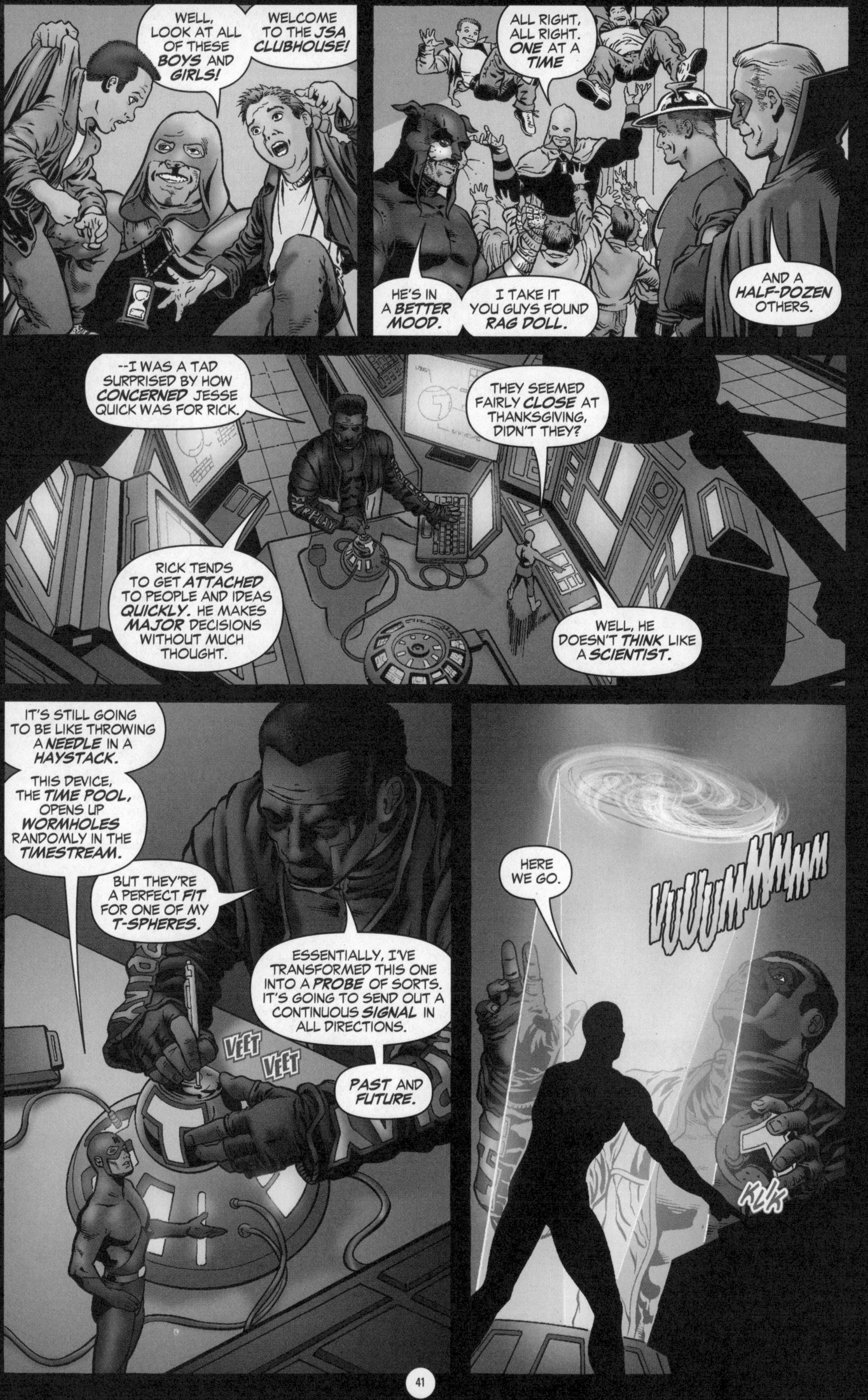
WELL, LOOK AT ALL OF THESE BOYS AND GIRLS!
WELCOME TO THE JSA CLUBHOUSE!
ALL RIGHT, ALL RIGHT. ONE AT A TIME
HE'S IN A BETTER MOOD.
I TAKE IT YOU GUYS FOUND RAG DOLL.
AND A HALF-DOZEN OTHERS.
--I WAS A TAD SURPRISED BY HOW CONCERNED JESSE QUICK WAS FOR RICK.
THEY SEEMED FAIRLY CLOSE AT THANKSGIVING, DIDN'T THEY?
RICK TENDS TO GET ATTACHED TO PEOPLE AND IDEAS QUICKLY. HE MAKES MAJOR DECISIONS WITHOUT MUCH THOUGHT.
WELL, HE DOESN'T THINK LIKE A SCIENTIST.
IT'S STILL GOING TO BE LIKE THROWING A NEEDLE IN A HAYSTACK.
THIS DEVICE, THE TIME POOL, OPENS UP WORMHOLES RANDOMLY IN THE TIMESTREAM.
BUT THEY'RE A PERFECT FIT FOR ONE OF MY T-SPHERES.
ESSENTIALLY, I'VE TRANSFORMED THIS ONE INTO A PROBE OF SORTS. IT'S GOING TO SEND OUT A CONTINUOUS SIGNAL IN ALL DIRECTIONS.
PAST AND FUTURE.
VEET
VEET
HERE WE GO.
VUUUMMMMM
KLIK

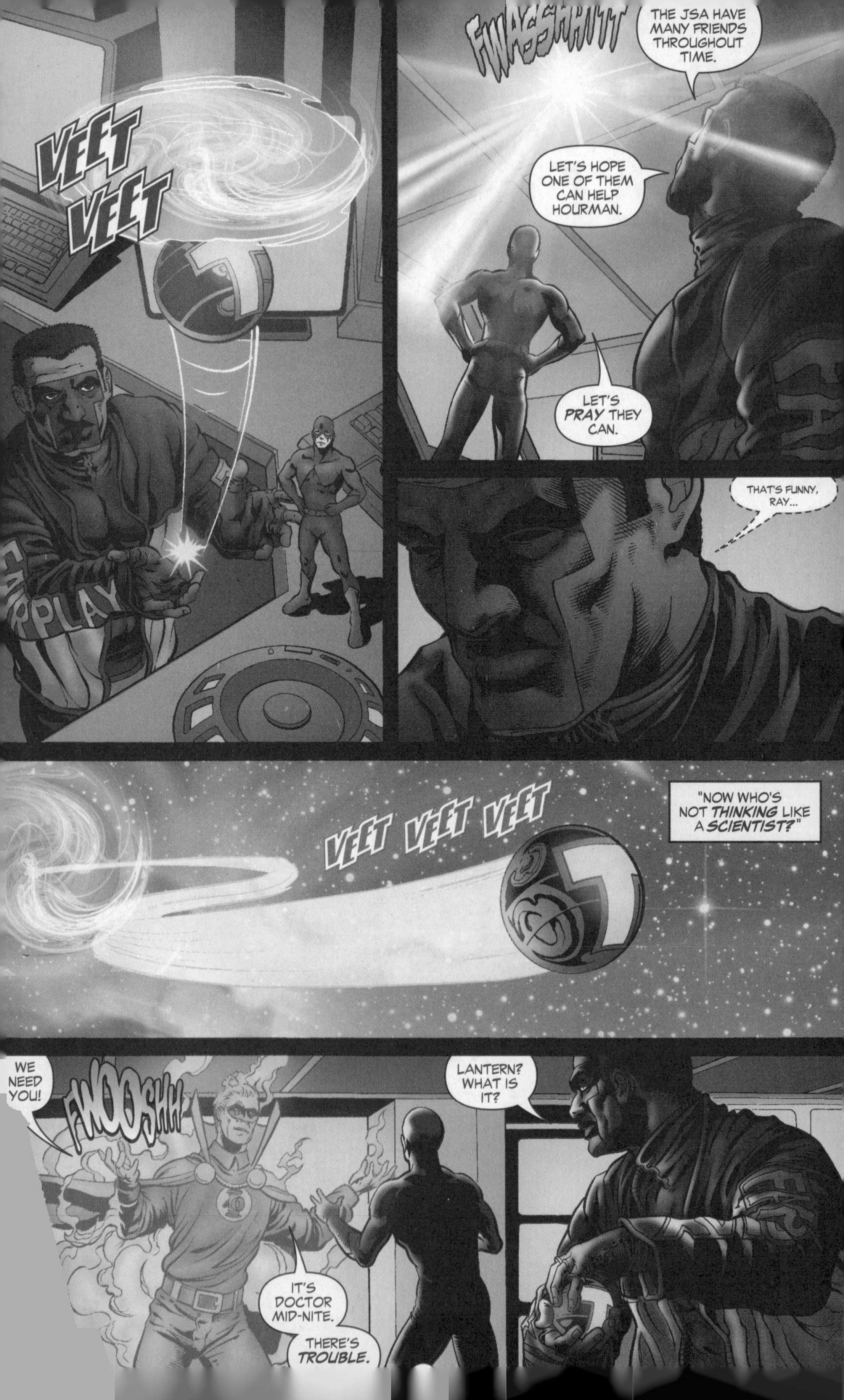
VEET
VEET
FWASHHTT
THE JSA HAVE MANY FRIENDS THROUGHOUT TIME.
LET'S HOPE ONE OF THEM CAN HELP HOURMAN.
LET'S PRAY THEY CAN.
THAT'S FUNNY, RAY...
"NOW WHO'S NOT THINKING LIKE A SCIENTIST?"
VEET VEET VEET
WE NEED YOU!
FWOOSHH
LANTERN? WHAT IS IT?
IT'S DOCTOR MID-NITE.
THERE'S TROUBLE.

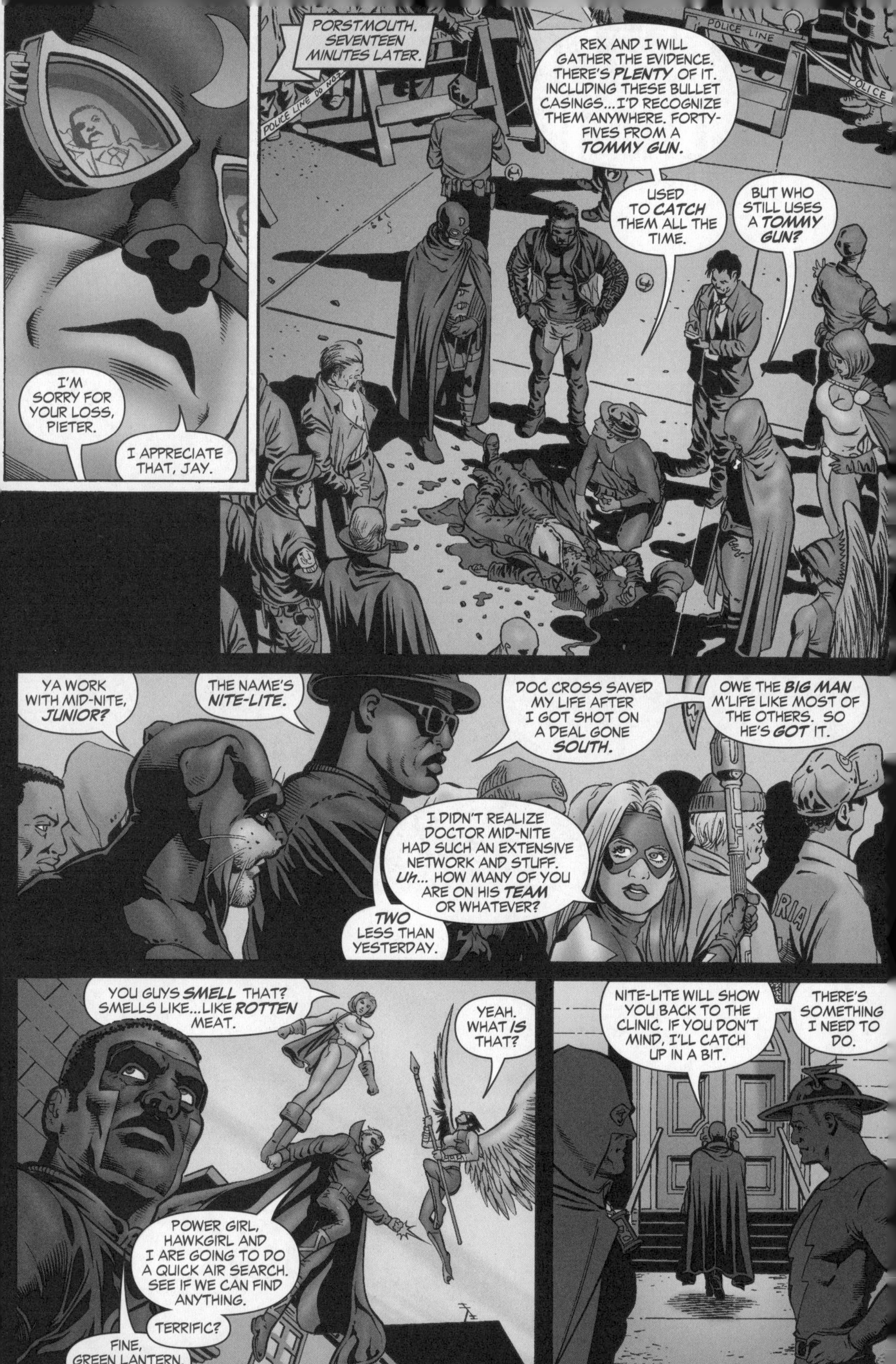
I'M SORRY FOR YOUR LOSS, PIETER.
I APPRECIATE THAT, JAY.
PORSTMOUTH. SEVENTEEN MINUTES LATER.
REX AND I WILL GATHER THE EVIDENCE. THERE'S PLENTY OF IT. INCLUDING THESE BULLET CASINGS...I'D RECOGNIZE THEM ANYWHERE. FORTY-FIVES FROM A TOMMY GUN.
USED TO CATCH THEM ALL THE TIME.
BUT WHO STILL USES A TOMMY GUN?
YA WORK WITH MID-NITE, JUNIOR?
THE NAME'S NITE-LITE.
DOC CROSS SAVED MY LIFE AFTER I GOT SHOT ON A DEAL GONE SOUTH.
OWE THE BIG MAN M'LIFE LIKE MOST OF THE OTHERS. SO HE'S GOT IT.
I DIDN'T REALIZE DOCTOR MID-NITE HAD SUCH AN EXTENSIVE NETWORK AND STUFF. Uh... HOW MANY OF YOU ARE ON HIS TEAM OR WHATEVER?
TWO LESS THAN YESTERDAY.
YOU GUYS SMELL THAT? SMELLS LIKE...LIKE ROTTEN MEAT.
YEAH. WHAT IS THAT?
POWER GIRL, HAWKGIRL AND I ARE GOING TO DO A QUICK AIR SEARCH. SEE IF WE CAN FIND ANYTHING.
TERRIFIC?
FINE, GREEN LANTERN.
NITE-LITE WILL SHOW YOU BACK TO THE CLINIC. IF YOU DON'T MIND, I'LL CATCH UP IN A BIT.
THERE'S SOMETHING I NEED TO DO.

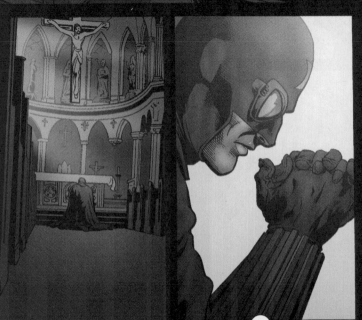

WHAT ARE YOU DOING?

I'M PRAYING.

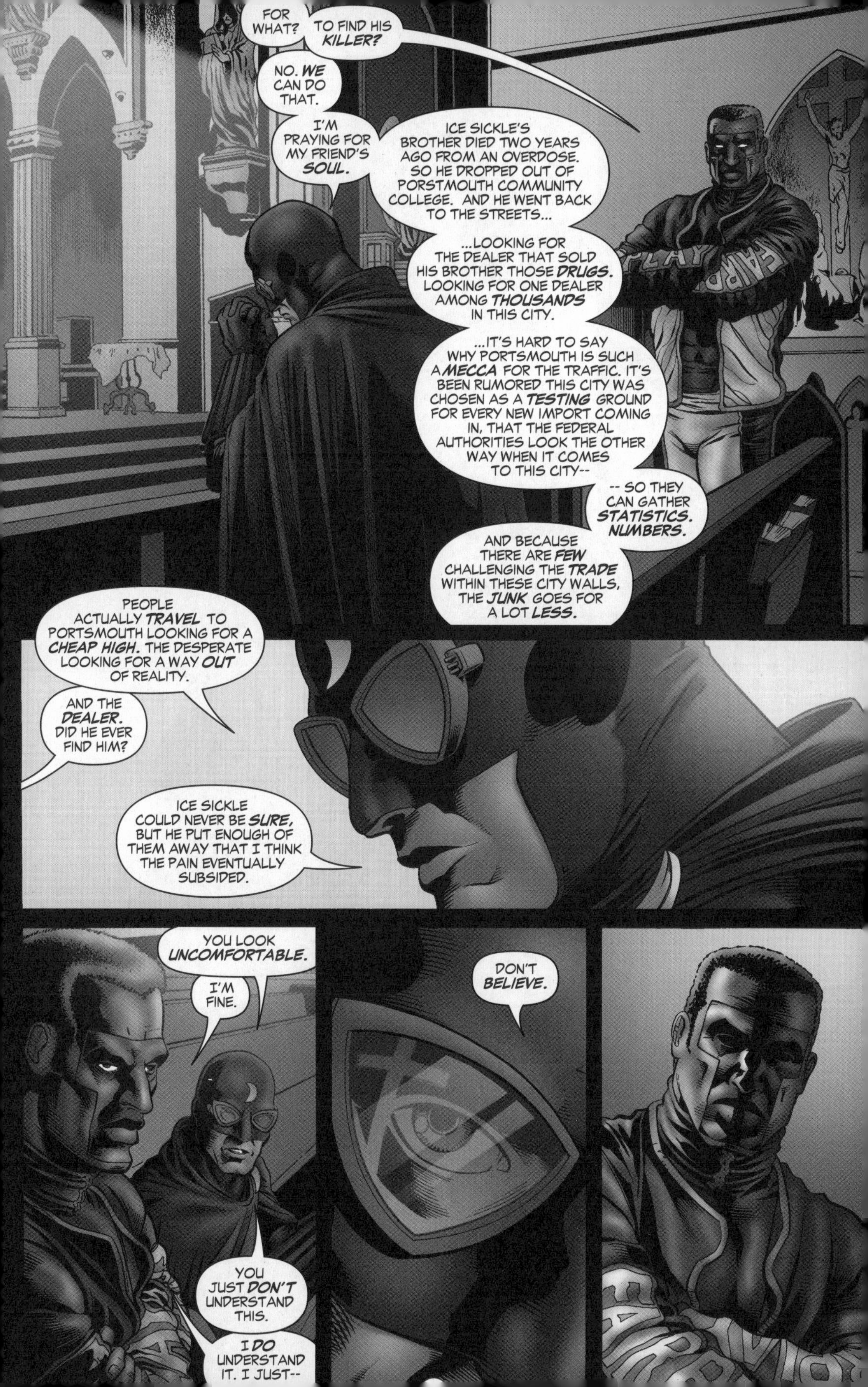
FOR WHAT?
TO FIND HIS KILLER?
NO. WE CAN DO THAT.
I'M PRAYING FOR MY FRIEND'S SOUL.
ICE SICKLE'S BROTHER DIED TWO YEARS AGO FROM AN OVERDOSE. SO HE DROPPED OUT OF PORTSMOUTH COMMUNITY COLLEGE. AND HE WENT BACK TO THE STREETS...
...LOOKING FOR THE DEALER THAT SOLD HIS BROTHER THOSE DRUGS. LOOKING FOR ONE DEALER AMONG THOUSANDS IN THIS CITY.
...IT'S HARD TO SAY WHY PORTSMOUTH IS SUCH A MECCA FOR THE TRAFFIC. IT'S BEEN RUMORED THIS CITY WAS CHOSEN AS A TESTING GROUND FOR EVERY NEW IMPORT COMING IN, THAT THE FEDERAL AUTHORITIES LOOK THE OTHER WAY WHEN IT COMES TO THIS CITY--
-- SO THEY CAN GATHER STATISTICS. NUMBERS.
AND BECAUSE THERE ARE FEW CHALLENGING THE TRADE WITHIN THESE CITY WALLS, THE JUNK GOES FOR A LOT LESS.
PEOPLE ACTUALLY TRAVEL TO PORTSMOUTH LOOKING FOR A CHEAP HIGH. THE DESPERATE LOOKING FOR A WAY OUT OF REALITY.
AND THE DEALER. DID HE EVER FIND HIM?
ICE SICKLE COULD NEVER BE SURE, BUT HE PUT ENOUGH OF THEM AWAY THAT I THINK THE PAIN EVENTUALLY SUBSIDED.
YOU LOOK UNCOMFORTABLE.
I'M FINE.
YOU JUST DON'T UNDERSTAND THIS.
I DO UNDERSTAND IT. I JUST--
DON'T BELIEVE.

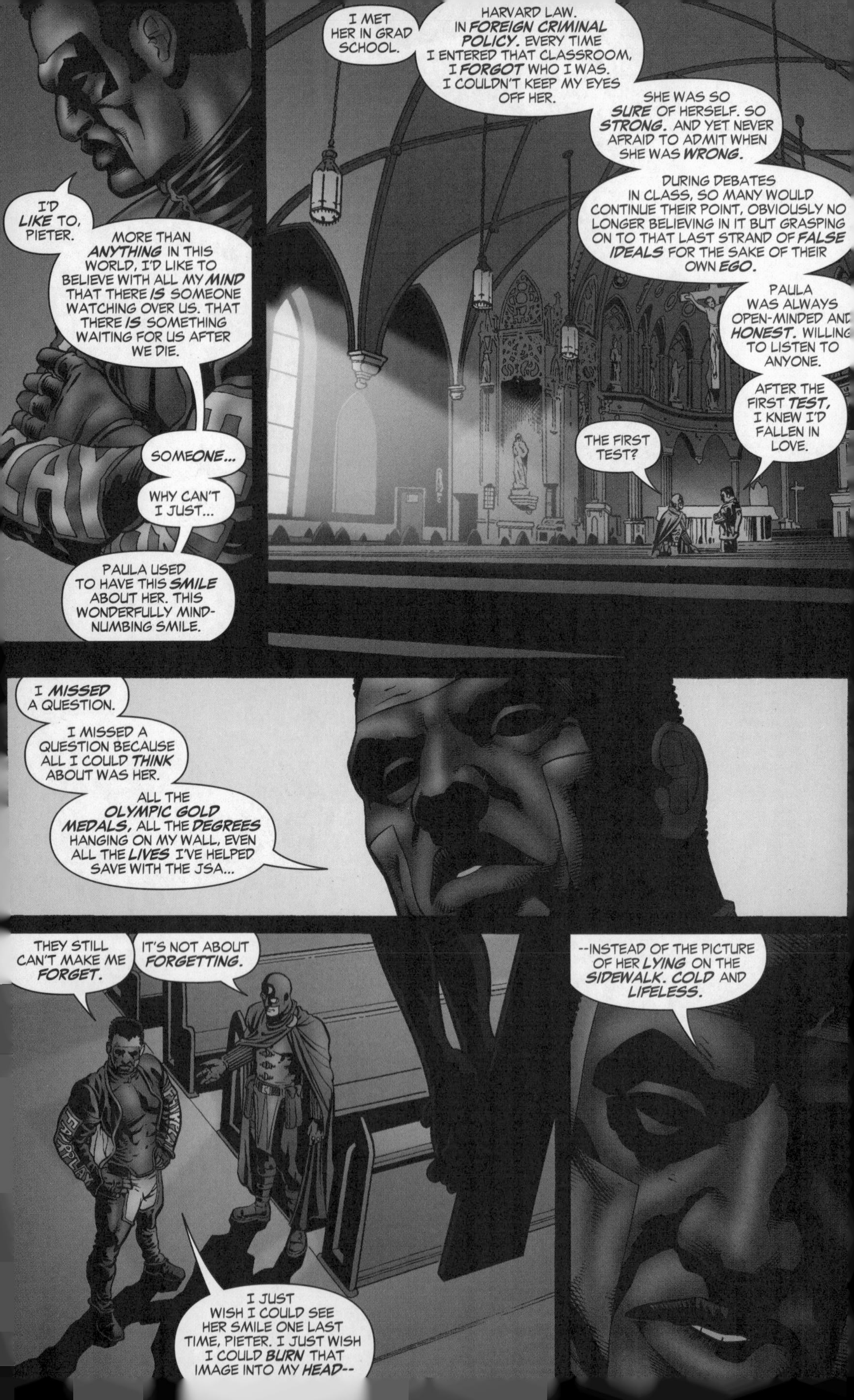
I'D LIKE TO, PIETER.
MORE THAN ANYTHING IN THIS WORLD, I'D LIKE TO BELIEVE WITH ALL MY MIND THAT THERE IS SOMEONE WATCHING OVER US. THAT THERE IS SOMETHING WAITING FOR US AFTER WE DIE.
SOMEONE...
WHY CAN'T I JUST...
PAULA USED TO HAVE THIS SMILE ABOUT HER. THIS WONDERFULLY MIND-NUMBING SMILE.
I MET HER IN GRAD SCHOOL.
HARVARD LAW. IN FOREIGN CRIMINAL POLICY. EVERY TIME I ENTERED THAT CLASSROOM, I FORGOT WHO I WAS. I COULDN'T KEEP MY EYES OFF HER.
SHE WAS SO SURE OF HERSELF. SO STRONG. AND YET NEVER AFRAID TO ADMIT WHEN SHE WAS WRONG.
DURING DEBATES IN CLASS, SO MANY WOULD CONTINUE THEIR POINT, OBVIOUSLY NO LONGER BELIEVING IN IT BUT GRASPING ON TO THAT LAST STRAND OF FALSE IDEALS FOR THE SAKE OF THEIR OWN EGO.
PAULA WAS ALWAYS OPEN-MINDED AND HONEST. WILLING TO LISTEN TO ANYONE.
AFTER THE FIRST TEST, I KNEW I'D FALLEN IN LOVE.
THE FIRST TEST?
I MISSED A QUESTION.
I MISSED A QUESTION BECAUSE ALL I COULD THINK ABOUT WAS HER.
ALL THE OLYMPIC GOLD MEDALS, ALL THE DEGREES HANGING ON MY WALL, EVEN ALL THE LIVES I'VE HELPED SAVE WITH THE JSA...
THEY STILL CAN'T MAKE ME FORGET.
IT'S NOT ABOUT FORGETTING.
I JUST WISH I COULD SEE HER SMILE ONE LAST TIME, PIETER. I JUST WISH I COULD BURN THAT IMAGE INTO MY HEAD--
--INSTEAD OF THE PICTURE OF HER LYING ON THE SIDEWALK. COLD AND LIFELESS.

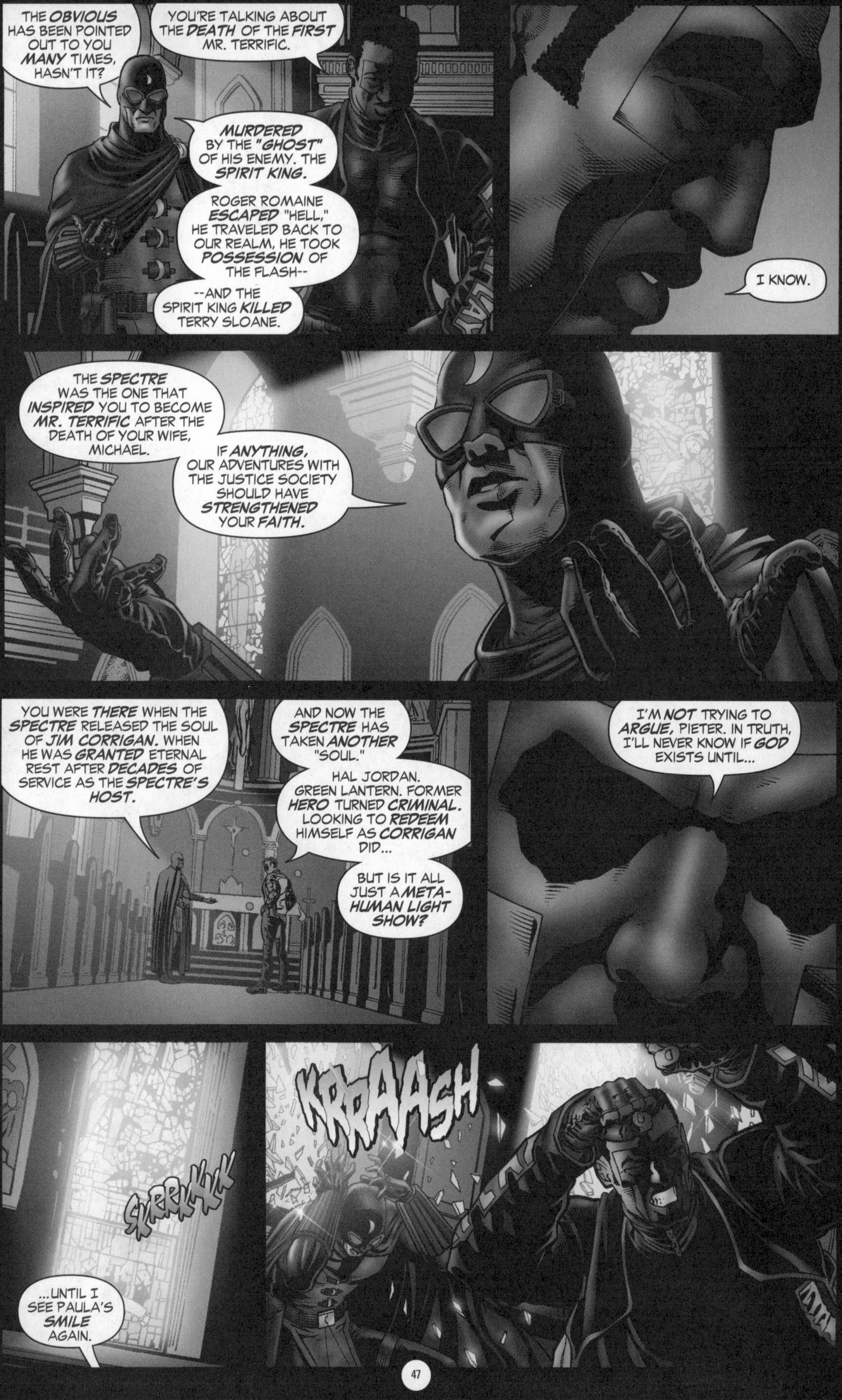

THE OBVIOUS HAS BEEN POINTED OUT TO YOU MANY TIMES, HASN'T IT?
YOU'RE TALKING ABOUT THE DEATH OF THE FIRST MR. TERRIFIC.
MURDERED BY THE "GHOST" OF HIS ENEMY. THE SPIRIT KING.
ROGER ROMAINE ESCAPED "HELL," HE TRAVELED BACK TO OUR REALM, HE TOOK POSSESSION OF THE FLASH--
--AND THE SPIRIT KING KILLED TERRY SLOANE.
I KNOW.
THE SPECTRE WAS THE ONE THAT INSPIRED YOU TO BECOME MR. TERRIFIC AFTER THE DEATH OF YOUR WIFE, MICHAEL.
IF ANYTHING, OUR ADVENTURES WITH THE JUSTICE SOCIETY SHOULD HAVE STRENGTHENED YOUR FAITH.
YOU WERE THERE WHEN THE SPECTRE RELEASED THE SOUL OF JIM CORRIGAN. WHEN HE WAS GRANTED ETERNAL REST AFTER DECADES OF SERVICE AS THE SPECTRE'S HOST.
AND NOW THE SPECTRE HAS TAKEN ANOTHER "SOUL."
HAL JORDAN. GREEN LANTERN. FORMER HERO TURNED CRIMINAL. LOOKING TO REDEEM HIMSELF AS CORRIGAN DID...
BUT IS IT ALL JUST A META-HUMAN LIGHT SHOW?
I'M NOT TRYING TO ARGUE, PIETER. IN TRUTH, I'LL NEVER KNOW IF GOD EXISTS UNTIL...
SKRRKKK
...UNTIL I SEE PAULA'S SMILE AGAIN.
KRRAASH

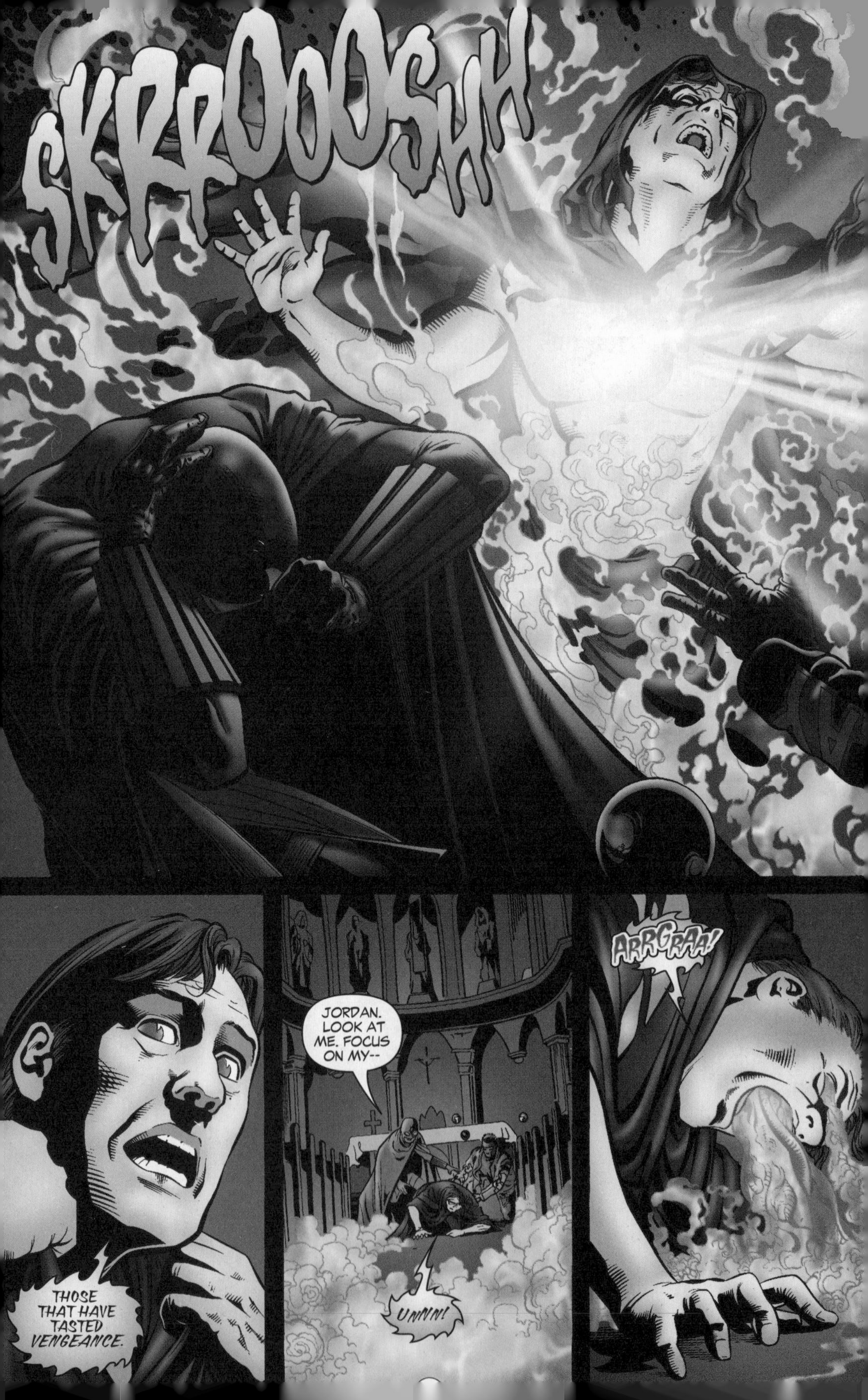
SKRROOOSHH
THOSE THAT HAVE TASTED VENGEANCE.
JORDAN. LOOK AT ME. FOCUS ON MY--
UNNN!
ARRGRAA!

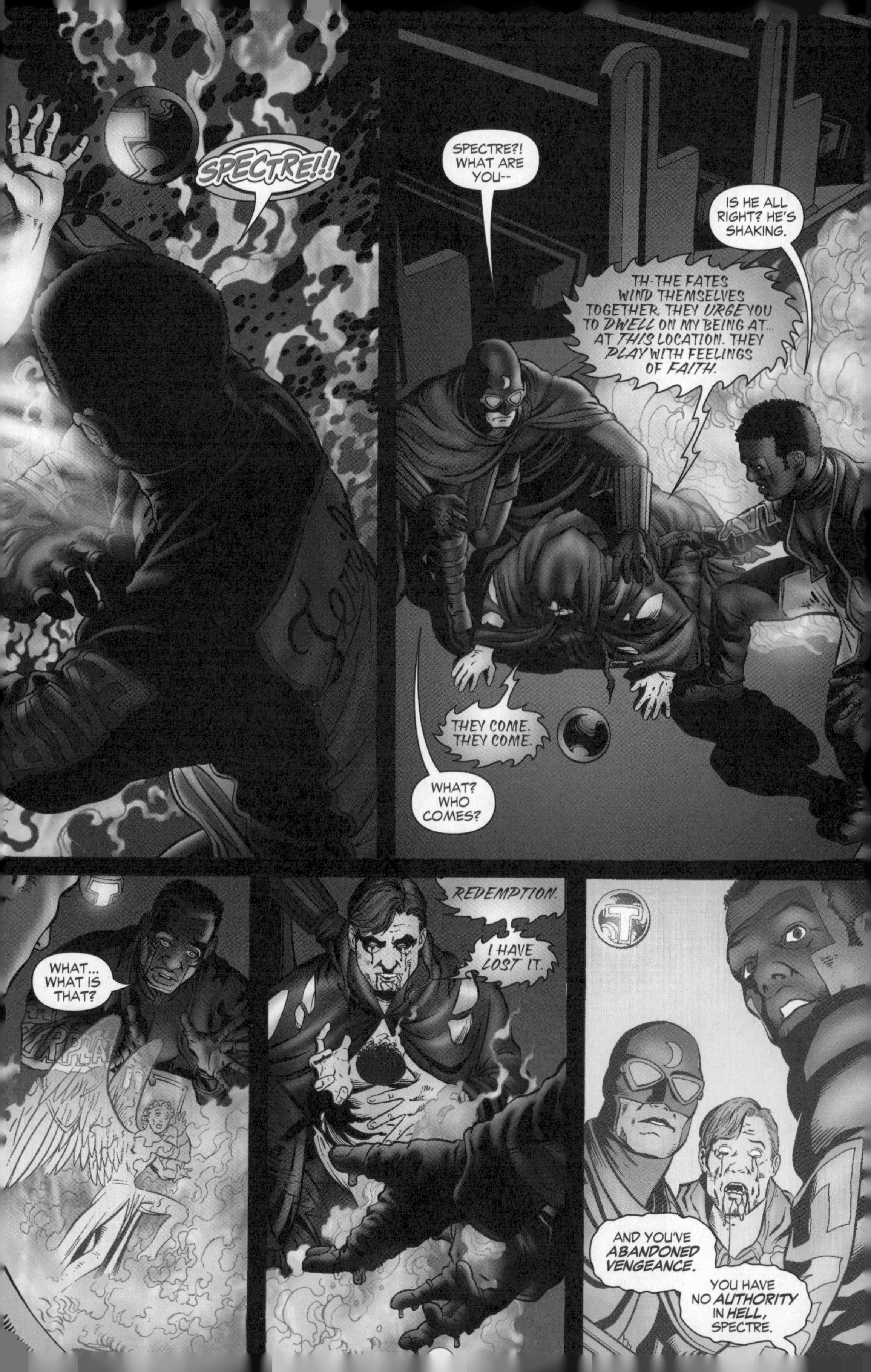
SPECTRE!!!
SPECTRE?! WHAT ARE YOU--
IS HE ALL RIGHT? HE'S SHAKING.
TH-THE FATES WIND THEMSELVES TOGETHER. THEY URGE YOU TO DWELL ON MY BEING AT... AT THIS LOCATION. THEY PLAY WITH FEELINGS OF FAITH.
THEY COME. THEY COME.
WHAT? WHO COMES?
WHAT... WHAT IS THAT?
REDEMPTION.
I HAVE LOST IT.
AND YOU'VE ABANDONED VENGEANCE.
YOU HAVE NO AUTHORITY IN HELL, SPECTRE.

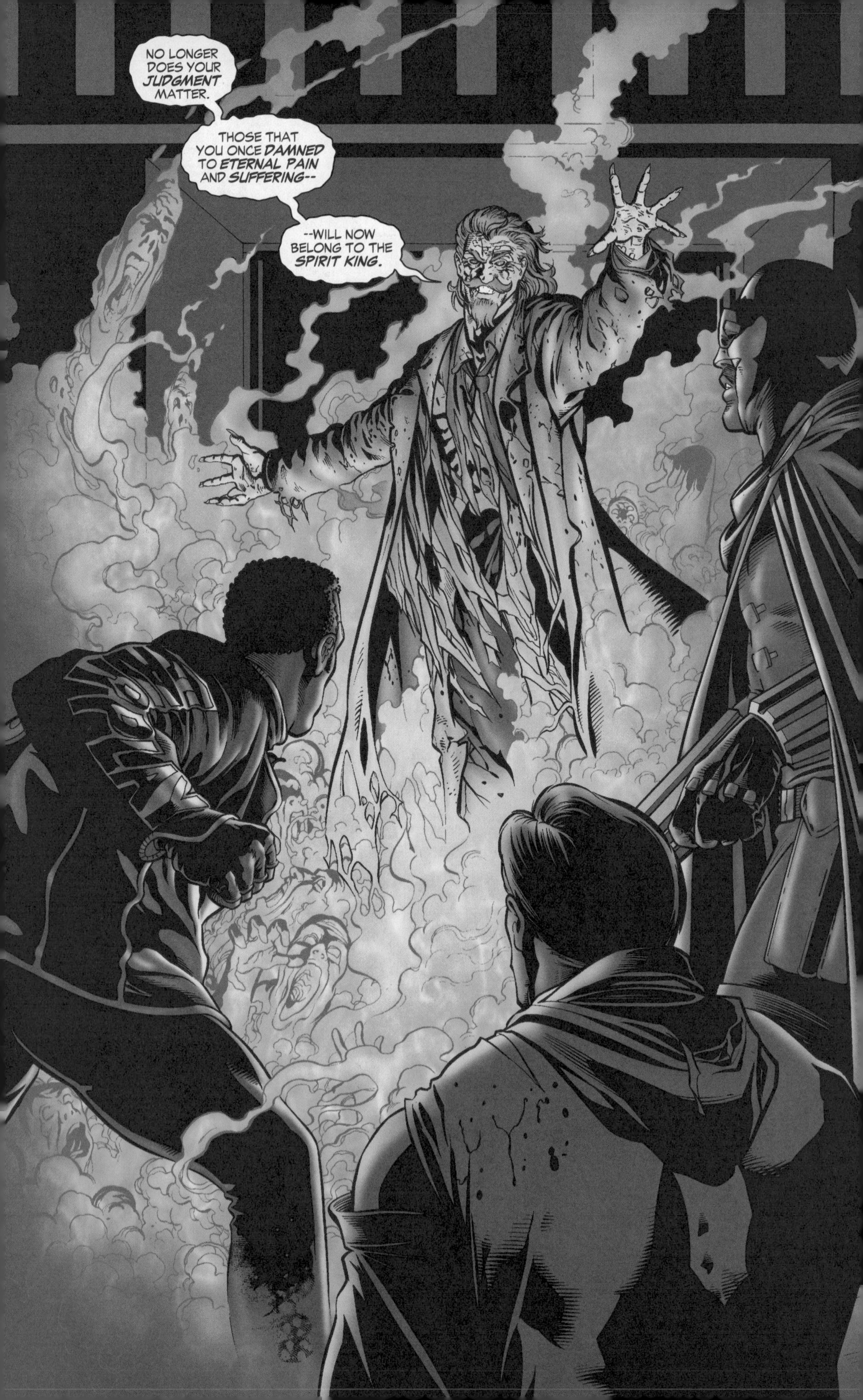
NO LONGER DOES YOUR JUDGMENT MATTER.
THOSE THAT YOU ONCE DAMNED TO ETERNAL PAIN AND SUFFERING--
--WILL NOW BELONG TO THE SPIRIT KING.

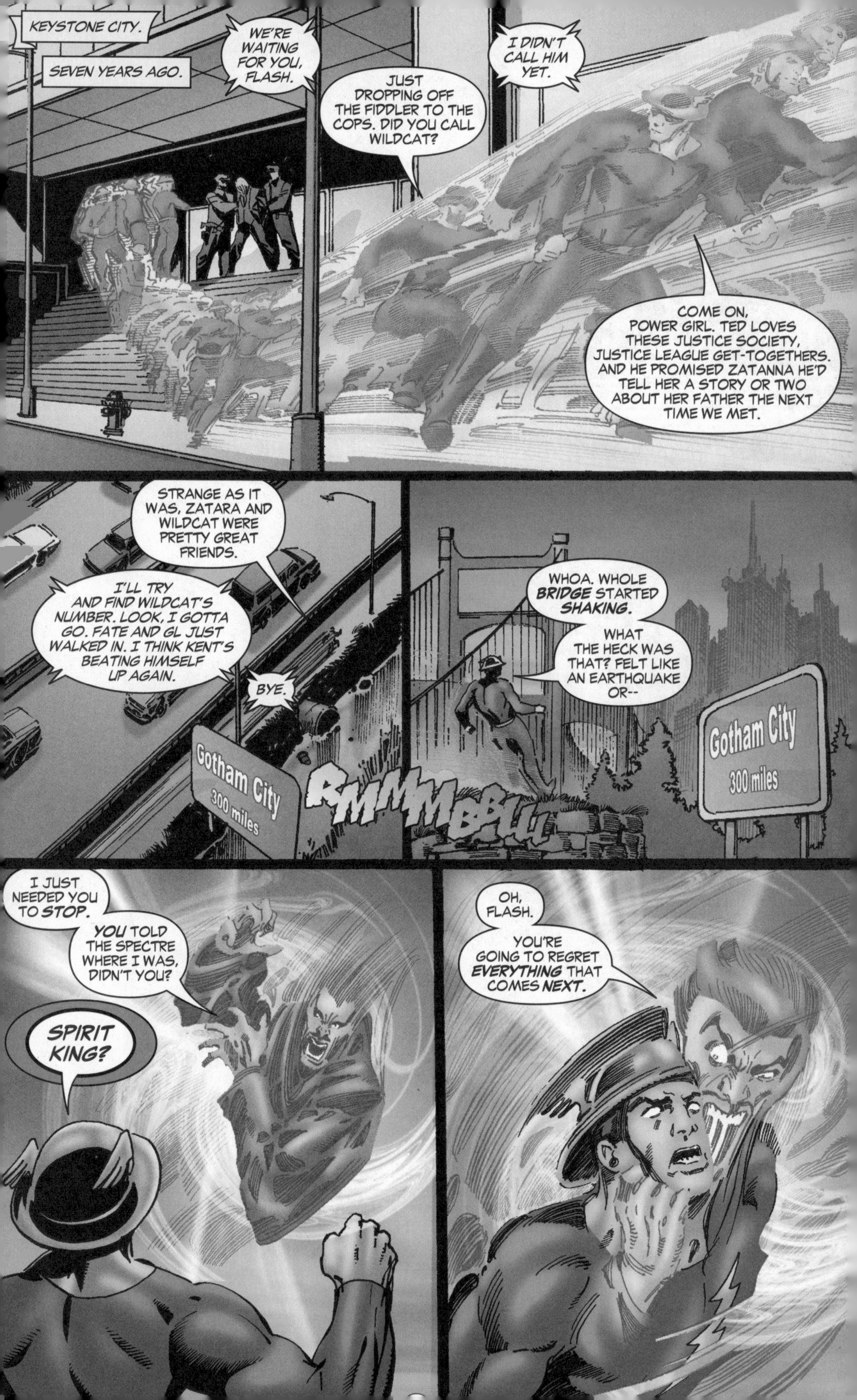

KEYSTONE CITY.
SEVEN YEARS AGO.
WE'RE WAITING FOR YOU, FLASH.
JUST DROPPING OFF THE FIDDLER TO THE COPS. DID YOU CALL WILDCAT?
I DIDN'T CALL HIM YET.
COME ON, POWER GIRL. TED LOVES THESE JUSTICE SOCIETY, JUSTICE LEAGUE GET-TOGETHERS. AND HE PROMISED ZATANNA HE'D TELL HER A STORY OR TWO ABOUT HER FATHER THE NEXT TIME WE MET.
STRANGE AS IT WAS, ZATARA AND WILDCAT WERE PRETTY GREAT FRIENDS.
I'LL TRY AND FIND WILDCAT'S NUMBER. LOOK, I GOTTA GO. FATE AND GL JUST WALKED IN. I THINK KENT'S BEATING HIMSELF UP AGAIN.
BYE.
Gotham City 300 miles
RMMMMBBLLL
WHOA. WHOLE BRIDGE STARTED SHAKING.
WHAT THE HECK WAS THAT? FELT LIKE AN EARTHQUAKE OR--
Gotham City 300 miles
I JUST NEEDED YOU TO STOP.
YOU TOLD THE SPECTRE WHERE I WAS, DIDN'T YOU?
SPIRIT KING?
OH, FLASH.
YOU'RE GOING TO REGRET EVERYTHING THAT COMES NEXT.

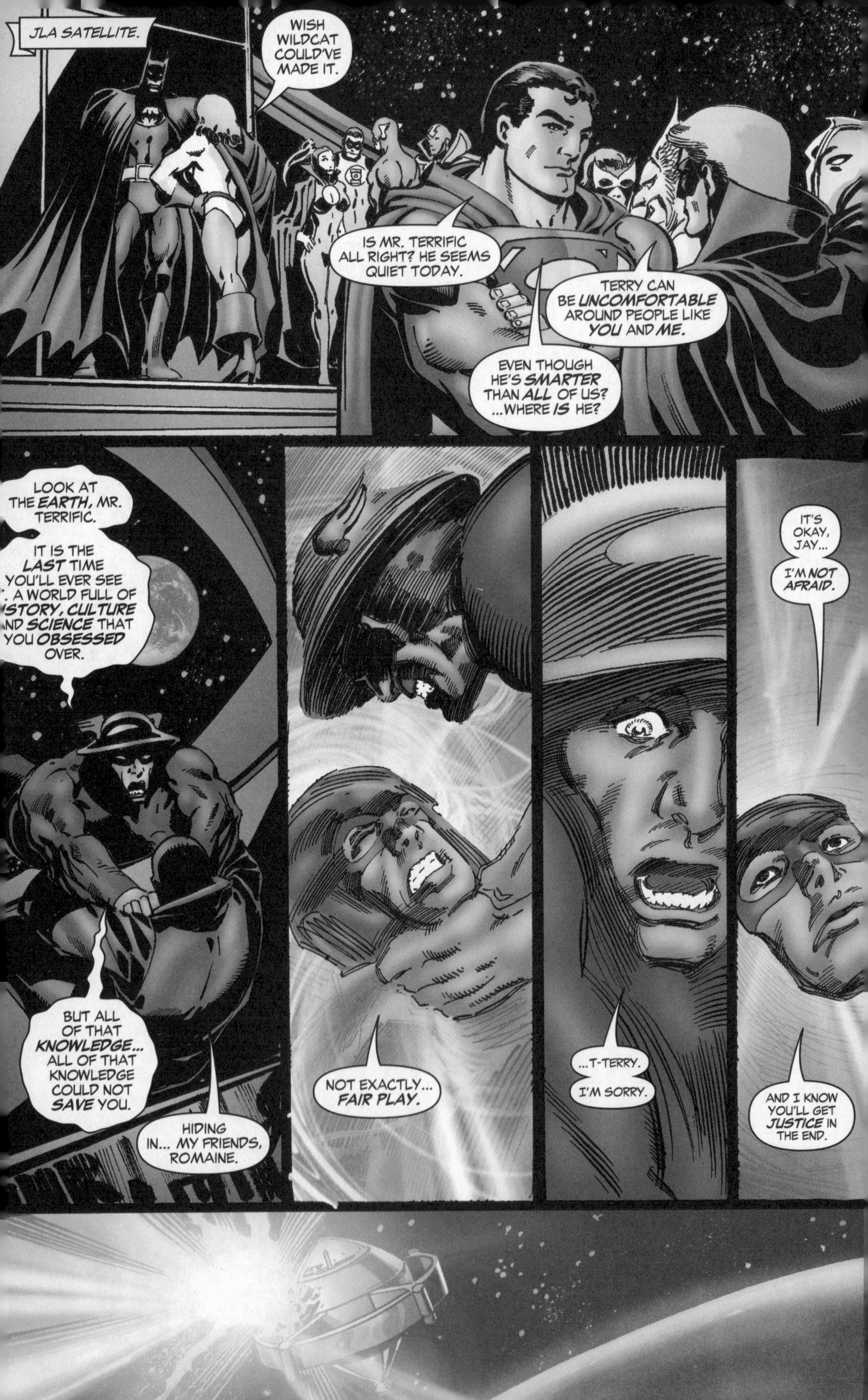
JLA SATELLITE.
WISH WILDCAT COULD'VE MADE IT.
IS MR. TERRIFIC ALL RIGHT? HE SEEMS QUIET TODAY.
TERRY CAN BE UNCOMFORTABLE AROUND PEOPLE LIKE YOU AND ME.
EVEN THOUGH HE'S SMARTER THAN ALL OF US? ...WHERE IS HE?
LOOK AT THE EARTH, MR. TERRIFIC.
IT IS THE LAST TIME YOU'LL EVER SEE T. A WORLD FULL OF STORY, CULTURE ND SCIENCE THAT YOU OBSESSED OVER.
BUT ALL OF THAT KNOWLEDGE... ALL OF THAT KNOWLEDGE COULD NOT SAVE YOU.
HIDING IN... MY FRIENDS, ROMAINE.
NOT EXACTLY... FAIR PLAY.
...T-TERRY.
I'M SORRY.
IT'S OKAY, JAY...
I'M NOT AFRAID.
AND I KNOW YOU'LL GET JUSTICE IN THE END.

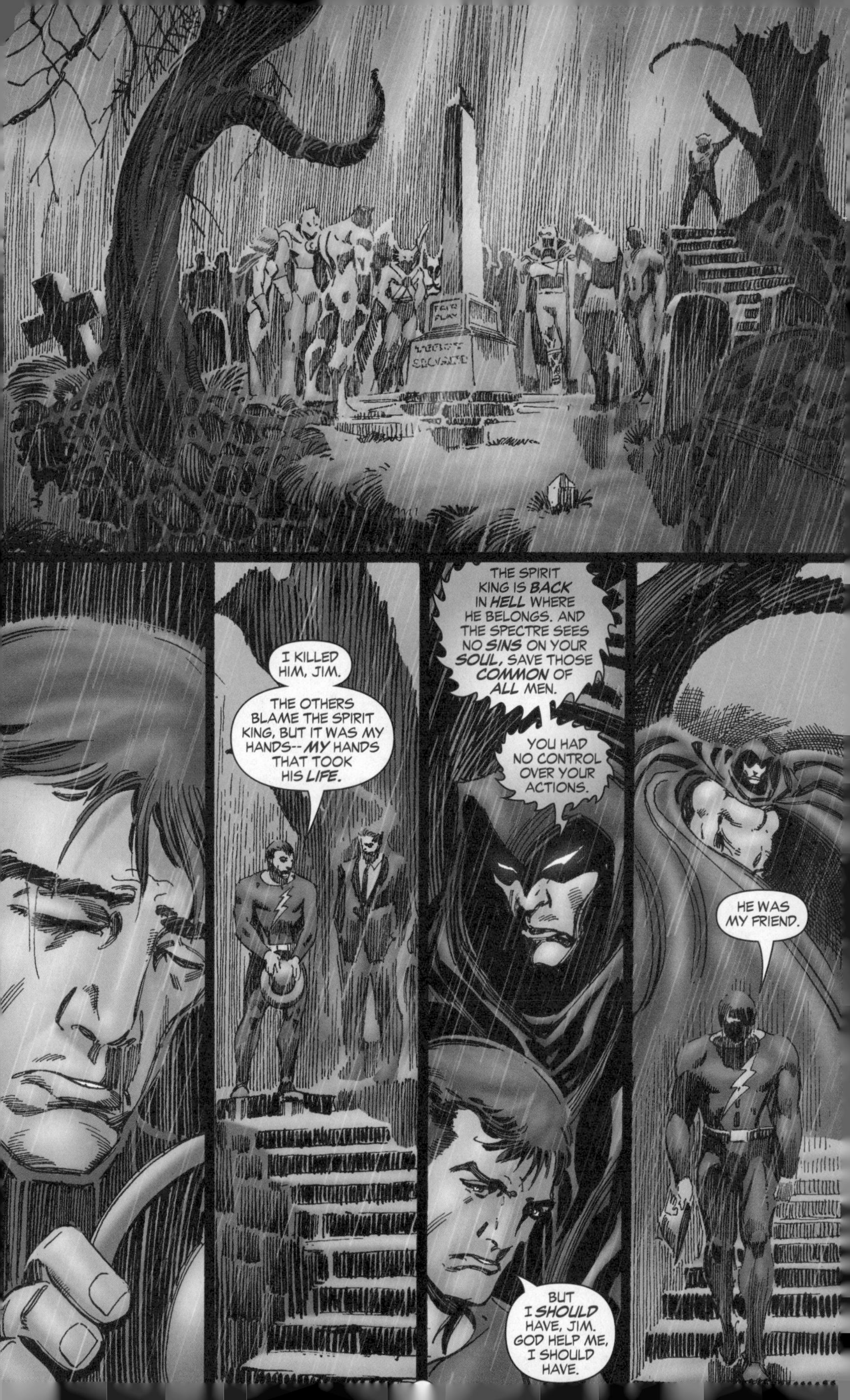
I KILLED HIM, JIM.
THE OTHERS BLAME THE SPIRIT KING, BUT IT WAS MY HANDS-- MY HANDS THAT TOOK HIS LIFE.
THE SPIRIT KING IS BACK IN HELL WHERE HE BELONGS. AND THE SPECTRE SEES NO SINS ON YOUR SOUL, SAVE THOSE COMMON OF ALL MEN.
YOU HAD NO CONTROL OVER YOUR ACTIONS.
BUT I SHOULD HAVE, JIM. GOD HELP ME, I SHOULD HAVE.
HE WAS MY FRIEND.

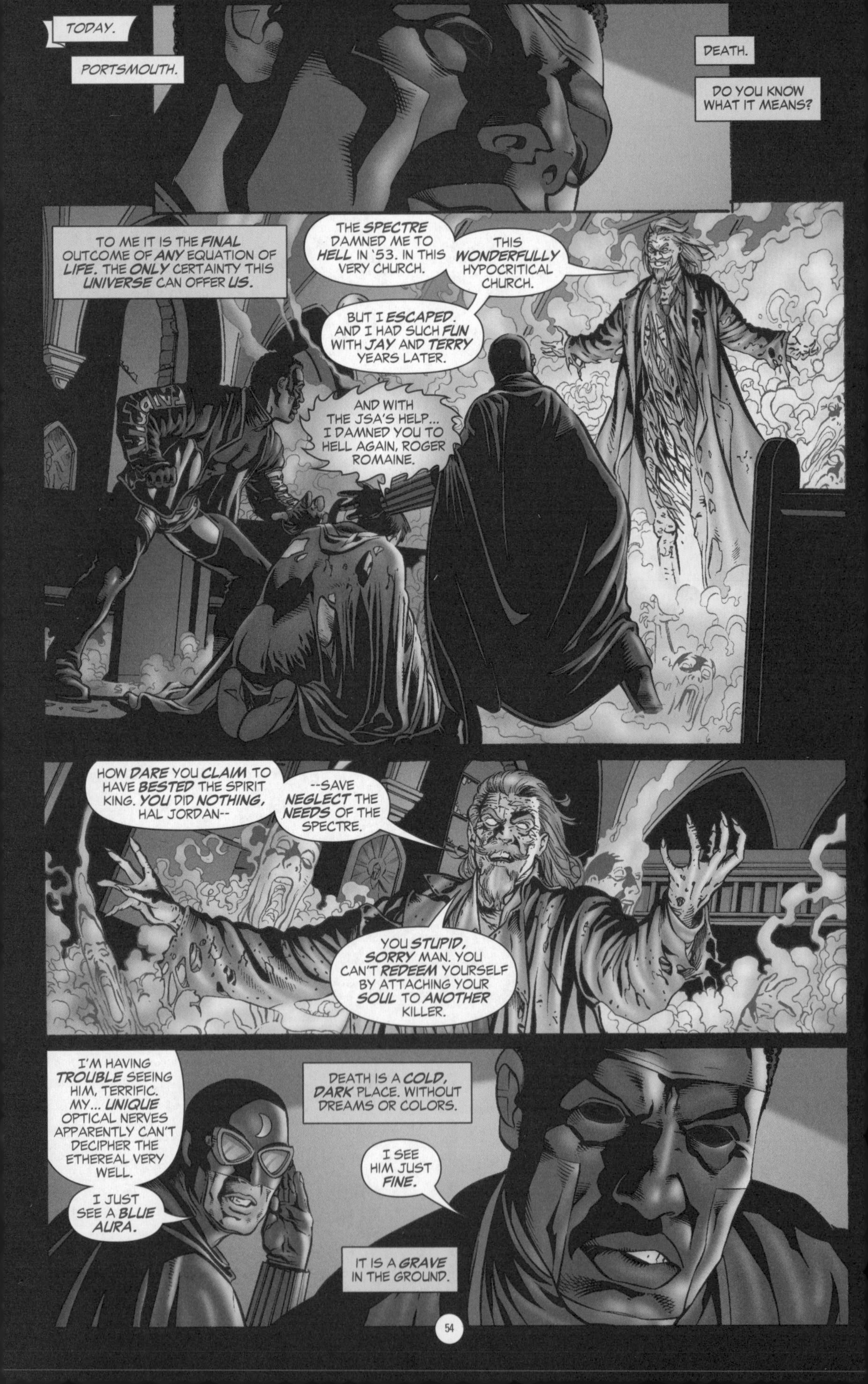
TODAY.
PORTSMOUTH.
DEATH.
DO YOU KNOW WHAT IT MEANS?
TO ME IT IS THE FINAL OUTCOME OF ANY EQUATION OF LIFE. THE ONLY CERTAINTY THIS UNIVERSE CAN OFFER US.
THE SPECTRE DAMNED ME TO HELL IN '53. IN THIS VERY CHURCH.
THIS WONDERFULLY HYPOCRITICAL CHURCH.
BUT I ESCAPED. AND I HAD SUCH FUN WITH JAY AND TERRY YEARS LATER.
AND WITH THE JSA'S HELP... I DAMNED YOU TO HELL AGAIN, ROGER ROMAINE.
HOW DARE YOU CLAIM TO HAVE BESTED THE SPIRIT KING. YOU DID NOTHING, HAL JORDAN--
--SAVE NEGLECT THE NEEDS OF THE SPECTRE.
YOU STUPID, SORRY MAN. YOU CAN'T REDEEM YOURSELF BY ATTACHING YOUR SOUL TO ANOTHER KILLER.
I'M HAVING TROUBLE SEEING HIM, TERRIFIC. MY... UNIQUE OPTICAL NERVES APPARENTLY CAN'T DECIPHER THE ETHEREAL VERY WELL.
I JUST SEE A BLUE AURA.
DEATH IS A COLD, DARK PLACE. WITHOUT DREAMS OR COLORS.
I SEE HIM JUST FINE.
IT IS A GRAVE IN THE GROUND.

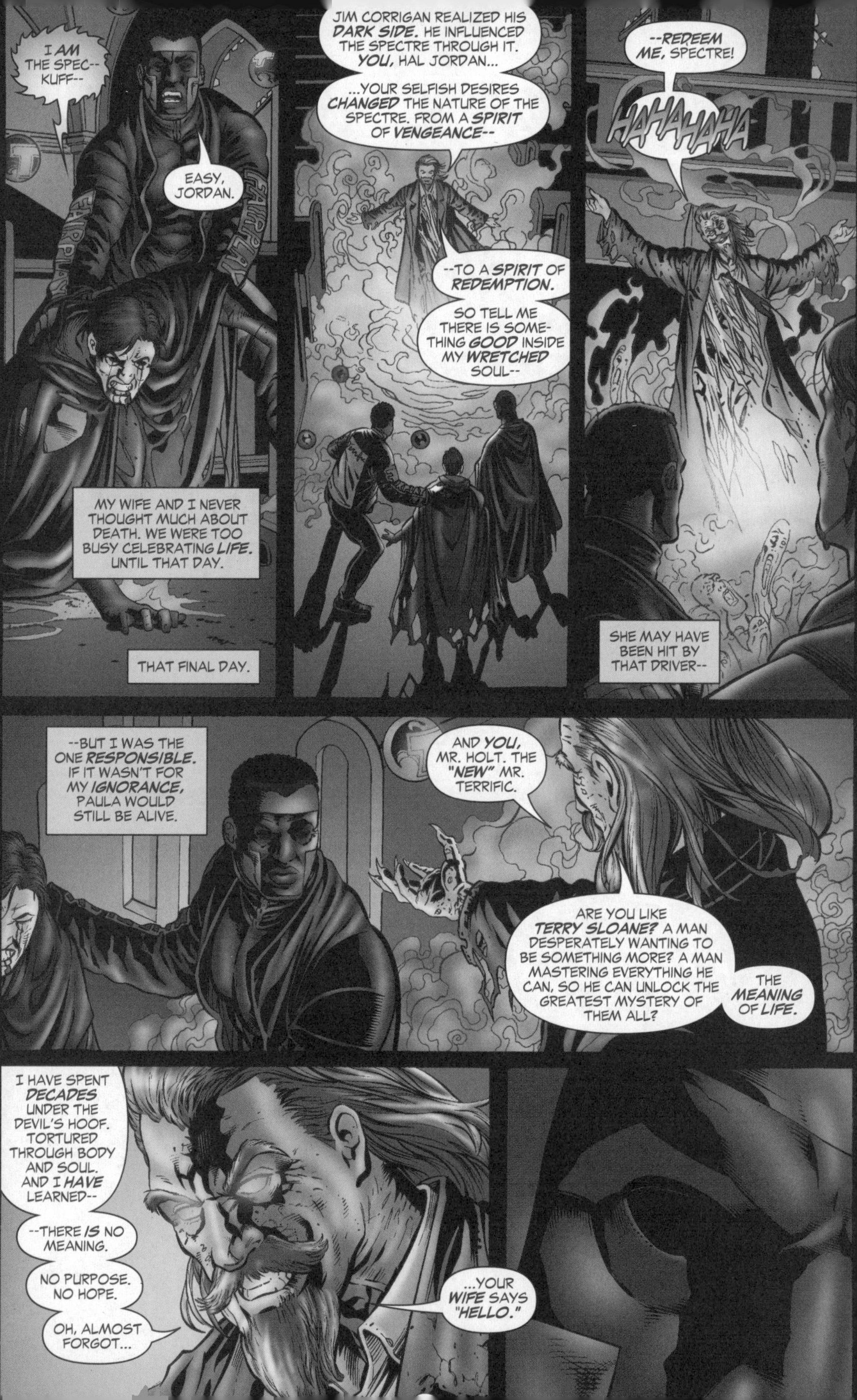
I AM THE SPEC-- KUFF--
EASY, JORDAN.
MY WIFE AND I NEVER THOUGHT MUCH ABOUT DEATH. WE WERE TOO BUSY CELEBRATING LIFE. UNTIL THAT DAY.
THAT FINAL DAY.
JIM CORRIGAN REALIZED HIS DARK SIDE. HE INFLUENCED THE SPECTRE THROUGH IT. YOU, HAL JORDAN...
...YOUR SELFISH DESIRES CHANGED THE NATURE OF THE SPECTRE. FROM A SPIRIT OF VENGEANCE--
--TO A SPIRIT OF REDEMPTION.
SO TELL ME THERE IS SOME-THING GOOD INSIDE MY WRETCHED SOUL--
--REDEEM ME, SPECTRE!
HAHAHAHA
SHE MAY HAVE BEEN HIT BY THAT DRIVER--
--BUT I WAS THE ONE RESPONSIBLE. IF IT WASN'T FOR MY IGNORANCE, PAULA WOULD STILL BE ALIVE.
AND YOU, MR. HOLT. THE "NEW" MR. TERRIFIC.
ARE YOU LIKE TERRY SLOANE? A MAN DESPERATELY WANTING TO BE SOMETHING MORE? A MAN MASTERING EVERYTHING HE CAN, SO HE CAN UNLOCK THE GREATEST MYSTERY OF THEM ALL?
THE MEANING OF LIFE.
I HAVE SPENT DECADES UNDER THE DEVIL'S HOOF. TORTURED THROUGH BODY AND SOUL. AND I HAVE LEARNED--
--THERE IS NO MEANING.
NO PURPOSE. NO HOPE.
OH, ALMOST FORGOT...
...YOUR WIFE SAYS "HELLO."

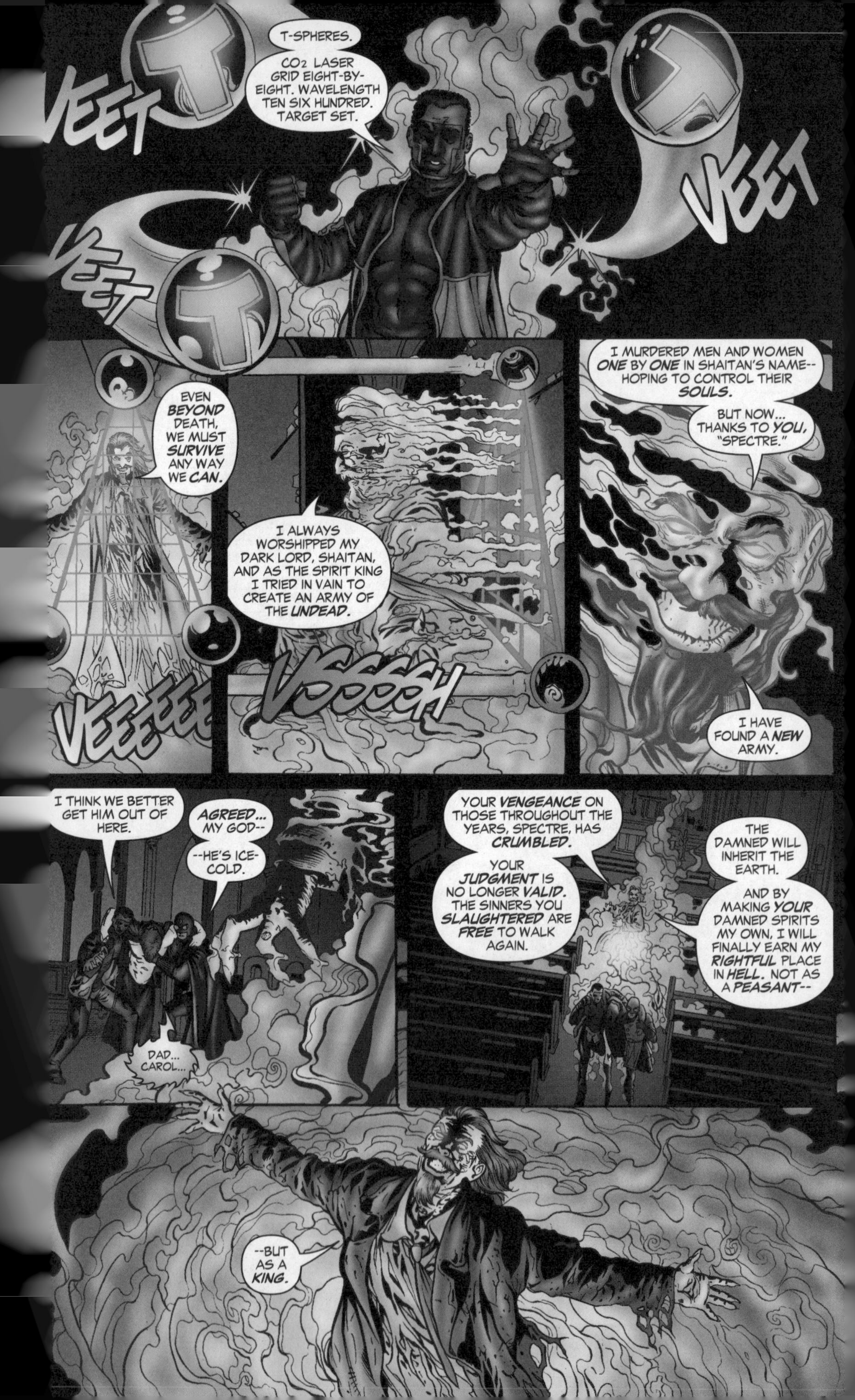
VEET
T-SPHERES.
CO2 LASER GRID EIGHT-BY-EIGHT. WAVELENGTH TEN SIX HUNDRED. TARGET SET.
VEET
VEET
EVEN BEYOND DEATH, WE MUST SURVIVE ANY WAY WE CAN.
VEEEEEEE
I ALWAYS WORSHIPPED MY DARK LORD, SHAITAN, AND AS THE SPIRIT KING I TRIED IN VAIN TO CREATE AN ARMY OF THE UNDEAD.
VSSSSH
I MURDERED MEN AND WOMEN ONE BY ONE IN SHAITAN'S NAME--HOPING TO CONTROL THEIR SOULS.
BUT NOW... THANKS TO YOU, "SPECTRE."
I HAVE FOUND A NEW ARMY.
I THINK WE BETTER GET HIM OUT OF HERE.
AGREED... MY GOD--
--HE'S ICE-COLD.
DAD... CAROL...
YOUR VENGEANCE ON THOSE THROUGHOUT THE YEARS, SPECTRE, HAS CRUMBLED.
YOUR JUDGMENT IS NO LONGER VALID. THE SINNERS YOU SLAUGHTERED ARE FREE TO WALK AGAIN.
THE DAMNED WILL INHERIT THE EARTH.
AND BY MAKING YOUR DAMNED SPIRITS MY OWN, I WILL FINALLY EARN MY RIGHTFUL PLACE IN HELL. NOT AS A PEASANT--
--BUT AS A KING.

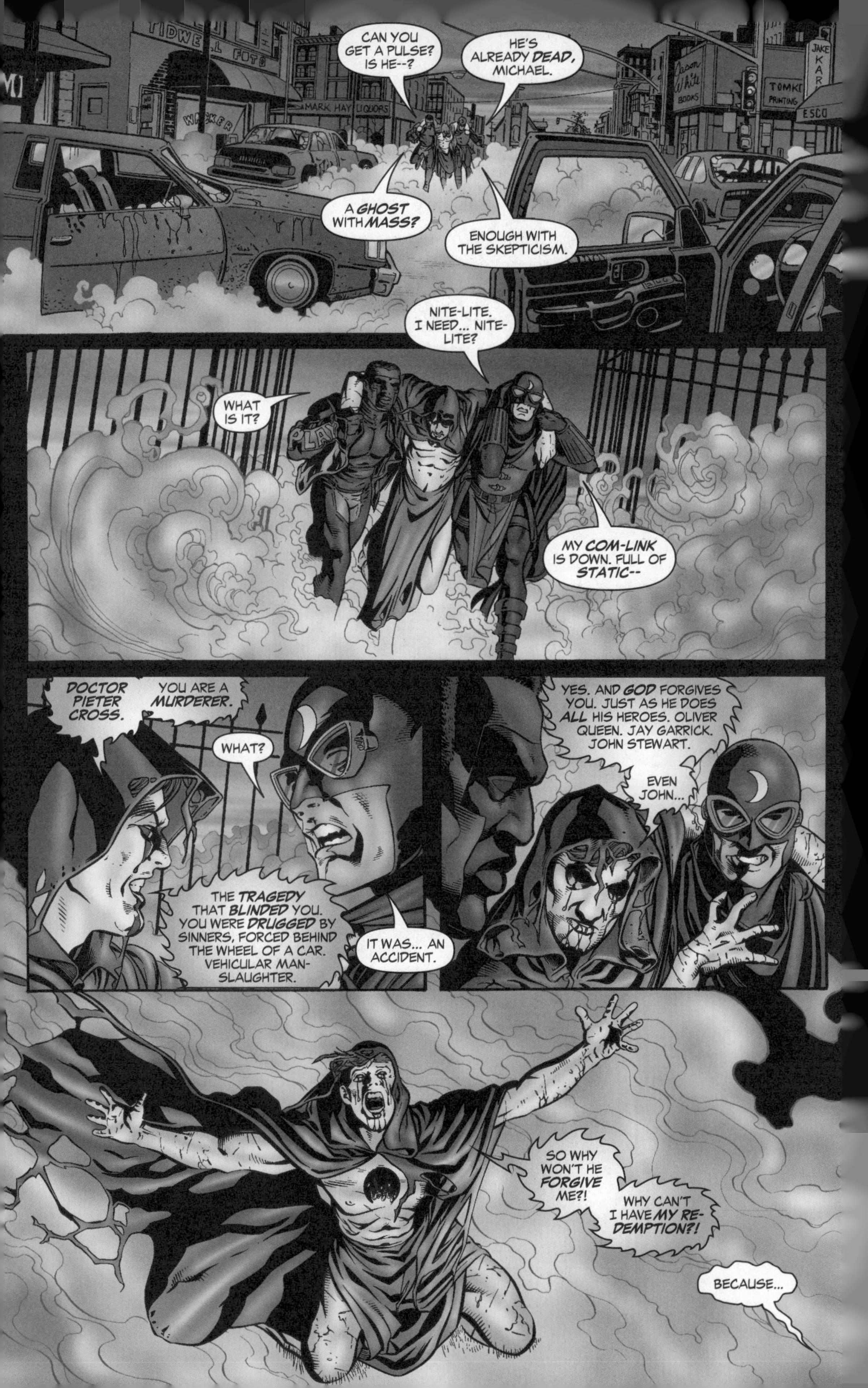

TIDWELL FOTO
MARK HAY LIQUORS
WACKER
JASON WHITE BOOKS
TOMKO PRINTING
ESCO
CAN YOU GET A PULSE? IS HE--?
HE'S ALREADY DEAD, MICHAEL.
A GHOST WITH MASS?
ENOUGH WITH THE SKEPTICISM.
NITE-LITE. I NEED... NITE-LITE?
WHAT IS IT?
MY COM-LINK IS DOWN. FULL OF STATIC--
DOCTOR PIETER CROSS.
YOU ARE A MURDERER.
WHAT?
THE TRAGEDY THAT BLINDED YOU. YOU WERE DRUGGED BY SINNERS, FORCED BEHIND THE WHEEL OF A CAR. VEHICULAR MAN-SLAUGHTER.
IT WAS... AN ACCIDENT.
YES. AND GOD FORGIVES YOU. JUST AS HE DOES ALL HIS HEROES. OLIVER QUEEN. JAY GARRICK. JOHN STEWART.
EVEN JOHN...
SO WHY WON'T HE FORGIVE ME?!
WHY CAN'T I HAVE MY RE-DEMPTION?!
BECAUSE...

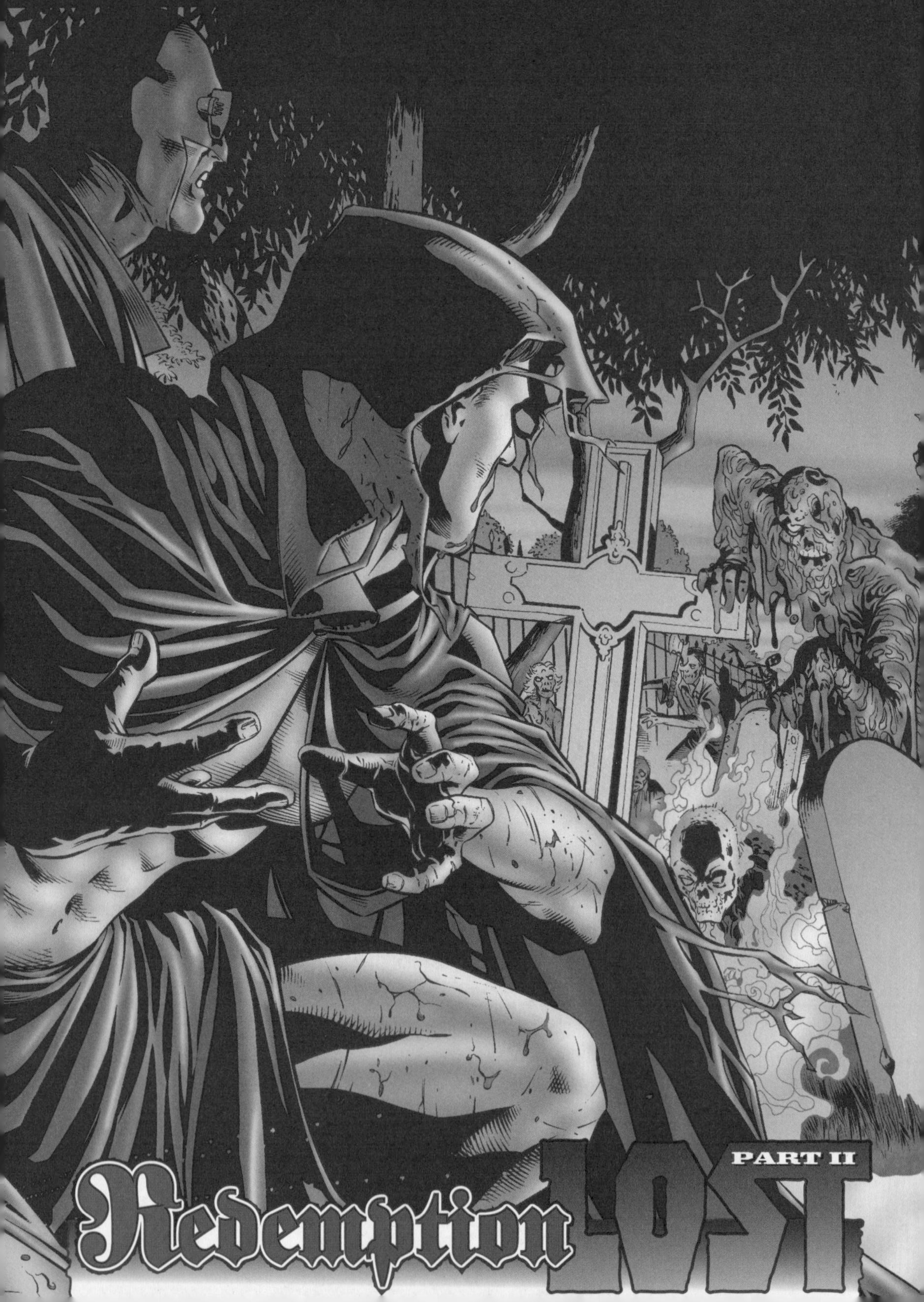
PART II
Redemption LOST

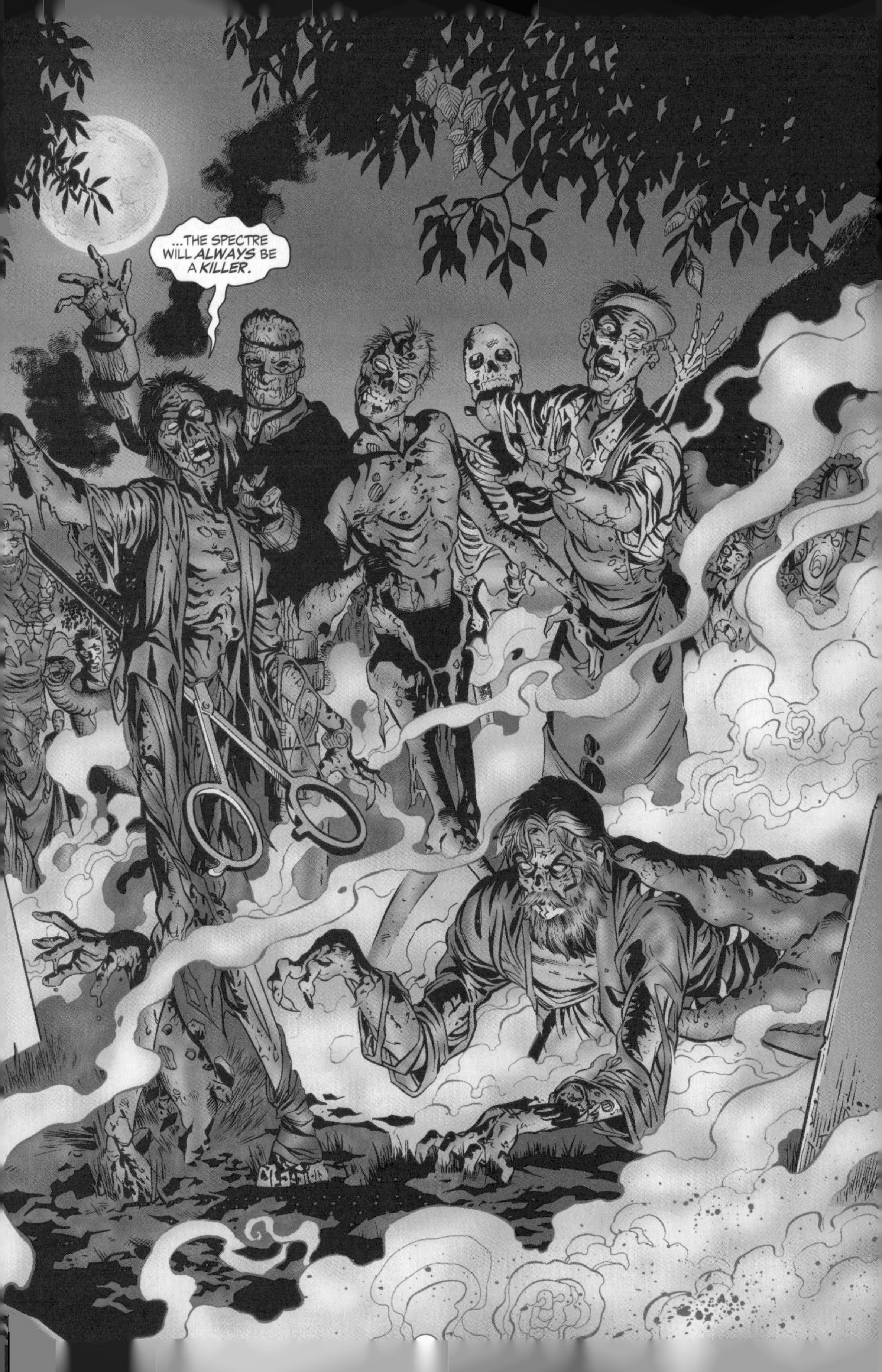
...THE SPECTRE WILL ALWAYS BE A KILLER.

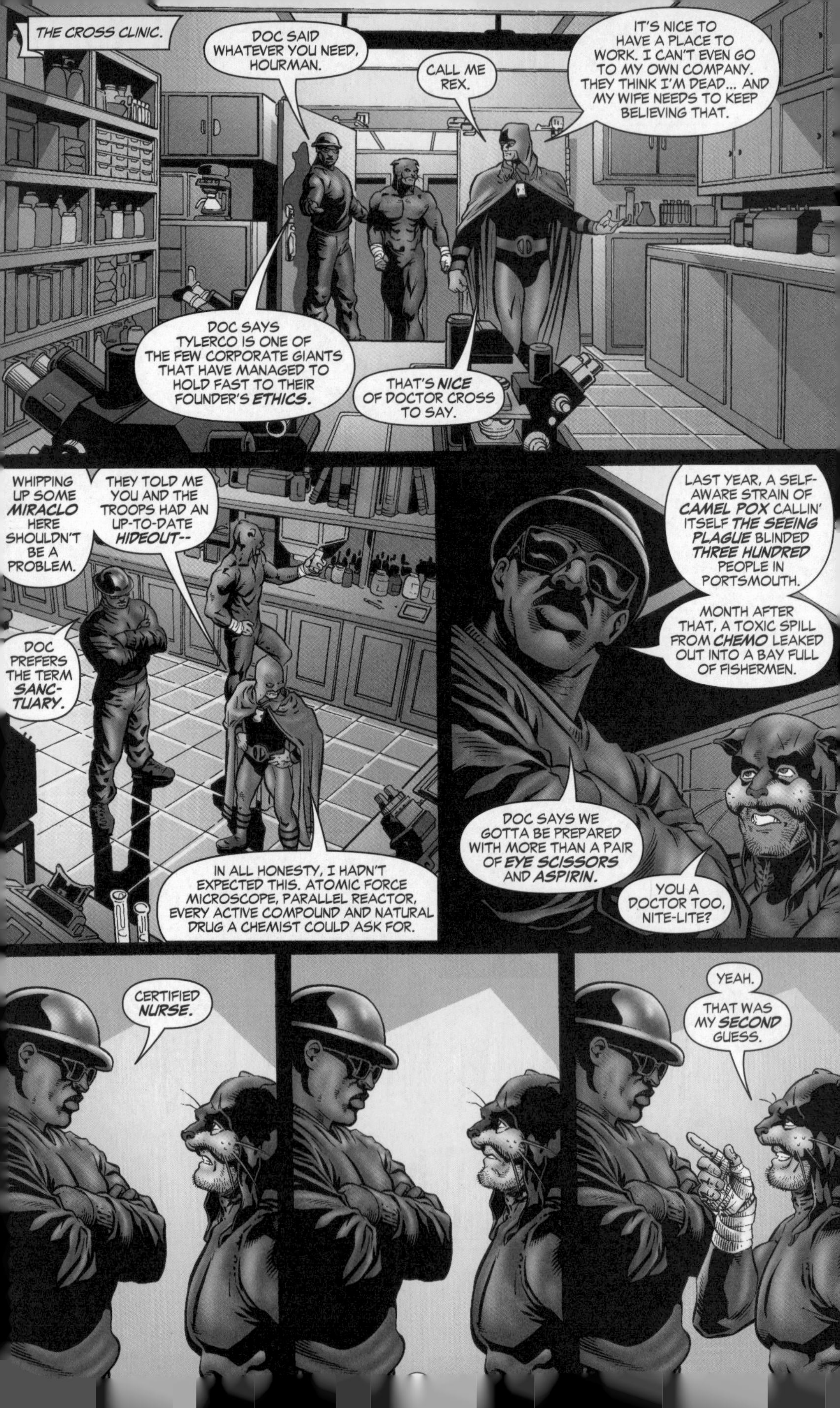
THE CROSS CLINIC.
DOC SAID WHATEVER YOU NEED, HOURMAN.
CALL ME REX.
IT'S NICE TO HAVE A PLACE TO WORK. I CAN'T EVEN GO TO MY OWN COMPANY. THEY THINK I'M DEAD... AND MY WIFE NEEDS TO KEEP BELIEVING THAT.
DOC SAYS TYLERCO IS ONE OF THE FEW CORPORATE GIANTS THAT HAVE MANAGED TO HOLD FAST TO THEIR FOUNDER'S ETHICS.
THAT'S NICE OF DOCTOR CROSS TO SAY.
WHIPPING UP SOME MIRACLO HERE SHOULDN'T BE A PROBLEM.
THEY TOLD ME YOU AND THE TROOPS HAD AN UP-TO-DATE HIDEOUT--
DOC PREFERS THE TERM SANCTUARY.
IN ALL HONESTY, I HADN'T EXPECTED THIS. ATOMIC FORCE MICROSCOPE, PARALLEL REACTOR, EVERY ACTIVE COMPOUND AND NATURAL DRUG A CHEMIST COULD ASK FOR.
LAST YEAR, A SELF-AWARE STRAIN OF CAMEL POX CALLIN' ITSELF THE SEEING PLAGUE BLINDED THREE HUNDRED PEOPLE IN PORTSMOUTH.
MONTH AFTER THAT, A TOXIC SPILL FROM CHEMO LEAKED OUT INTO A BAY FULL OF FISHERMEN.
DOC SAYS WE GOTTA BE PREPARED WITH MORE THAN A PAIR OF EYE SCISSORS AND ASPIRIN.
YOU A DOCTOR TOO, NITE-LITE?
CERTIFIED NURSE.
YEAH.
THAT WAS MY SECOND GUESS.

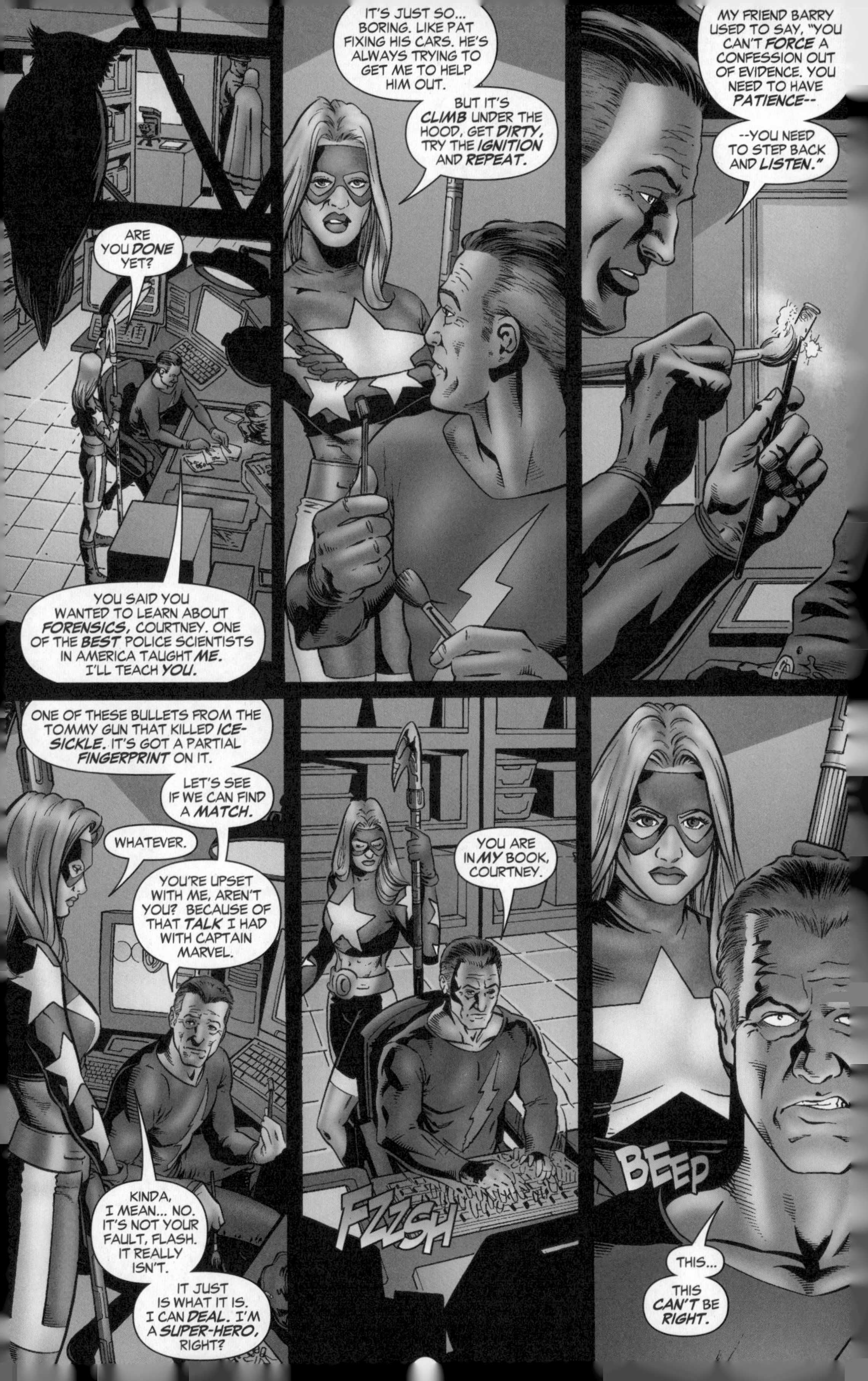
ARE YOU DONE YET?
YOU SAID YOU WANTED TO LEARN ABOUT FORENSICS, COURTNEY. ONE OF THE BEST POLICE SCIENTISTS IN AMERICA TAUGHT ME. I'LL TEACH YOU.
IT'S JUST SO... BORING. LIKE PAT FIXING HIS CARS. HE'S ALWAYS TRYING TO GET ME TO HELP HIM OUT.
BUT IT'S CLIMB UNDER THE HOOD, GET DIRTY, TRY THE IGNITION AND REPEAT.
MY FRIEND BARRY USED TO SAY, "YOU CAN'T FORCE A CONFESSION OUT OF EVIDENCE. YOU NEED TO HAVE PATIENCE--
--YOU NEED TO STEP BACK AND LISTEN."
ONE OF THESE BULLETS FROM THE TOMMY GUN THAT KILLED ICE-SICKLE. IT'S GOT A PARTIAL FINGERPRINT ON IT.
LET'S SEE IF WE CAN FIND A MATCH.
WHATEVER.
YOU'RE UPSET WITH ME, AREN'T YOU? BECAUSE OF THAT TALK I HAD WITH CAPTAIN MARVEL.
KINDA, I MEAN... NO. IT'S NOT YOUR FAULT, FLASH. IT REALLY ISN'T.
IT JUST IS WHAT IT IS. I CAN DEAL. I'M A SUPER-HERO, RIGHT?
YOU ARE IN MY BOOK, COURTNEY.
FZZSH
BEEP
THIS...
THIS CAN'T BE RIGHT.

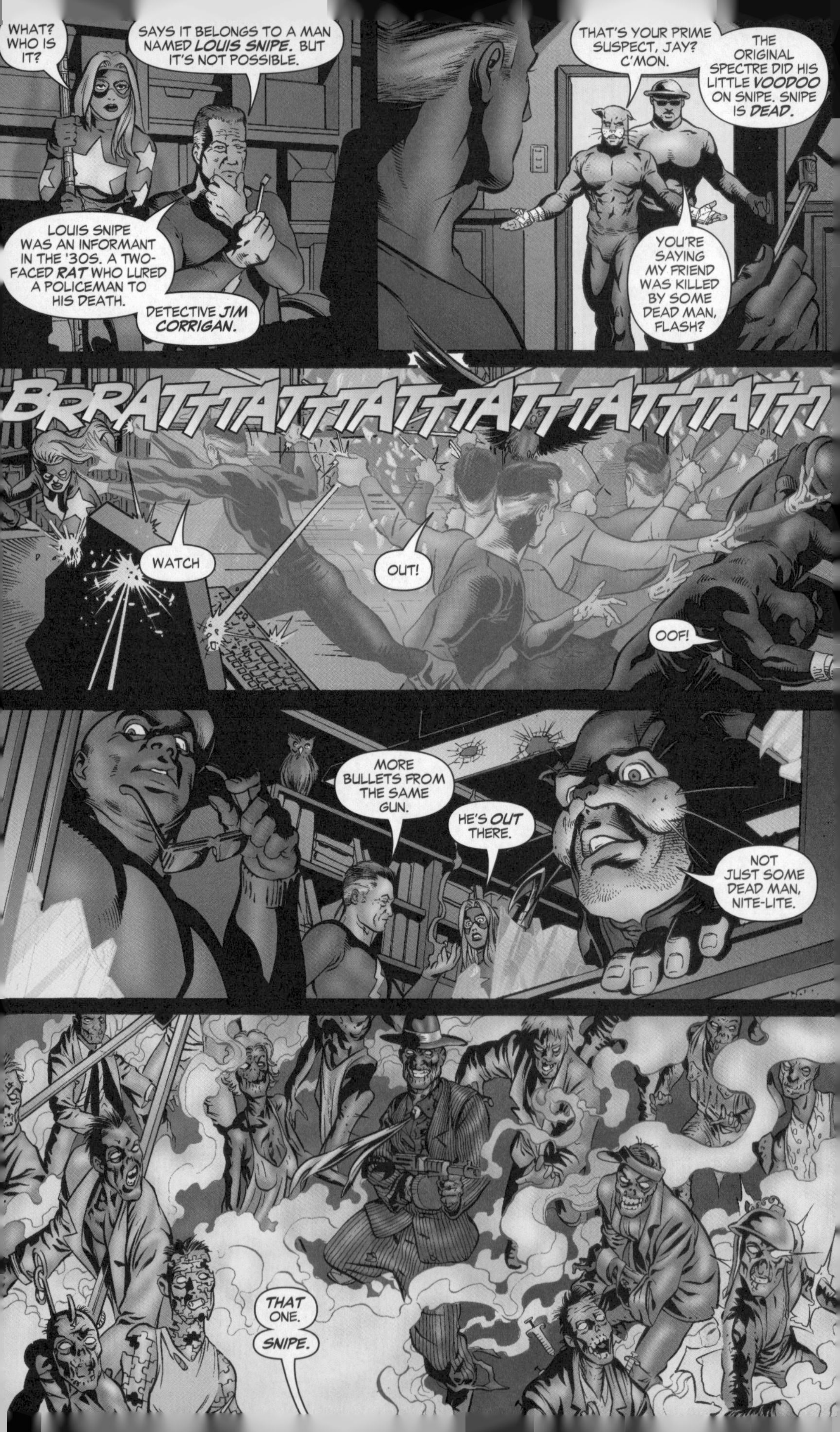
WHAT? WHO IS IT?
SAYS IT BELONGS TO A MAN NAMED LOUIS SNIPE. BUT IT'S NOT POSSIBLE.
LOUIS SNIPE WAS AN INFORMANT IN THE '30S. A TWO-FACED RAT WHO LURED A POLICEMAN TO HIS DEATH.
DETECTIVE JIM CORRIGAN.
THAT'S YOUR PRIME SUSPECT, JAY? C'MON.
THE ORIGINAL SPECTRE DID HIS LITTLE VOODOO ON SNIPE. SNIPE IS DEAD.
YOU'RE SAYING MY FRIEND WAS KILLED BY SOME DEAD MAN, FLASH?
BRRATTTTATTTTATTTTATTTTATTTTATTT
WATCH
OUT!
OOF!
MORE BULLETS FROM THE SAME GUN.
HE'S OUT THERE.
NOT JUST SOME DEAD MAN, NITE-LITE.
THAT ONE.
SNIPE.

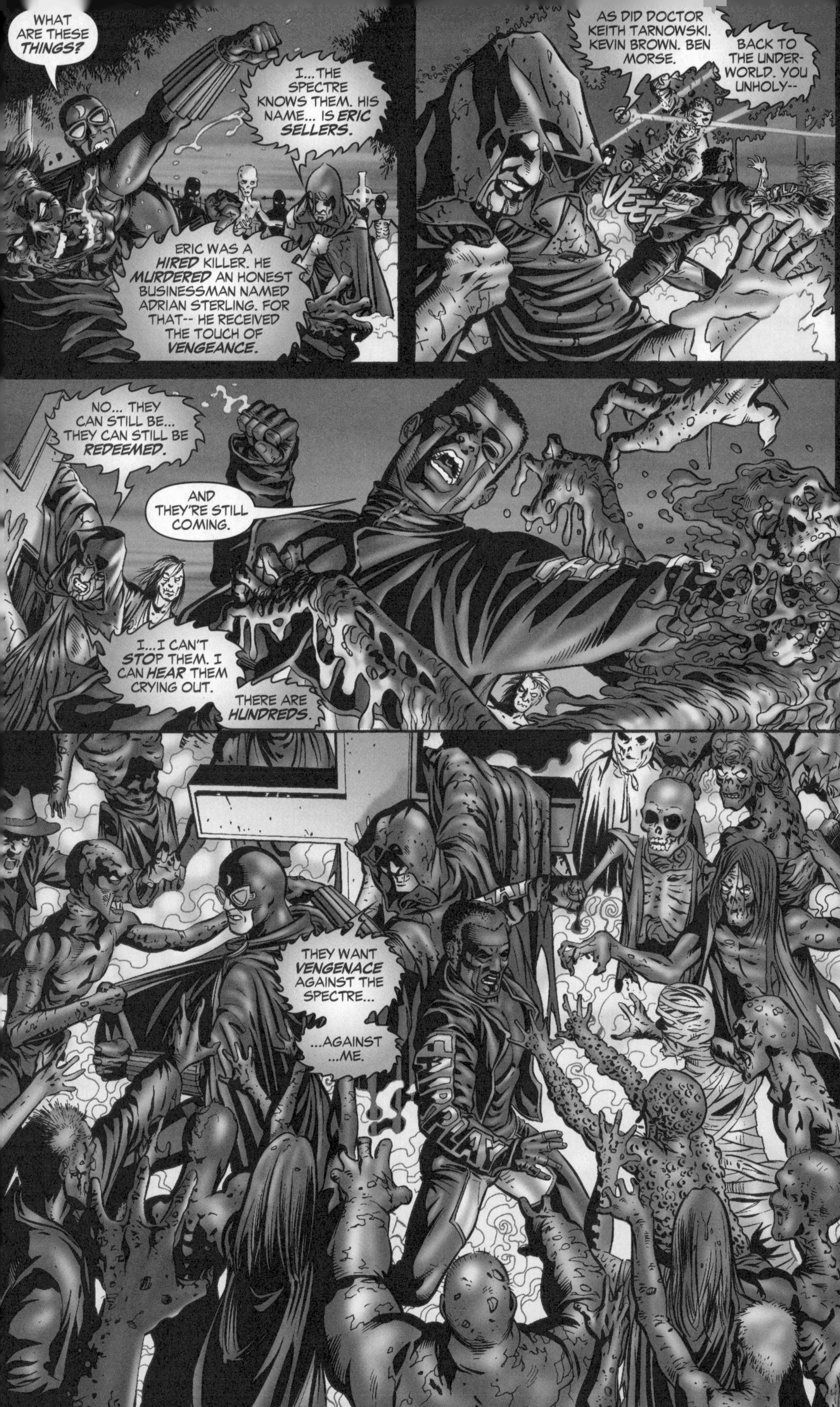
WHAT ARE THESE THINGS?
I... THE SPECTRE KNOWS THEM. HIS NAME... IS ERIC SELLERS.
ERIC WAS A HIRED KILLER. HE MURDERED AN HONEST BUSINESSMAN NAMED ADRIAN STERLING. FOR THAT-- HE RECEIVED THE TOUCH OF VENGEANCE.
AS DID DOCTOR KEITH TARNOWSKI. KEVIN BROWN. BEN MORSE.
BACK TO THE UNDER-WORLD. YOU UNHOLY--
VEET
NO... THEY CAN STILL BE... THEY CAN STILL BE REDEEMED.
AND THEY'RE STILL COMING.
I...I CAN'T STOP THEM. I CAN HEAR THEM CRYING OUT.
THERE ARE HUNDREDS.
THEY WANT VENGENACE AGAINST THE SPECTRE...
...AGAINST ...ME.

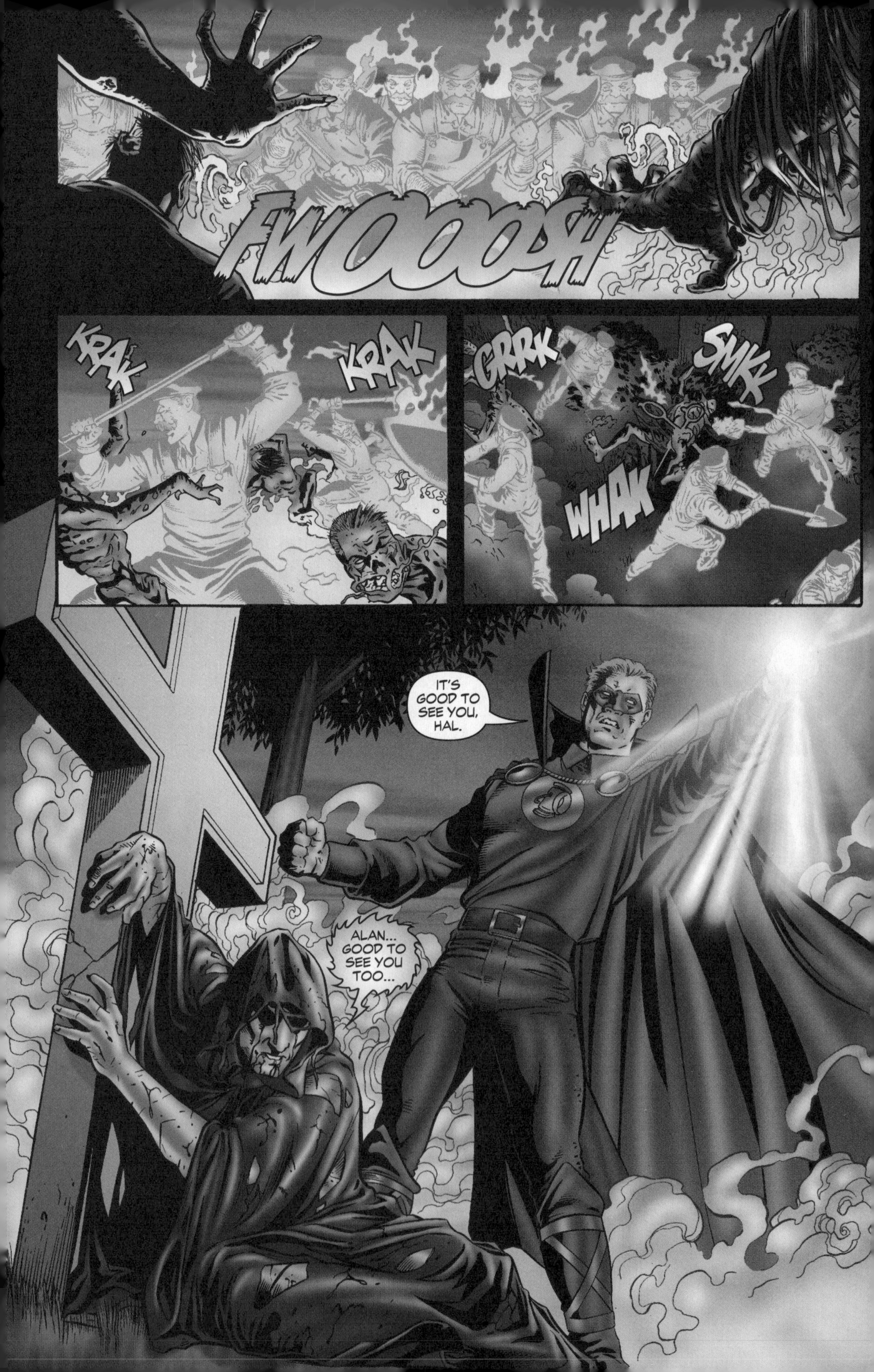
FWOOOSH
KRAK
KRAK
GRRK
SMKK
WHAK
IT'S GOOD TO SEE YOU, HAL.
ALAN... GOOD TO SEE YOU TOO...

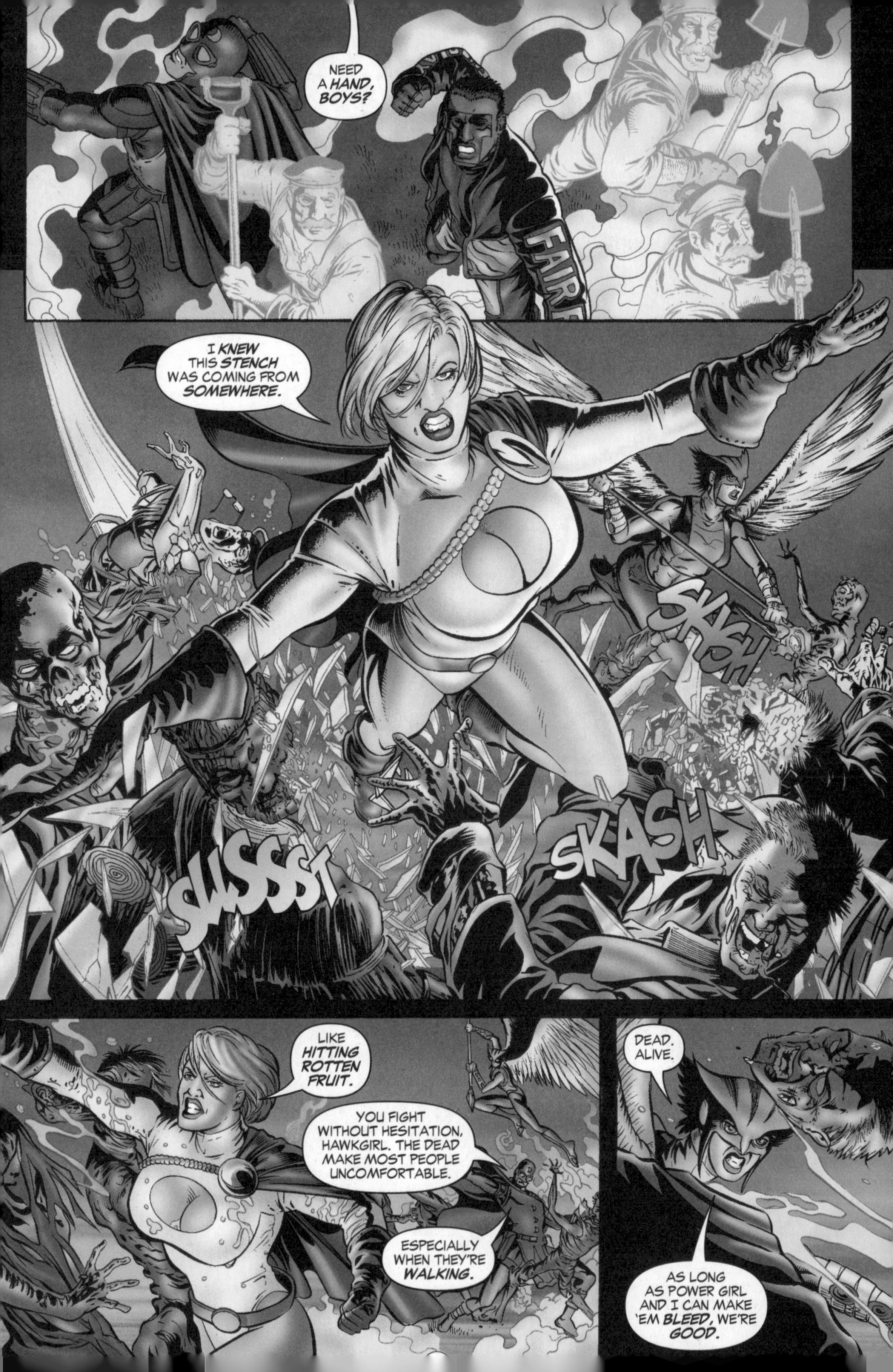
NEED A HAND, BOYS?
I KNEW THIS STENCH WAS COMING FROM SOMEWHERE.
SKASH
SUSSST
SKASH
LIKE HITTING ROTTEN FRUIT.
YOU FIGHT WITHOUT HESITATION, HAWKGIRL. THE DEAD MAKE MOST PEOPLE UNCOMFORTABLE.
ESPECIALLY WHEN THEY'RE WALKING.
DEAD. ALIVE.
AS LONG AS POWER GIRL AND I CAN MAKE 'EM BLEED, WE'RE GOOD.

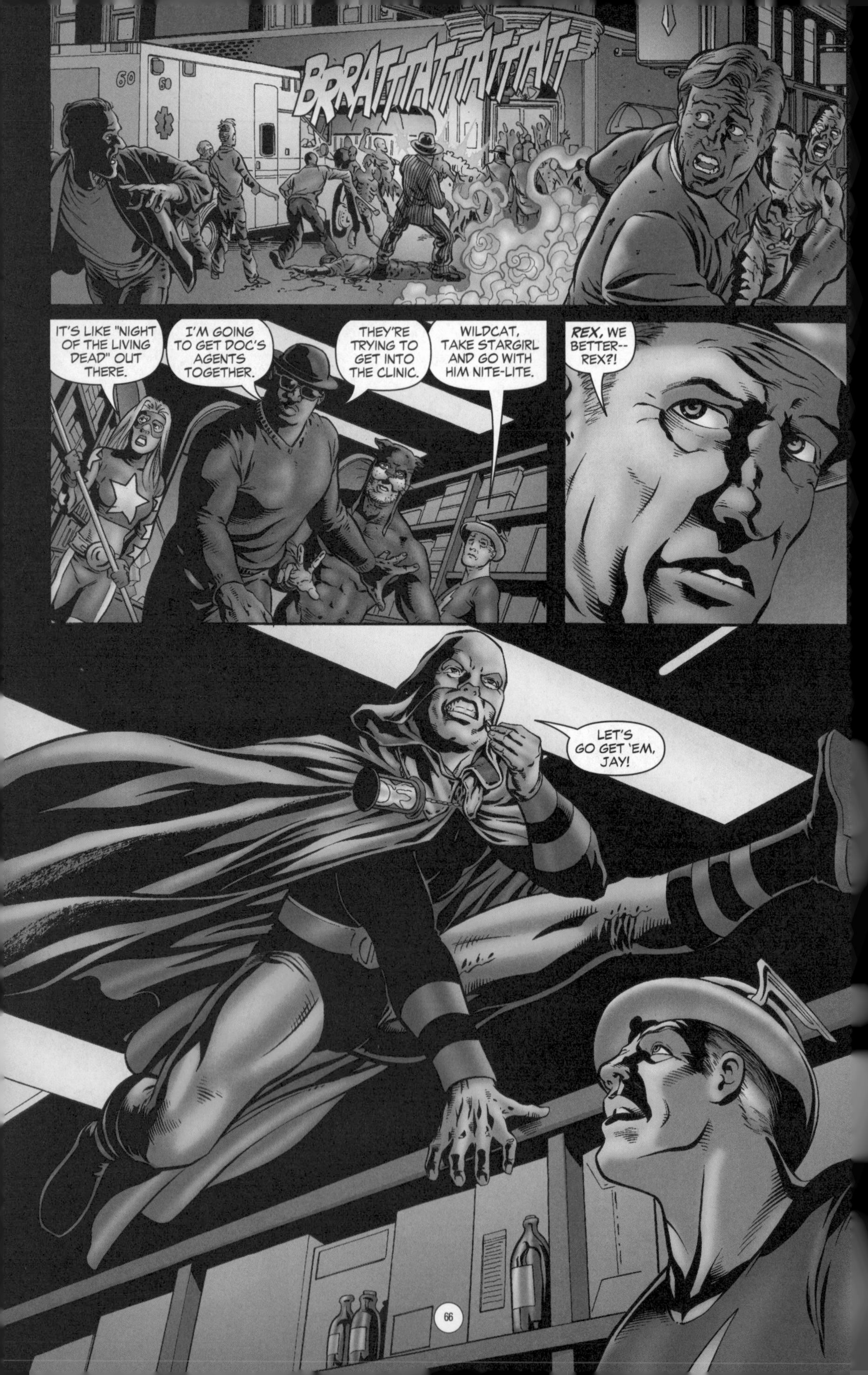
BRRATTTATTATTAT
IT'S LIKE "NIGHT OF THE LIVING DEAD" OUT THERE.
I'M GOING TO GET DOC'S AGENTS TOGETHER.
THEY'RE TRYING TO GET INTO THE CLINIC.
WILDCAT, TAKE STARGIRL AND GO WITH HIM NITE-LITE.
REX, WE BETTER-- REX?!
LET'S GO GET 'EM, JAY!

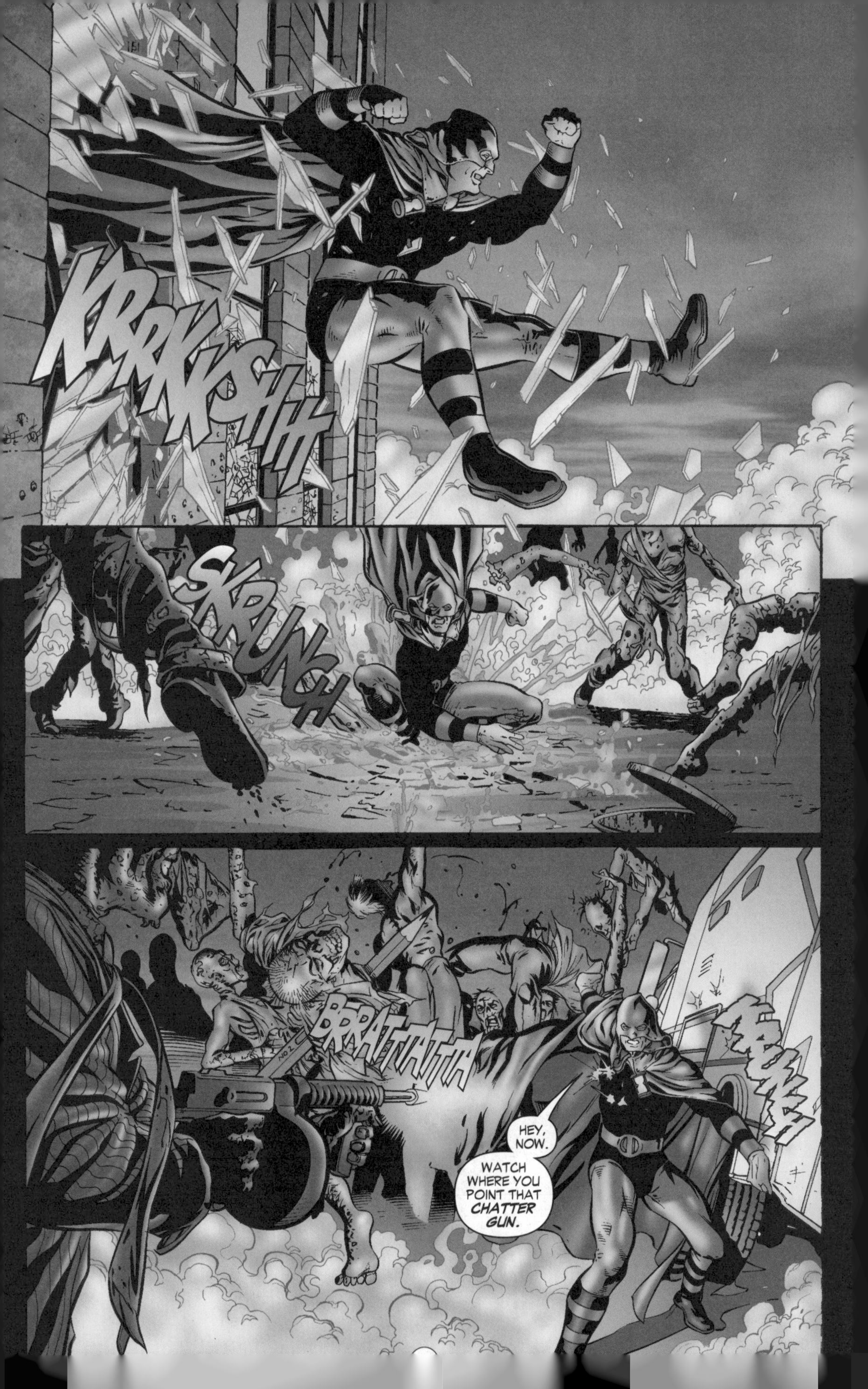
KRRKSHH
SKRUNCH
BRRATTATTA
HEY, NOW.
WATCH WHERE YOU POINT THAT CHATTER GUN.
KRUNCH

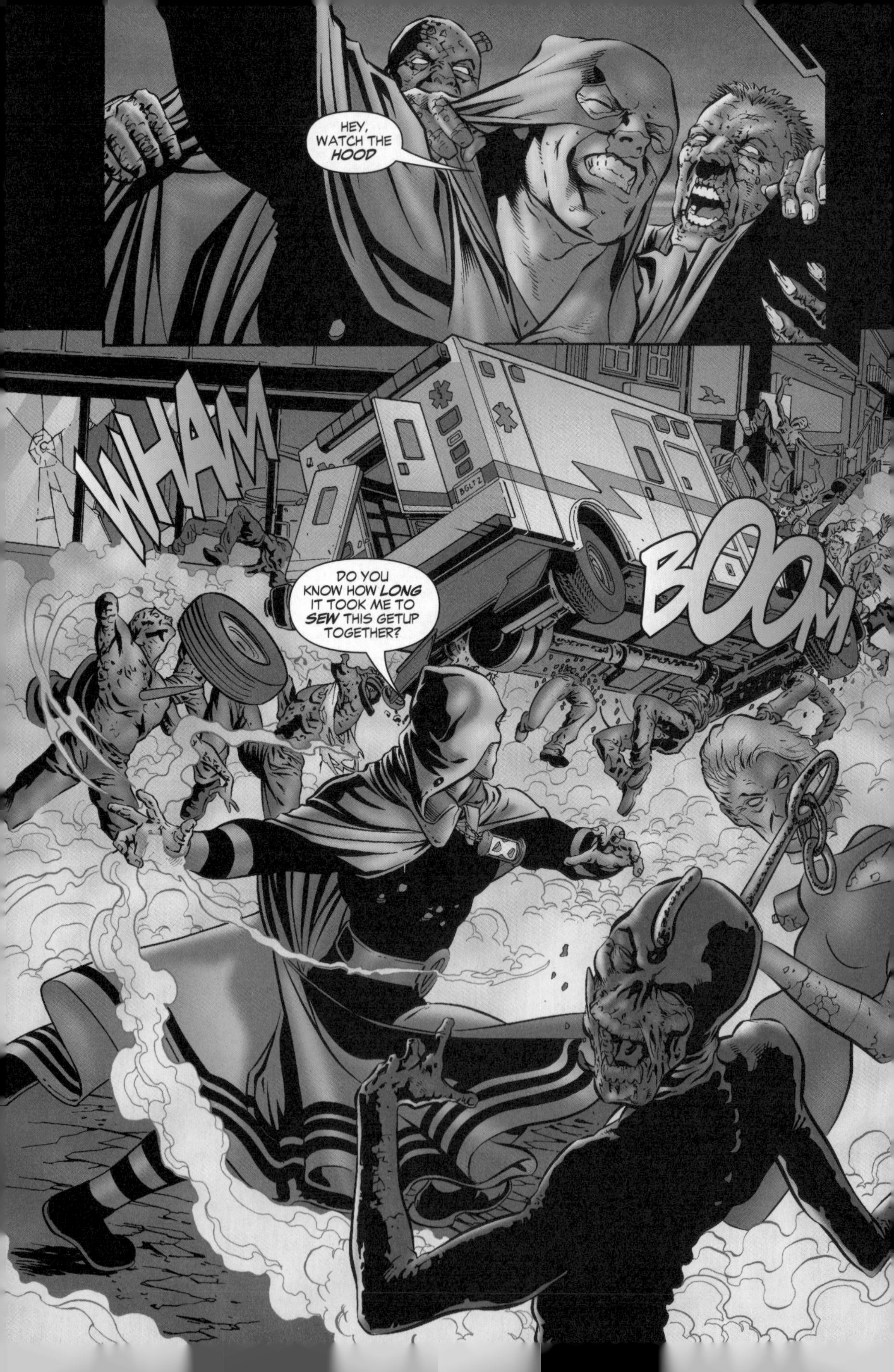
HEY, WATCH THE HOOD
WHAM
BOOM
DO YOU KNOW HOW LONG IT TOOK ME TO SEW THIS GETUP TOGETHER?

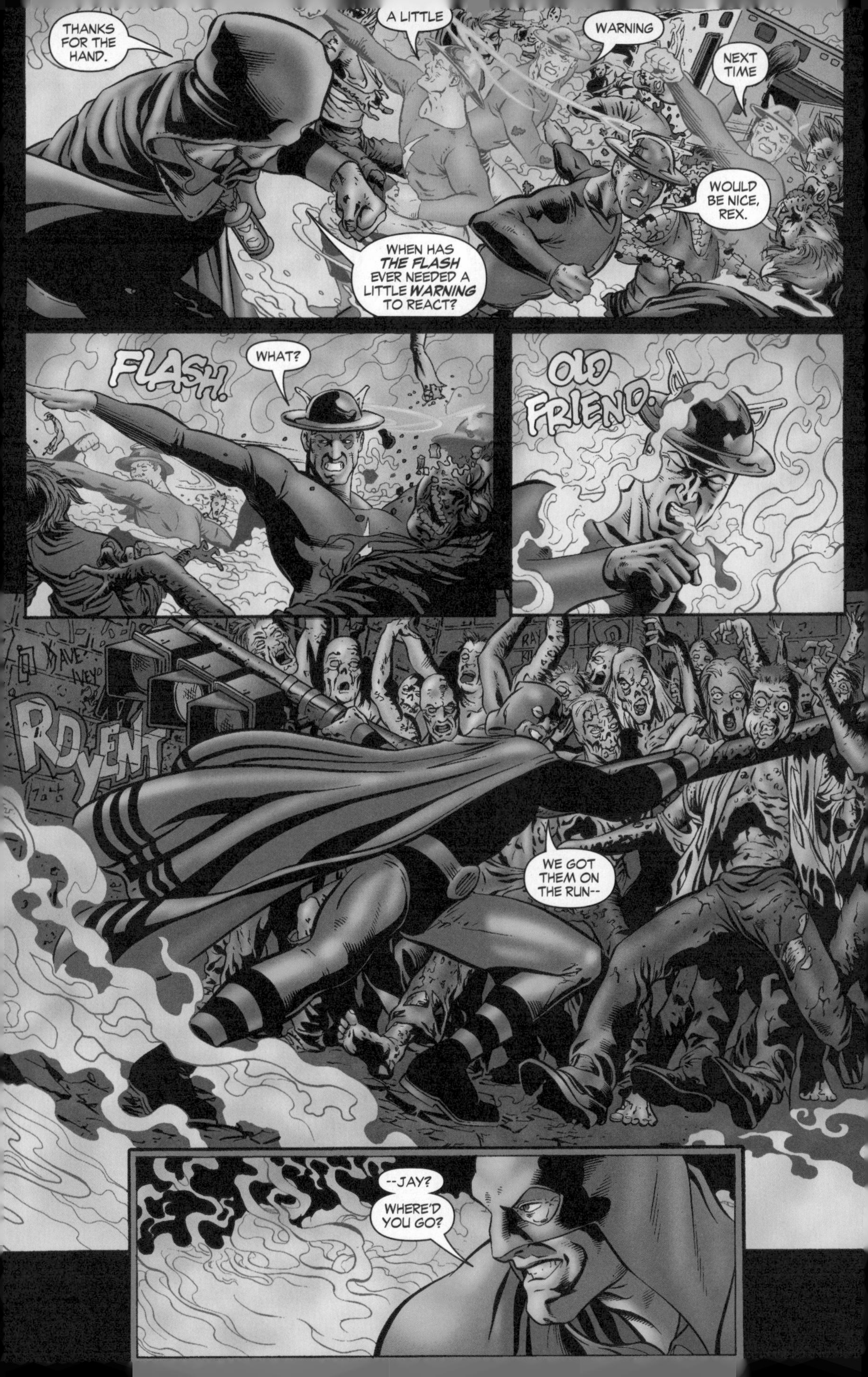
THANKS FOR THE HAND.
A LITTLE
WARNING
NEXT TIME
WOULD BE NICE, REX.
WHEN HAS THE FLASH EVER NEEDED A LITTLE WARNING TO REACT?
FLASH!
WHAT?
OLD FRIEND.
WE GOT THEM ON THE RUN--
--JAY?
WHERE'D YOU GO?

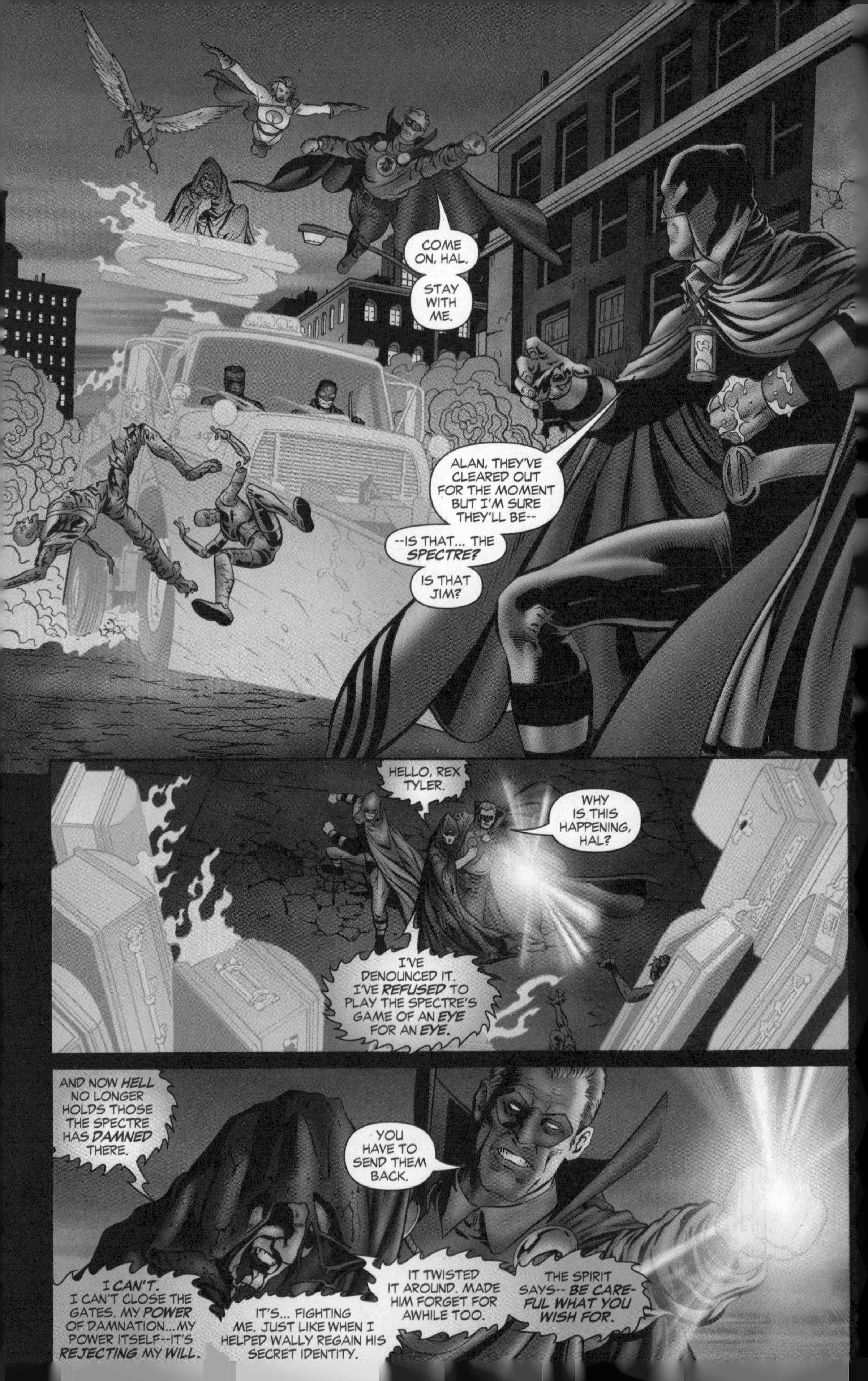

COME ON, HAL.
STAY WITH ME.
ALAN, THEY'VE CLEARED OUT FOR THE MOMENT BUT I'M SURE THEY'LL BE--
--IS THAT... THE SPECTRE?
IS THAT JIM?
HELLO, REX TYLER.
WHY IS THIS HAPPENING, HAL?
I'VE DENOUNCED IT. I'VE REFUSED TO PLAY THE SPECTRE'S GAME OF AN EYE FOR AN EYE.
AND NOW HELL NO LONGER HOLDS THOSE THE SPECTRE HAS DAMNED THERE.
YOU HAVE TO SEND THEM BACK.
I CAN'T. I CAN'T CLOSE THE GATES. MY POWER OF DAMNATION...MY POWER ITSELF--IT'S REJECTING MY WILL.
IT'S... FIGHTING ME. JUST LIKE WHEN I HELPED WALLY REGAIN HIS SECRET IDENTITY.
IT TWISTED IT AROUND. MADE HIM FORGET FOR AWHILE TOO.
THE SPIRIT SAYS-- BE CARE-FUL WHAT YOU WISH FOR.

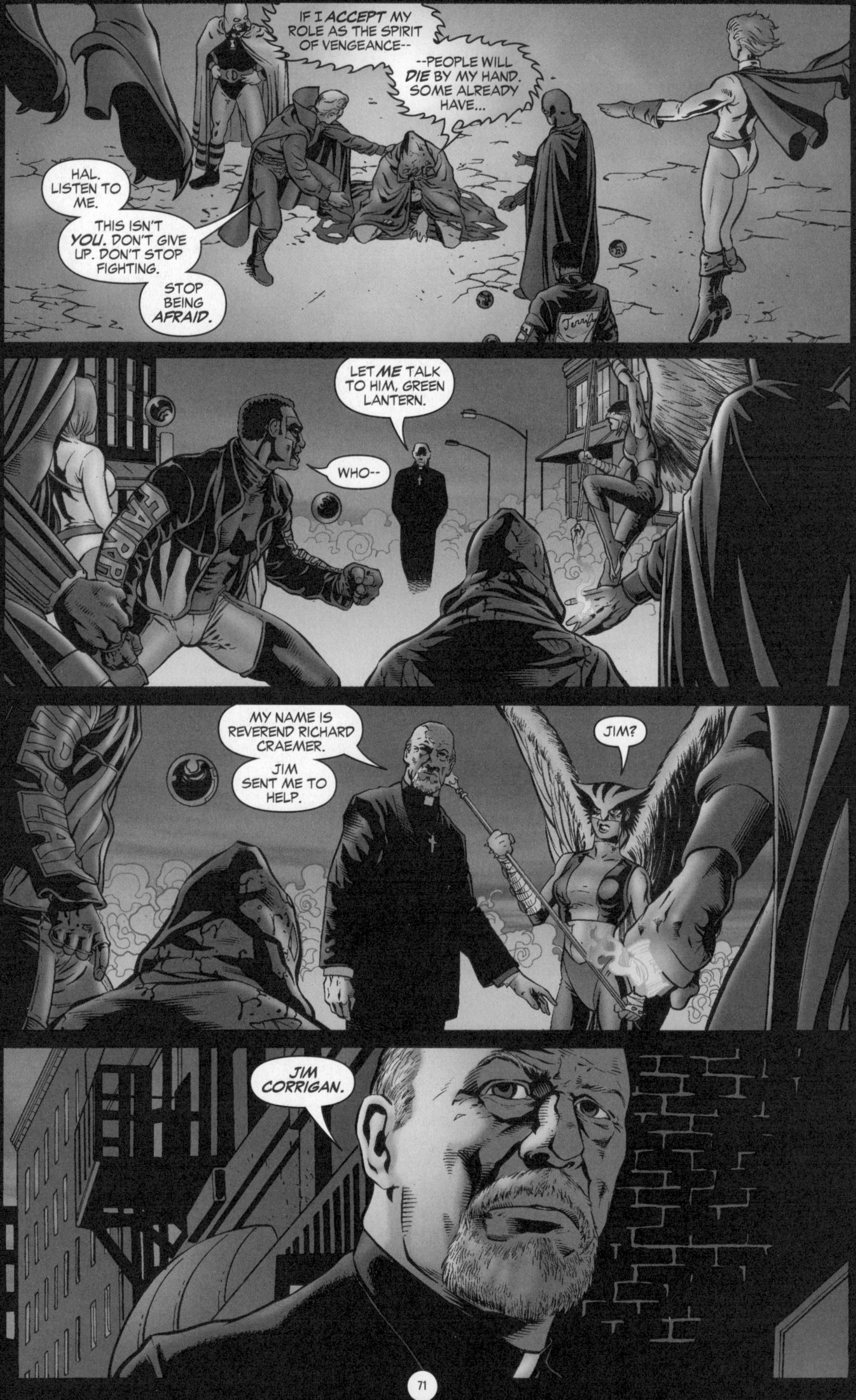

IF I ACCEPT MY ROLE AS THE SPIRIT OF VENGEANCE--
--PEOPLE WILL DIE BY MY HAND. SOME ALREADY HAVE...
HAL. LISTEN TO ME.
THIS ISN'T YOU. DON'T GIVE UP. DON'T STOP FIGHTING.
STOP BEING AFRAID.
LET ME TALK TO HIM, GREEN LANTERN.
WHO--
MY NAME IS REVEREND RICHARD CRAEMER.
JIM SENT ME TO HELP.
JIM?
JIM CORRIGAN.

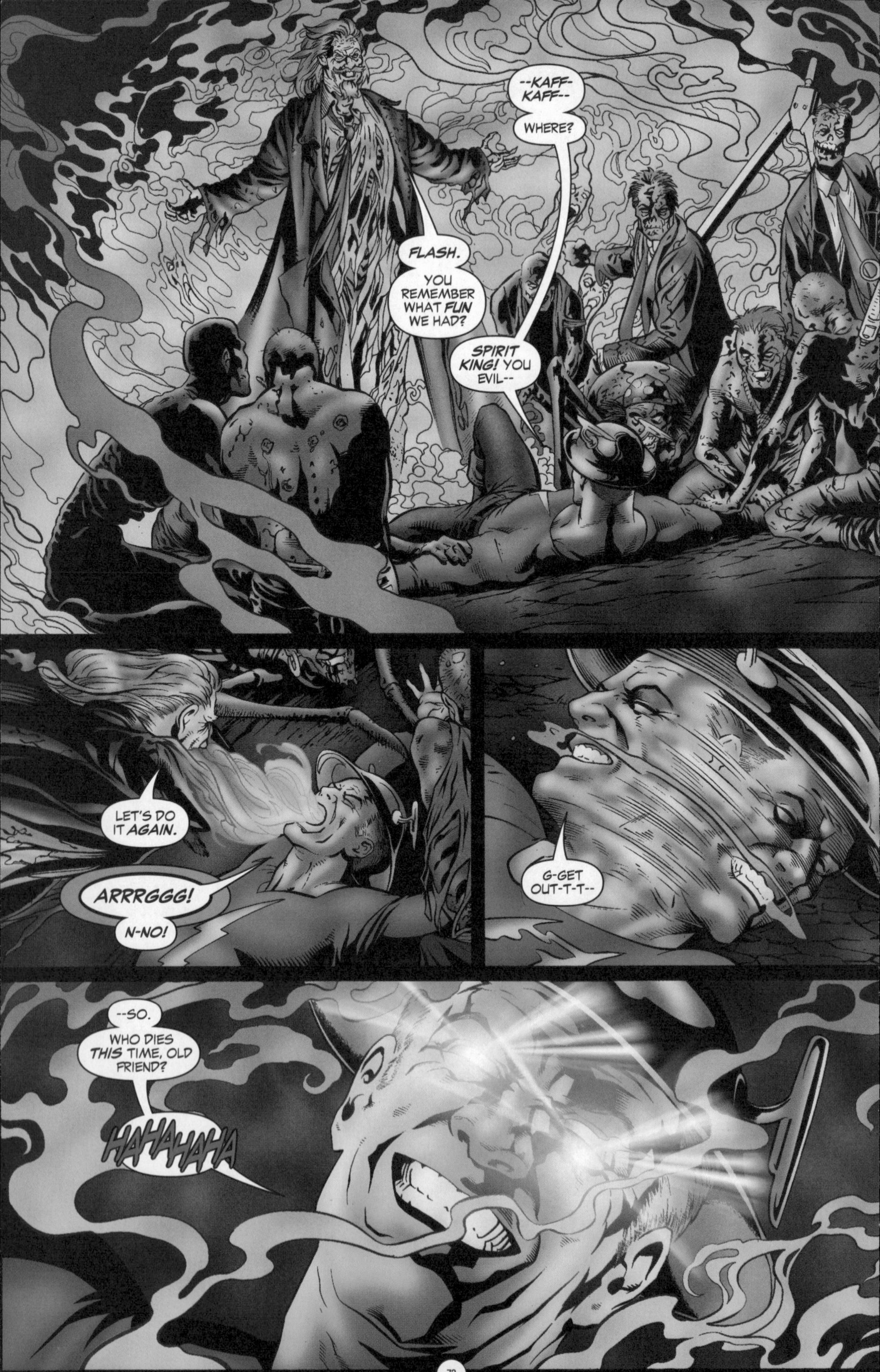

--KAFF-KAFF--
WHERE?
FLASH.
YOU REMEMBER WHAT FUN WE HAD?
SPIRIT KING! YOU EVIL--
LET'S DO IT AGAIN.
ARRRGGG!
N-NO!
G-GET OUT-T-T--
--SO.
WHO DIES THIS TIME, OLD FRIEND?
HAHAHAHA

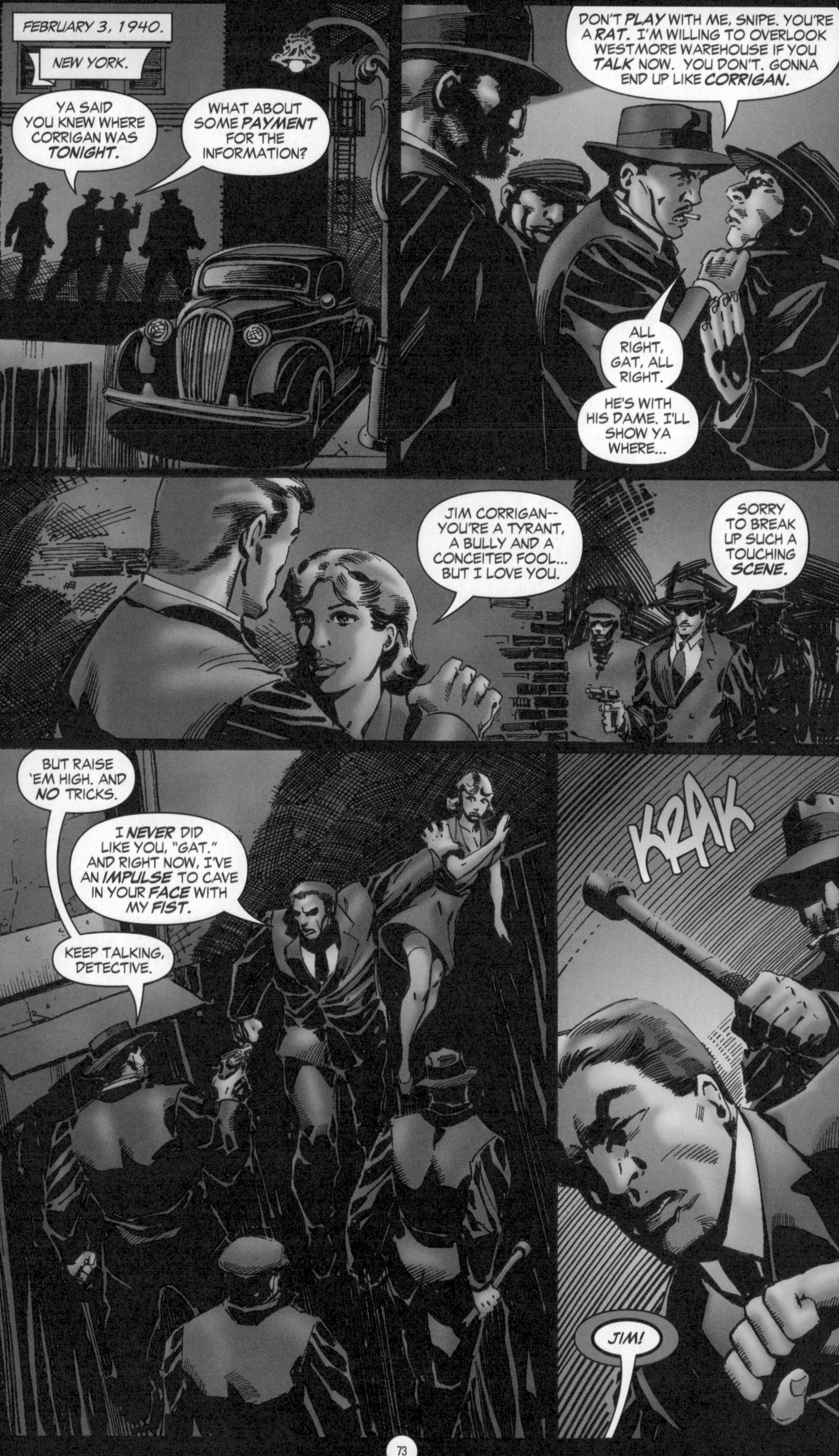

FEBRUARY 3, 1940.
NEW YORK.
YA SAID YOU KNEW WHERE CORRIGAN WAS TONIGHT.
WHAT ABOUT SOME PAYMENT FOR THE INFORMATION?
DON'T PLAY WITH ME, SNIPE. YOU'RE A RAT. I'M WILLING TO OVERLOOK WESTMORE WAREHOUSE IF YOU TALK NOW. YOU DON'T. GONNA END UP LIKE CORRIGAN.
ALL RIGHT, GAT, ALL RIGHT.
HE'S WITH HIS DAME. I'LL SHOW YA WHERE...
JIM CORRIGAN-- YOU'RE A TYRANT, A BULLY AND A CONCEITED FOOL... BUT I LOVE YOU.
SORRY TO BREAK UP SUCH A TOUCHING SCENE.
BUT RAISE 'EM HIGH. AND NO TRICKS.
I NEVER DID LIKE YOU, "GAT." AND RIGHT NOW, I'VE AN IMPULSE TO CAVE IN YOUR FACE WITH MY FIST.
KEEP TALKING, DETECTIVE.
KRAK
JIM!

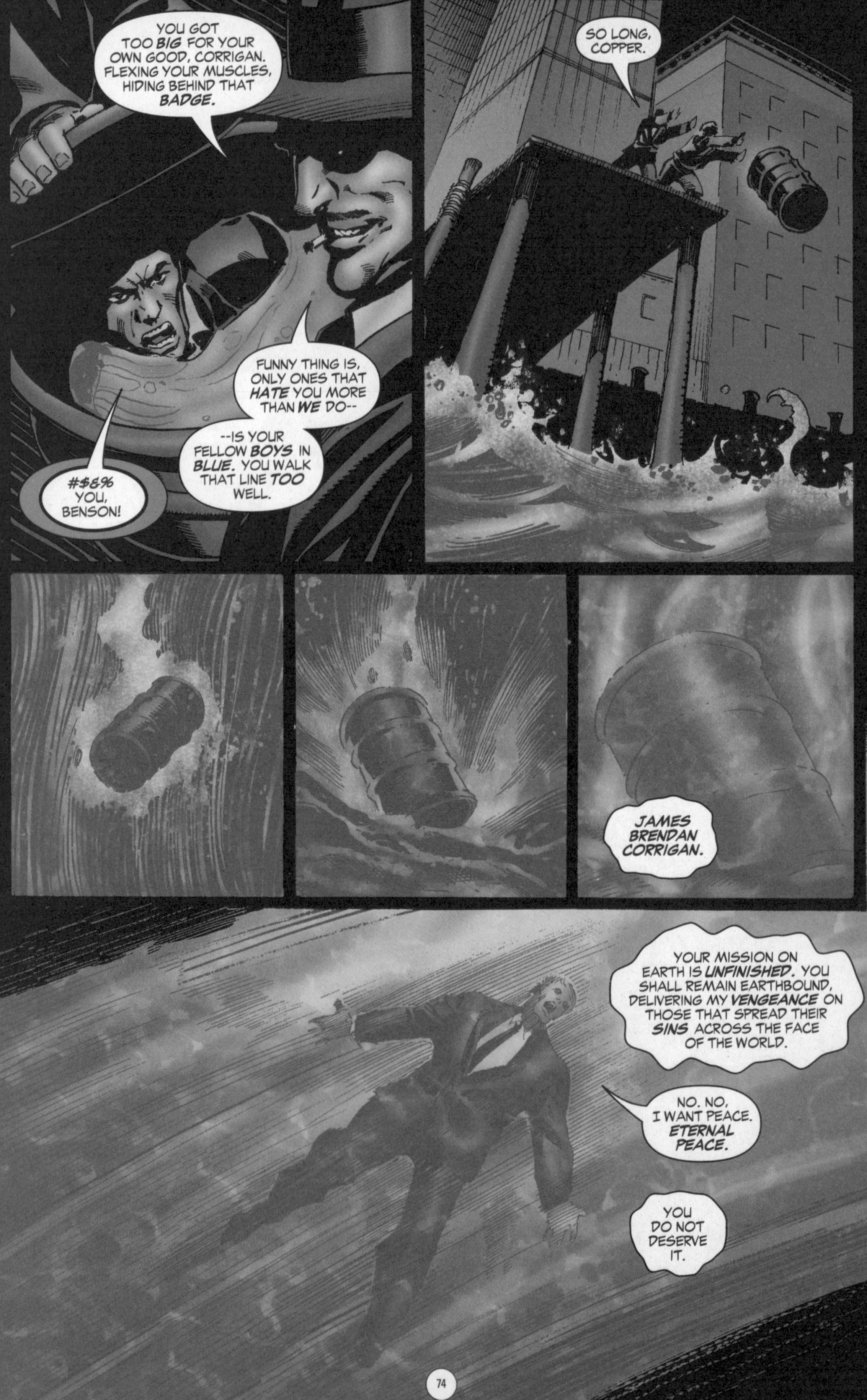
YOU GOT TOO BIG FOR YOUR OWN GOOD, CORRIGAN. FLEXING YOUR MUSCLES, HIDING BEHIND THAT BADGE.
FUNNY THING IS, ONLY ONES THAT HATE YOU MORE THAN WE DO--
--IS YOUR FELLOW BOYS IN BLUE. YOU WALK THAT LINE TOO WELL.
#$&% YOU, BENSON!
SO LONG, COPPER.
JAMES BRENDAN CORRIGAN.
YOUR MISSION ON EARTH IS UNFINISHED. YOU SHALL REMAIN EARTHBOUND, DELIVERING MY VENGEANCE ON THOSE THAT SPREAD THEIR SINS ACROSS THE FACE OF THE WORLD.
NO. NO, I WANT PEACE. ETERNAL PEACE.
YOU DO NOT DESERVE IT.

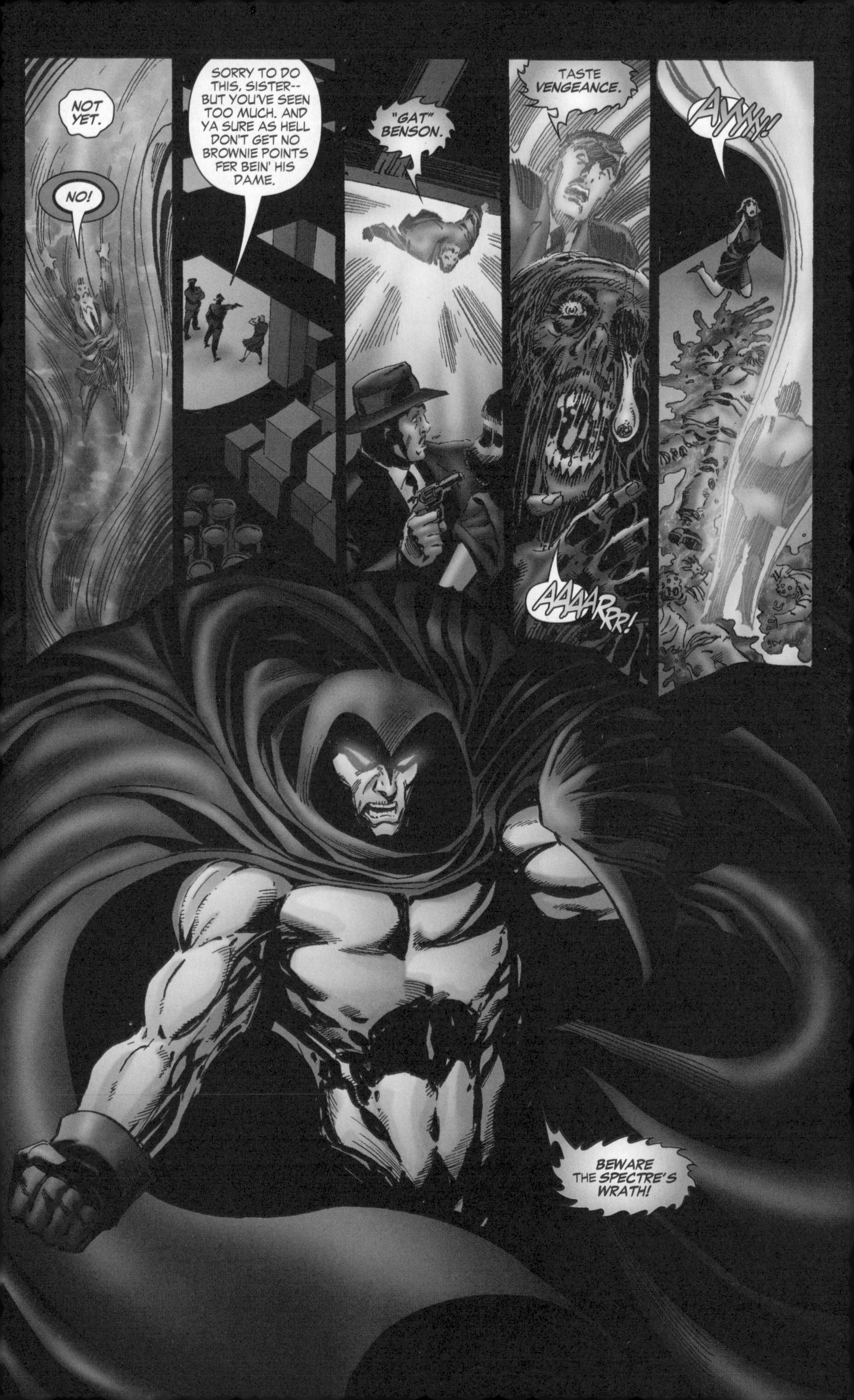
NOT YET.
NO!
SORRY TO DO THIS, SISTER-- BUT YOU'VE SEEN TOO MUCH. AND YA SURE AS HELL DON'T GET NO BROWNIE POINTS FER BEIN' HIS DAME.
"GAT" BENSON.
TASTE VENGEANCE.
AAAARRR!
AYYYY!
BEWARE THE SPECTRE'S WRATH!

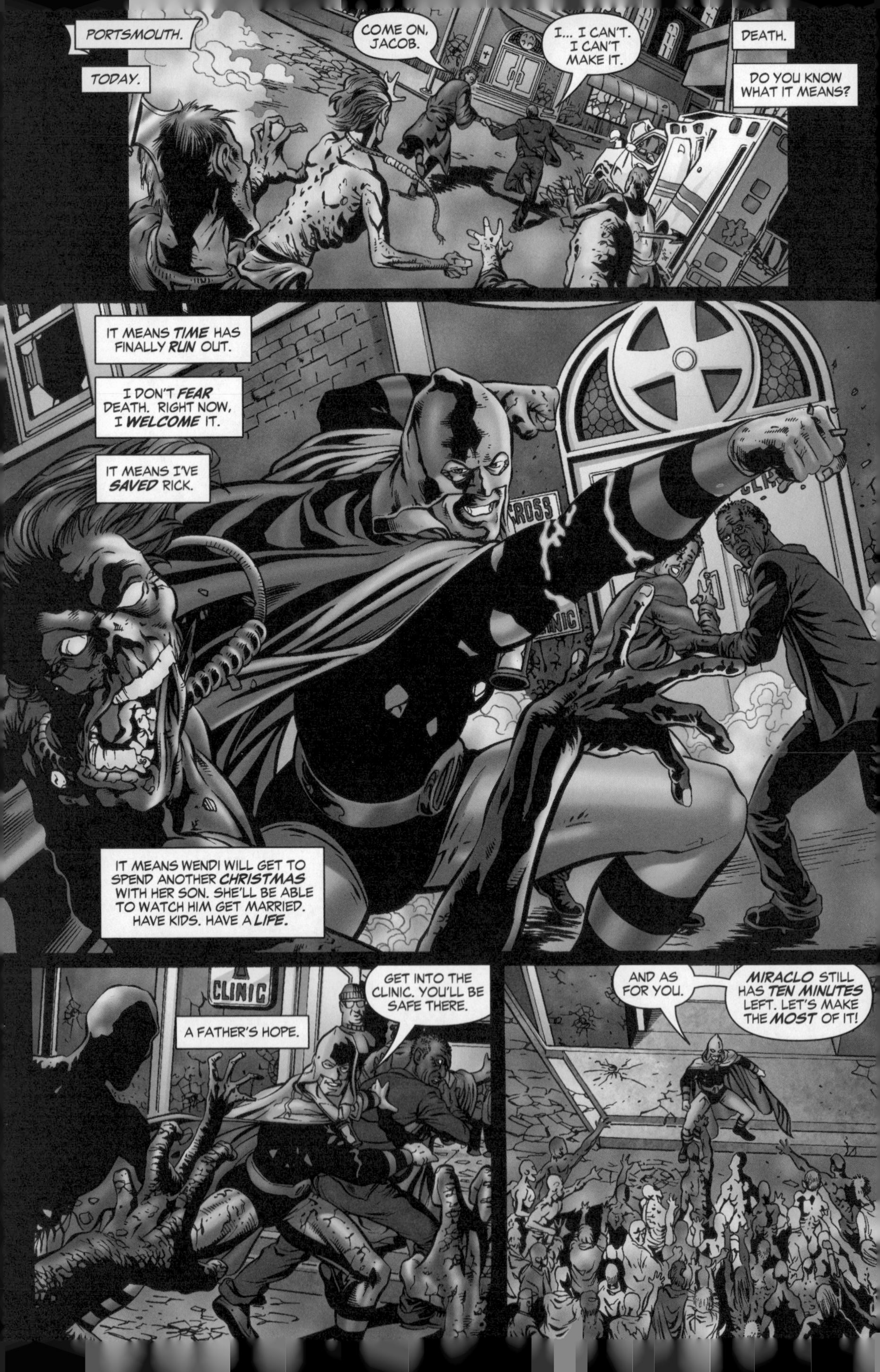
PORTSMOUTH.
TODAY.
COME ON, JACOB.
I... I CAN'T. I CAN'T MAKE IT.
DEATH.
DO YOU KNOW WHAT IT MEANS?
IT MEANS TIME HAS FINALLY RUN OUT.
I DON'T FEAR DEATH. RIGHT NOW, I WELCOME IT.
IT MEANS I'VE SAVED RICK.
CROSS
CLINIC
IT MEANS WENDI WILL GET TO SPEND ANOTHER CHRISTMAS WITH HER SON. SHE'LL BE ABLE TO WATCH HIM GET MARRIED. HAVE KIDS. HAVE A LIFE.
CLINIC
A FATHER'S HOPE.
GET INTO THE CLINIC. YOU'LL BE SAFE THERE.
AND AS FOR YOU.
MIRACLO STILL HAS TEN MINUTES LEFT. LET'S MAKE THE MOST OF IT!

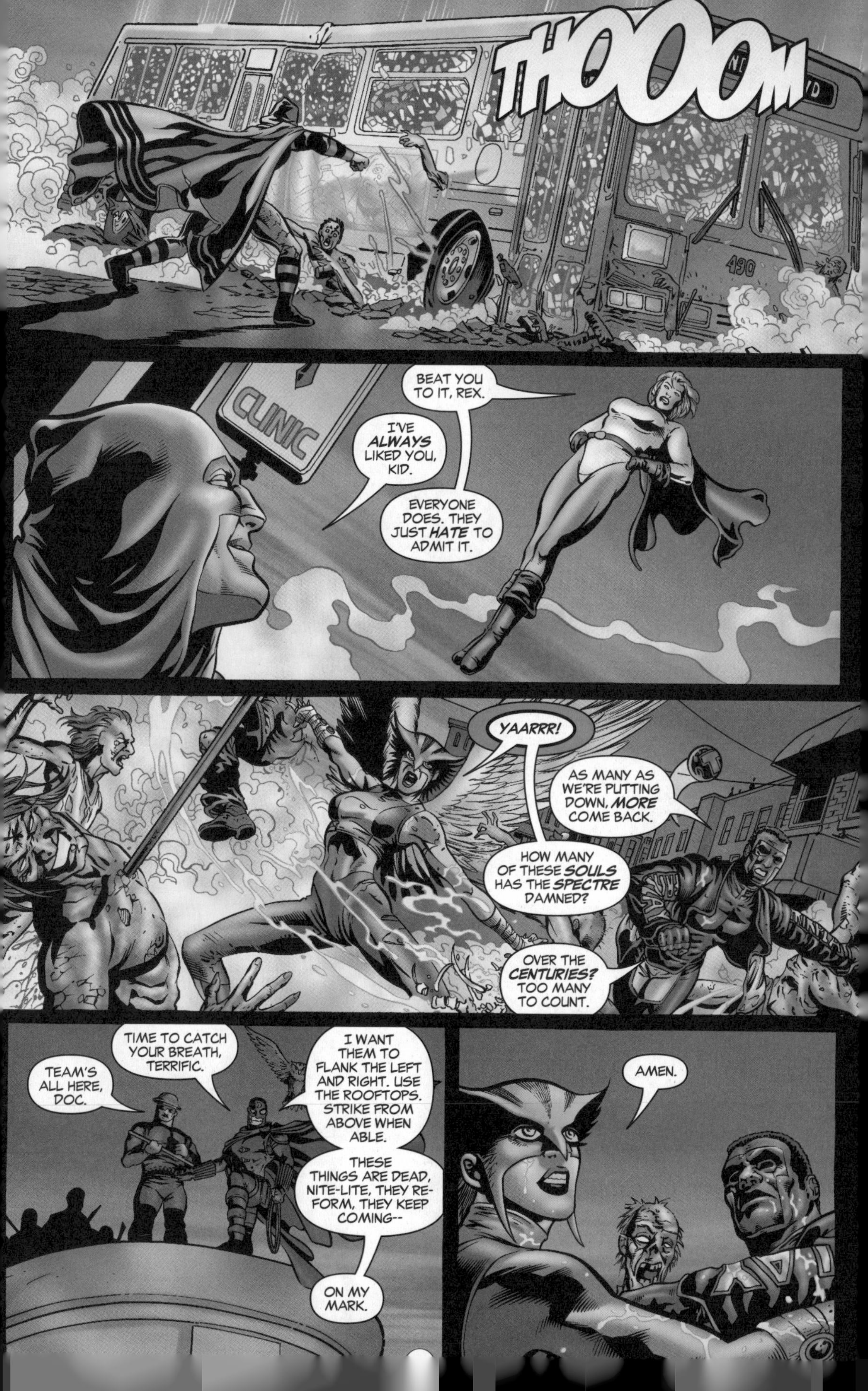
THOOOM
CLINIC
BEAT YOU TO IT, REX.
I'VE ALWAYS LIKED YOU, KID.
EVERYONE DOES. THEY JUST HATE TO ADMIT IT.
YAARRR!
AS MANY AS WE'RE PUTTING DOWN, MORE COME BACK.
HOW MANY OF THESE SOULS HAS THE SPECTRE DAMNED?
OVER THE CENTURIES? TOO MANY TO COUNT.
TEAM'S ALL HERE, DOC.
TIME TO CATCH YOUR BREATH, TERRIFIC.
I WANT THEM TO FLANK THE LEFT AND RIGHT. USE THE ROOFTOPS. STRIKE FROM ABOVE WHEN ABLE.
THESE THINGS ARE DEAD, NITE-LITE, THEY RE-FORM, THEY KEEP COMING--
ON MY MARK.
AMEN.

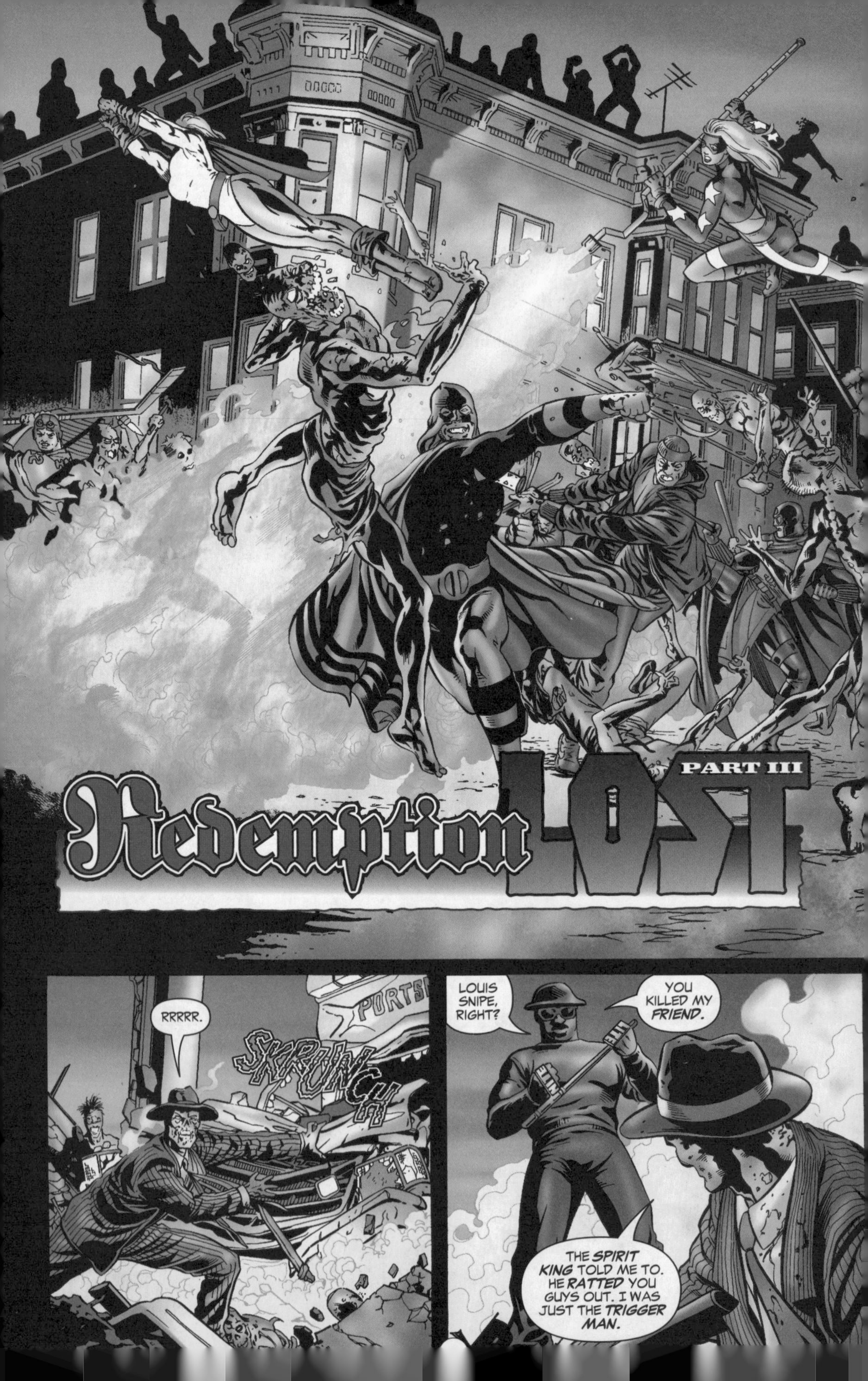
PART III
Redemption LOST
PORTS
RRRRR.
SKRUNCH
LOUIS SNIPE, RIGHT?
YOU KILLED MY FRIEND.
THE SPIRIT KING TOLD ME TO. HE RATTED YOU GUYS OUT. I WAS JUST THE TRIGGER MAN.

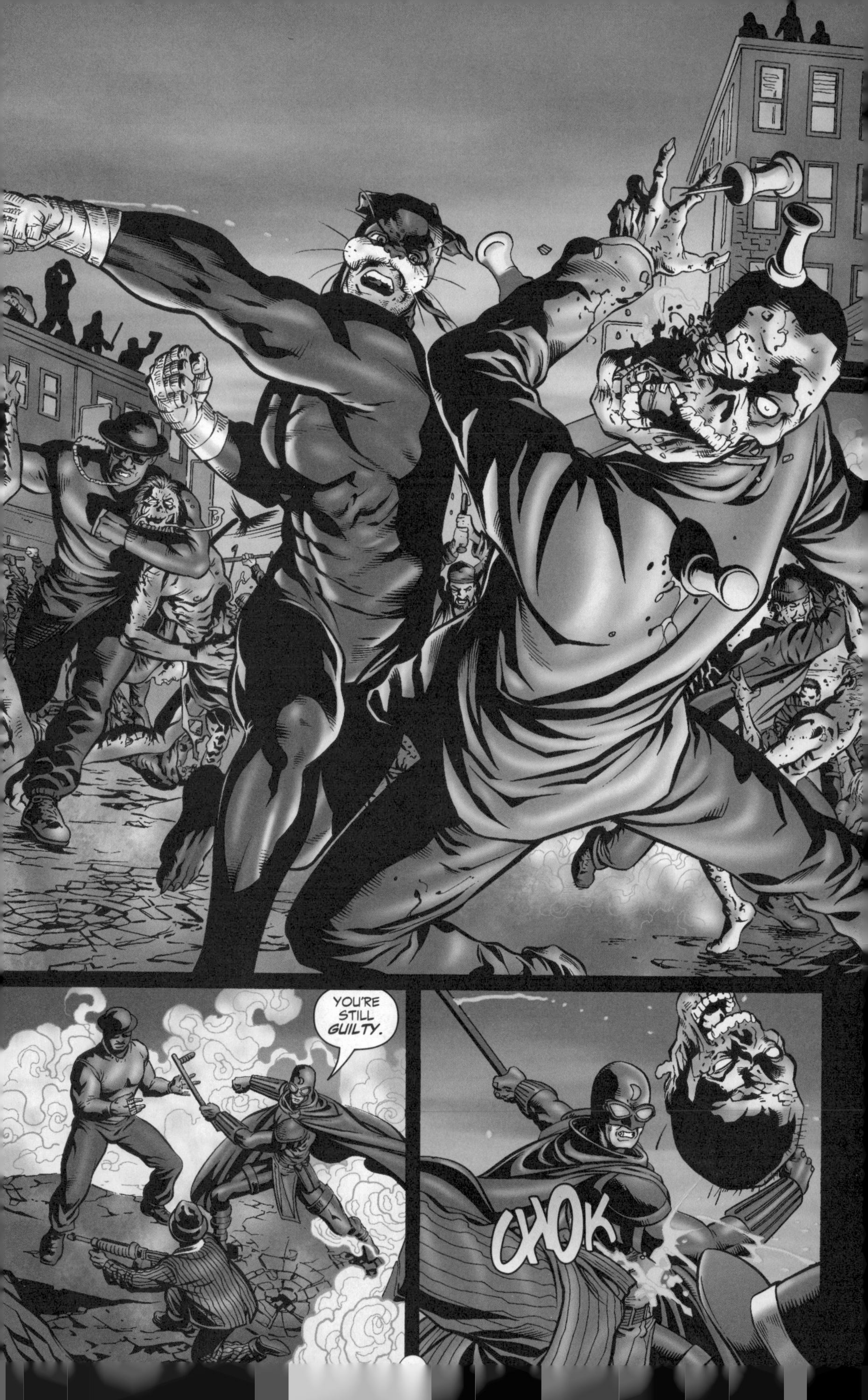
YOU'RE STILL GUILTY.
CHOK

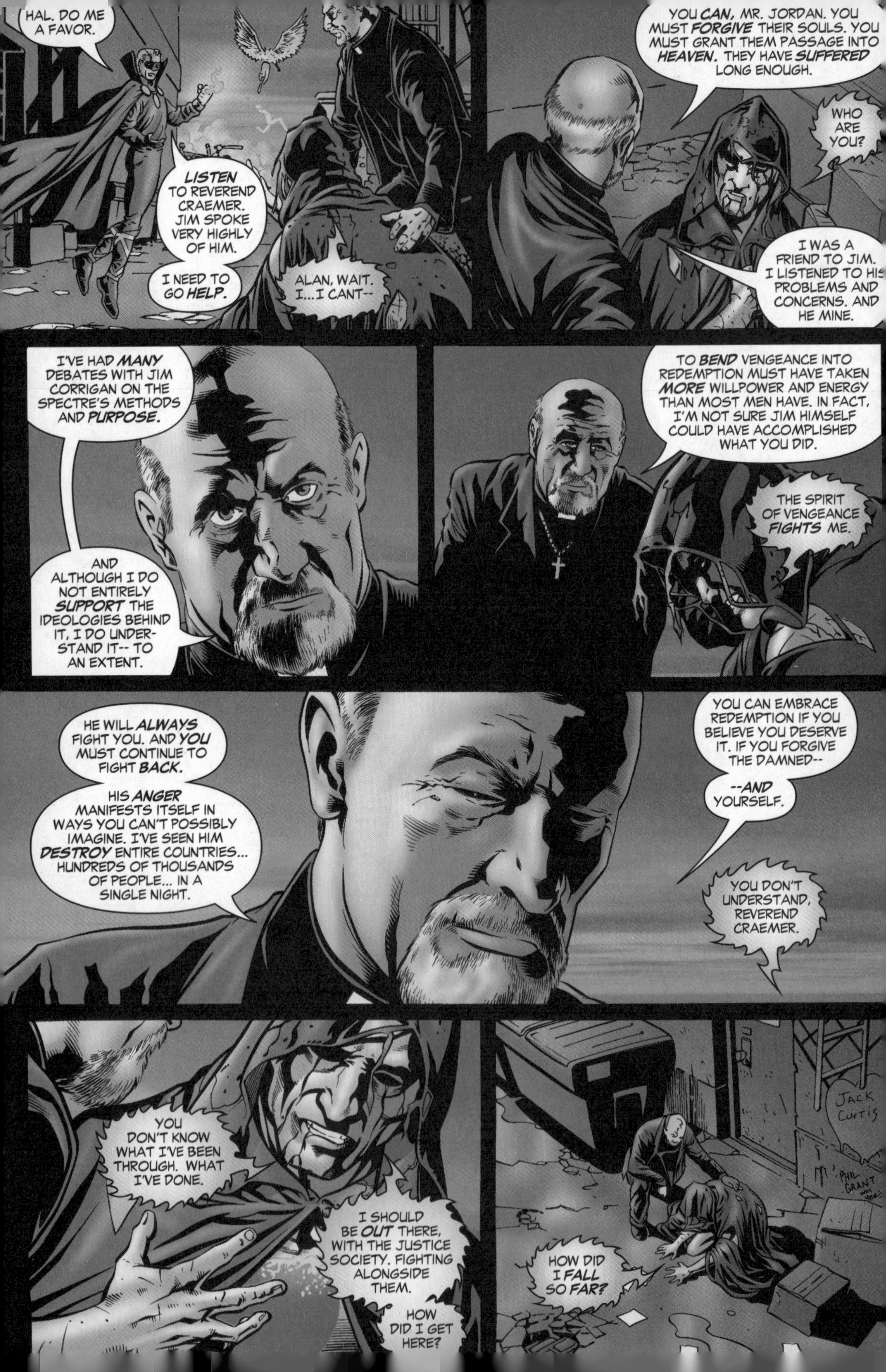
HAL. DO ME A FAVOR.
LISTEN TO REVEREND CRAEMER. JIM SPOKE VERY HIGHLY OF HIM.
I NEED TO GO HELP.
ALAN, WAIT. I...I CANT--
YOU CAN, MR. JORDAN. YOU MUST FORGIVE THEIR SOULS. YOU MUST GRANT THEM PASSAGE INTO HEAVEN. THEY HAVE SUFFERED LONG ENOUGH.
WHO ARE YOU?
I WAS A FRIEND TO JIM. I LISTENED TO HIS PROBLEMS AND CONCERNS. AND HE MINE.
I'VE HAD MANY DEBATES WITH JIM CORRIGAN ON THE SPECTRE'S METHODS AND PURPOSE.
AND ALTHOUGH I DO NOT ENTIRELY SUPPORT THE IDEOLOGIES BEHIND IT, I DO UNDERSTAND IT-- TO AN EXTENT.
TO BEND VENGEANCE INTO REDEMPTION MUST HAVE TAKEN MORE WILLPOWER AND ENERGY THAN MOST MEN HAVE. IN FACT, I'M NOT SURE JIM HIMSELF COULD HAVE ACCOMPLISHED WHAT YOU DID.
THE SPIRIT OF VENGEANCE FIGHTS ME.
HE WILL ALWAYS FIGHT YOU. AND YOU MUST CONTINUE TO FIGHT BACK.
HIS ANGER MANIFESTS ITSELF IN WAYS YOU CAN'T POSSIBLY IMAGINE. I'VE SEEN HIM DESTROY ENTIRE COUNTRIES... HUNDREDS OF THOUSANDS OF PEOPLE... IN A SINGLE NIGHT.
YOU CAN EMBRACE REDEMPTION IF YOU BELIEVE YOU DESERVE IT. IF YOU FORGIVE THE DAMNED--
--AND YOURSELF.
YOU DON'T UNDERSTAND, REVEREND CRAEMER.
YOU DON'T KNOW WHAT I'VE BEEN THROUGH. WHAT I'VE DONE.
I SHOULD BE OUT THERE, WITH THE JUSTICE SOCIETY. FIGHTING ALONGSIDE THEM.
HOW DID I GET HERE?
JACK CURTIS
HOW DID I FALL SO FAR?

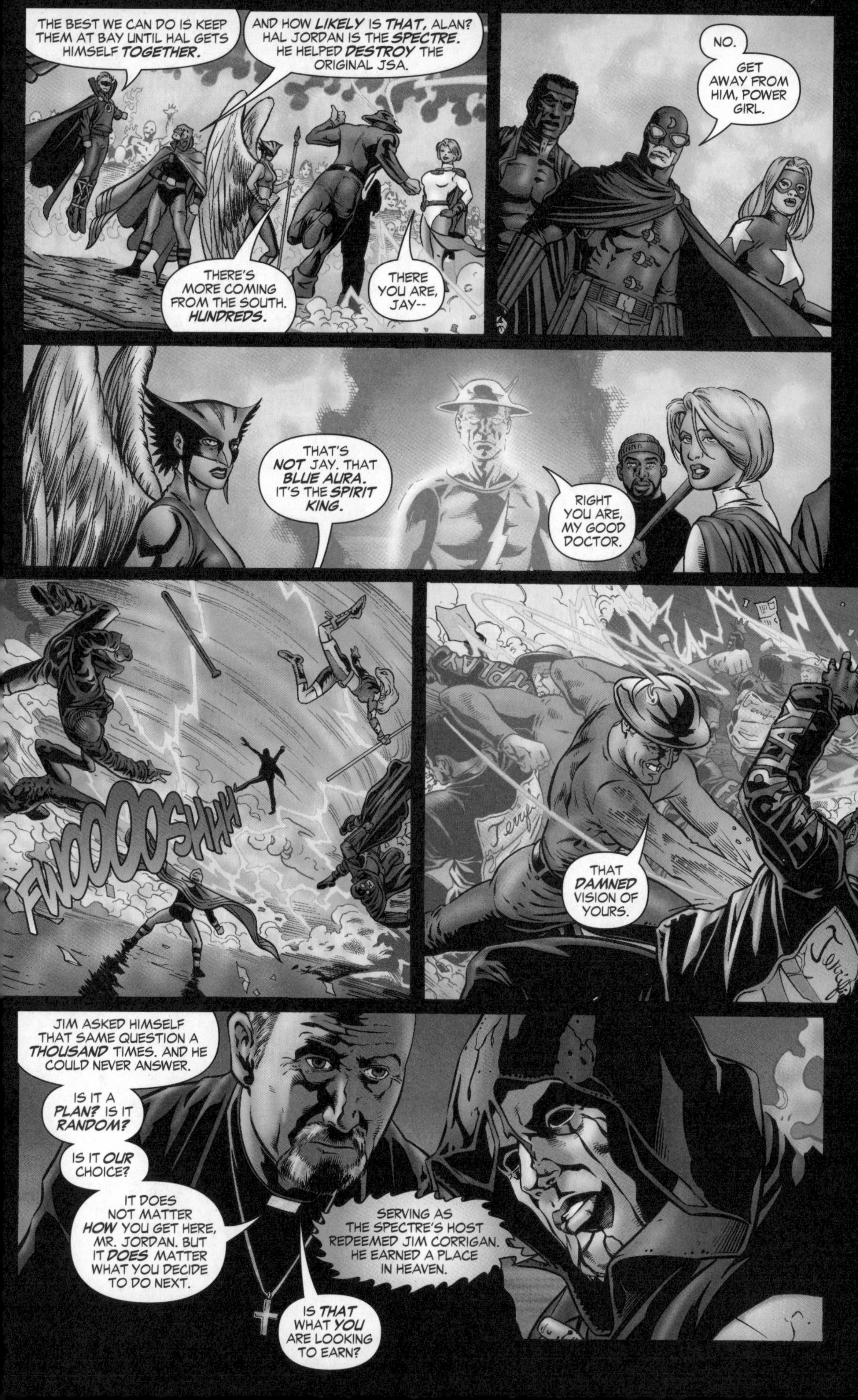
THE BEST WE CAN DO IS KEEP THEM AT BAY UNTIL HAL GETS HIMSELF TOGETHER.
AND HOW LIKELY IS THAT, ALAN? HAL JORDAN IS THE SPECTRE. HE HELPED DESTROY THE ORIGINAL JSA.
THERE'S MORE COMING FROM THE SOUTH. HUNDREDS.
THERE YOU ARE, JAY--
NO.
GET AWAY FROM HIM, POWER GIRL.
THAT'S NOT JAY. THAT BLUE AURA. IT'S THE SPIRIT KING.
RIGHT YOU ARE, MY GOOD DOCTOR.
FWOOOOSHHH
THAT DAMNED VISION OF YOURS.
JIM ASKED HIMSELF THAT SAME QUESTION A THOUSAND TIMES. AND HE COULD NEVER ANSWER.
IS IT A PLAN? IS IT RANDOM?
IS IT OUR CHOICE?
IT DOES NOT MATTER HOW YOU GET HERE, MR. JORDAN. BUT IT DOES MATTER WHAT YOU DECIDE TO DO NEXT.
SERVING AS THE SPECTRE'S HOST REDEEMED JIM CORRIGAN. HE EARNED A PLACE IN HEAVEN.
IS THAT WHAT YOU ARE LOOKING TO EARN?

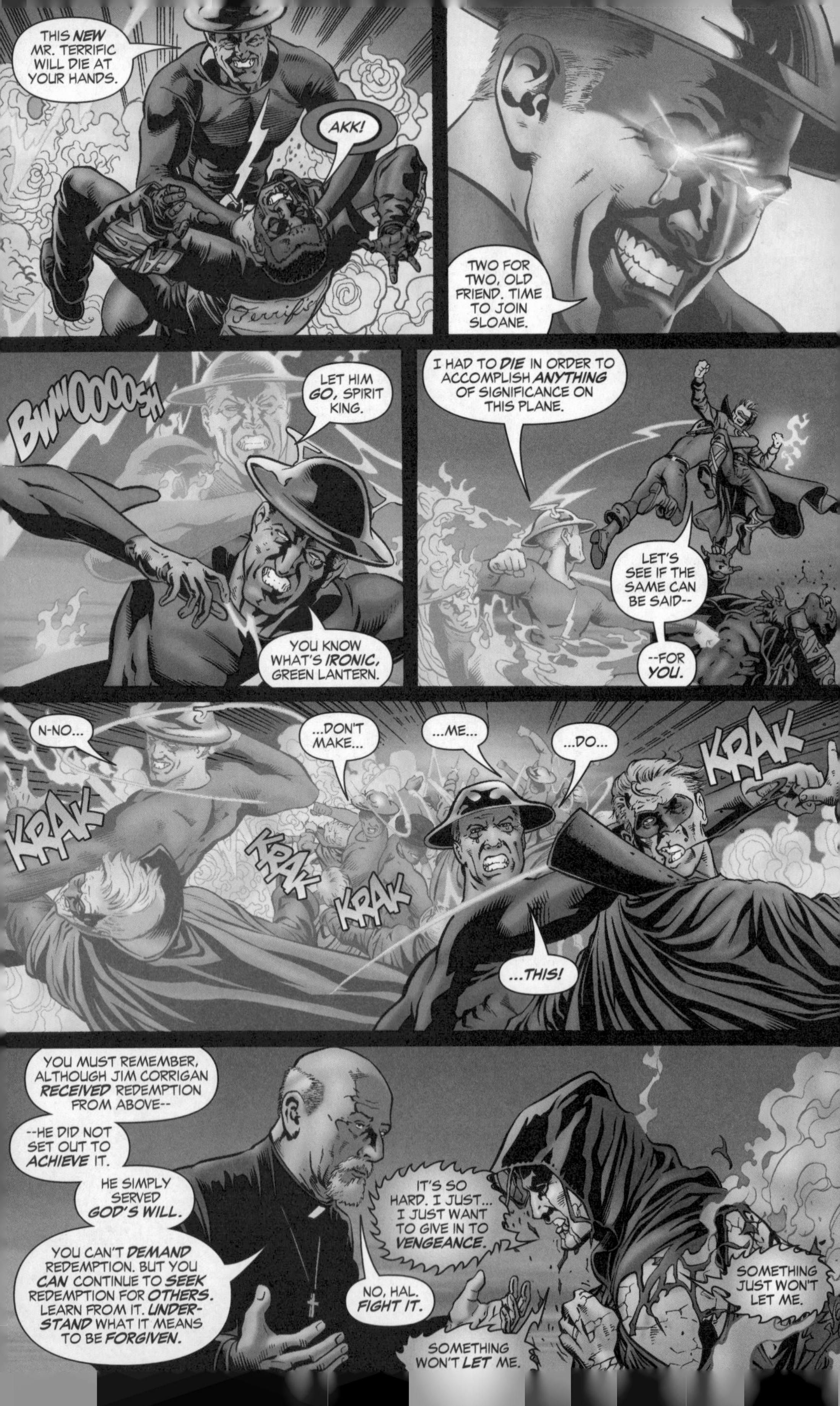
THIS NEW MR. TERRIFIC WILL DIE AT YOUR HANDS.
AKK!
TWO FOR TWO, OLD FRIEND. TIME TO JOIN SLOANE.
BWWOOOOSH
LET HIM GO, SPIRIT KING.
YOU KNOW WHAT'S IRONIC, GREEN LANTERN.
I HAD TO DIE IN ORDER TO ACCOMPLISH ANYTHING OF SIGNIFICANCE ON THIS PLANE.
LET'S SEE IF THE SAME CAN BE SAID--
--FOR YOU.
N-NO...
...DON'T MAKE...
...ME...
...DO...
KRAK
KRAK
KRAK
KRAK
...THIS!
YOU MUST REMEMBER, ALTHOUGH JIM CORRIGAN RECEIVED REDEMPTION FROM ABOVE--
--HE DID NOT SET OUT TO ACHIEVE IT.
HE SIMPLY SERVED GOD'S WILL.
YOU CAN'T DEMAND REDEMPTION. BUT YOU CAN CONTINUE TO SEEK REDEMPTION FOR OTHERS. LEARN FROM IT. UNDERSTAND WHAT IT MEANS TO BE FORGIVEN.
IT'S SO HARD. I JUST... I JUST WANT TO GIVE IN TO VENGEANCE.
NO, HAL. FIGHT IT.
SOMETHING JUST WON'T LET ME.
SOMETHING WON'T LET ME.

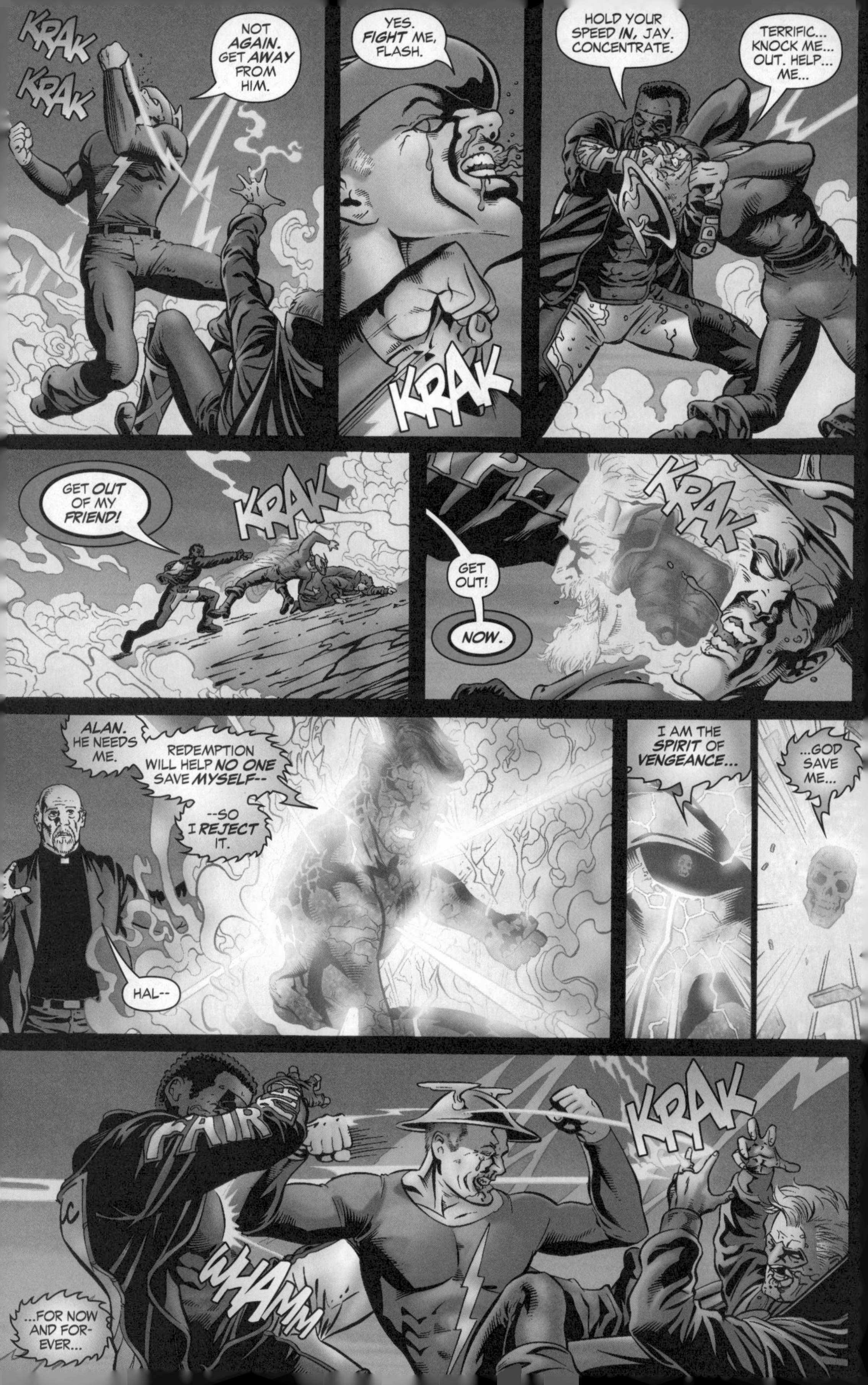
KRAK
KRAK
NOT AGAIN. GET AWAY FROM HIM.
YES. FIGHT ME, FLASH.
KRAK
HOLD YOUR SPEED IN, JAY. CONCENTRATE.
TERRIFIC... KNOCK ME... OUT. HELP... ME...
GET OUT OF MY FRIEND!
KRAK
KRAK
GET OUT!
NOW.
ALAN. HE NEEDS ME.
REDEMPTION WILL HELP NO ONE SAVE MYSELF--
--SO I REJECT IT.
HAL--
I AM THE SPIRIT OF VENGEANCE...
...GOD SAVE ME...
KRAK
WHAMM
...FOR NOW AND FOR-EVER...

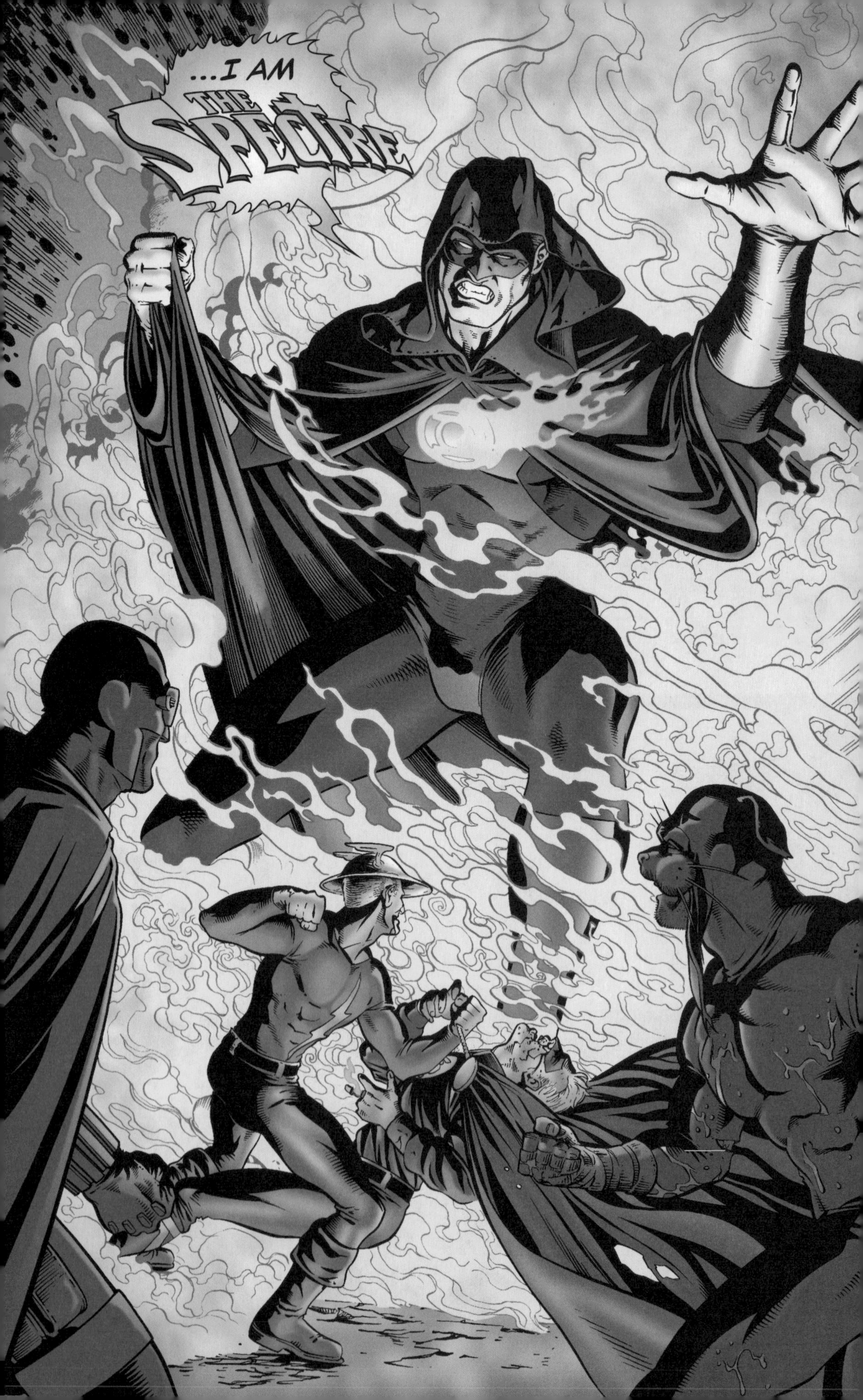
...I AM
THE SPECTRE

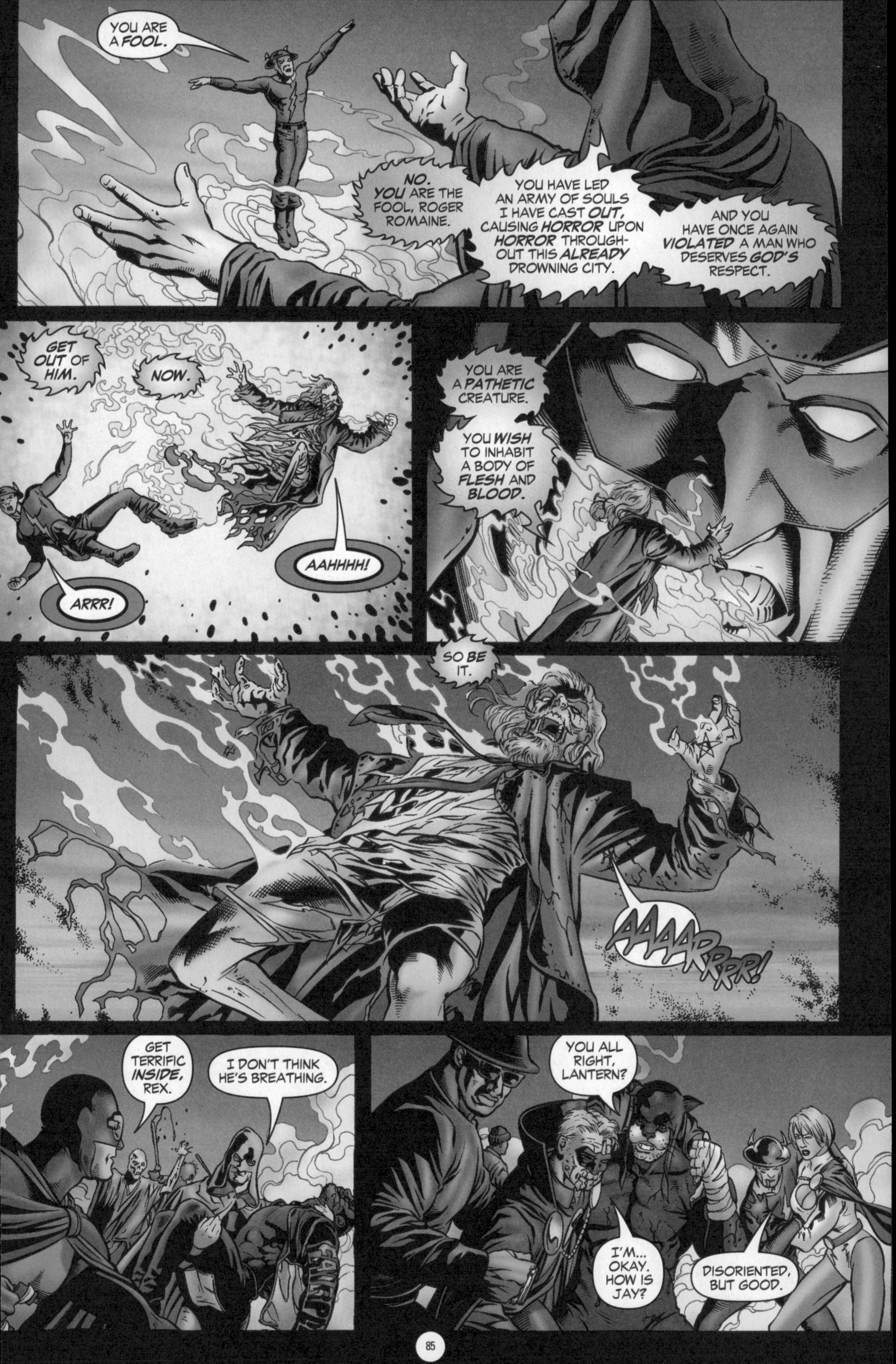

YOU ARE A FOOL.
NO. YOU ARE THE FOOL, ROGER ROMAINE.
YOU HAVE LED AN ARMY OF SOULS I HAVE CAST OUT, CAUSING HORROR UPON HORROR THROUGH-OUT THIS ALREADY DROWNING CITY.
AND YOU HAVE ONCE AGAIN VIOLATED A MAN WHO DESERVES GOD'S RESPECT.
GET OUT OF HIM.
NOW.
AAHHHH!
ARRR!
YOU ARE A PATHETIC CREATURE.
YOU WISH TO INHABIT A BODY OF FLESH AND BLOOD.
SO BE IT.
AAAARRRR!
GET TERRIFIC INSIDE, REX.
I DON'T THINK HE'S BREATHING.
YOU ALL RIGHT, LANTERN?
I'M... OKAY. HOW IS JAY?
DISORIENTED, BUT GOOD.

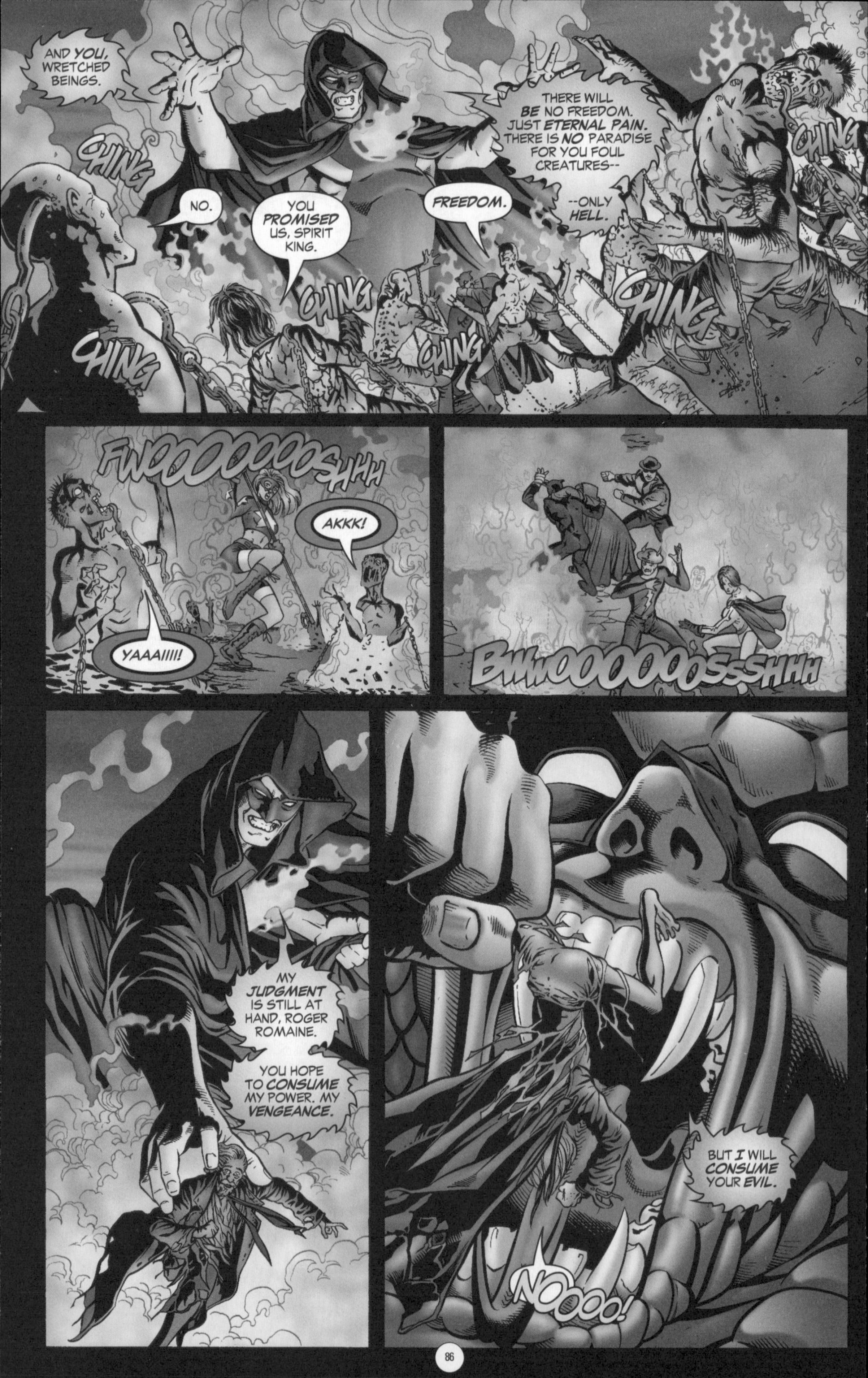
AND YOU, WRETCHED BEINGS.
CHING
NO.
YOU PROMISED US, SPIRIT KING.
FREEDOM.
THERE WILL BE NO FREEDOM. JUST ETERNAL PAIN. THERE IS NO PARADISE FOR YOU FOUL CREATURES--
--ONLY HELL.
CHING
CHING
CHING
CHING
CHING
FWOOOOOOOOSHHH
AKKK!
YAAAIIII!
BWWOOOOOOOSSSHHH
MY JUDGMENT IS STILL AT HAND, ROGER ROMAINE.
YOU HOPE TO CONSUME MY POWER. MY VENGEANCE.
BUT I WILL CONSUME YOUR EVIL.
NOOOO!

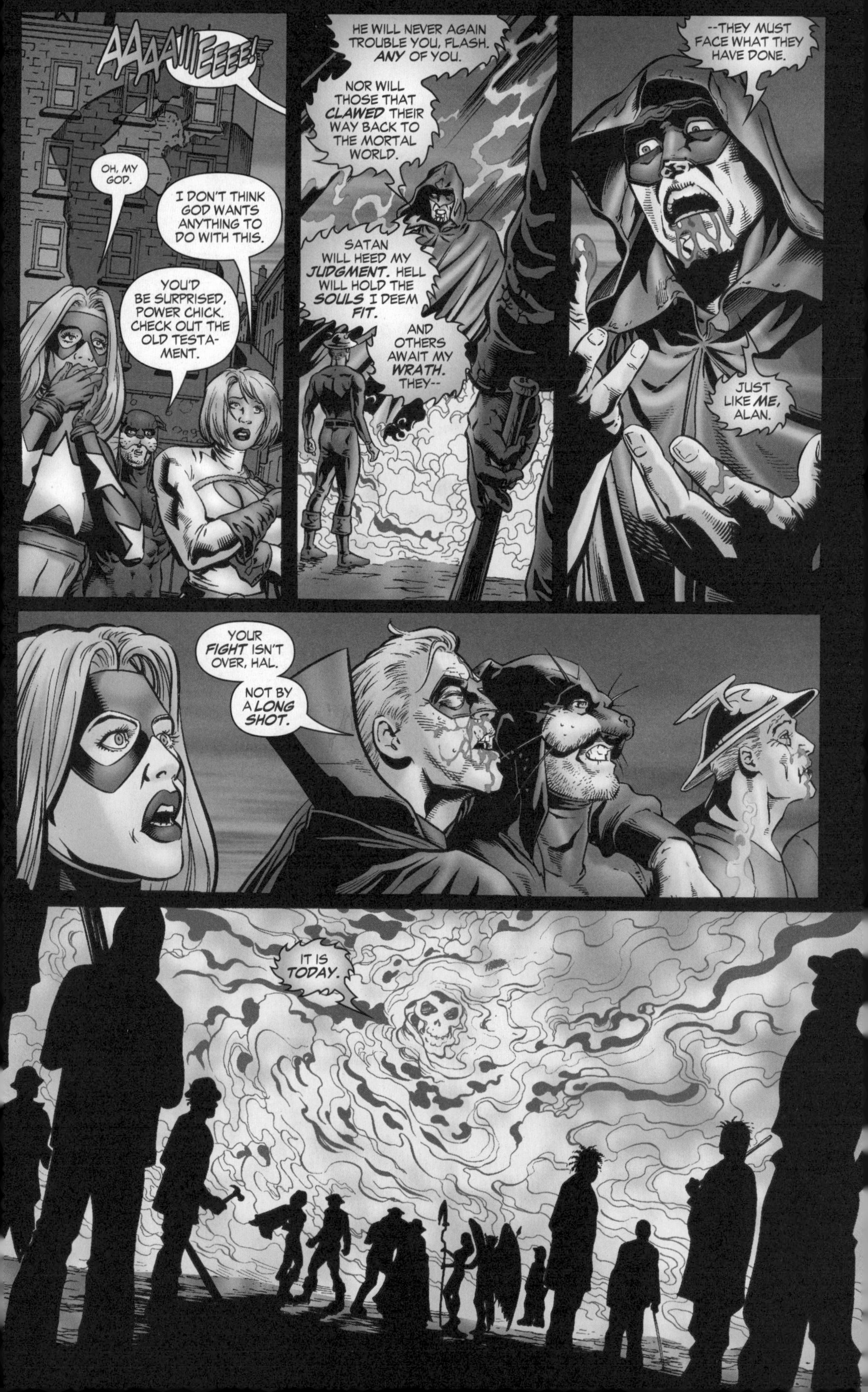

AAAAIIIEEEE!
OH, MY GOD.
I DON'T THINK GOD WANTS ANYTHING TO DO WITH THIS.
YOU'D BE SURPRISED, POWER CHICK. CHECK OUT THE OLD TESTA-MENT.
HE WILL NEVER AGAIN TROUBLE YOU, FLASH. ANY OF YOU.
NOR WILL THOSE THAT CLAWED THEIR WAY BACK TO THE MORTAL WORLD.
SATAN WILL HEED MY JUDGMENT. HELL WILL HOLD THE SOULS I DEEM FIT.
AND OTHERS AWAIT MY WRATH. THEY--
--THEY MUST FACE WHAT THEY HAVE DONE.
JUST LIKE ME, ALAN.
YOUR FIGHT ISN'T OVER, HAL.
NOT BY A LONG SHOT.
IT IS TODAY.

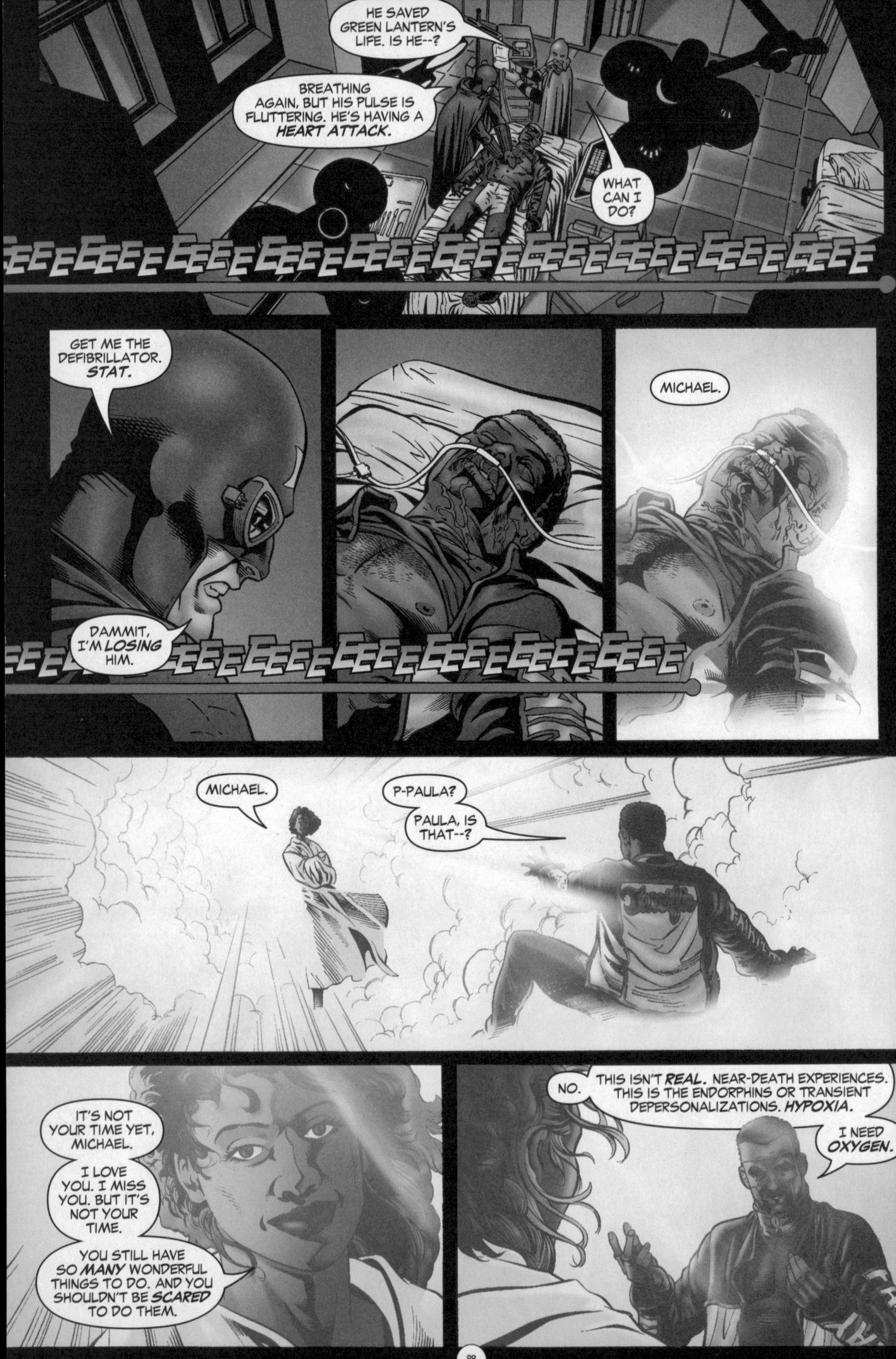
HE SAVED GREEN LANTERN'S LIFE. IS HE--?
BREATHING AGAIN, BUT HIS PULSE IS FLUTTERING. HE'S HAVING A *HEART ATTACK.*
WHAT CAN I DO?
EEEEEEEEEEEEEEEEEEEEEEEEEEEEEEEEEEEE
GET ME THE DEFIBRILLATOR. *STAT.*
DAMMIT, I'M *LOSING* HIM.
EEEEEEEEEEEEEEEEEEEEEEEEEEEEE
MICHAEL.
MICHAEL.
P-PAULA?
PAULA, IS THAT--?
IT'S NOT YOUR TIME YET, MICHAEL.
I LOVE YOU. I MISS YOU. BUT IT'S NOT YOUR TIME.
YOU STILL HAVE SO *MANY* WONDERFUL THINGS TO DO. AND YOU SHOULDN'T BE *SCARED* TO DO THEM.
NO.
THIS ISN'T *REAL.* NEAR-DEATH EXPERIENCES. THIS IS THE ENDORPHINS OR TRANSIENT DEPERSONALIZATIONS. *HYPOXIA.*
I NEED *OXYGEN.*

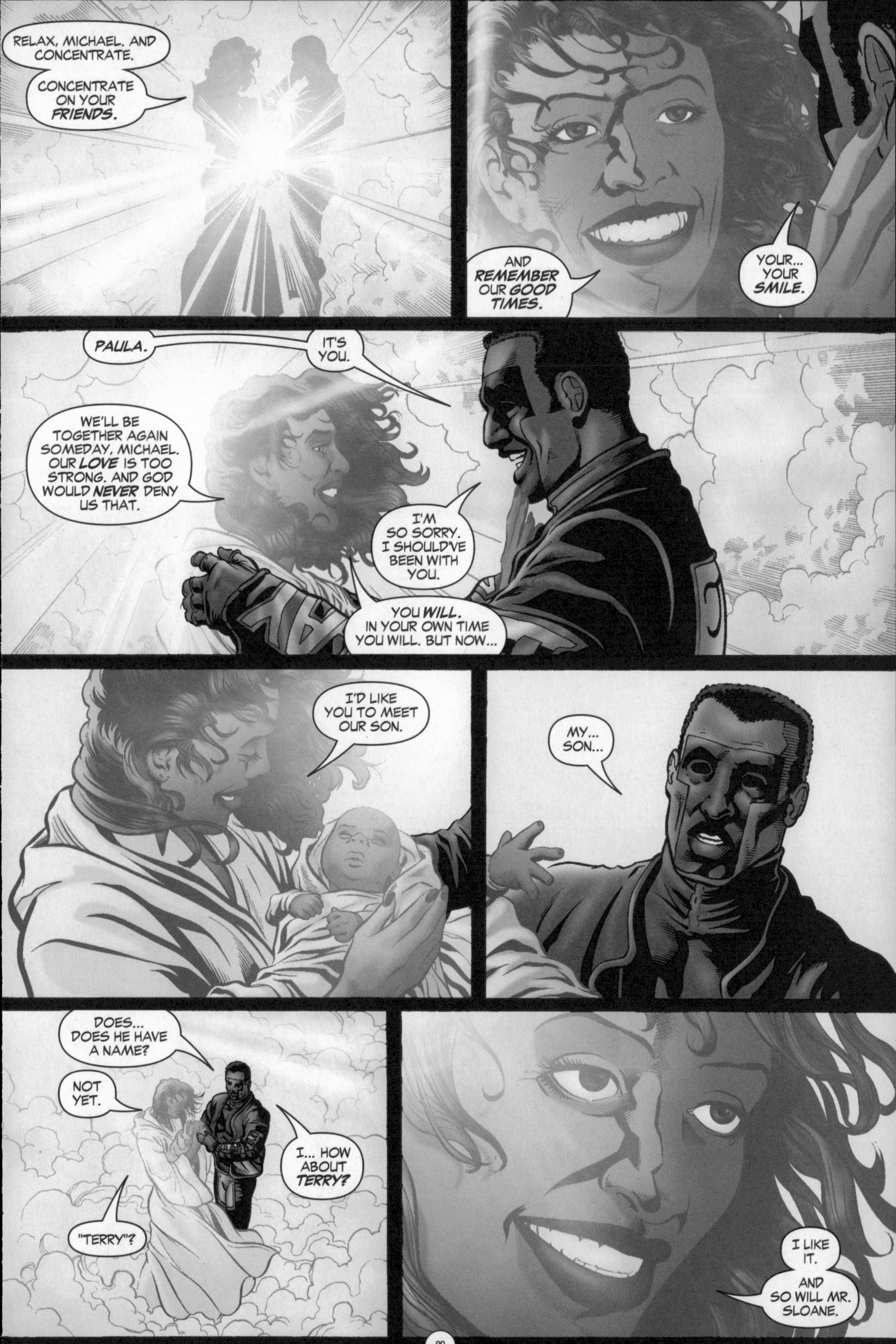
RELAX, MICHAEL. AND CONCENTRATE.
CONCENTRATE ON YOUR FRIENDS.
AND REMEMBER OUR GOOD TIMES.
YOUR... YOUR SMILE.
PAULA.
IT'S YOU.
WE'LL BE TOGETHER AGAIN SOMEDAY, MICHAEL. OUR LOVE IS TOO STRONG. AND GOD WOULD NEVER DENY US THAT.
I'M SO SORRY. I SHOULD'VE BEEN WITH YOU.
YOU WILL. IN YOUR OWN TIME YOU WILL. BUT NOW...
I'D LIKE YOU TO MEET OUR SON.
MY... SON...
DOES... DOES HE HAVE A NAME?
NOT YET.
I... HOW ABOUT TERRY?
"TERRY"?
I LIKE IT.
AND SO WILL MR. SLOANE.

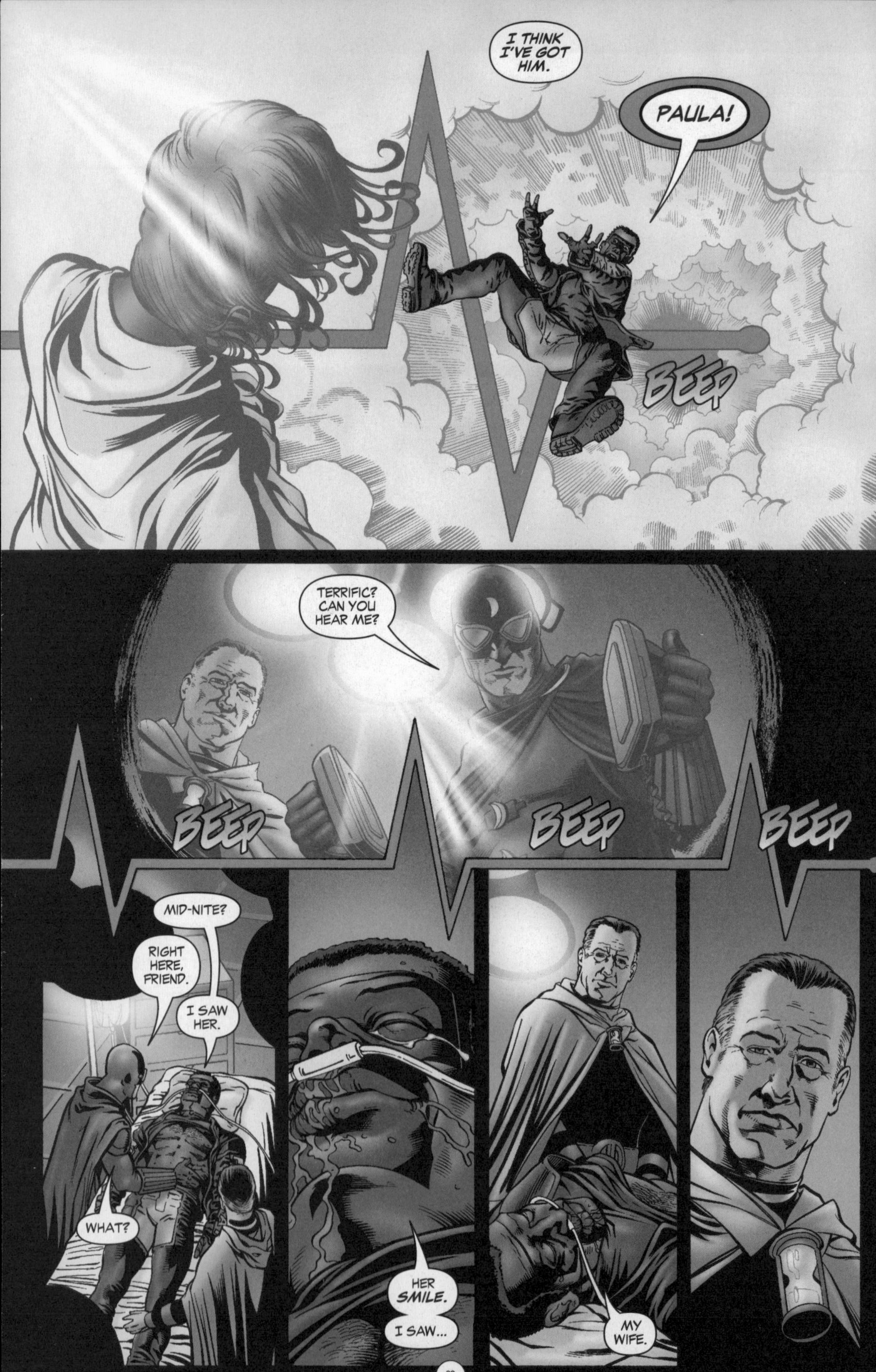
I THINK I'VE GOT HIM.
PAULA!
BEEP
TERRIFIC? CAN YOU HEAR ME?
BEEP
BEEP
BEEP
MID-NITE?
RIGHT HERE, FRIEND.
I SAW HER.
WHAT?
HER SMILE.
I SAW...
MY WIFE.

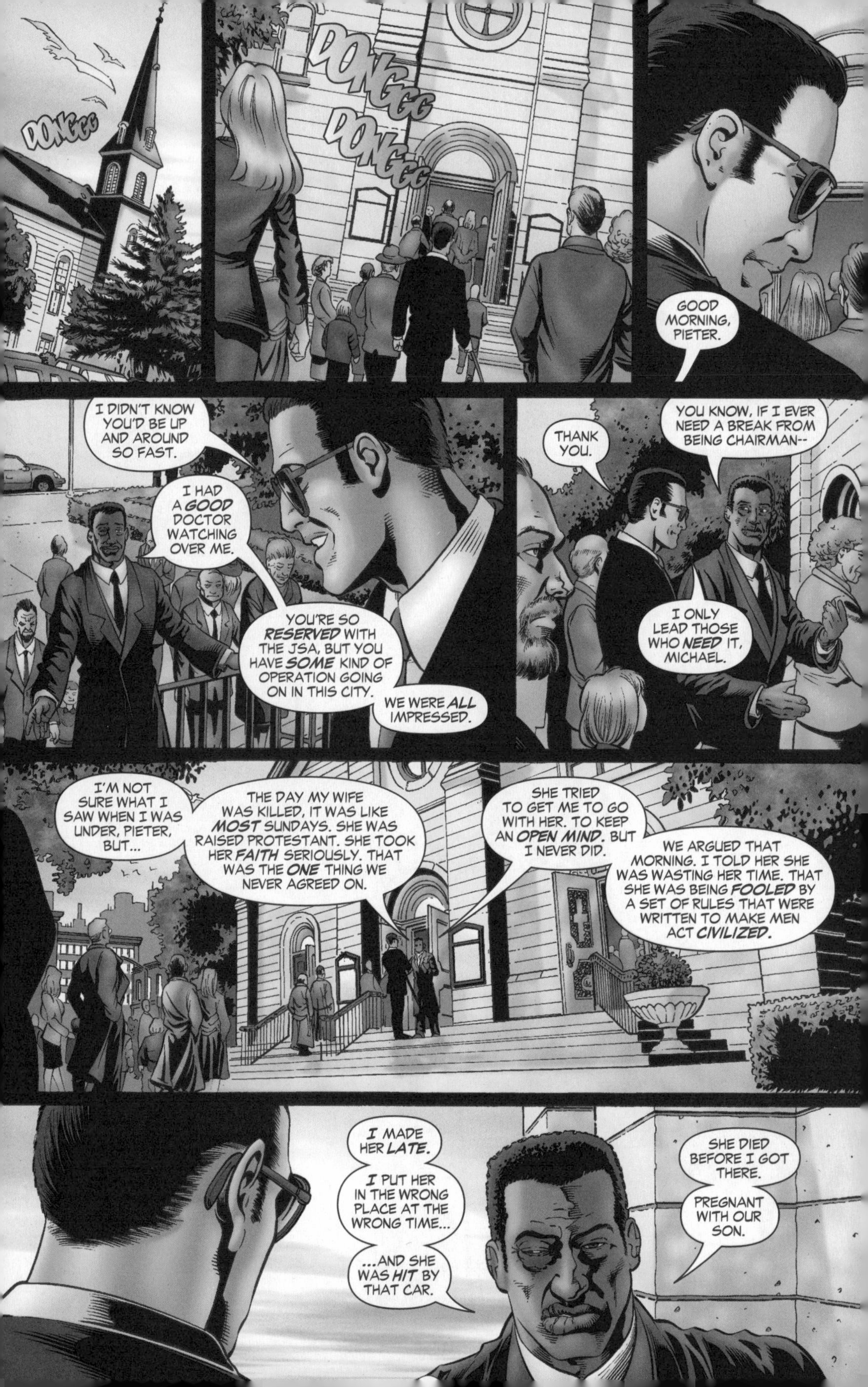
DONGGG
DONGGG
DONGGG
GOOD MORNING, PIETER.
I DIDN'T KNOW YOU'D BE UP AND AROUND SO FAST.
I HAD A GOOD DOCTOR WATCHING OVER ME.
YOU'RE SO RESERVED WITH THE JSA, BUT YOU HAVE SOME KIND OF OPERATION GOING ON IN THIS CITY.
WE WERE ALL IMPRESSED.
THANK YOU.
YOU KNOW, IF I EVER NEED A BREAK FROM BEING CHAIRMAN--
I ONLY LEAD THOSE WHO NEED IT, MICHAEL.
I'M NOT SURE WHAT I SAW WHEN I WAS UNDER, PIETER, BUT...
THE DAY MY WIFE WAS KILLED, IT WAS LIKE MOST SUNDAYS. SHE WAS RAISED PROTESTANT. SHE TOOK HER FAITH SERIOUSLY. THAT WAS THE ONE THING WE NEVER AGREED ON.
SHE TRIED TO GET ME TO GO WITH HER. TO KEEP AN OPEN MIND. BUT I NEVER DID.
WE ARGUED THAT MORNING. I TOLD HER SHE WAS WASTING HER TIME. THAT SHE WAS BEING FOOLED BY A SET OF RULES THAT WERE WRITTEN TO MAKE MEN ACT CIVILIZED.
I MADE HER LATE.
I PUT HER IN THE WRONG PLACE AT THE WRONG TIME...
...AND SHE WAS HIT BY THAT CAR.
SHE DIED BEFORE I GOT THERE.
PREGNANT WITH OUR SON.

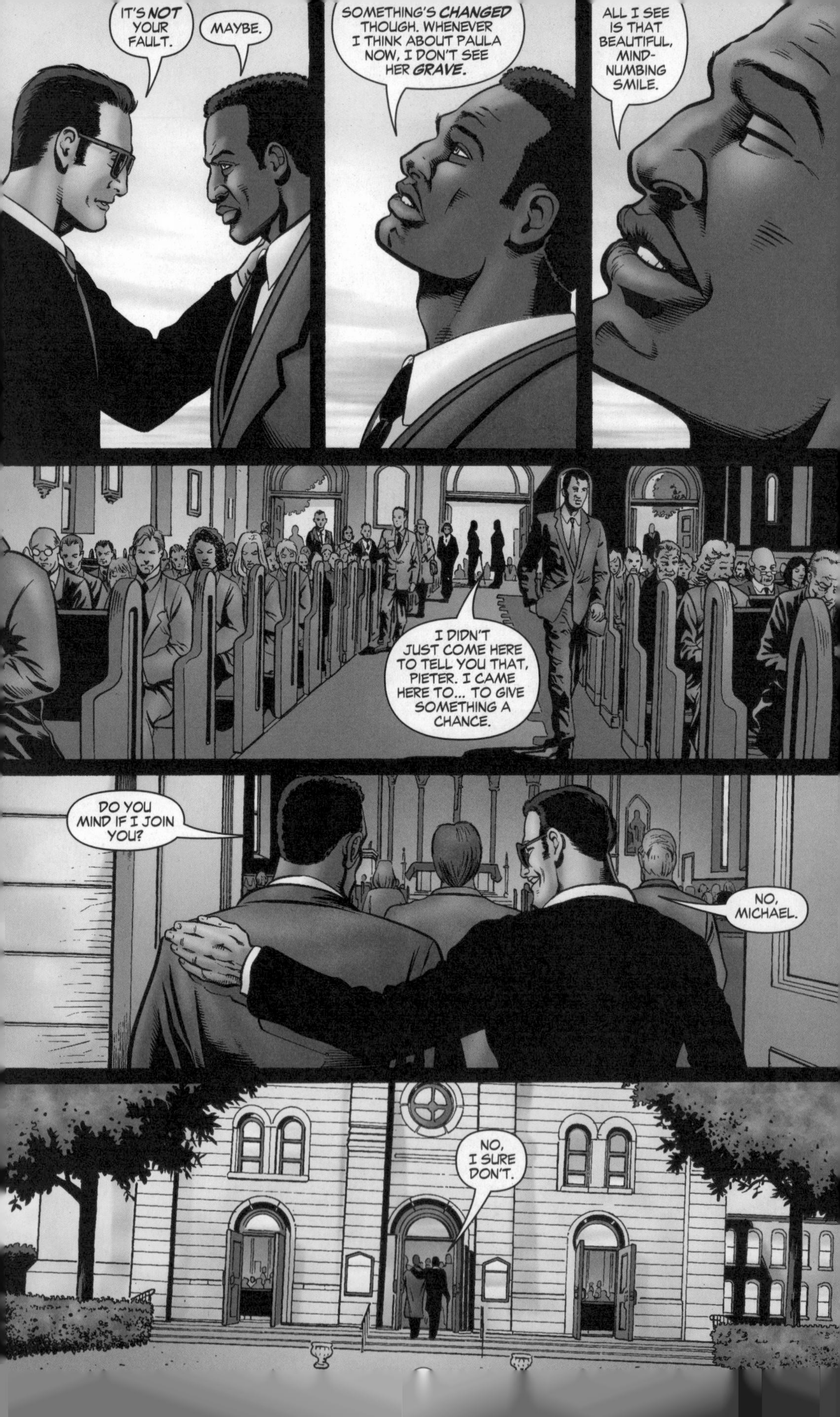

IT'S NOT YOUR FAULT.
MAYBE.
SOMETHING'S CHANGED THOUGH. WHENEVER I THINK ABOUT PAULA NOW, I DON'T SEE HER GRAVE.
ALL I SEE IS THAT BEAUTIFUL, MIND-NUMBING SMILE.
I DIDN'T JUST COME HERE TO TELL YOU THAT, PIETER. I CAME HERE TO... TO GIVE SOMETHING A CHANCE.
DO YOU MIND IF I JOIN YOU?
NO, MICHAEL.
NO, I SURE DON'T.

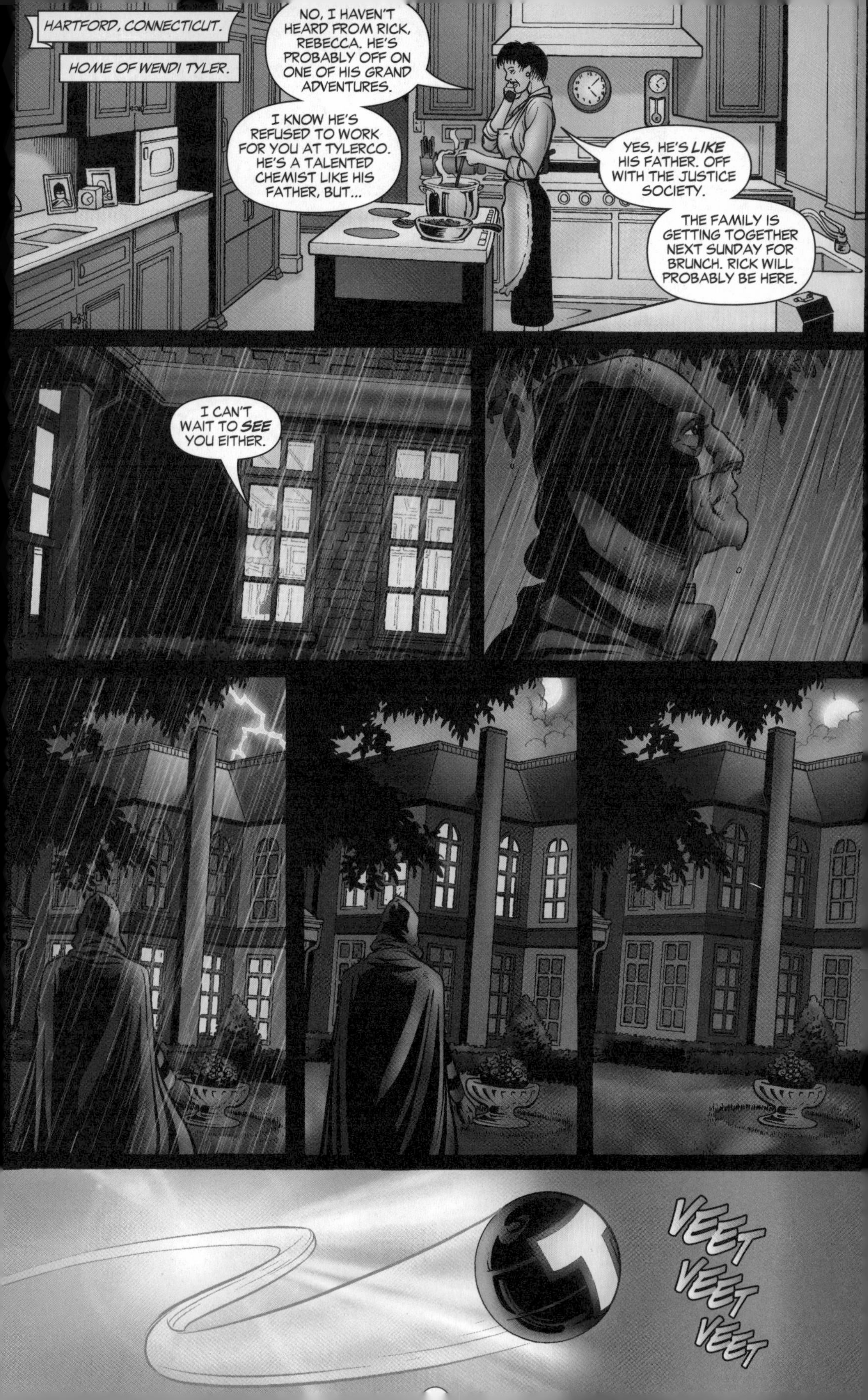
HARTFORD, CONNECTICUT.
HOME OF WENDI TYLER.
NO, I HAVEN'T HEARD FROM RICK, REBECCA. HE'S PROBABLY OFF ON ONE OF HIS GRAND ADVENTURES.
I KNOW HE'S REFUSED TO WORK FOR YOU AT TYLERCO. HE'S A TALENTED CHEMIST LIKE HIS FATHER, BUT...
YES, HE'S LIKE HIS FATHER. OFF WITH THE JUSTICE SOCIETY.
THE FAMILY IS GETTING TOGETHER NEXT SUNDAY FOR BRUNCH. RICK WILL PROBABLY BE HERE.
I CAN'T WAIT TO SEE YOU EITHER.
VEET VEET VEET

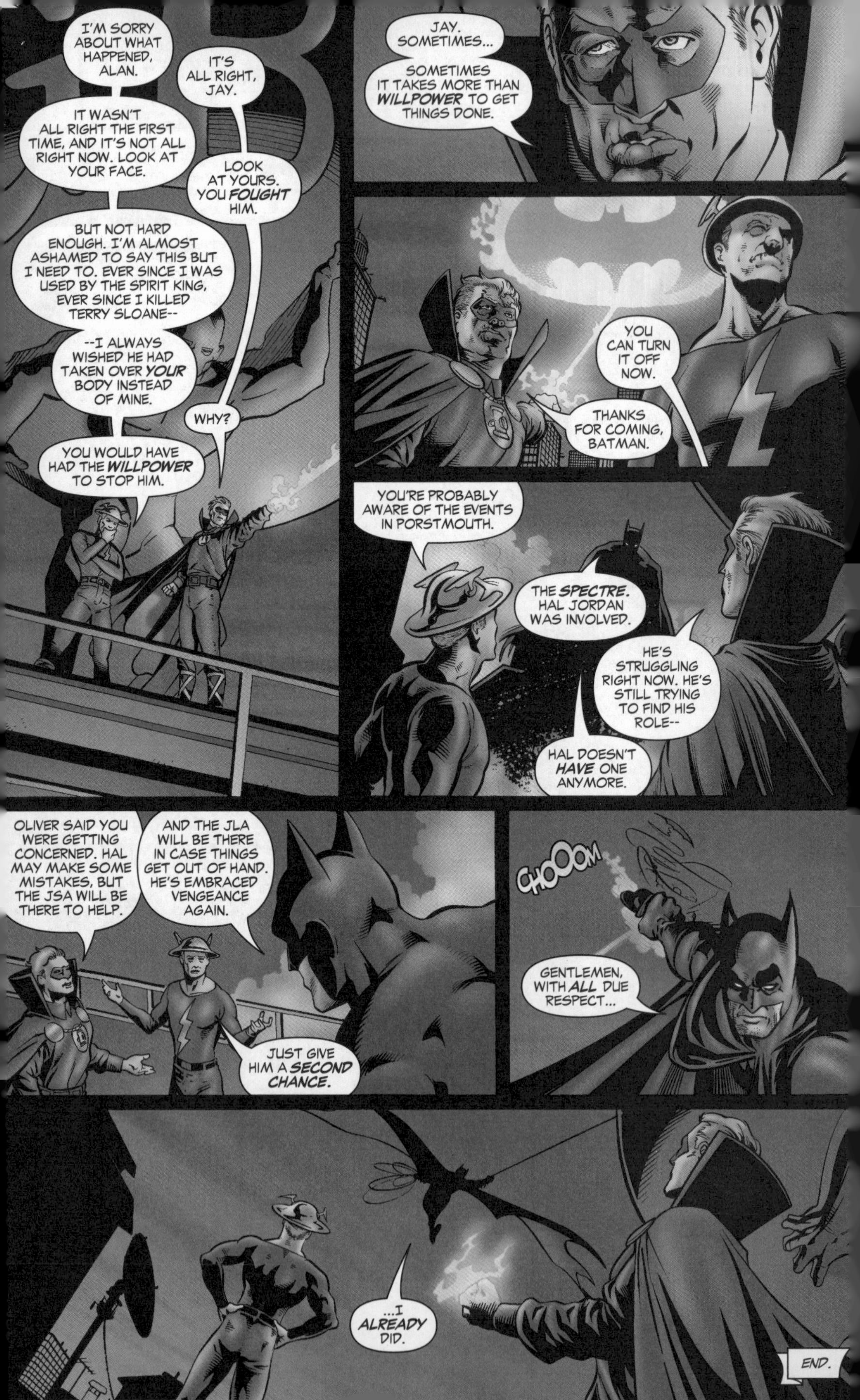
I'M SORRY ABOUT WHAT HAPPENED, ALAN.
IT'S ALL RIGHT, JAY.
IT WASN'T ALL RIGHT THE FIRST TIME, AND IT'S NOT ALL RIGHT NOW. LOOK AT YOUR FACE.
LOOK AT YOURS. YOU FOUGHT HIM.
BUT NOT HARD ENOUGH. I'M ALMOST ASHAMED TO SAY THIS BUT I NEED TO. EVER SINCE I WAS USED BY THE SPIRIT KING, EVER SINCE I KILLED TERRY SLOANE--
--I ALWAYS WISHED HE HAD TAKEN OVER YOUR BODY INSTEAD OF MINE.
WHY?
YOU WOULD HAVE HAD THE WILLPOWER TO STOP HIM.
JAY. SOMETIMES...
SOMETIMES IT TAKES MORE THAN WILLPOWER TO GET THINGS DONE.
YOU CAN TURN IT OFF NOW.
THANKS FOR COMING, BATMAN.
YOU'RE PROBABLY AWARE OF THE EVENTS IN PORSTMOUTH.
THE SPECTRE. HAL JORDAN WAS INVOLVED.
HE'S STRUGGLING RIGHT NOW. HE'S STILL TRYING TO FIND HIS ROLE--
HAL DOESN'T HAVE ONE ANYMORE.
OLIVER SAID YOU WERE GETTING CONCERNED. HAL MAY MAKE SOME MISTAKES, BUT THE JSA WILL BE THERE TO HELP.
AND THE JLA WILL BE THERE IN CASE THINGS GET OUT OF HAND. HE'S EMBRACED VENGEANCE AGAIN.
JUST GIVE HIM A SECOND CHANCE.
CHOOOM
GENTLEMEN, WITH ALL DUE RESPECT...
...I ALREADY DID.
END.

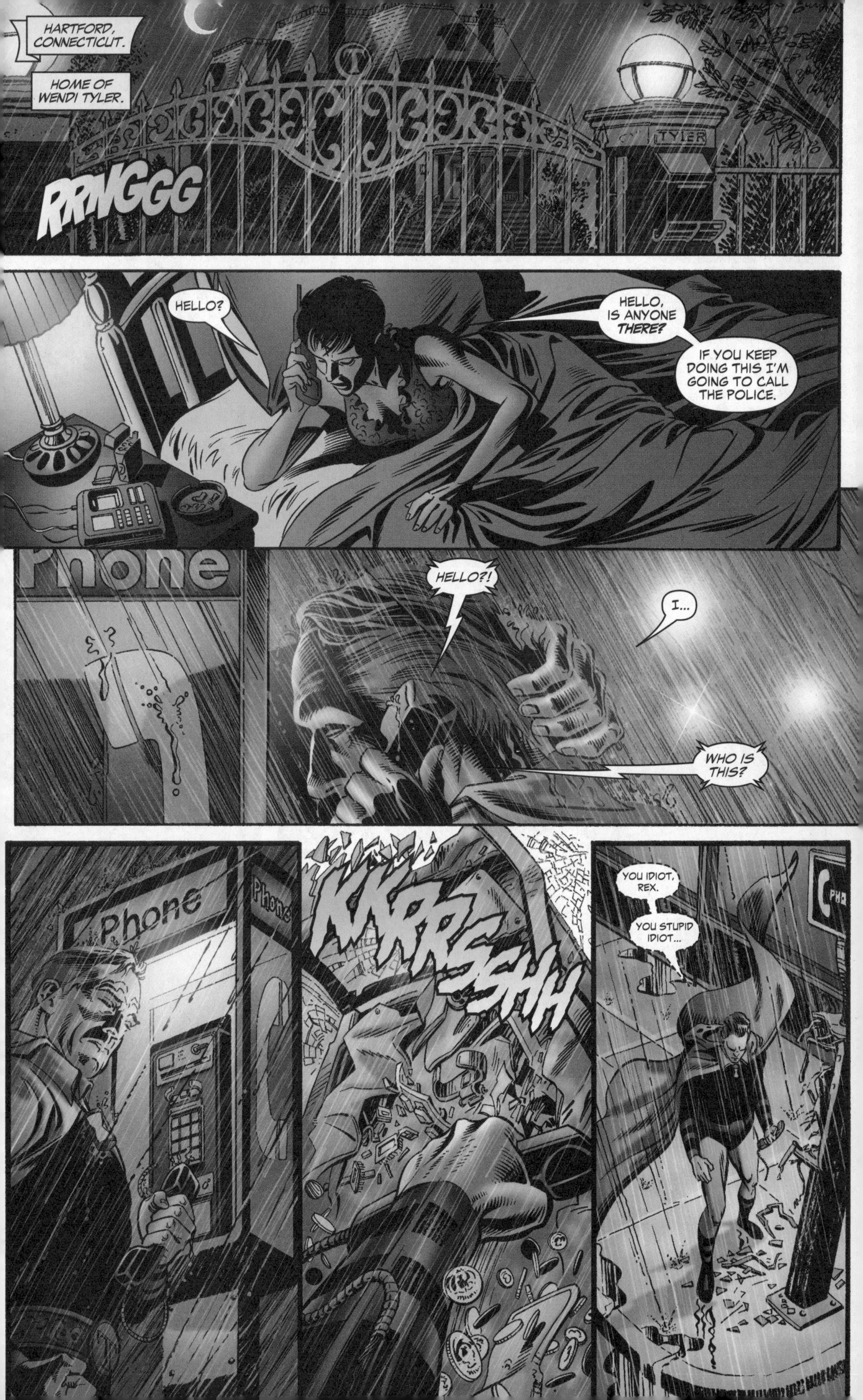
HARTFORD, CONNECTICUT.
HOME OF WENDI TYLER.
TYLER
RRRNGGG
HELLO?
HELLO, IS ANYONE THERE?
IF YOU KEEP DOING THIS I'M GOING TO CALL THE POLICE.
Phone
HELLO?!
I...
WHO IS THIS?
Phone
Phone
KARRSCHH
YOU IDIOT, REX.
YOU STUPID IDIOT...

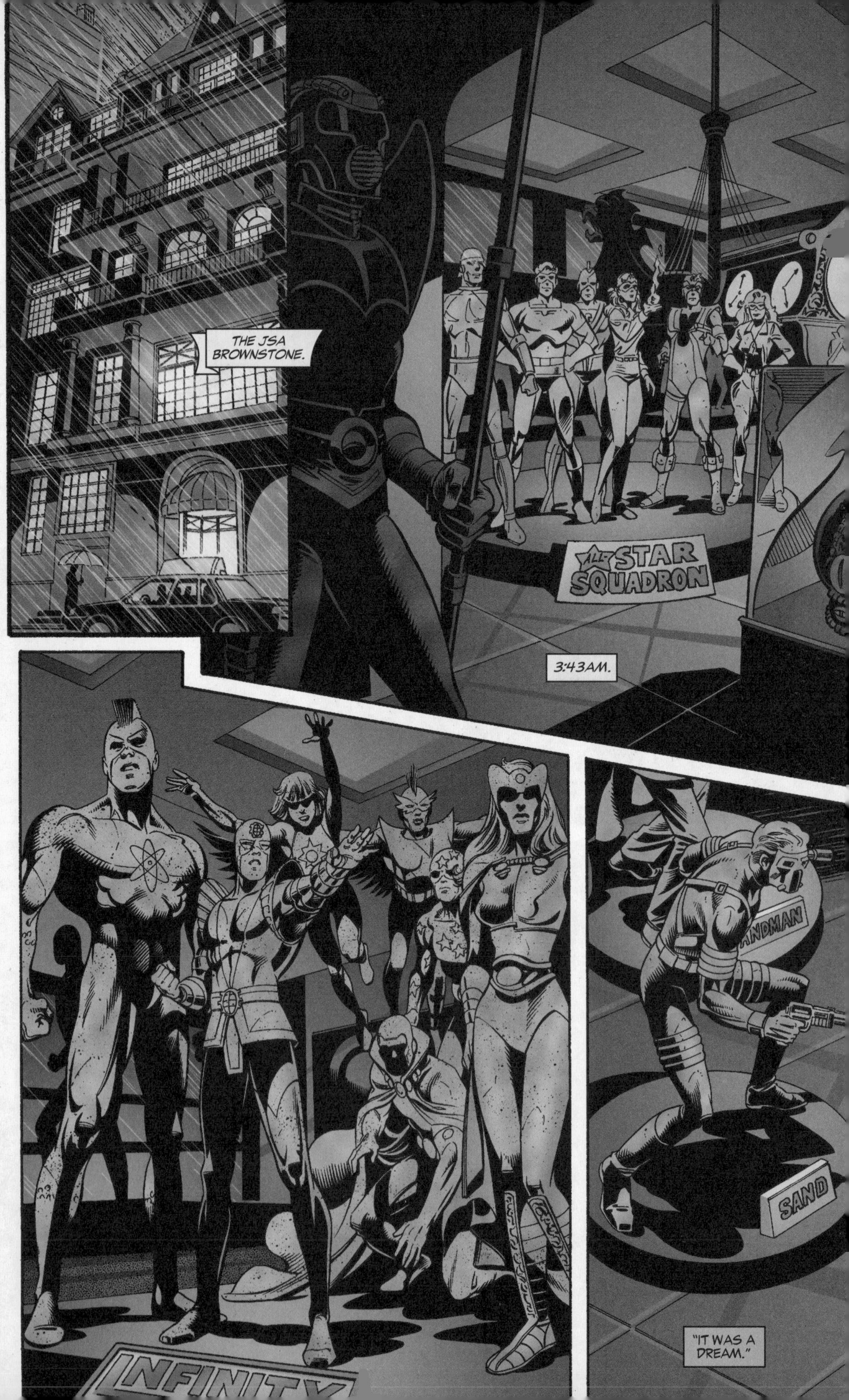
THE JSA BROWNSTONE.
ALL-STAR SQUADRON
3:43AM.
SANDMAN
SAND
"IT WAS A DREAM."
INFINITY

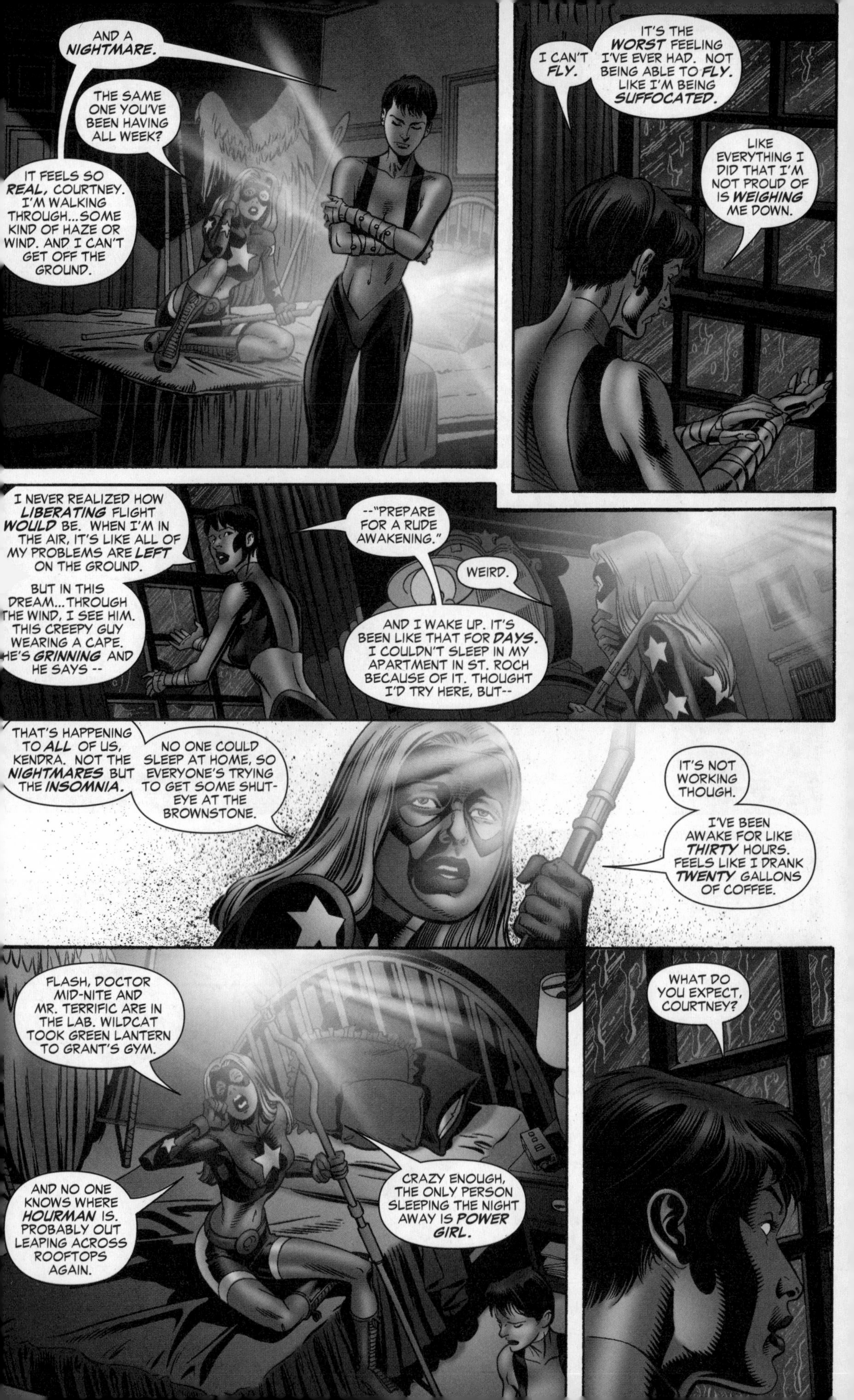
AND A NIGHTMARE.
THE SAME ONE YOU'VE BEEN HAVING ALL WEEK?
IT FEELS SO REAL, COURTNEY. I'M WALKING THROUGH...SOME KIND OF HAZE OR WIND. AND I CAN'T GET OFF THE GROUND.
I CAN'T FLY.
IT'S THE WORST FEELING I'VE EVER HAD. NOT BEING ABLE TO FLY. LIKE I'M BEING SUFFOCATED.
LIKE EVERYTHING I DID THAT I'M NOT PROUD OF IS WEIGHING ME DOWN.
I NEVER REALIZED HOW LIBERATING FLIGHT WOULD BE. WHEN I'M IN THE AIR, IT'S LIKE ALL OF MY PROBLEMS ARE LEFT ON THE GROUND.
BUT IN THIS DREAM...THROUGH THE WIND, I SEE HIM. THIS CREEPY GUY WEARING A CAPE. HE'S GRINNING AND HE SAYS --
--"PREPARE FOR A RUDE AWAKENING."
AND I WAKE UP. IT'S BEEN LIKE THAT FOR DAYS. I COULDN'T SLEEP IN MY APARTMENT IN ST. ROCH BECAUSE OF IT. THOUGHT I'D TRY HERE, BUT--
WEIRD.
THAT'S HAPPENING TO ALL OF US, KENDRA. NOT THE NIGHTMARES BUT THE INSOMNIA.
NO ONE COULD SLEEP AT HOME, SO EVERYONE'S TRYING TO GET SOME SHUT-EYE AT THE BROWNSTONE.
IT'S NOT WORKING THOUGH.
I'VE BEEN AWAKE FOR LIKE THIRTY HOURS. FEELS LIKE I DRANK TWENTY GALLONS OF COFFEE.
FLASH, DOCTOR MID-NITE AND MR. TERRIFIC ARE IN THE LAB. WILDCAT TOOK GREEN LANTERN TO GRANT'S GYM.
AND NO ONE KNOWS WHERE HOURMAN IS. PROBABLY OUT LEAPING ACROSS ROOFTOPS AGAIN.
CRAZY ENOUGH, THE ONLY PERSON SLEEPING THE NIGHT AWAY IS POWER GIRL.
WHAT DO YOU EXPECT, COURTNEY?

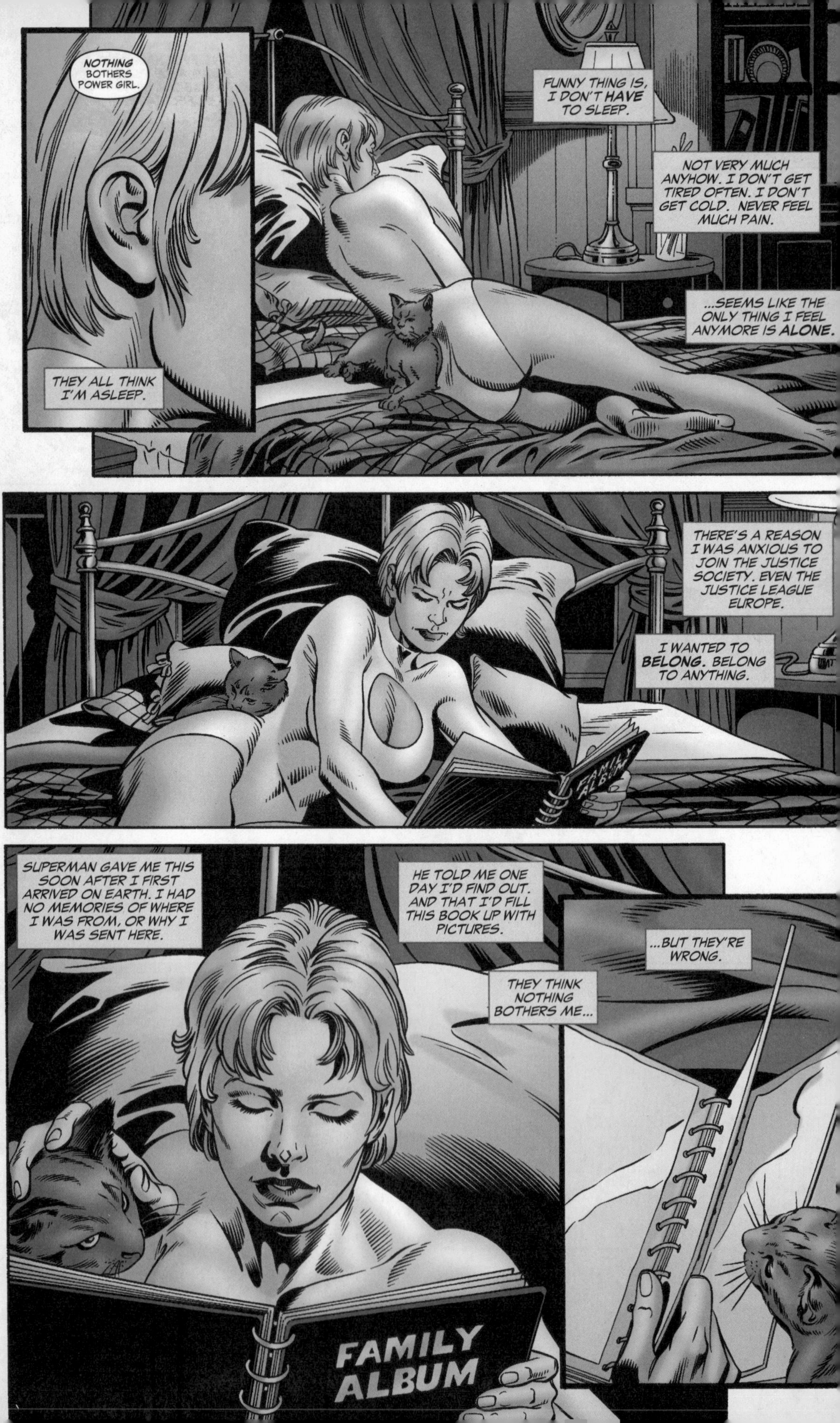
NOTHING BOTHERS POWER GIRL.
THEY ALL THINK I'M ASLEEP.
FUNNY THING IS, I DON'T HAVE TO SLEEP.
NOT VERY MUCH ANYHOW. I DON'T GET TIRED OFTEN. I DON'T GET COLD. NEVER FEEL MUCH PAIN.
...SEEMS LIKE THE ONLY THING I FEEL ANYMORE IS ALONE.
THERE'S A REASON I WAS ANXIOUS TO JOIN THE JUSTICE SOCIETY. EVEN THE JUSTICE LEAGUE EUROPE.
I WANTED TO BELONG. BELONG TO ANYTHING.
FAMILY ALBUM
SUPERMAN GAVE ME THIS SOON AFTER I FIRST ARRIVED ON EARTH. I HAD NO MEMORIES OF WHERE I WAS FROM, OR WHY I WAS SENT HERE.
HE TOLD ME ONE DAY I'D FIND OUT. AND THAT I'D FILL THIS BOOK UP WITH PICTURES.
THEY THINK NOTHING BOTHERS ME...
...BUT THEY'RE WRONG.
FAMILY ALBUM

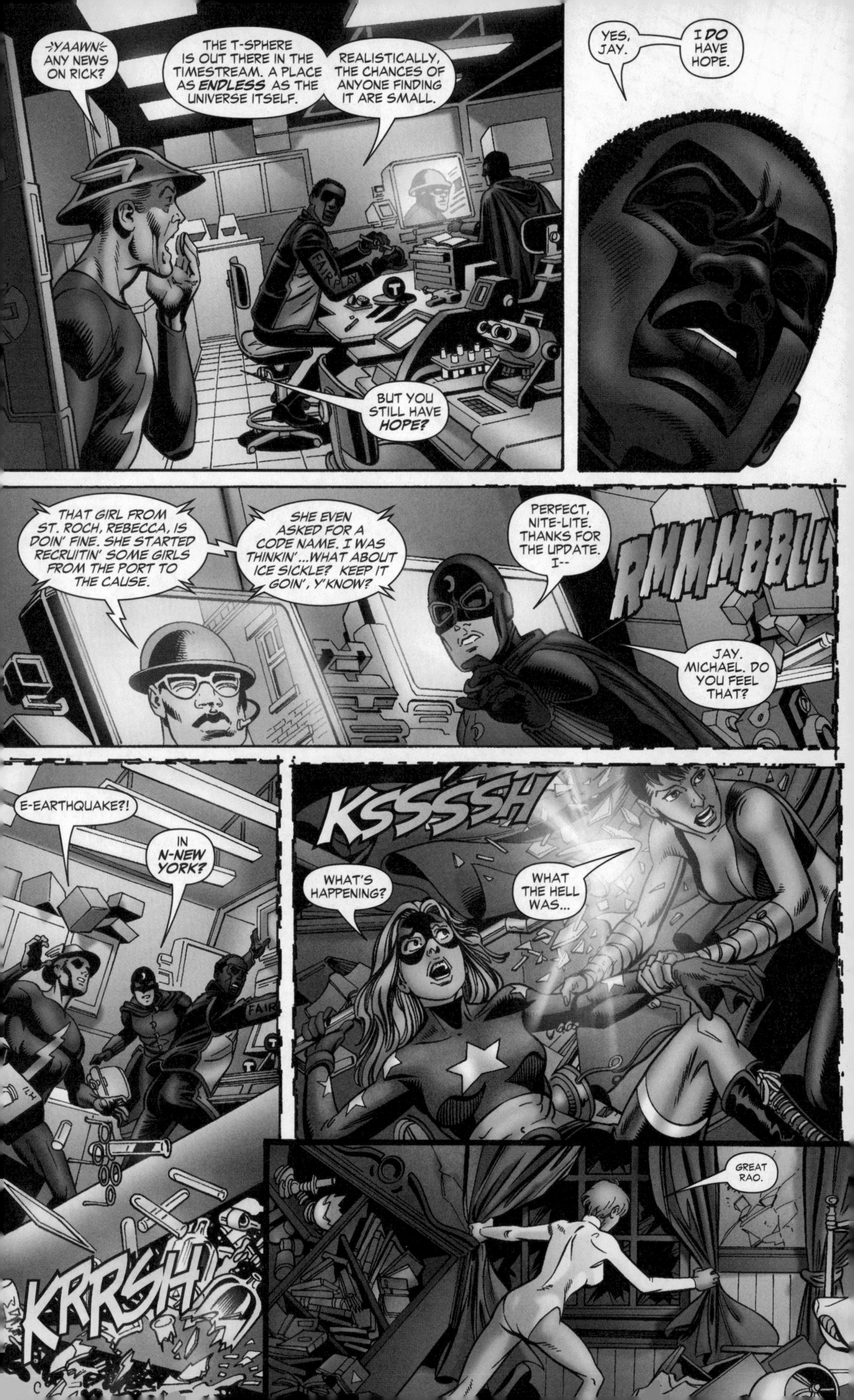

~YAAWN~ ANY NEWS ON RICK?
THE T-SPHERE IS OUT THERE IN THE TIMESTREAM. A PLACE AS ENDLESS AS THE UNIVERSE ITSELF.
REALISTICALLY, THE CHANCES OF ANYONE FINDING IT ARE SMALL.
BUT YOU STILL HAVE HOPE?
YES, JAY.
I DO HAVE HOPE.
THAT GIRL FROM ST. ROCH, REBECCA, IS DOIN' FINE. SHE STARTED RECRUITIN' SOME GIRLS FROM THE PORT TO THE CAUSE.
SHE EVEN ASKED FOR A CODE NAME. I WAS THINKIN' ...WHAT ABOUT ICE SICKLE? KEEP IT GOIN', Y'KNOW?
PERFECT, NITE-LITE. THANKS FOR THE UPDATE. I--
RMMMBBLL
JAY. MICHAEL. DO YOU FEEL THAT?
E-EARTHQUAKE?!
IN N-NEW YORK?
KSSSSH
WHAT'S HAPPENING?
WHAT THE HELL WAS...
KRRSH
GREAT RAO.

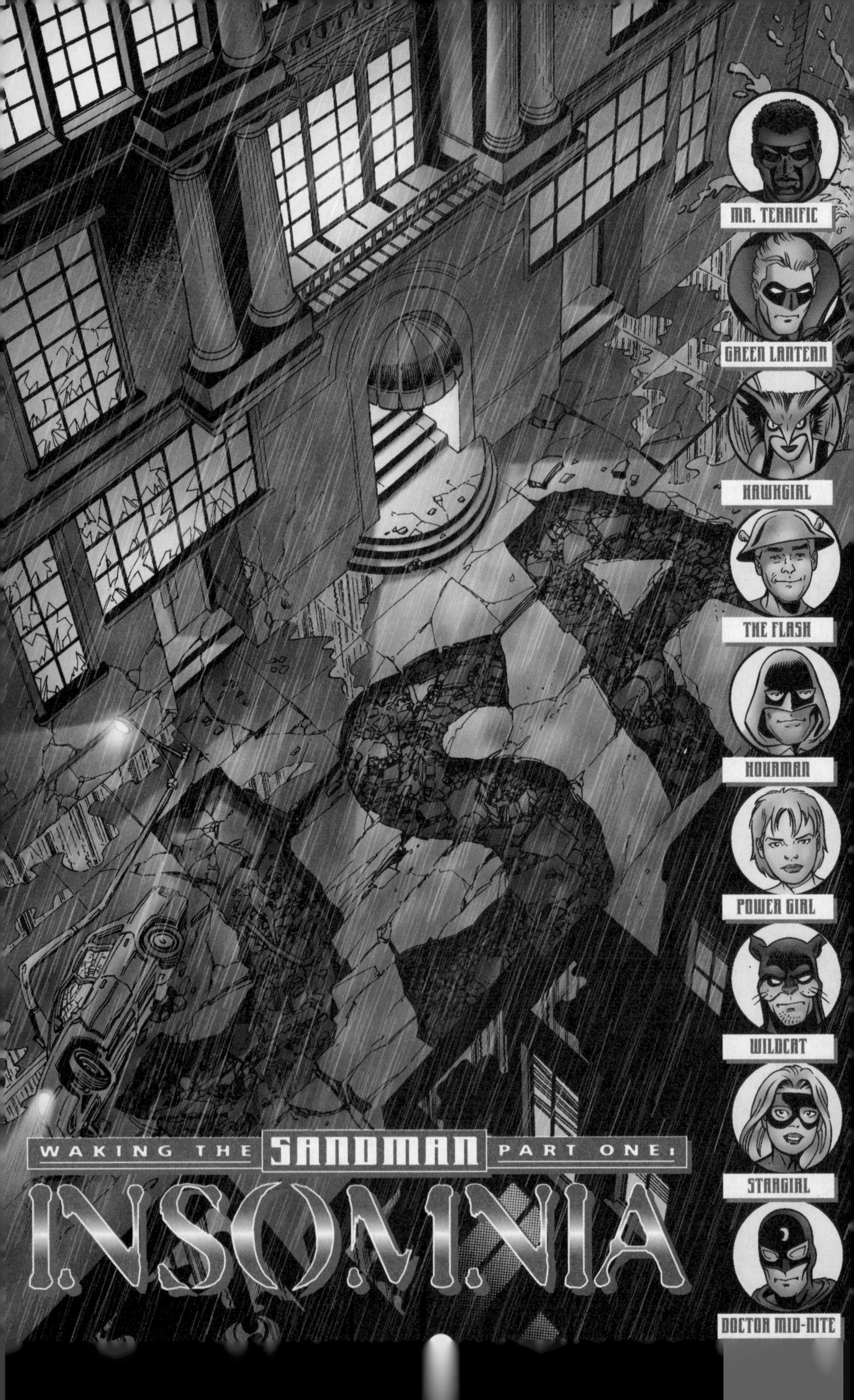
MR. TERRIFIC
GREEN LANTERN
HAWKGIRL
THE FLASH
HOURMAN
POWER GIRL
WILDCAT
STARGIRL
DOCTOR MID-NITE
WAKING THE SANDMAN PART ONE:
INSOMNIA

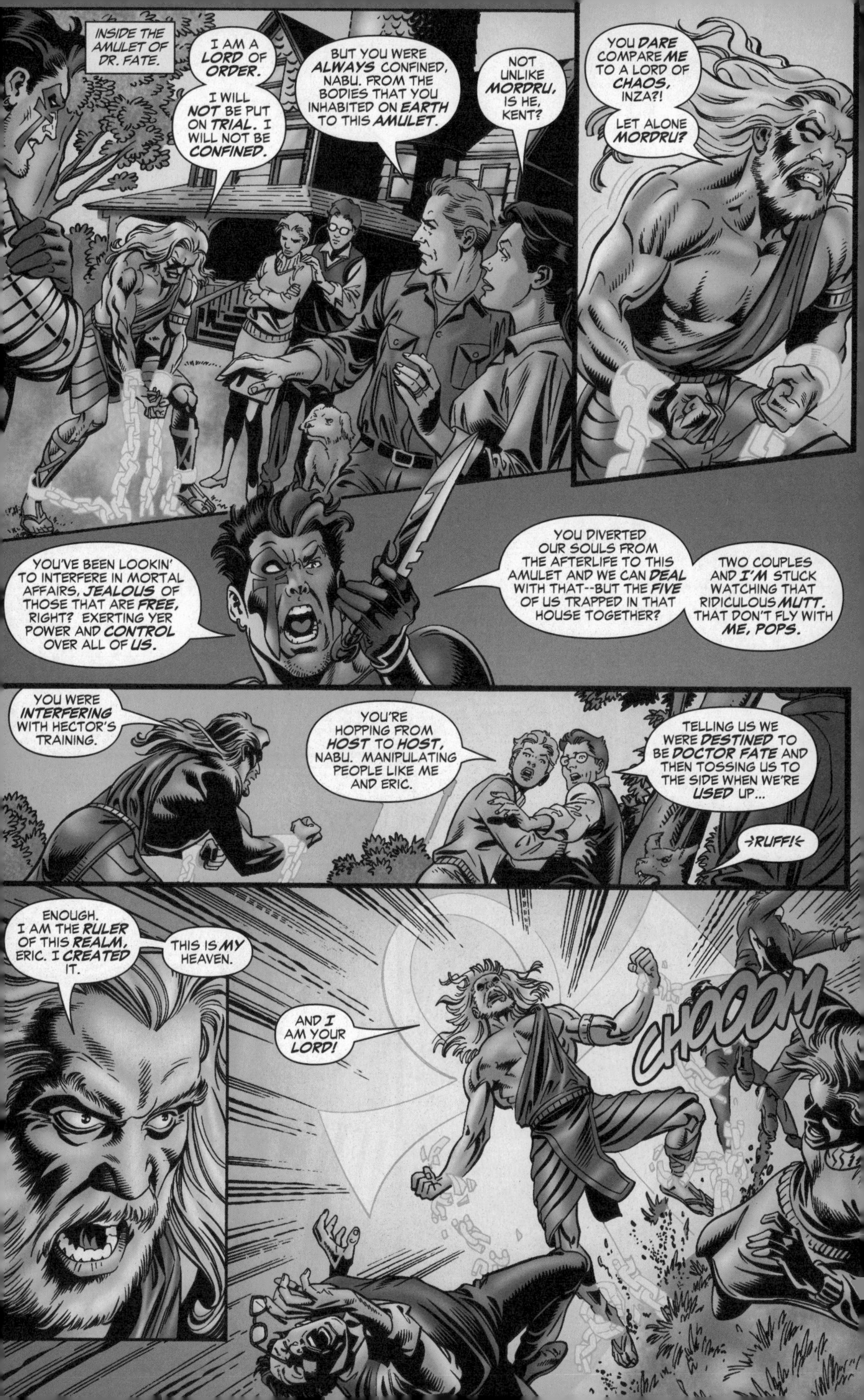
INSIDE THE AMULET OF DR. FATE.
I AM A LORD OF ORDER.
I WILL NOT BE PUT ON TRIAL. I WILL NOT BE CONFINED.
BUT YOU WERE ALWAYS CONFINED, NABU. FROM THE BODIES THAT YOU INHABITED ON EARTH TO THIS AMULET.
NOT UNLIKE MORDRU, IS HE, KENT?
YOU DARE COMPARE ME TO A LORD OF CHAOS, INZA?!
LET ALONE MORDRU?
YOU'VE BEEN LOOKIN' TO INTERFERE IN MORTAL AFFAIRS, JEALOUS OF THOSE THAT ARE FREE, RIGHT? EXERTING YER POWER AND CONTROL OVER ALL OF US.
YOU DIVERTED OUR SOULS FROM THE AFTERLIFE TO THIS AMULET AND WE CAN DEAL WITH THAT--BUT THE FIVE OF US TRAPPED IN THAT HOUSE TOGETHER?
TWO COUPLES AND I'M STUCK WATCHING THAT RIDICULOUS MUTT. THAT DON'T FLY WITH ME, POPS.
YOU WERE INTERFERING WITH HECTOR'S TRAINING.
YOU'RE HOPPING FROM HOST TO HOST, NABU. MANIPULATING PEOPLE LIKE ME AND ERIC.
TELLING US WE WERE DESTINED TO BE DOCTOR FATE AND THEN TOSSING US TO THE SIDE WHEN WE'RE USED UP...
>RUFF!<
ENOUGH. I AM THE RULER OF THIS REALM, ERIC. I CREATED IT.
THIS IS MY HEAVEN.
AND I AM YOUR LORD!
CHOOOM

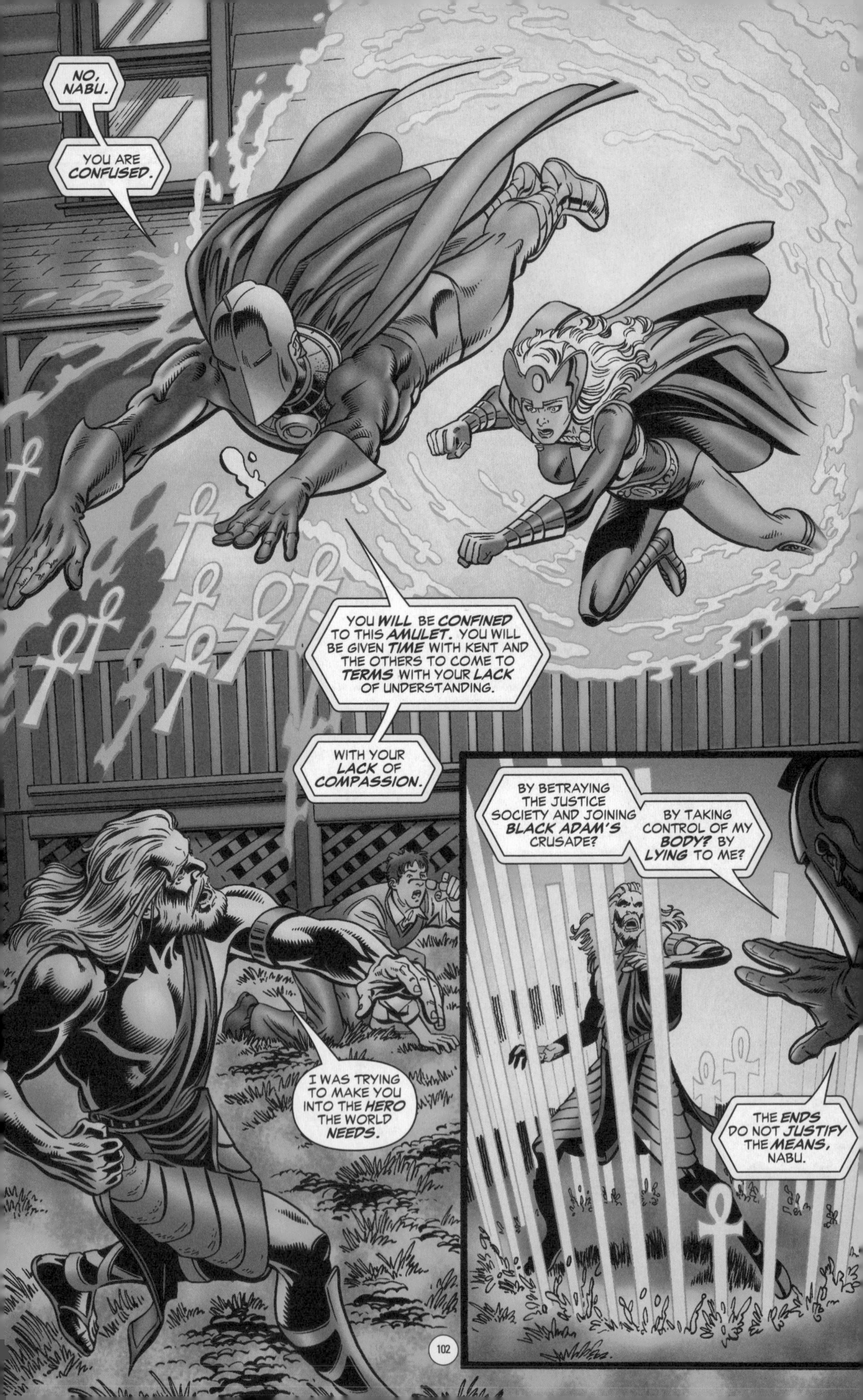
NO, NABU.
YOU ARE CONFUSED.
YOU WILL BE CONFINED TO THIS AMULET. YOU WILL BE GIVEN TIME WITH KENT AND THE OTHERS TO COME TO TERMS WITH YOUR LACK OF UNDERSTANDING.
WITH YOUR LACK OF COMPASSION.
I WAS TRYING TO MAKE YOU INTO THE HERO THE WORLD NEEDS.
BY BETRAYING THE JUSTICE SOCIETY AND JOINING BLACK ADAM'S CRUSADE?
BY TAKING CONTROL OF MY BODY? BY LYING TO ME?
THE ENDS DO NOT JUSTIFY THE MEANS, NABU.

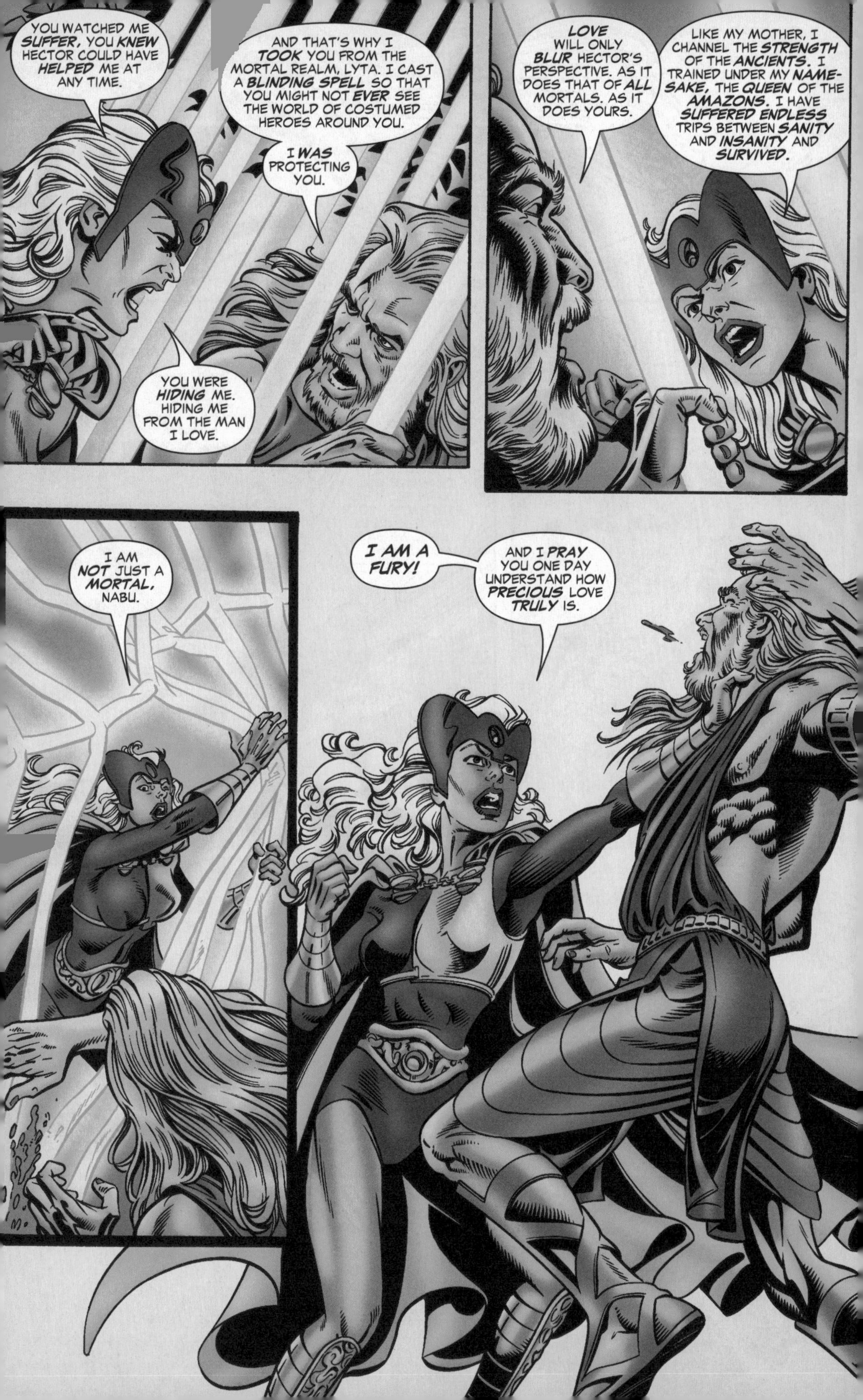
YOU WATCHED ME SUFFER, YOU KNEW HECTOR COULD HAVE HELPED ME AT ANY TIME.
AND THAT'S WHY I TOOK YOU FROM THE MORTAL REALM, LYTA. I CAST A BLINDING SPELL SO THAT YOU MIGHT NOT EVER SEE THE WORLD OF COSTUMED HEROES AROUND YOU.
I WAS PROTECTING YOU.
YOU WERE HIDING ME. HIDING ME FROM THE MAN I LOVE.
LOVE WILL ONLY BLUR HECTOR'S PERSPECTIVE. AS IT DOES THAT OF ALL MORTALS. AS IT DOES YOURS.
LIKE MY MOTHER, I CHANNEL THE STRENGTH OF THE ANCIENTS. I TRAINED UNDER MY NAMESAKE, THE QUEEN OF THE AMAZONS. I HAVE SUFFERED ENDLESS TRIPS BETWEEN SANITY AND INSANITY AND SURVIVED.
I AM NOT JUST A MORTAL, NABU.
I AM A FURY!
AND I PRAY YOU ONE DAY UNDERSTAND HOW PRECIOUS LOVE TRULY IS.

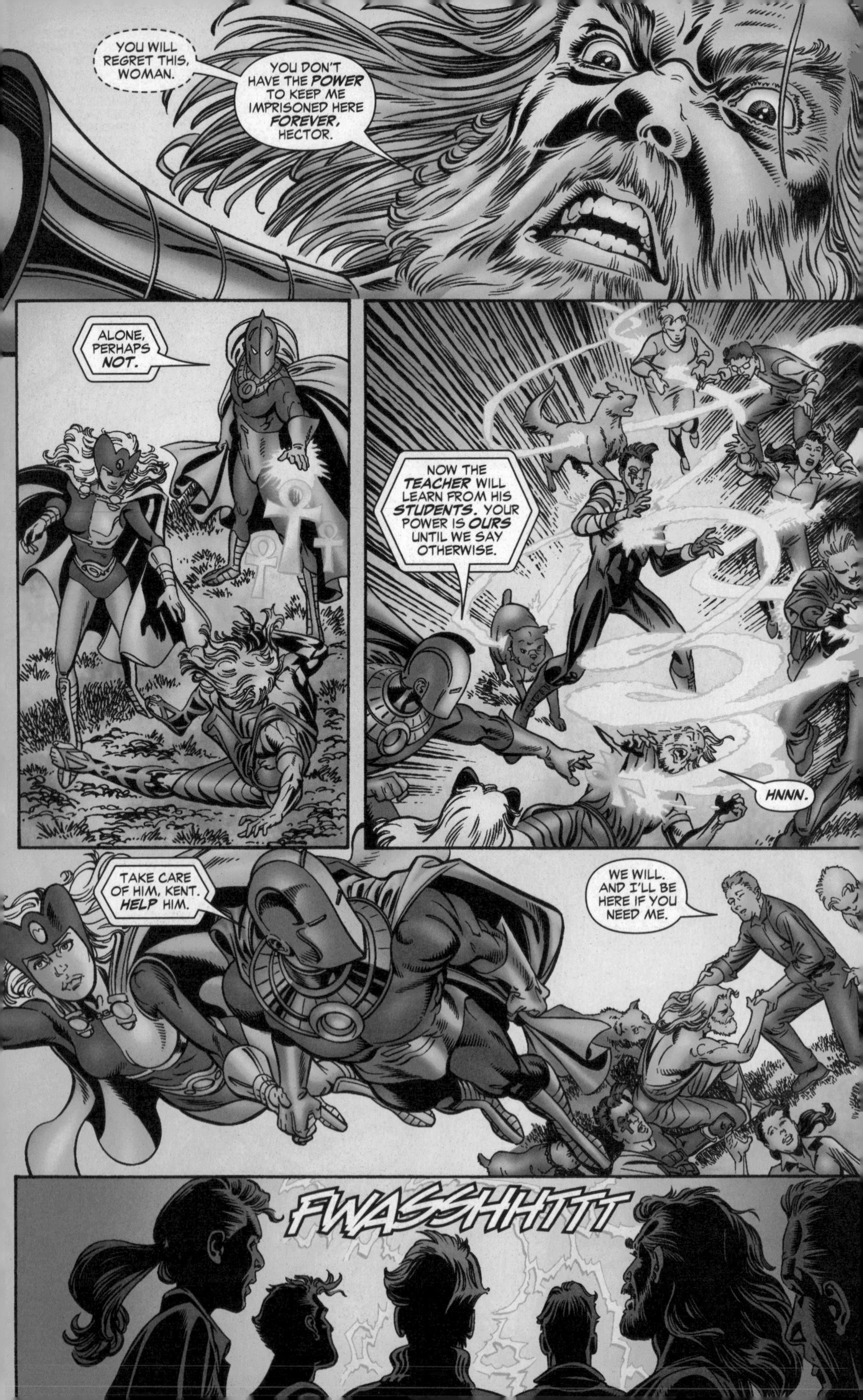
YOU WILL REGRET THIS, WOMAN.
YOU DON'T HAVE THE POWER TO KEEP ME IMPRISONED HERE FOREVER, HECTOR.
ALONE, PERHAPS NOT.
NOW THE TEACHER WILL LEARN FROM HIS STUDENTS. YOUR POWER IS OURS UNTIL WE SAY OTHERWISE.
HNNN.
TAKE CARE OF HIM, KENT. HELP HIM.
WE WILL. AND I'LL BE HERE IF YOU NEED ME.
FWASSHHTTT

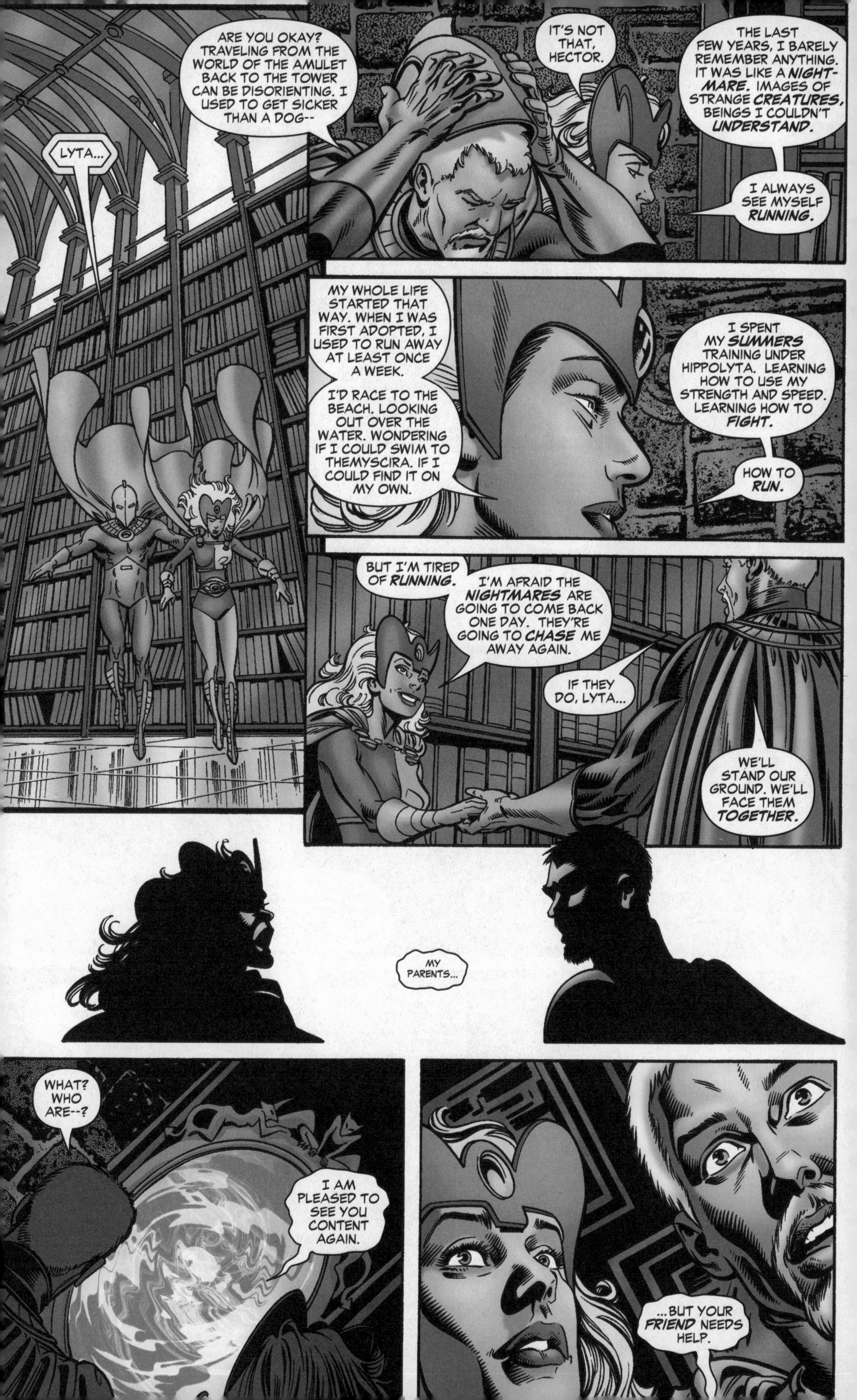
ARE YOU OKAY? TRAVELING FROM THE WORLD OF THE AMULET BACK TO THE TOWER CAN BE DISORIENTING. I USED TO GET SICKER THAN A DOG--
LYTA...
IT'S NOT THAT, HECTOR.
THE LAST FEW YEARS, I BARELY REMEMBER ANYTHING. IT WAS LIKE A NIGHTMARE. IMAGES OF STRANGE CREATURES, BEINGS I COULDN'T UNDERSTAND.
I ALWAYS SEE MYSELF RUNNING.
MY WHOLE LIFE STARTED THAT WAY. WHEN I WAS FIRST ADOPTED, I USED TO RUN AWAY AT LEAST ONCE A WEEK.
I'D RACE TO THE BEACH. LOOKING OUT OVER THE WATER. WONDERING IF I COULD SWIM TO THEMYSCIRA. IF I COULD FIND IT ON MY OWN.
I SPENT MY SUMMERS TRAINING UNDER HIPPOLYTA. LEARNING HOW TO USE MY STRENGTH AND SPEED. LEARNING HOW TO FIGHT.
HOW TO RUN.
BUT I'M TIRED OF RUNNING.
I'M AFRAID THE NIGHTMARES ARE GOING TO COME BACK ONE DAY. THEY'RE GOING TO CHASE ME AWAY AGAIN.
IF THEY DO, LYTA...
WE'LL STAND OUR GROUND. WE'LL FACE THEM TOGETHER.
MY PARENTS...
WHAT? WHO ARE--?
I AM PLEASED TO SEE YOU CONTENT AGAIN.
...BUT YOUR FRIEND NEEDS HELP.

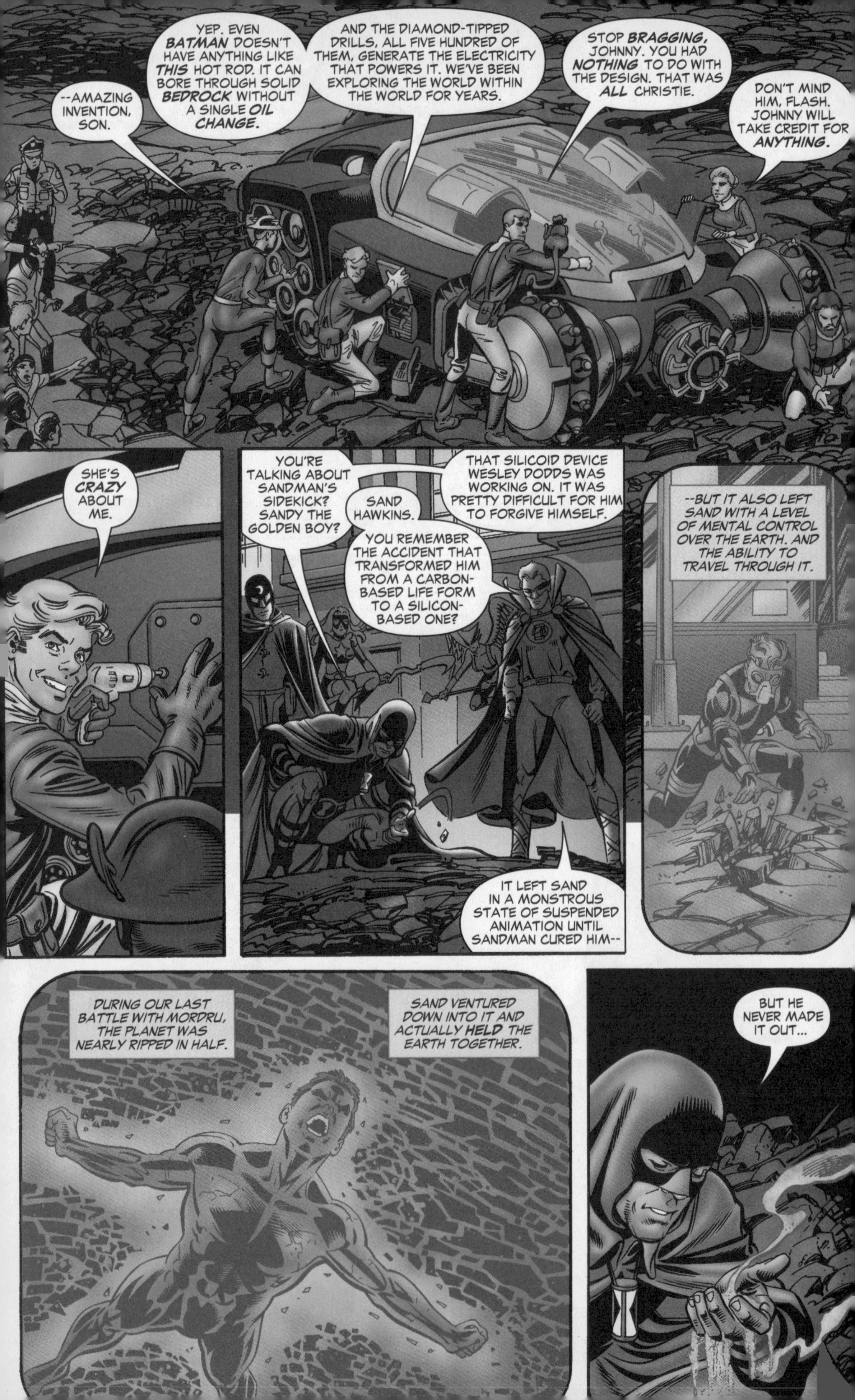
--AMAZING INVENTION, SON.
YEP. EVEN BATMAN DOESN'T HAVE ANYTHING LIKE THIS HOT ROD. IT CAN BORE THROUGH SOLID BEDROCK WITHOUT A SINGLE OIL CHANGE.
AND THE DIAMOND-TIPPED DRILLS, ALL FIVE HUNDRED OF THEM, GENERATE THE ELECTRICITY THAT POWERS IT. WE'VE BEEN EXPLORING THE WORLD WITHIN THE WORLD FOR YEARS.
STOP BRAGGING, JOHNNY. YOU HAD NOTHING TO DO WITH THE DESIGN. THAT WAS ALL CHRISTIE.
DON'T MIND HIM, FLASH. JOHNNY WILL TAKE CREDIT FOR ANYTHING.
SHE'S CRAZY ABOUT ME.
YOU'RE TALKING ABOUT SANDMAN'S SIDEKICK? SANDY THE GOLDEN BOY?
SAND HAWKINS.
THAT SILICOID DEVICE WESLEY DODDS WAS WORKING ON. IT WAS PRETTY DIFFICULT FOR HIM TO FORGIVE HIMSELF.
YOU REMEMBER THE ACCIDENT THAT TRANSFORMED HIM FROM A CARBON-BASED LIFE FORM TO A SILICON-BASED ONE?
IT LEFT SAND IN A MONSTROUS STATE OF SUSPENDED ANIMATION UNTIL SANDMAN CURED HIM--
--BUT IT ALSO LEFT SAND WITH A LEVEL OF MENTAL CONTROL OVER THE EARTH. AND THE ABILITY TO TRAVEL THROUGH IT.
DURING OUR LAST BATTLE WITH MORDRU, THE PLANET WAS NEARLY RIPPED IN HALF.
SAND VENTURED DOWN INTO IT AND ACTUALLY HELD THE EARTH TOGETHER.
BUT HE NEVER MADE IT OUT...

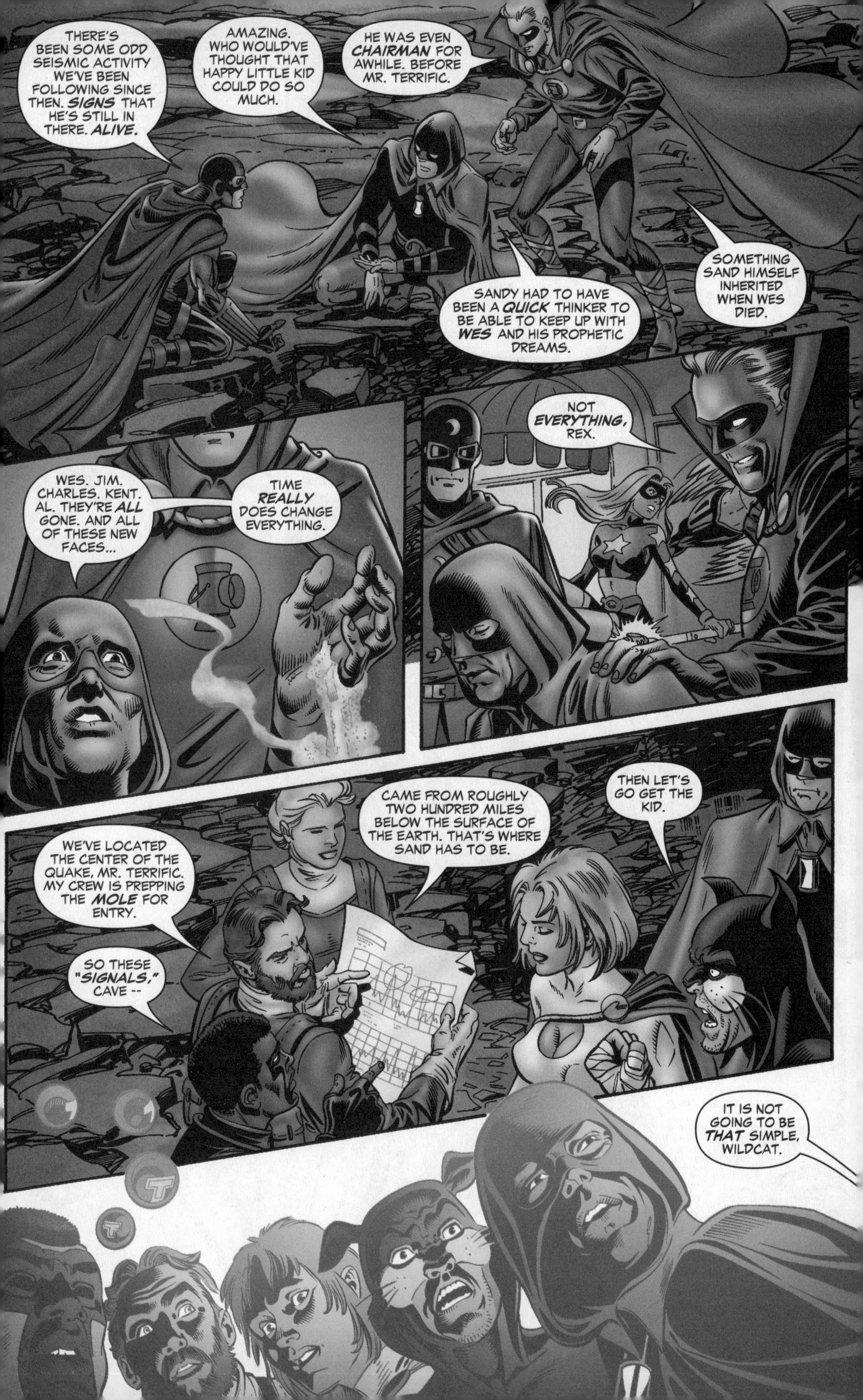

THERE'S BEEN SOME ODD SEISMIC ACTIVITY WE'VE BEEN FOLLOWING SINCE THEN. SIGNS THAT HE'S STILL IN THERE. ALIVE.
AMAZING. WHO WOULD'VE THOUGHT THAT HAPPY LITTLE KID COULD DO SO MUCH.
HE WAS EVEN CHAIRMAN FOR AWHILE. BEFORE MR. TERRIFIC.
SANDY HAD TO HAVE BEEN A QUICK THINKER TO BE ABLE TO KEEP UP WITH WES AND HIS PROPHETIC DREAMS.
SOMETHING SAND HIMSELF INHERITED WHEN WES DIED.
WES. JIM. CHARLES. KENT. AL. THEY'RE ALL GONE. AND ALL OF THESE NEW FACES...
TIME REALLY DOES CHANGE EVERYTHING.
NOT EVERYTHING, REX.
WE'VE LOCATED THE CENTER OF THE QUAKE, MR. TERRIFIC. MY CREW IS PREPPING THE MOLE FOR ENTRY.
SO THESE "SIGNALS," CAVE --
CAME FROM ROUGHLY TWO HUNDRED MILES BELOW THE SURFACE OF THE EARTH. THAT'S WHERE SAND HAS TO BE.
THEN LET'S GO GET THE KID.
IT IS NOT GOING TO BE THAT SIMPLE, WILDCAT.

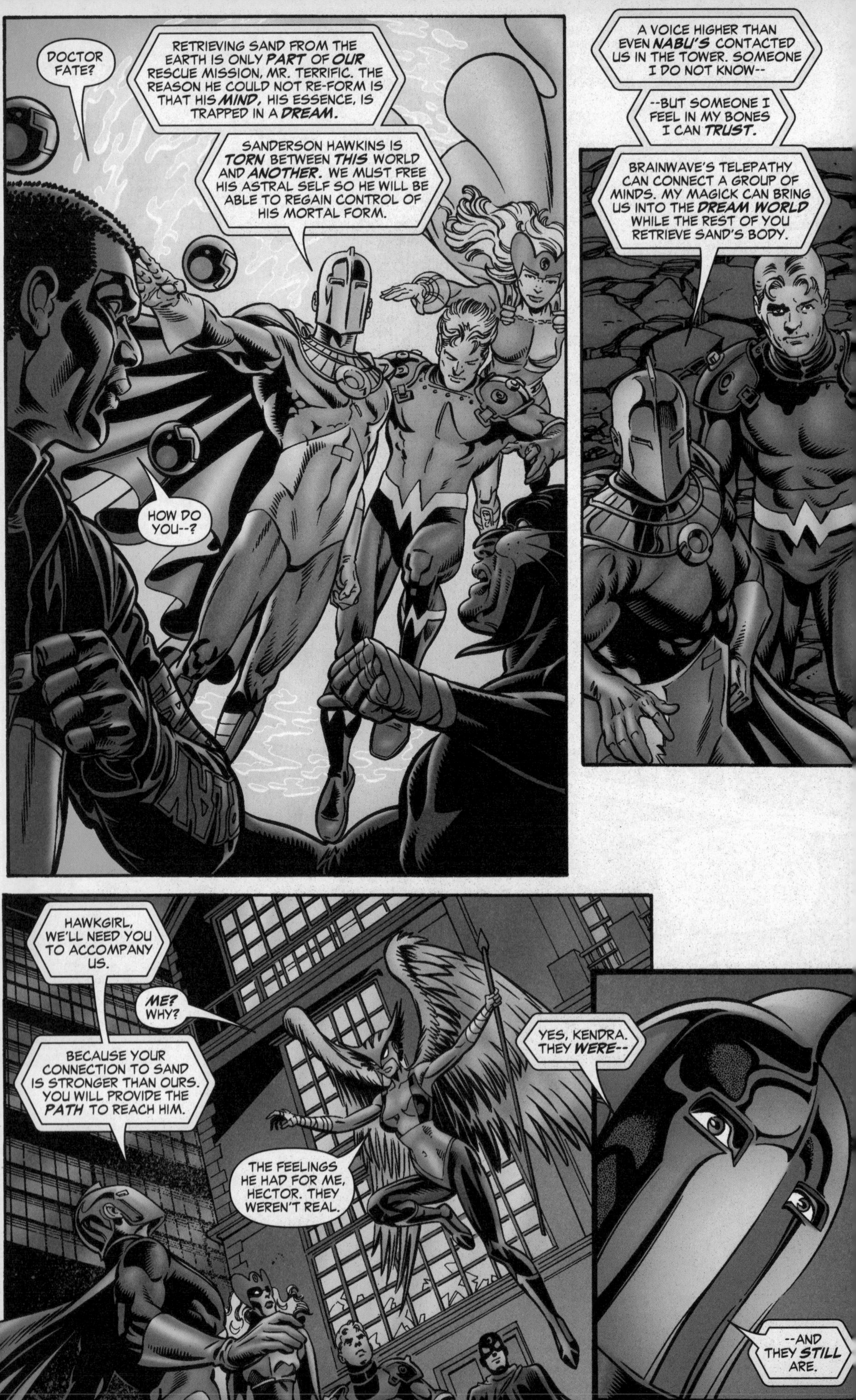
DOCTOR FATE?
RETRIEVING SAND FROM THE EARTH IS ONLY PART OF OUR RESCUE MISSION, MR. TERRIFIC. THE REASON HE COULD NOT RE-FORM IS THAT HIS MIND, HIS ESSENCE, IS TRAPPED IN A DREAM.
SANDERSON HAWKINS IS TORN BETWEEN THIS WORLD AND ANOTHER. WE MUST FREE HIS ASTRAL SELF SO HE WILL BE ABLE TO REGAIN CONTROL OF HIS MORTAL FORM.
HOW DO YOU--?
A VOICE HIGHER THAN EVEN NABU'S CONTACTED US IN THE TOWER. SOMEONE I DO NOT KNOW--
--BUT SOMEONE I FEEL IN MY BONES I CAN TRUST.
BRAINWAVE'S TELEPATHY CAN CONNECT A GROUP OF MINDS. MY MAGICK CAN BRING US INTO THE DREAM WORLD WHILE THE REST OF YOU RETRIEVE SAND'S BODY.
HAWKGIRL, WE'LL NEED YOU TO ACCOMPANY US.
ME? WHY?
BECAUSE YOUR CONNECTION TO SAND IS STRONGER THAN OURS. YOU WILL PROVIDE THE PATH TO REACH HIM.
THE FEELINGS HE HAD FOR ME, HECTOR. THEY WEREN'T REAL.
YES, KENDRA. THEY WERE--
--AND THEY STILL ARE.

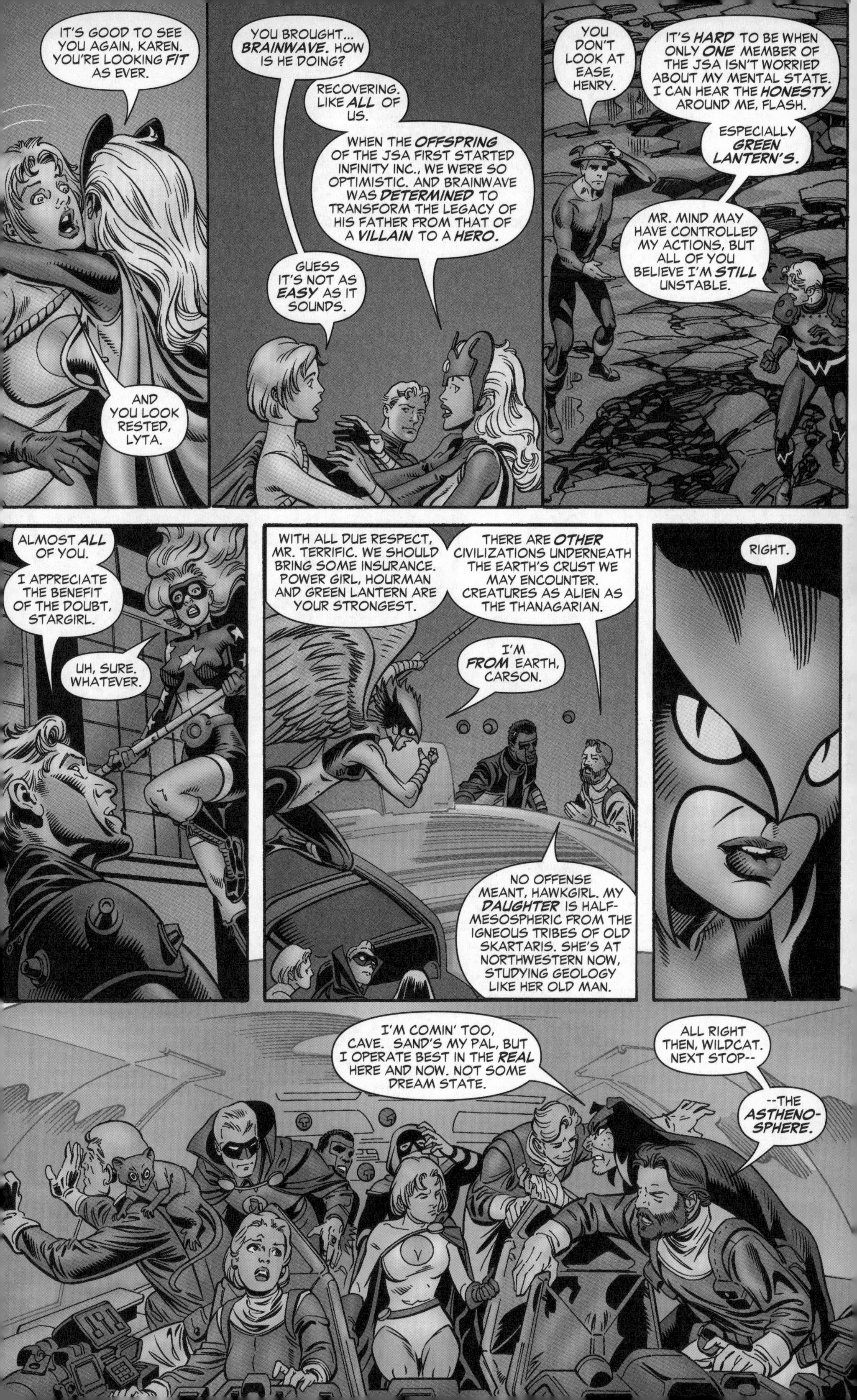
IT'S GOOD TO SEE YOU AGAIN, KAREN. YOU'RE LOOKING FIT AS EVER.
AND YOU LOOK RESTED, LYTA.
YOU BROUGHT... BRAINWAVE. HOW IS HE DOING?
RECOVERING. LIKE ALL OF US.
WHEN THE OFFSPRING OF THE JSA FIRST STARTED INFINITY INC., WE WERE SO OPTIMISTIC. AND BRAINWAVE WAS DETERMINED TO TRANSFORM THE LEGACY OF HIS FATHER FROM THAT OF A VILLAIN TO A HERO.
GUESS IT'S NOT AS EASY AS IT SOUNDS.
YOU DON'T LOOK AT EASE, HENRY.
IT'S HARD TO BE WHEN ONLY ONE MEMBER OF THE JSA ISN'T WORRIED ABOUT MY MENTAL STATE. I CAN HEAR THE HONESTY AROUND ME, FLASH.
ESPECIALLY GREEN LANTERN'S.
MR. MIND MAY HAVE CONTROLLED MY ACTIONS, BUT ALL OF YOU BELIEVE I'M STILL UNSTABLE.
ALMOST ALL OF YOU.
I APPRECIATE THE BENEFIT OF THE DOUBT, STARGIRL.
UH, SURE. WHATEVER.
WITH ALL DUE RESPECT, MR. TERRIFIC. WE SHOULD BRING SOME INSURANCE. POWER GIRL, HOURMAN AND GREEN LANTERN ARE YOUR STRONGEST.
THERE ARE OTHER CIVILIZATIONS UNDERNEATH THE EARTH'S CRUST WE MAY ENCOUNTER. CREATURES AS ALIEN AS THE THANAGARIAN.
I'M FROM EARTH, CARSON.
NO OFFENSE MEANT, HAWKGIRL. MY DAUGHTER IS HALF-MESOSPHERIC FROM THE IGNEOUS TRIBES OF OLD SKARTARIS. SHE'S AT NORTHWESTERN NOW, STUDYING GEOLOGY LIKE HER OLD MAN.
RIGHT.
I'M COMIN' TOO, CAVE. SAND'S MY PAL, BUT I OPERATE BEST IN THE REAL HERE AND NOW. NOT SOME DREAM STATE.
ALL RIGHT THEN, WILDCAT. NEXT STOP--
--THE ASTHENO-SPHERE.

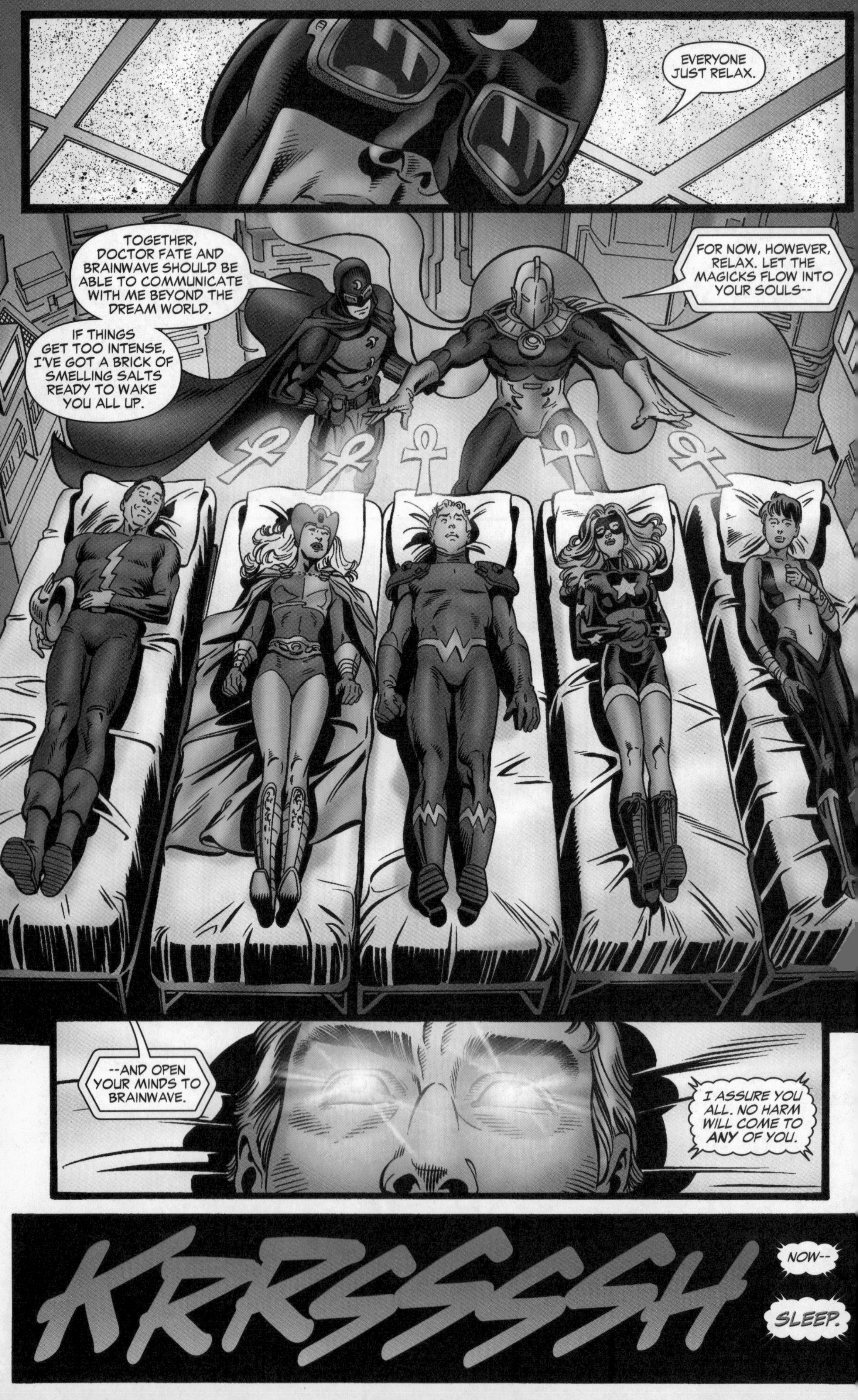
EVERYONE JUST RELAX.
TOGETHER, DOCTOR FATE AND BRAINWAVE SHOULD BE ABLE TO COMMUNICATE WITH ME BEYOND THE DREAM WORLD.
IF THINGS GET TOO INTENSE, I'VE GOT A BRICK OF SMELLING SALTS READY TO WAKE YOU ALL UP.
FOR NOW, HOWEVER, RELAX. LET THE MAGICKS FLOW INTO YOUR SOULS--
--AND OPEN YOUR MINDS TO BRAINWAVE.
I ASSURE YOU ALL. NO HARM WILL COME TO ANY OF YOU.
KRRSSSH
NOW--
SLEEP.

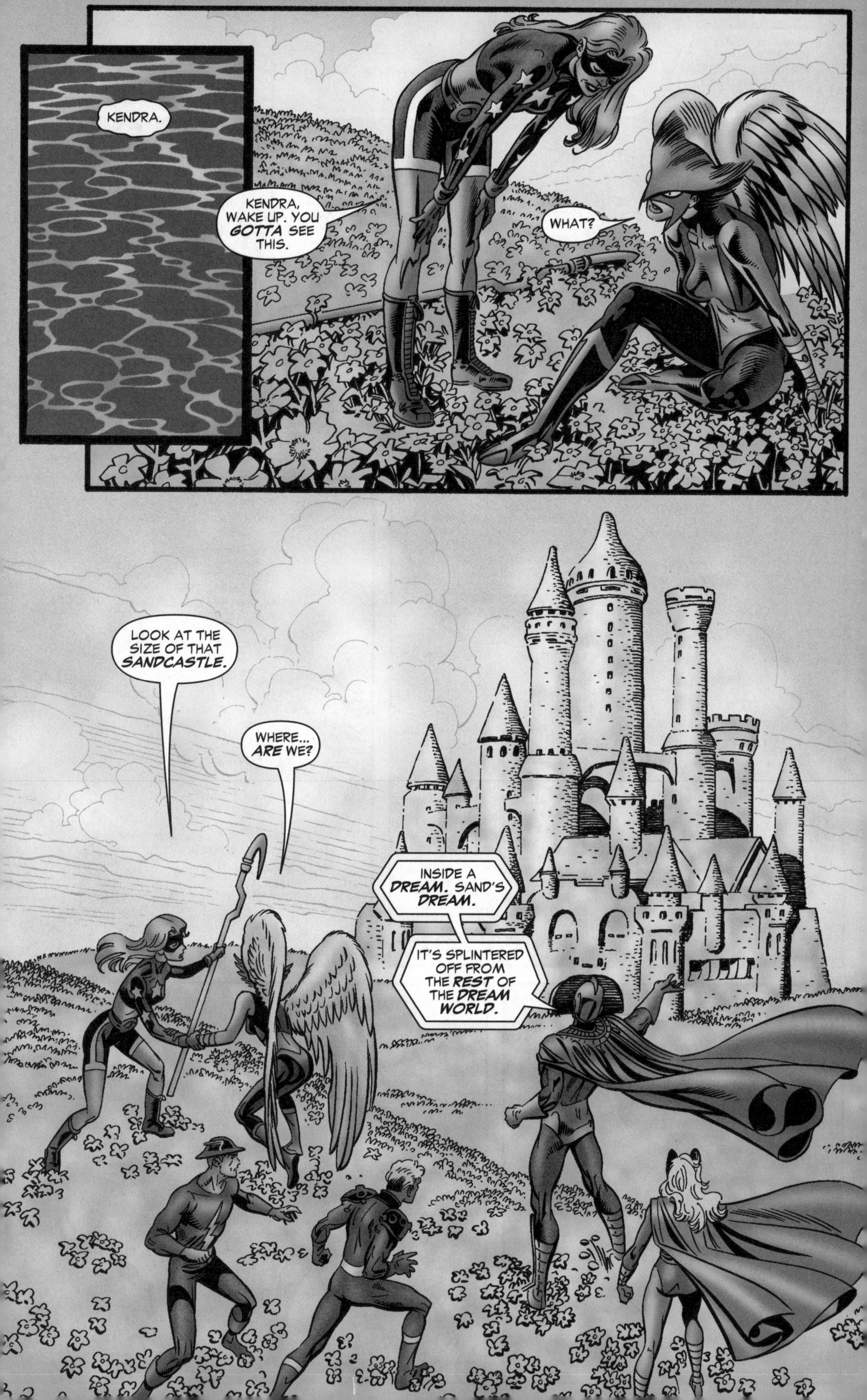
KENDRA.
KENDRA, WAKE UP. YOU GOTTA SEE THIS.
WHAT?
LOOK AT THE SIZE OF THAT SANDCASTLE.
WHERE... ARE WE?
INSIDE A DREAM. SAND'S DREAM.
IT'S SPLINTERED OFF FROM THE REST OF THE DREAM WORLD.

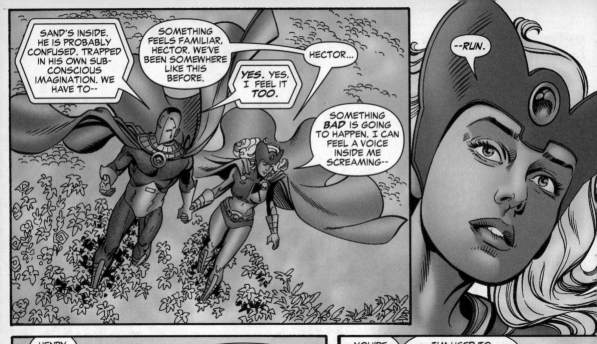

SAND'S INSIDE. HE IS PROBABLY CONFUSED. TRAPPED IN HIS OWN SUB-CONSCIOUS IMAGINATION. WE HAVE TO--

SOMETHING FEELS FAMILIAR, HECTOR. WE'VE BEEN SOMEWHERE LIKE THIS BEFORE.

HECTOR...

YES. YES, I FEEL IT TOO.

SOMETHING BAD IS GOING TO HAPPEN. I CAN FEEL A VOICE INSIDE ME SCREAMING--

--RUN.

HENRY. I DIDN'T MEAN TO--

OFFEND ME EARLIER. I KNOW, FLASH. AND IT'S HANK.

I KNOW YOU LOOK AT ME AS ONE OF YOUR MANY CHILDREN. YOU RESPECT ME FOR NOT FOLLOWING IN MY FATHER'S FOOTSTEPS.

I'VE TRIED MY BEST TO BE A HERO.

AND I'M PROUD OF YOU. I AM--

AND I DON'T MEAN TO READ YOUR MIND. IT JUST HAPPENS. I CAN'T TURN IT OFF AS WELL AS I USED TO.

YOU'RE WORRYING AGAIN. IT'S OKAY.

I'M USED TO PEOPLE TALKING BEHIND MY BACK. I LIVE WITH IT EVERY DAY NOW.

EVERY SECOND.

I LIVE A LIFE NOT MANY COULD HANDLE, FLASH. A WORLD BASED ON HONESTY INSTEAD OF LIES.

IN FACT...

I LIVE IN A DREAM.

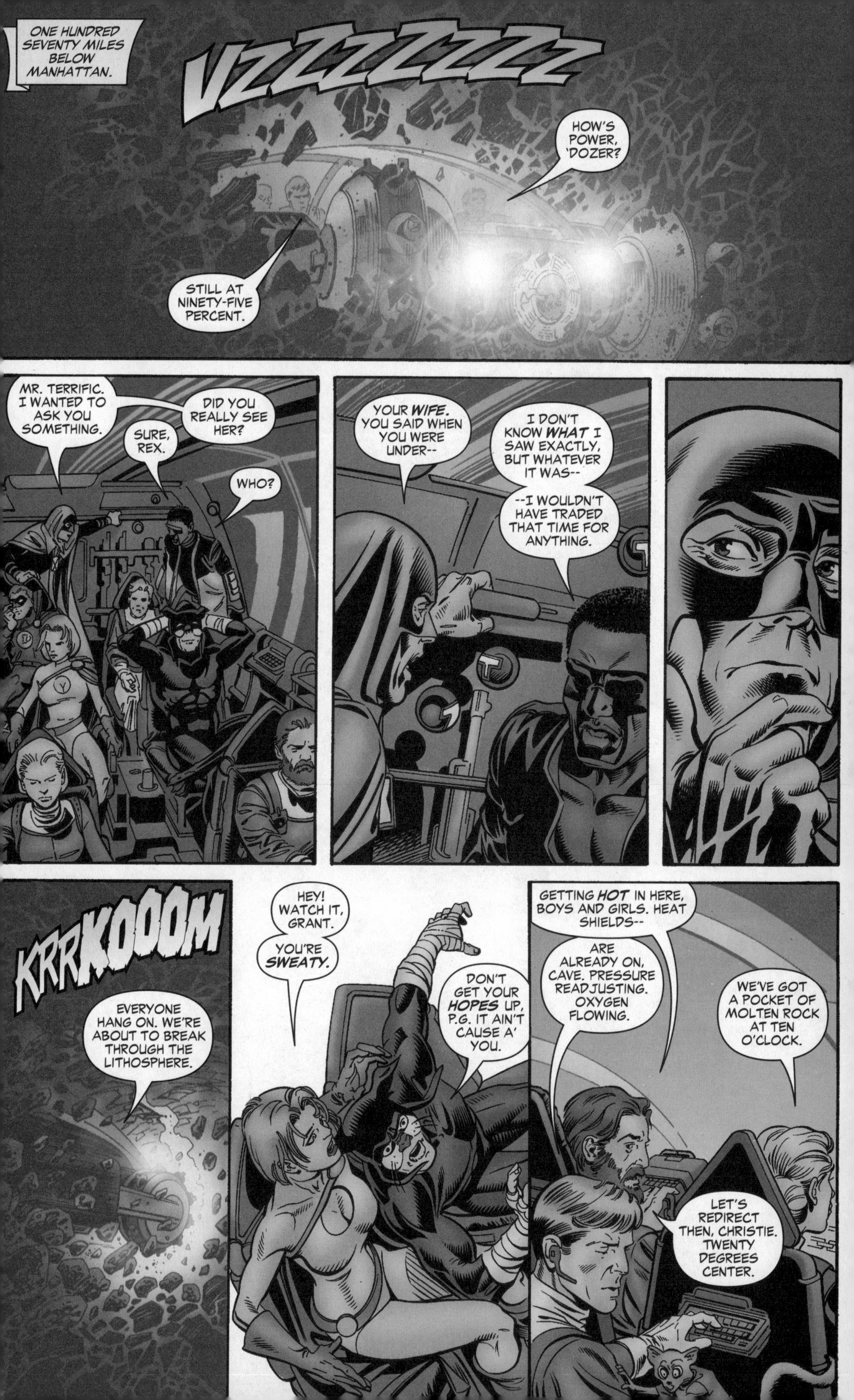
ONE HUNDRED SEVENTY MILES BELOW MANHATTAN.
VZZZZZZZZ
HOW'S POWER, 'DOZER?
STILL AT NINETY-FIVE PERCENT.
MR. TERRIFIC. I WANTED TO ASK YOU SOMETHING.
SURE, REX.
DID YOU REALLY SEE HER?
WHO?
YOUR WIFE. YOU SAID WHEN YOU WERE UNDER--
I DON'T KNOW WHAT I SAW EXACTLY, BUT WHATEVER IT WAS--
--I WOULDN'T HAVE TRADED THAT TIME FOR ANYTHING.
KRRKOOOM
EVERYONE HANG ON. WE'RE ABOUT TO BREAK THROUGH THE LITHOSPHERE.
HEY! WATCH IT, GRANT.
YOU'RE SWEATY.
DON'T GET YOUR HOPES UP, P.G. IT AIN'T CAUSE A' YOU.
GETTING HOT IN HERE, BOYS AND GIRLS. HEAT SHIELDS--
ARE ALREADY ON, CAVE. PRESSURE READJUSTING. OXYGEN FLOWING.
WE'VE GOT A POCKET OF MOLTEN ROCK AT TEN O'CLOCK.
LET'S REDIRECT THEN, CHRISTIE. TWENTY DEGREES CENTER.

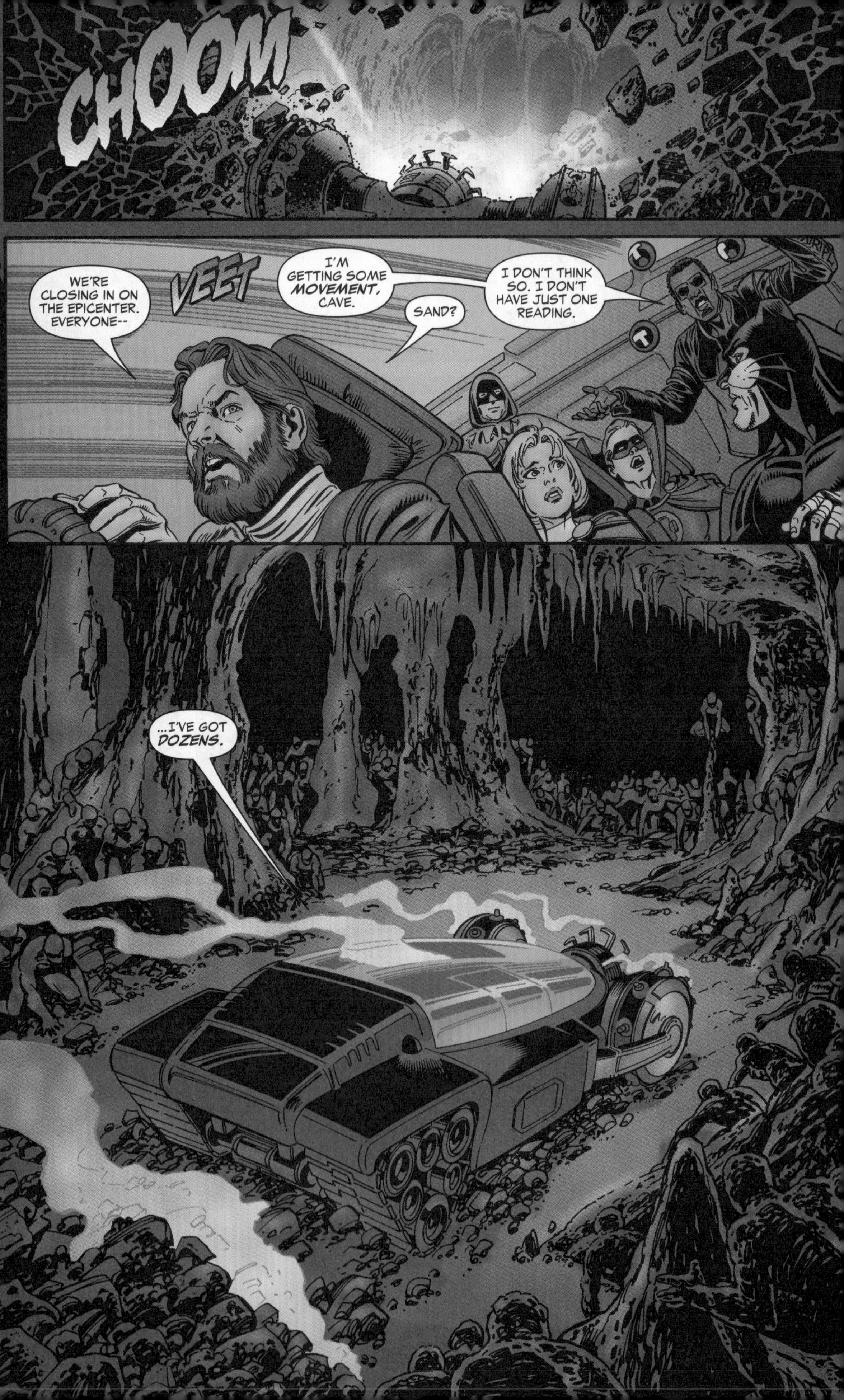
CHOOM
WE'RE CLOSING IN ON THE EPICENTER. EVERYONE--
VEET
I'M GETTING SOME MOVEMENT, CAVE.
SAND?
I DON'T THINK SO. I DON'T HAVE JUST ONE READING.
...I'VE GOT DOZENS.

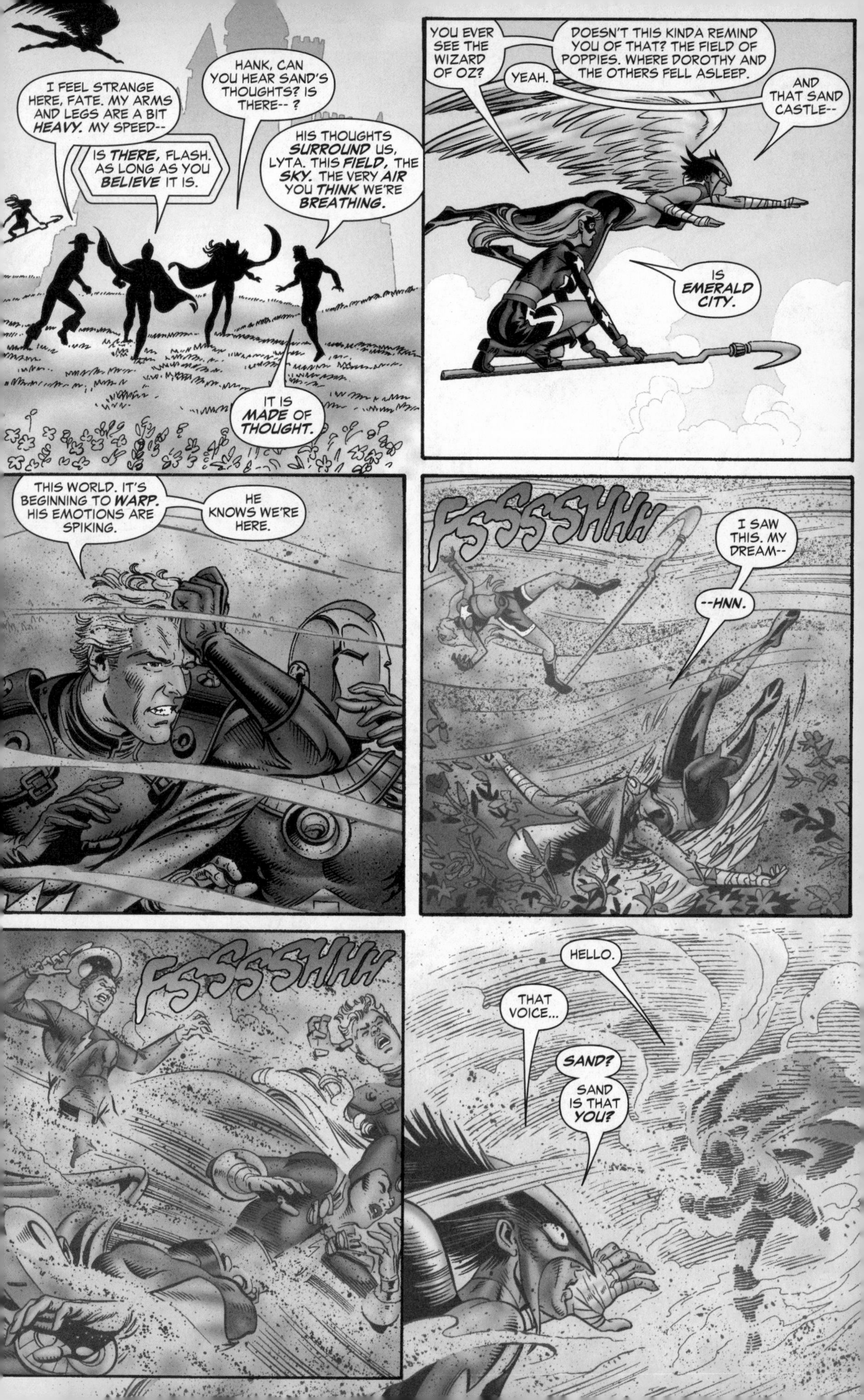

I FEEL STRANGE HERE, FATE. MY ARMS AND LEGS ARE A BIT HEAVY. MY SPEED--
IS THERE, FLASH. AS LONG AS YOU BELIEVE IT IS.
HANK, CAN YOU HEAR SAND'S THOUGHTS? IS THERE-- ?
HIS THOUGHTS SURROUND US, LYTA. THIS FIELD, THE SKY. THE VERY AIR YOU THINK WE'RE BREATHING.
IT IS MADE OF THOUGHT.
YOU EVER SEE THE WIZARD OF OZ?
YEAH.
DOESN'T THIS KINDA REMIND YOU OF THAT? THE FIELD OF POPPIES. WHERE DOROTHY AND THE OTHERS FELL ASLEEP.
AND THAT SAND CASTLE--
IS EMERALD CITY.
THIS WORLD. IT'S BEGINNING TO WARP. HIS EMOTIONS ARE SPIKING.
HE KNOWS WE'RE HERE.
FSSSSHHH
I SAW THIS. MY DREAM--
--HNN.
FSSSSHHH
HELLO.
THAT VOICE...
SAND?
SAND IS THAT YOU?

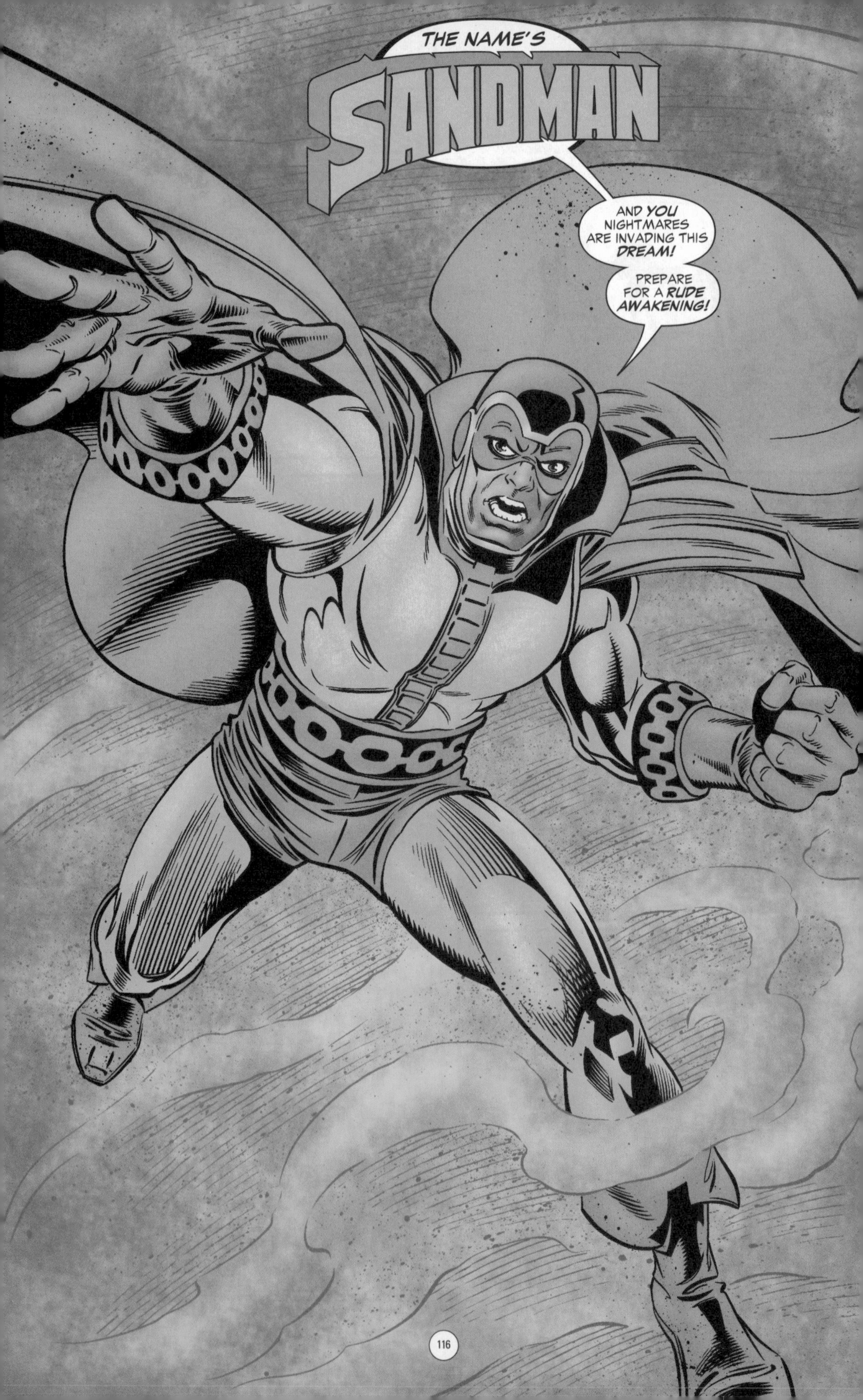
THE NAME'S SANDMAN
AND YOU NIGHTMARES ARE INVADING THIS DREAM!
PREPARE FOR A RUDE AWAKENING!

NEW YORK.

THE JSA BROWNSTONE.

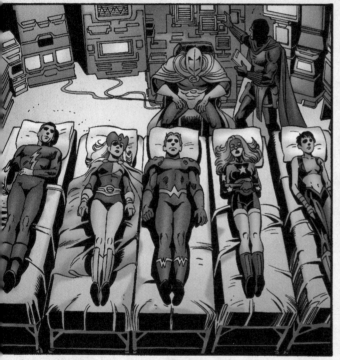

NN...ND, IS THAT YOU?

HAWKGIRL?

I CAN SEE *SAND* IN HER LUNGS? HOW...?

BETTER WAKE THEM UP--

>KAFF<

NO, DOCTOR MID-NITE.

BRAINWAVE?

NOT YET.

WHATEVER *CHAOS* THEY'RE EXPERIENCING INSIDE THAT *DREAM* IS AFFECTING THEIR BODIES HERE.

WOUNDS ARE *MANIFESTING*--

AND I CAN FEEL TWO FORCES *CLUTCHING* ON TO OUR PSYCHES AS WELL. YOU TRY TO WAKE US UP *NOW* AND JUST LIKE SAND--

--OUR *MINDS* WILL BE IMPRISONED IN A *NIGHTMARE*.

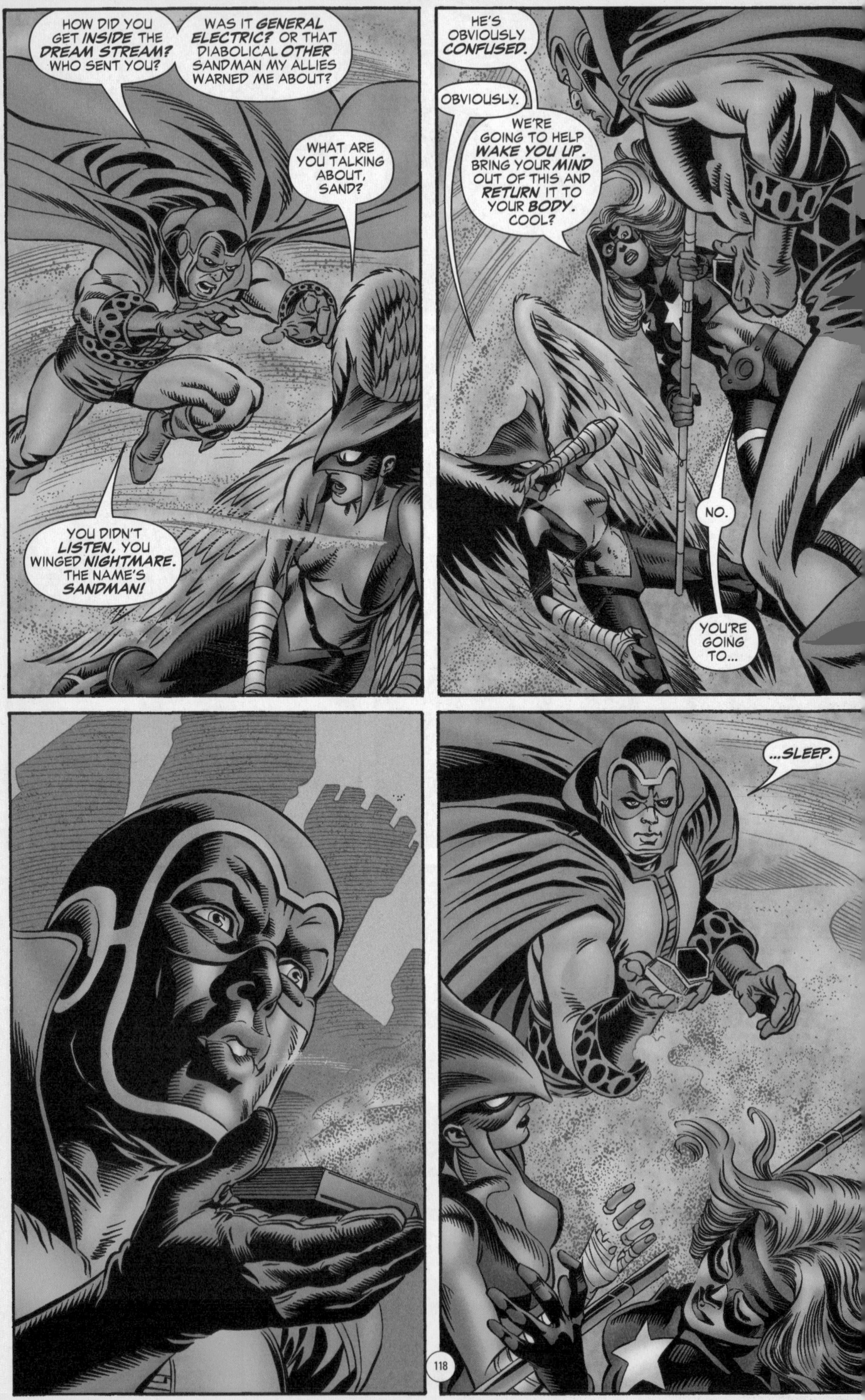

HOW DID YOU GET INSIDE THE DREAM STREAM? WHO SENT YOU?
WAS IT GENERAL ELECTRIC? OR THAT DIABOLICAL OTHER SANDMAN MY ALLIES WARNED ME ABOUT?
WHAT ARE YOU TALKING ABOUT, SAND?
YOU DIDN'T LISTEN, YOU WINGED NIGHTMARE. THE NAME'S SANDMAN!
HE'S OBVIOUSLY CONFUSED.
OBVIOUSLY.
WE'RE GOING TO HELP WAKE YOU UP. BRING YOUR MIND OUT OF THIS AND RETURN IT TO YOUR BODY. COOL?
NO.
YOU'RE GOING TO...
...SLEEP.

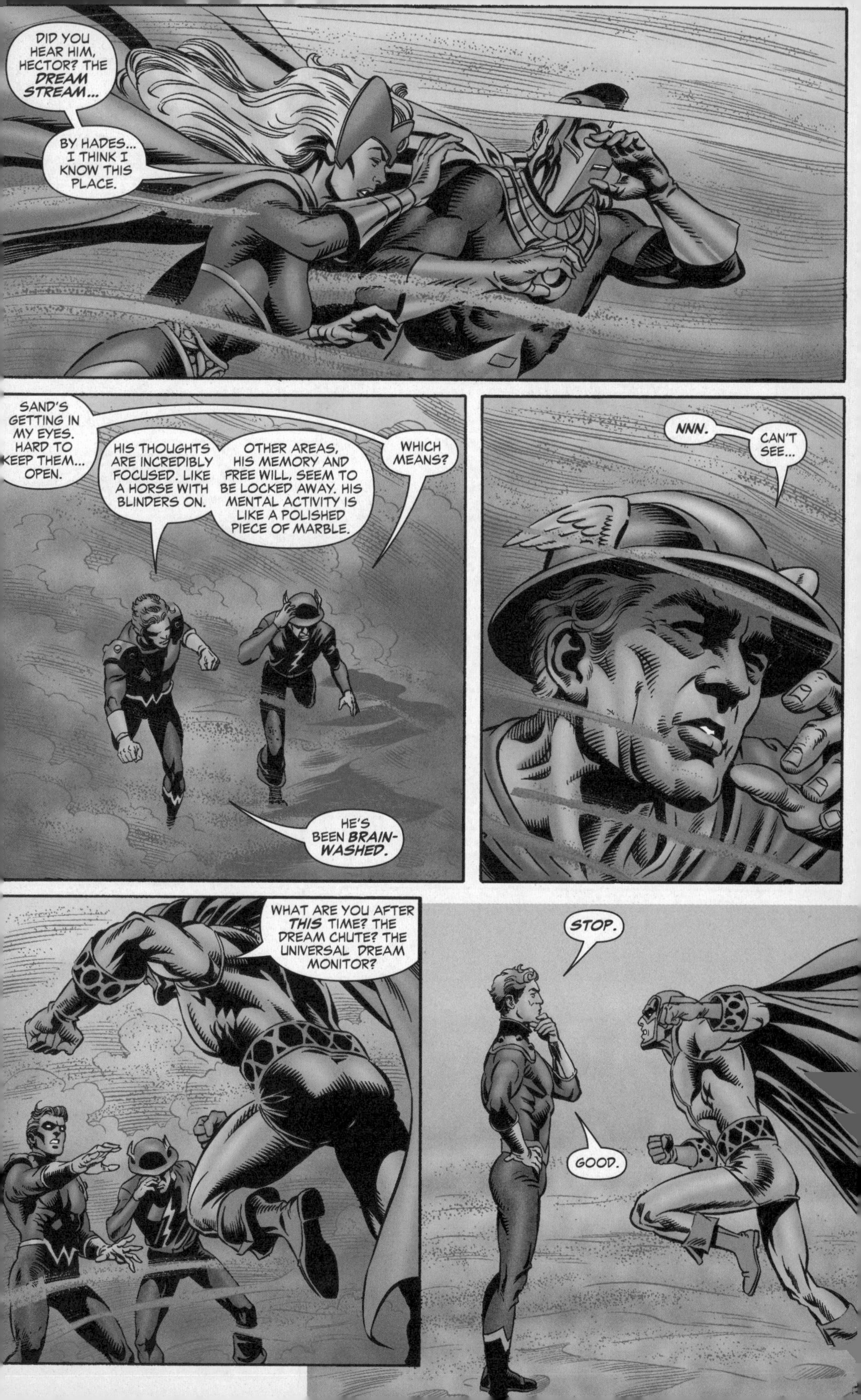
DID YOU HEAR HIM, HECTOR? THE *DREAM STREAM...*
BY HADES... I THINK I KNOW THIS PLACE.
SAND'S GETTING IN MY EYES. HARD TO KEEP THEM... OPEN.
HIS THOUGHTS ARE INCREDIBLY FOCUSED. LIKE A HORSE WITH BLINDERS ON.
OTHER AREAS, HIS MEMORY AND FREE WILL, SEEM TO BE LOCKED AWAY. HIS MENTAL ACTIVITY IS LIKE A POLISHED PIECE OF MARBLE.
WHICH MEANS?
HE'S BEEN *BRAIN-WASHED.*
*NNN.*
CAN'T SEE...
WHAT ARE YOU AFTER *THIS* TIME? THE DREAM CHUTE? THE UNIVERSAL DREAM MONITOR?
*STOP.*
GOOD.

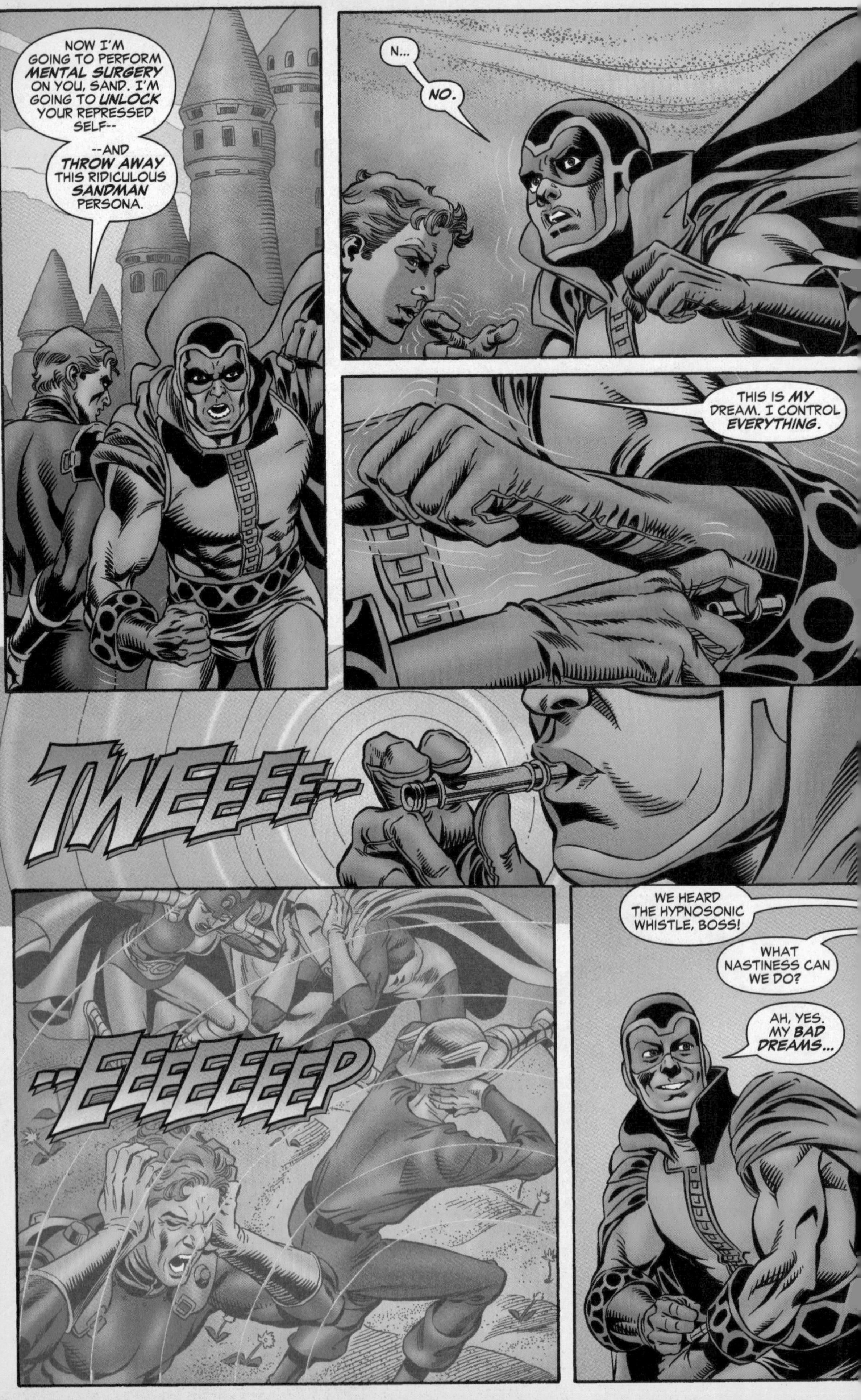
NOW I'M GOING TO PERFORM MENTAL SURGERY ON YOU, SAND. I'M GOING TO UNLOCK YOUR REPRESSED SELF--
--AND THROW AWAY THIS RIDICULOUS SANDMAN PERSONA.
N...
NO.
THIS IS MY DREAM. I CONTROL EVERYTHING.
TWEEEE--
--EEEEEEEP
WE HEARD THE HYPNOSONIC WHISTLE, BOSS!
WHAT NASTINESS CAN WE DO?
AH, YES. MY BAD DREAMS...

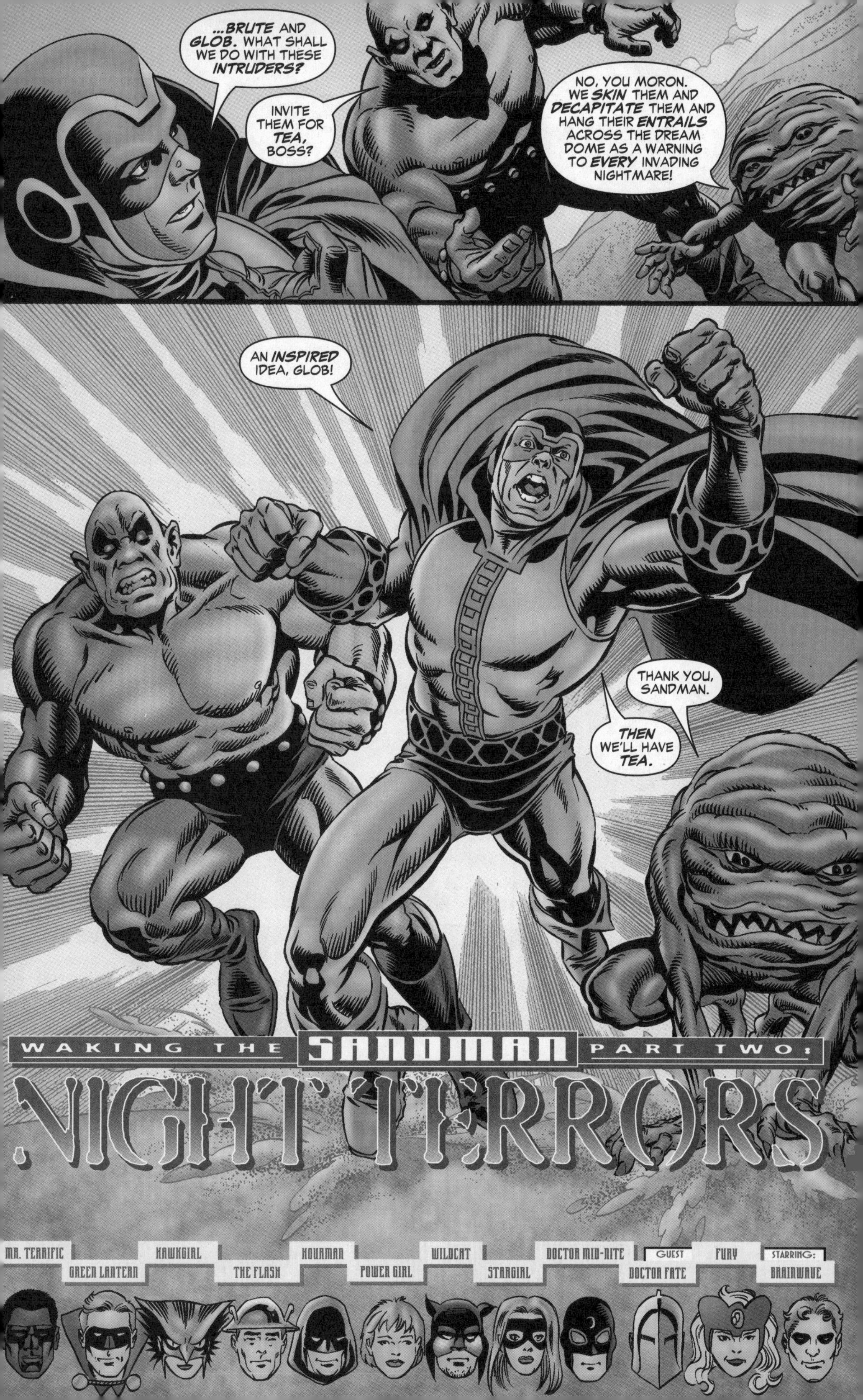
...BRUTE AND GLOB. WHAT SHALL WE DO WITH THESE INTRUDERS?
INVITE THEM FOR TEA, BOSS?
NO, YOU MORON. WE SKIN THEM AND DECAPITATE THEM AND HANG THEIR ENTRAILS ACROSS THE DREAM DOME AS A WARNING TO EVERY INVADING NIGHTMARE!
AN INSPIRED IDEA, GLOB!
THANK YOU, SANDMAN.
THEN WE'LL HAVE TEA.
WAKING THE SANDMAN PART TWO:
NIGHT TERRORS
MR. TERRIFIC
GREEN LANTERN
HAWKGIRL
THE FLASH
HOURMAN
POWER GIRL
WILDCAT
STARGIRL
DOCTOR MID-NITE
DOCTOR FATE
GUEST STARRING:
FURY
BRAINWAVE

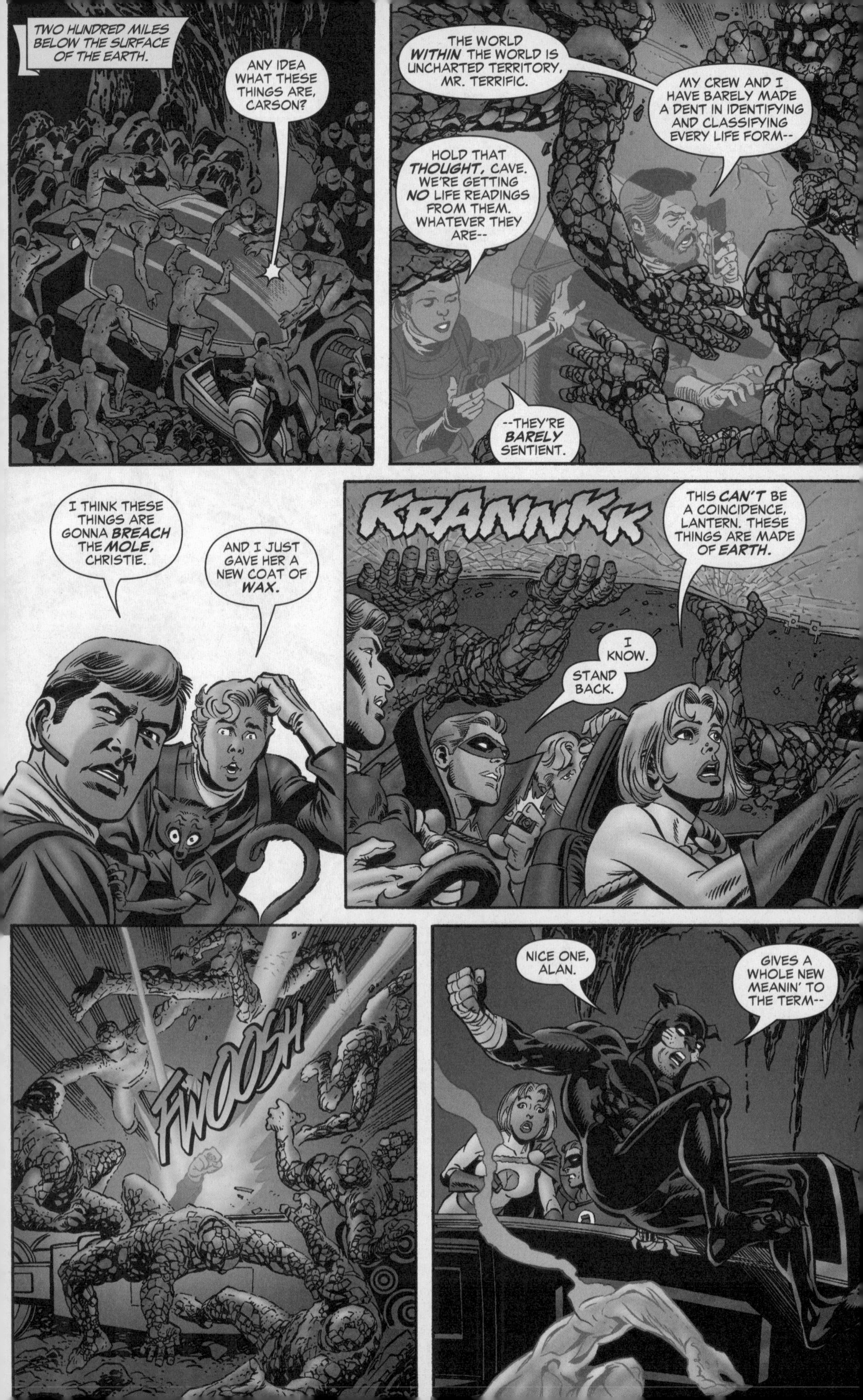
TWO HUNDRED MILES BELOW THE SURFACE OF THE EARTH.
ANY IDEA WHAT THESE THINGS ARE, CARSON?
THE WORLD WITHIN THE WORLD IS UNCHARTED TERRITORY, MR. TERRIFIC.
MY CREW AND I HAVE BARELY MADE A DENT IN IDENTIFYING AND CLASSIFYING EVERY LIFE FORM--
HOLD THAT THOUGHT, CAVE. WE'RE GETTING NO LIFE READINGS FROM THEM. WHATEVER THEY ARE--
--THEY'RE BARELY SENTIENT.
I THINK THESE THINGS ARE GONNA BREACH THE MOLE, CHRISTIE.
AND I JUST GAVE HER A NEW COAT OF WAX.
KRANNNKK
THIS CAN'T BE A COINCIDENCE, LANTERN. THESE THINGS ARE MADE OF EARTH.
I KNOW.
STAND BACK.
FWOOSH
NICE ONE, ALAN.
GIVES A WHOLE NEW MEANIN' TO THE TERM--

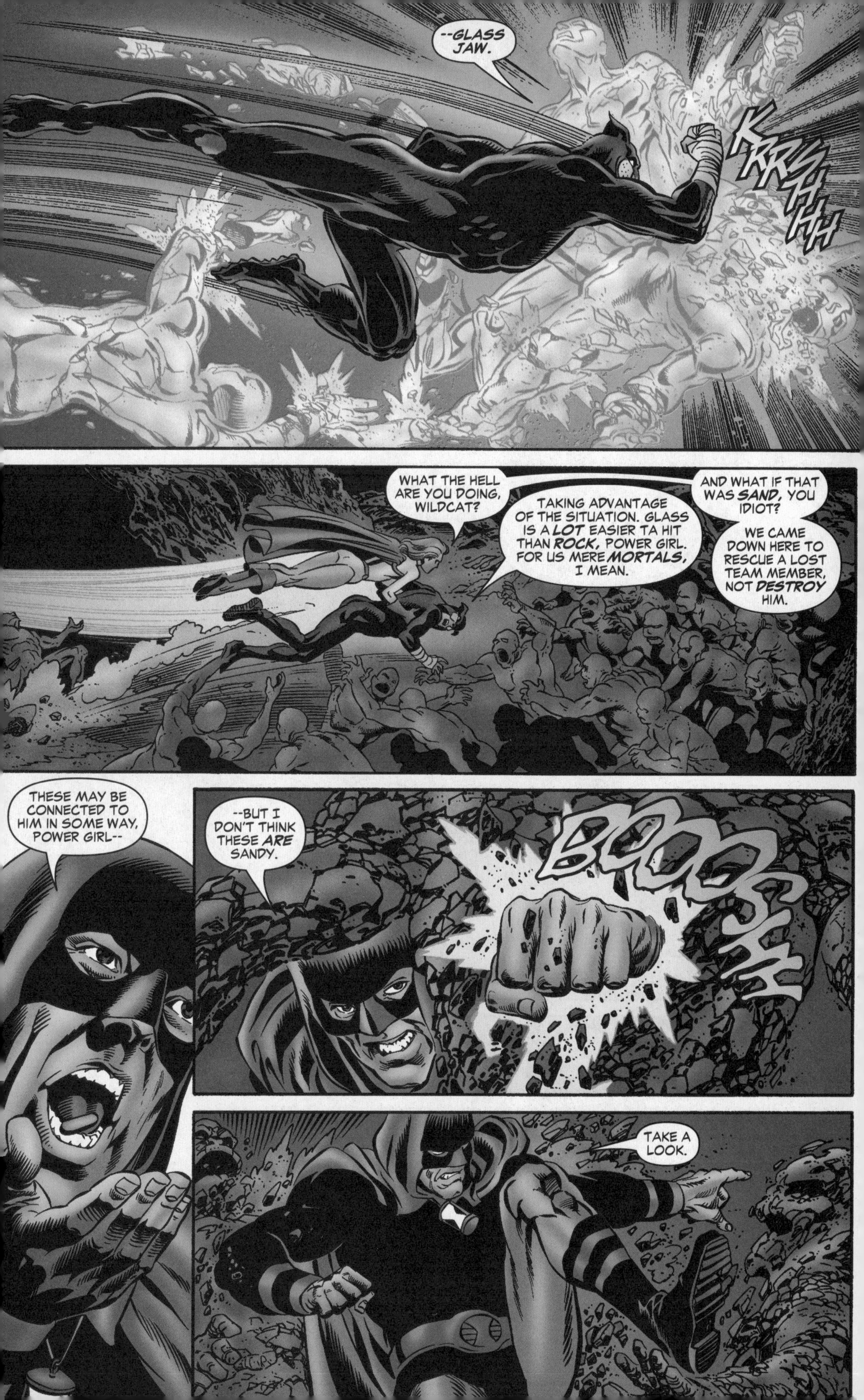
--GLASS JAW.
KRRSHHH
WHAT THE HELL ARE YOU DOING, WILDCAT?
TAKING ADVANTAGE OF THE SITUATION. GLASS IS A LOT EASIER TA HIT THAN ROCK, POWER GIRL. FOR US MERE MORTALS, I MEAN.
AND WHAT IF THAT WAS SAND, YOU IDIOT?
WE CAME DOWN HERE TO RESCUE A LOST TEAM MEMBER, NOT DESTROY HIM.
THESE MAY BE CONNECTED TO HIM IN SOME WAY, POWER GIRL--
--BUT I DON'T THINK THESE ARE SANDY.
BOOOSCHH
TAKE A LOOK.

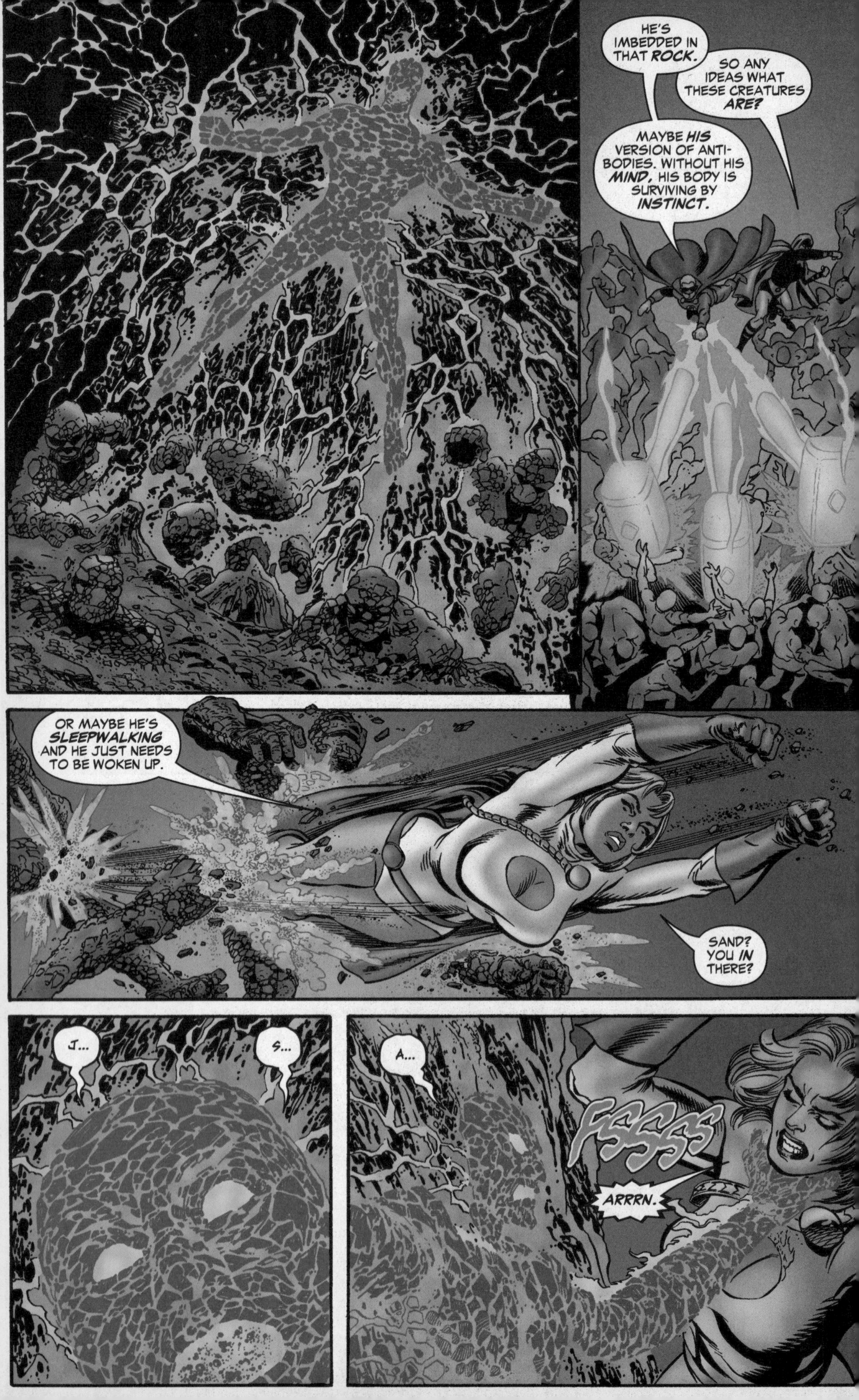
HE'S IMBEDDED IN THAT ROCK.
SO ANY IDEAS WHAT THESE CREATURES ARE?
MAYBE HIS VERSION OF ANTI-BODIES. WITHOUT HIS MIND, HIS BODY IS SURVIVING BY INSTINCT.
OR MAYBE HE'S SLEEPWALKING AND HE JUST NEEDS TO BE WOKEN UP.
SAND? YOU IN THERE?
J...
S...
A...
FSSSS
ARRRN.

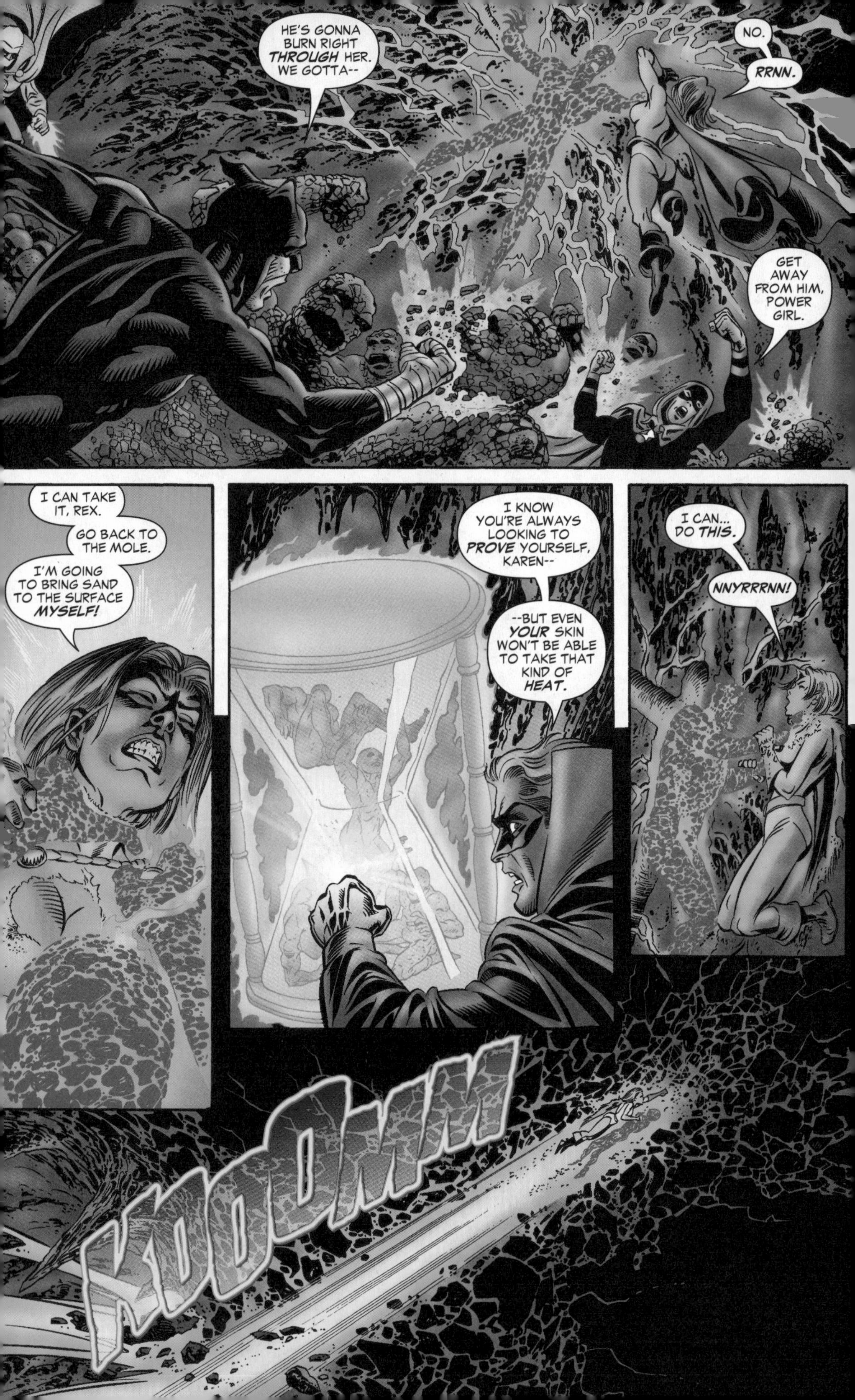
HE'S GONNA BURN RIGHT *THROUGH* HER. WE GOTTA--
NO.
*RRNN.*
GET AWAY FROM HIM, POWER GIRL.
I CAN TAKE IT, REX.
GO BACK TO THE MOLE.
I'M GOING TO BRING SAND TO THE SURFACE *MYSELF!*
I KNOW YOU'RE ALWAYS LOOKING TO *PROVE* YOURSELF, KAREN--
--BUT EVEN *YOUR* SKIN WON'T BE ABLE TO TAKE THAT KIND OF *HEAT*.
I CAN... DO *THIS*.
*NNYRRRNN!*
KROOMM

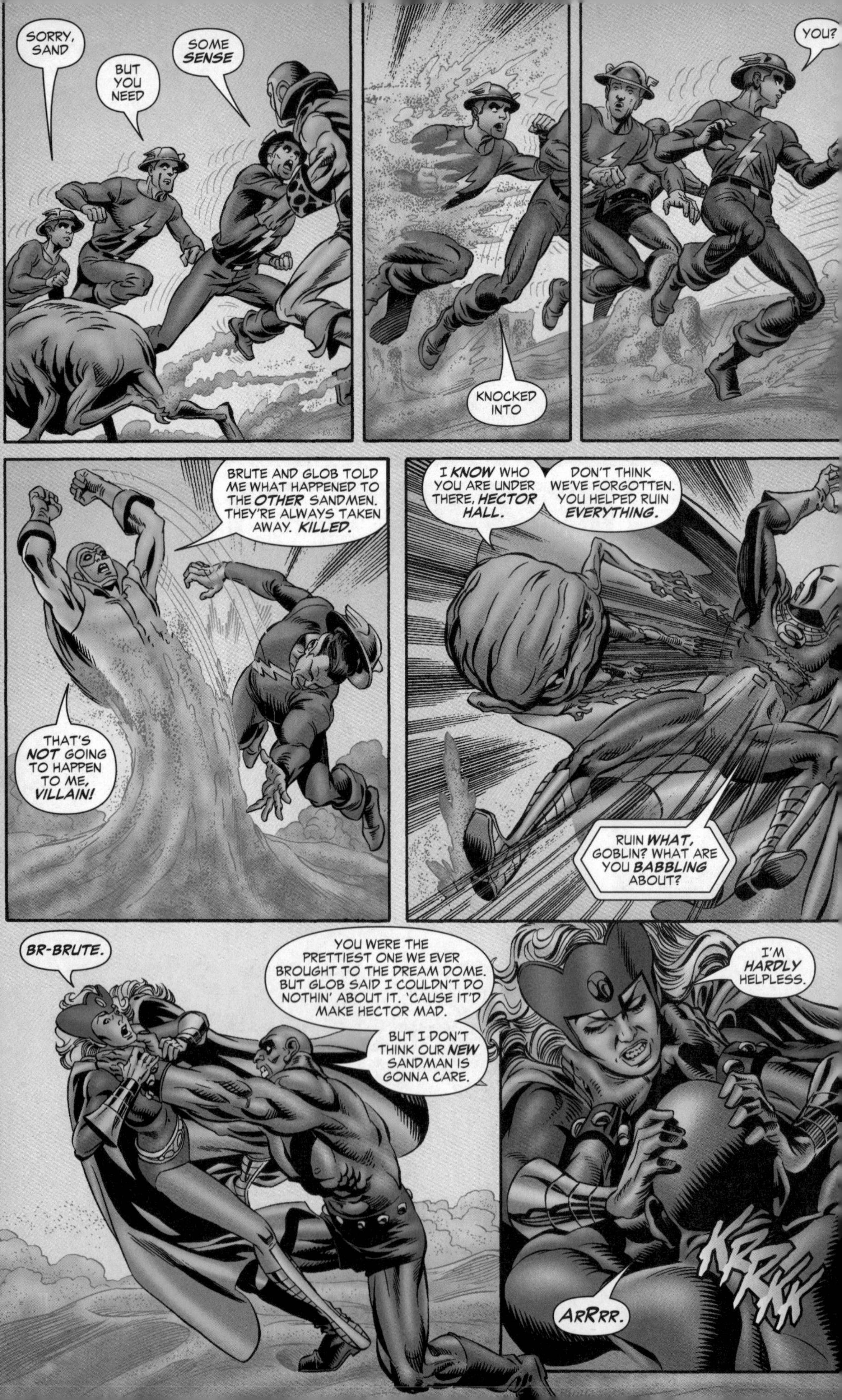
SORRY, SAND
BUT YOU NEED
SOME *SENSE*
KNOCKED INTO
YOU?
BRUTE AND GLOB TOLD ME WHAT HAPPENED TO THE *OTHER* SANDMEN. THEY'RE ALWAYS TAKEN AWAY. *KILLED.*
THAT'S *NOT* GOING TO HAPPEN TO ME, *VILLAIN!*
I *KNOW* WHO YOU ARE UNDER THERE, *HECTOR HALL.*
DON'T THINK WE'VE FORGOTTEN. YOU HELPED RUIN *EVERYTHING.*
RUIN *WHAT,* GOBLIN? WHAT ARE YOU *BABBLING* ABOUT?
*BR-BRUTE.*
YOU WERE THE PRETTIEST ONE WE EVER BROUGHT TO THE DREAM DOME. BUT GLOB SAID I COULDN'T DO NOTHIN' ABOUT IT. 'CAUSE IT'D MAKE HECTOR MAD.
BUT I DON'T THINK OUR *NEW* SANDMAN IS GONNA CARE.
I'M *HARDLY* HELPLESS.
KRRKK
*ARRRR.*

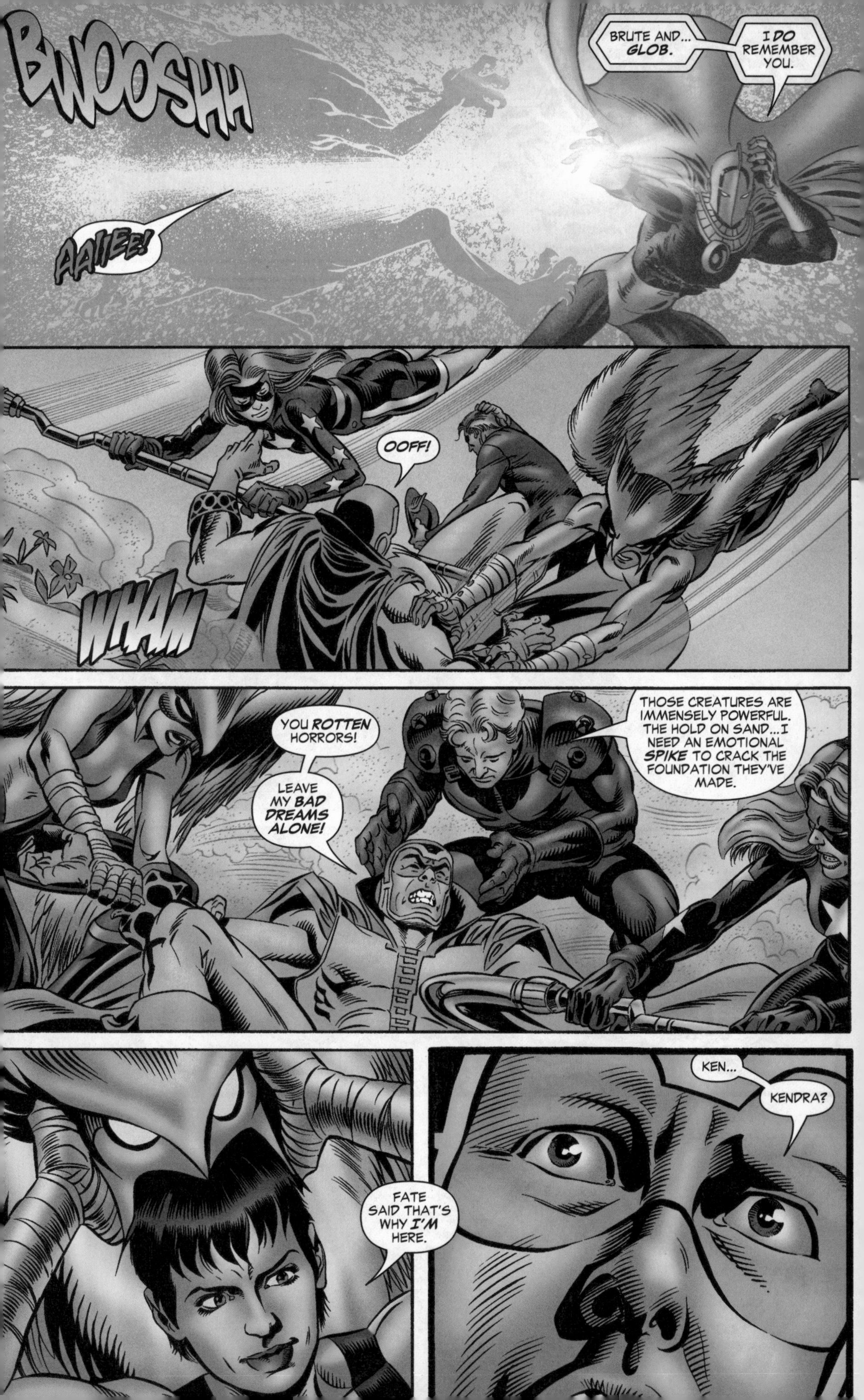
BWOOSHH
BRUTE AND... GLOB.
I DO REMEMBER YOU.
AAIIEE!
OOFF!
WHAM
YOU ROTTEN HORRORS!
LEAVE MY BAD DREAMS ALONE!
THOSE CREATURES ARE IMMENSELY POWERFUL. THE HOLD ON SAND...I NEED AN EMOTIONAL SPIKE TO CRACK THE FOUNDATION THEY'VE MADE.
FATE SAID THAT'S WHY I'M HERE.
KEN...
KENDRA?

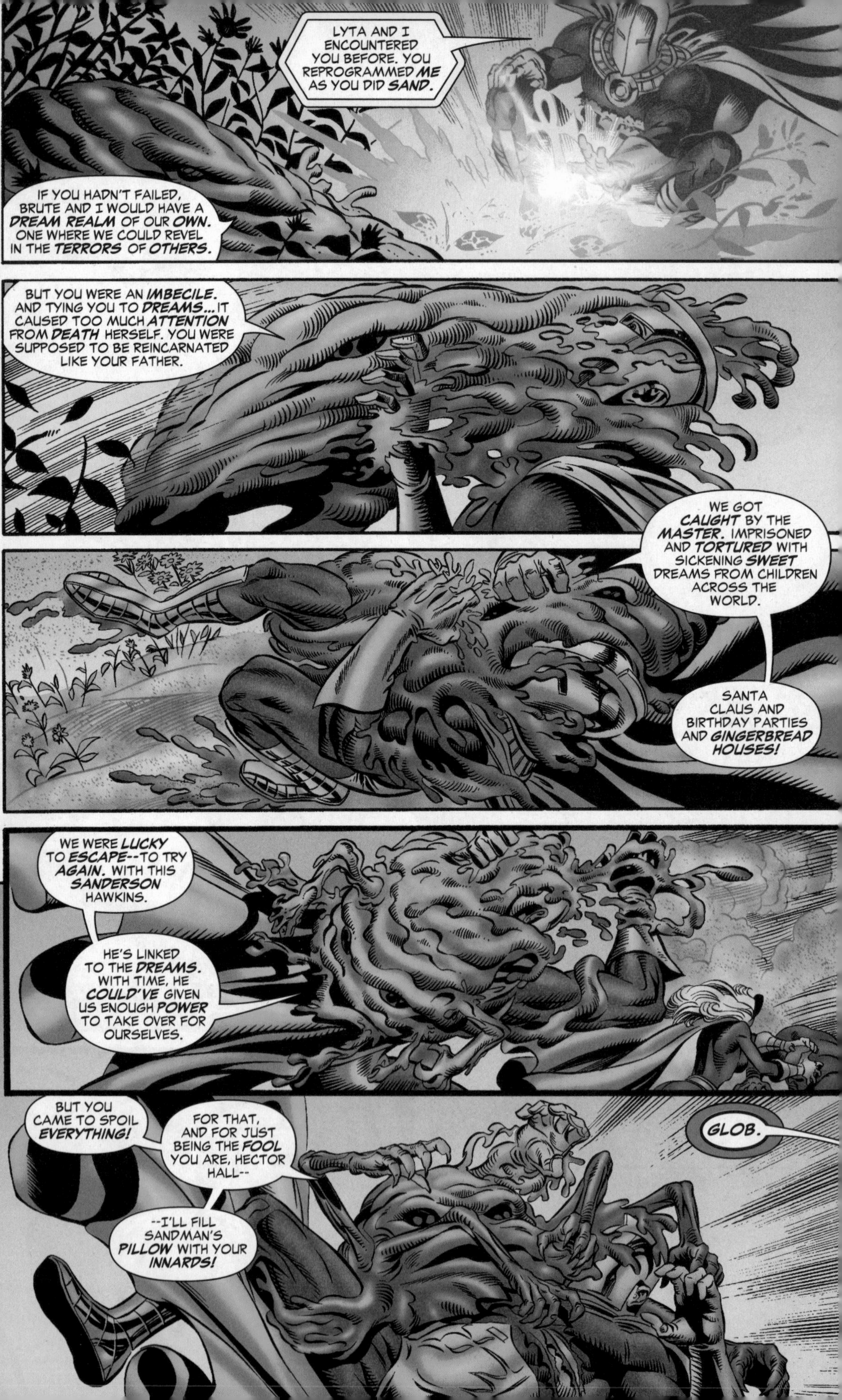
LYTA AND I ENCOUNTERED YOU BEFORE. YOU REPROGRAMMED ME AS YOU DID SAND.
IF YOU HADN'T FAILED, BRUTE AND I WOULD HAVE A DREAM REALM OF OUR OWN. ONE WHERE WE COULD REVEL IN THE TERRORS OF OTHERS.
BUT YOU WERE AN IMBECILE. AND TYING YOU TO DREAMS... IT CAUSED TOO MUCH ATTENTION FROM DEATH HERSELF. YOU WERE SUPPOSED TO BE REINCARNATED LIKE YOUR FATHER.
WE GOT CAUGHT BY THE MASTER. IMPRISONED AND TORTURED WITH SICKENING SWEET DREAMS FROM CHILDREN ACROSS THE WORLD.
SANTA CLAUS AND BIRTHDAY PARTIES AND GINGERBREAD HOUSES!
WE WERE LUCKY TO ESCAPE--TO TRY AGAIN. WITH THIS SANDERSON HAWKINS.
HE'S LINKED TO THE DREAMS. WITH TIME, HE COULD'VE GIVEN US ENOUGH POWER TO TAKE OVER FOR OURSELVES.
BUT YOU CAME TO SPOIL EVERYTHING!
FOR THAT, AND FOR JUST BEING THE FOOL YOU ARE, HECTOR HALL--
--I'LL FILL SANDMAN'S PILLOW WITH YOUR INNARDS!
GLOB.

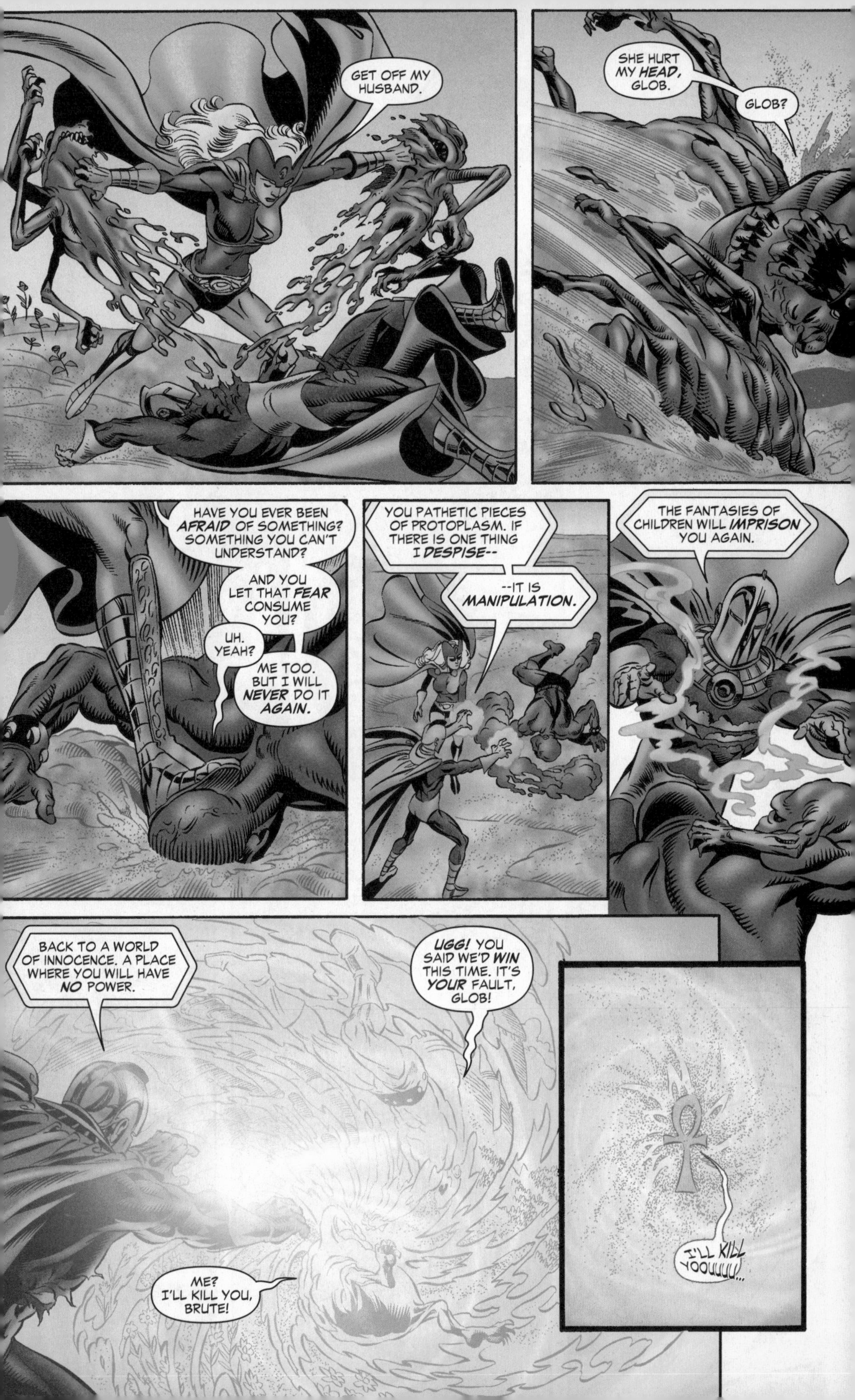
GET OFF MY HUSBAND.
SHE HURT MY HEAD, GLOB.
GLOB?
HAVE YOU EVER BEEN AFRAID OF SOMETHING? SOMETHING YOU CAN'T UNDERSTAND?
AND YOU LET THAT FEAR CONSUME YOU?
UH. YEAH?
ME TOO. BUT I WILL NEVER DO IT AGAIN.
YOU PATHETIC PIECES OF PROTOPLASM. IF THERE IS ONE THING I DESPISE--
--IT IS MANIPULATION.
THE FANTASIES OF CHILDREN WILL IMPRISON YOU AGAIN.
BACK TO A WORLD OF INNOCENCE. A PLACE WHERE YOU WILL HAVE NO POWER.
UGG! YOU SAID WE'D WIN THIS TIME. IT'S YOUR FAULT, GLOB!
ME? I'LL KILL YOU, BRUTE!
I'LL KILL YOOUUUU...

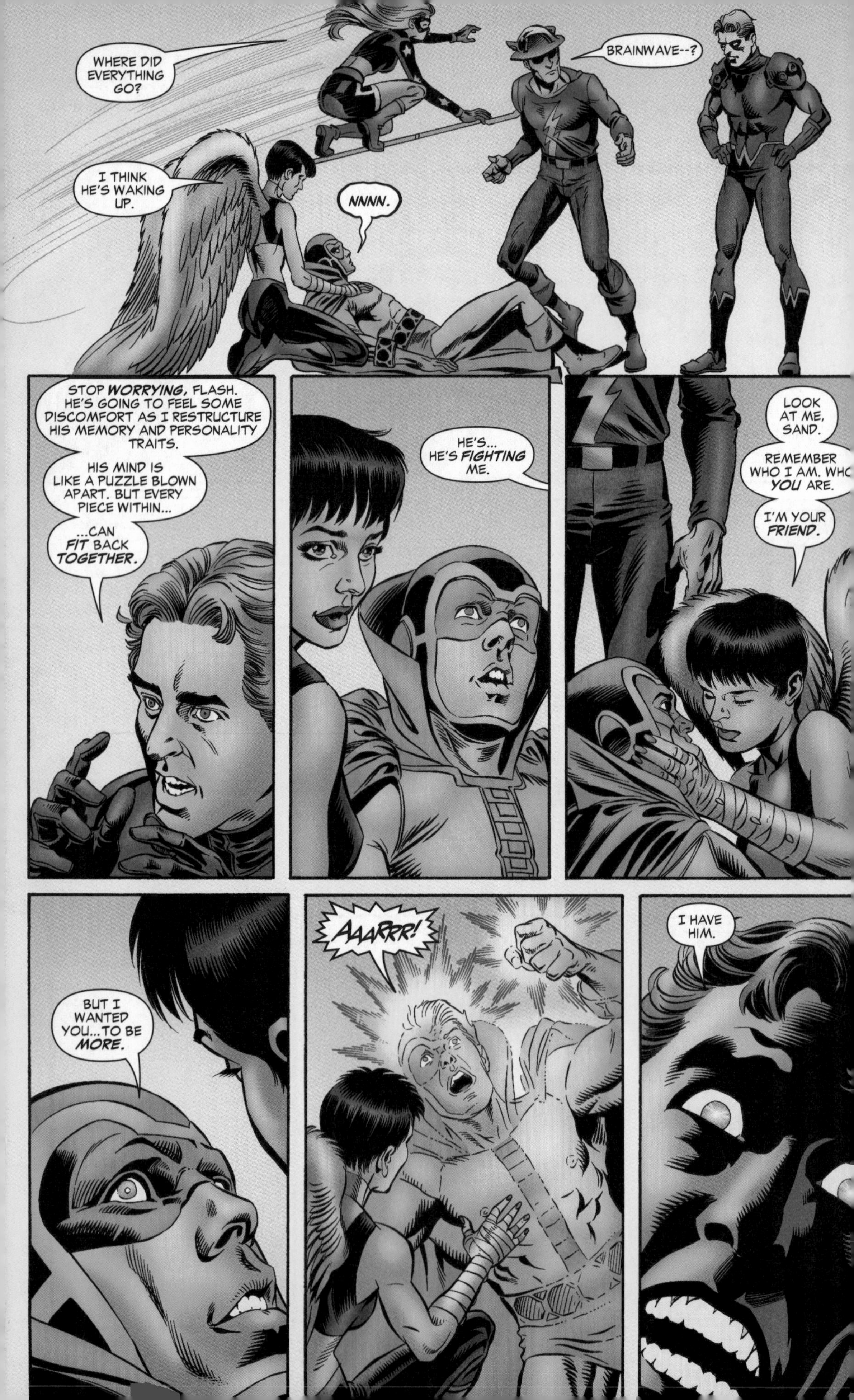
WHERE DID EVERYTHING GO?
BRAINWAVE--?
I THINK HE'S WAKING UP.
NNNN.
STOP WORRYING, FLASH. HE'S GOING TO FEEL SOME DISCOMFORT AS I RESTRUCTURE HIS MEMORY AND PERSONALITY TRAITS.
HIS MIND IS LIKE A PUZZLE BLOWN APART. BUT EVERY PIECE WITHIN...
...CAN FIT BACK TOGETHER.
HE'S... HE'S FIGHTING ME.
LOOK AT ME, SAND.
REMEMBER WHO I AM. WHO YOU ARE.
I'M YOUR FRIEND.
BUT I WANTED YOU...TO BE MORE.
AAARRR!
I HAVE HIM.

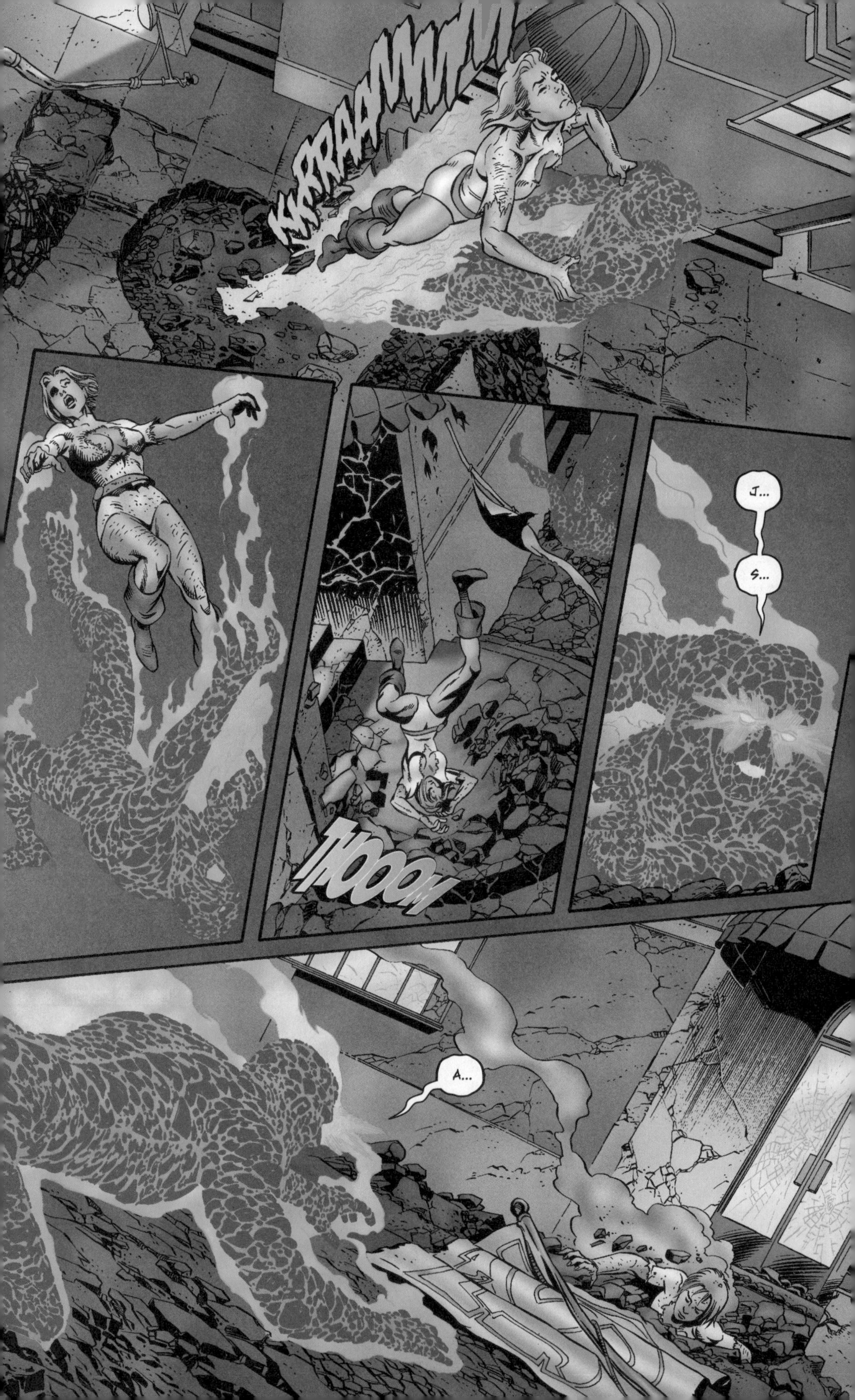
KRRAAMMM
THOOOM
J...
S...
A...

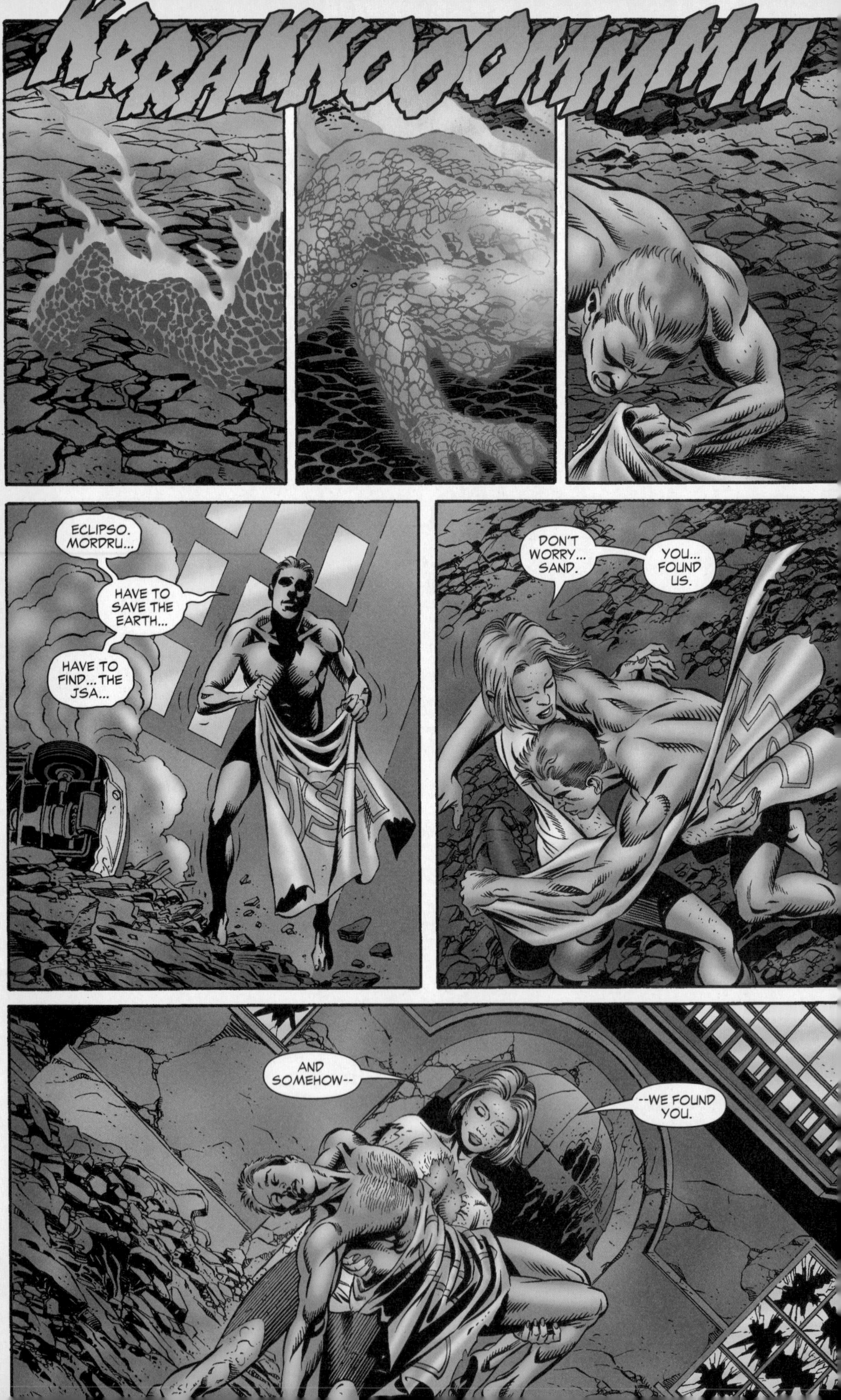
KRRAKKOOOOMMMMM
ECLIPSO. MORDRU...
HAVE TO SAVE THE EARTH...
HAVE TO FIND... THE JSA...
DON'T WORRY... SAND.
YOU... FOUND US.
AND SOMEHOW--
--WE FOUND YOU.

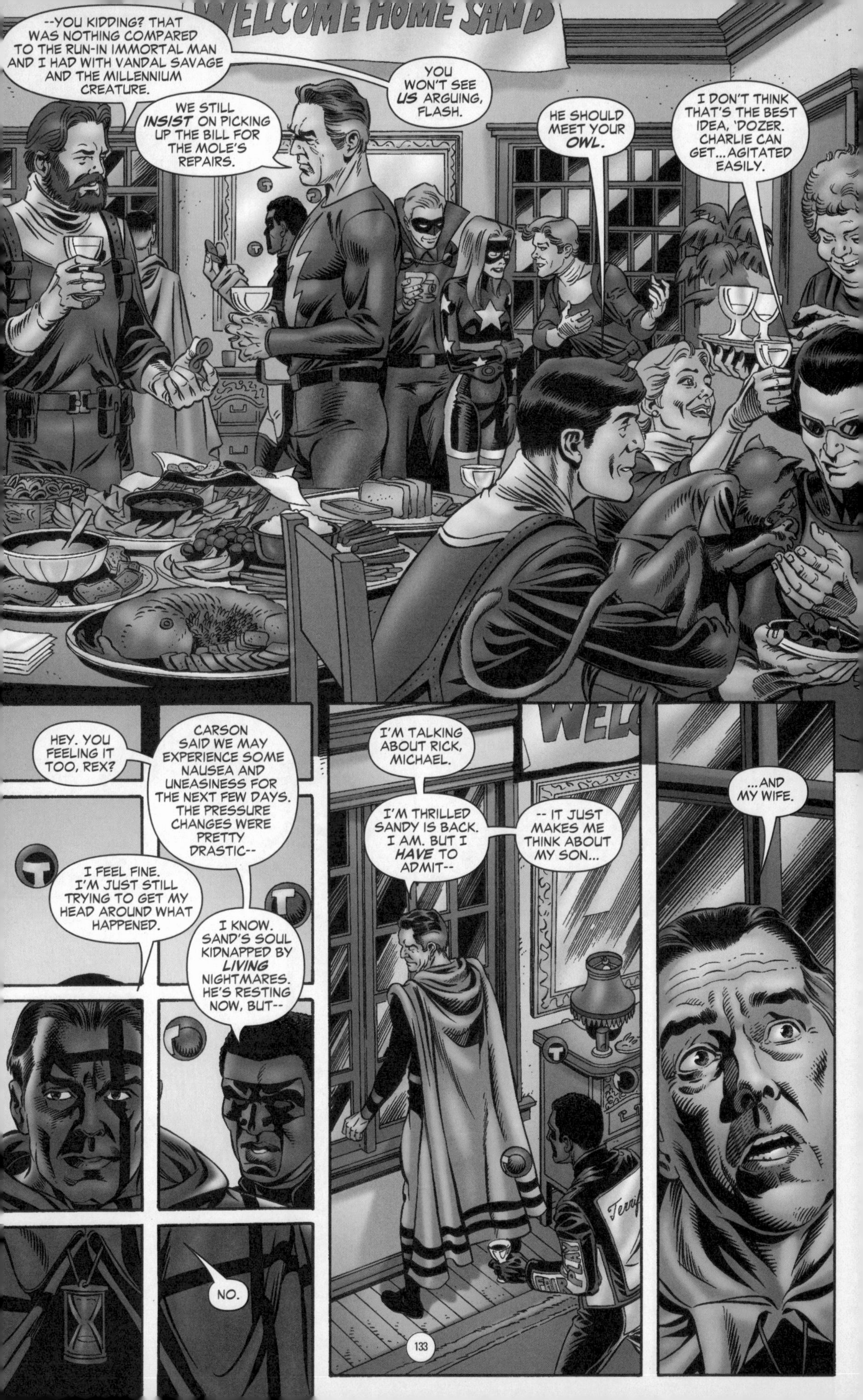
WELCOME HOME SAND
--YOU KIDDING? THAT WAS NOTHING COMPARED TO THE RUN-IN IMMORTAL MAN AND I HAD WITH VANDAL SAVAGE AND THE MILLENNIUM CREATURE.
YOU WON'T SEE US ARGUING, FLASH.
WE STILL INSIST ON PICKING UP THE BILL FOR THE MOLE'S REPAIRS.
HE SHOULD MEET YOUR OWL.
I DON'T THINK THAT'S THE BEST IDEA, 'DOZER. CHARLIE CAN GET...AGITATED EASILY.
HEY. YOU FEELING IT TOO, REX?
CARSON SAID WE MAY EXPERIENCE SOME NAUSEA AND UNEASINESS FOR THE NEXT FEW DAYS. THE PRESSURE CHANGES WERE PRETTY DRASTIC--
I FEEL FINE. I'M JUST STILL TRYING TO GET MY HEAD AROUND WHAT HAPPENED.
I KNOW. SAND'S SOUL KIDNAPPED BY LIVING NIGHTMARES. HE'S RESTING NOW, BUT--
NO.
WELC
I'M TALKING ABOUT RICK, MICHAEL.
I'M THRILLED SANDY IS BACK. I AM. BUT I HAVE TO ADMIT--
-- IT JUST MAKES ME THINK ABOUT MY SON...
...AND MY WIFE.
FAIR PLAY

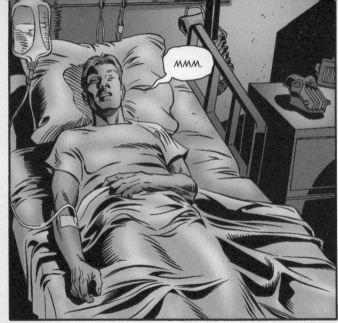

MMM.

SLEEPING BEAUTY LIVES.

KENDRA?

I'M SO GLAD YOU'RE BACK.

SAND?

SAND, ARE YOU AWAKE?

WHAT?

YOU SAID MY NAME. I WANTED TO MAKE SURE YOU WERE...

...YOU'RE BACK AT THE BROWNSTONE. EVERYONE'S CELEBRATING.

HAWKGIRL.

I HAD THE WEIRDEST DREAM.

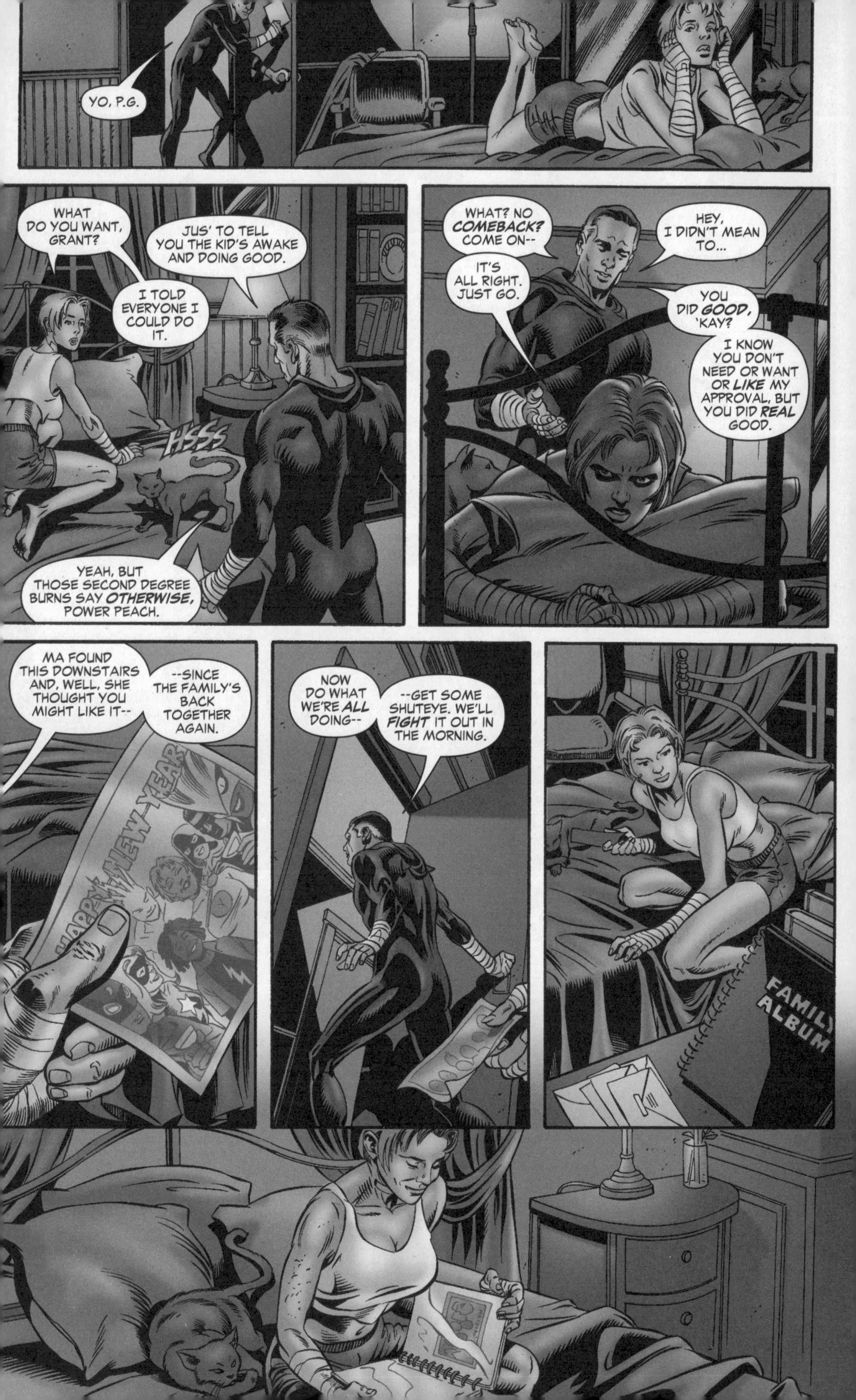

YO, P.G.
WHAT DO YOU WANT, GRANT?
JUS' TO TELL YOU THE KID'S AWAKE AND DOING GOOD.
I TOLD EVERYONE I COULD DO IT.
HSSS
YEAH, BUT THOSE SECOND DEGREE BURNS SAY OTHERWISE, POWER PEACH.
WHAT? NO COMEBACK? COME ON--
HEY, I DIDN'T MEAN TO...
IT'S ALL RIGHT. JUST GO.
YOU DID GOOD, 'KAY?
I KNOW YOU DON'T NEED OR WANT OR LIKE MY APPROVAL, BUT YOU DID REAL GOOD.
MA FOUND THIS DOWNSTAIRS AND, WELL, SHE THOUGHT YOU MIGHT LIKE IT--
--SINCE THE FAMILY'S BACK TOGETHER AGAIN.
HAPPY NEW YEAR
NOW DO WHAT WE'RE ALL DOING--
--GET SOME SHUTEYE. WE'LL FIGHT IT OUT IN THE MORNING.
FAMILY ALBUM

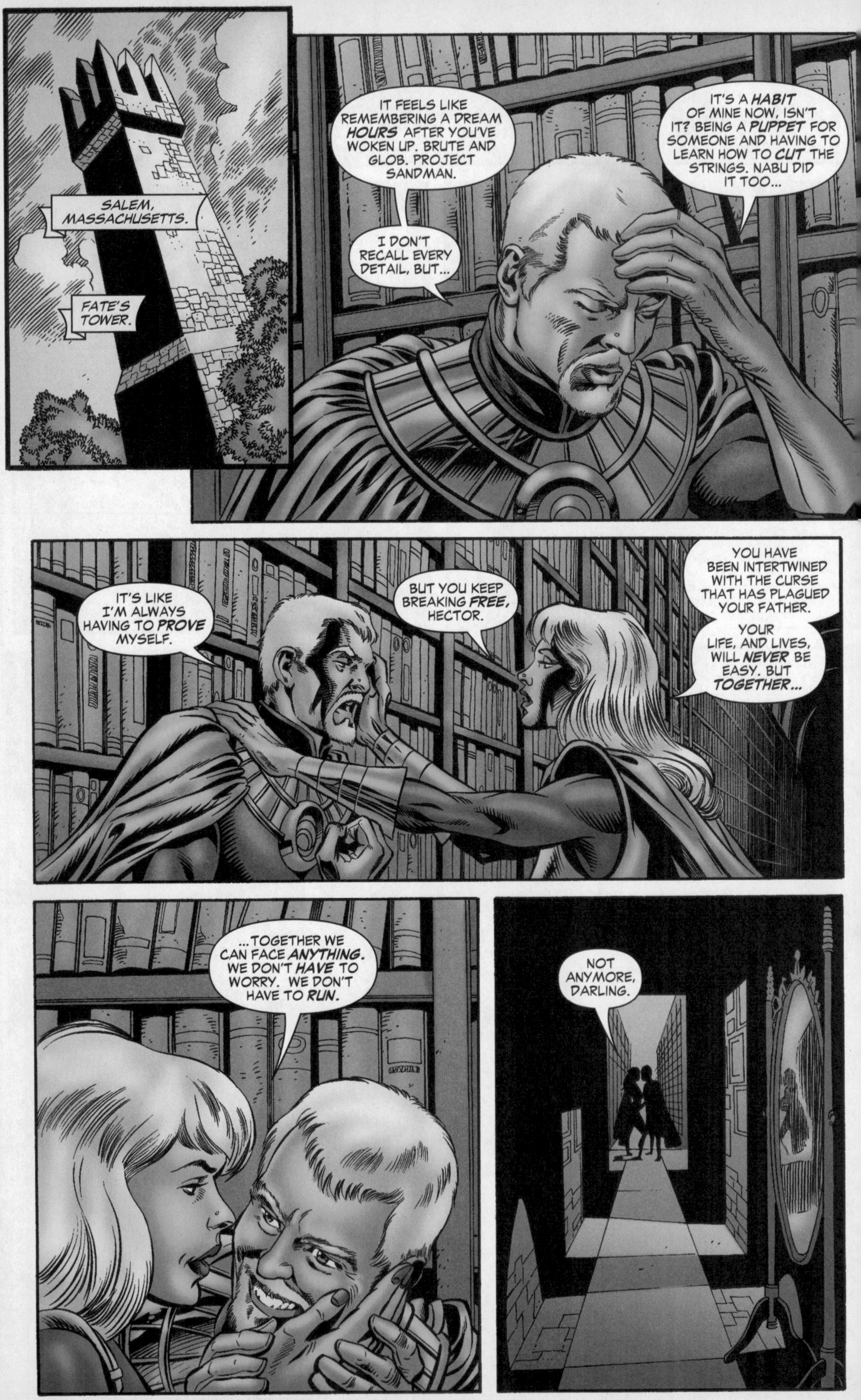
SALEM, MASSACHUSETTS.
FATE'S TOWER.
IT FEELS LIKE REMEMBERING A DREAM HOURS AFTER YOU'VE WOKEN UP. BRUTE AND GLOB. PROJECT SANDMAN.
I DON'T RECALL EVERY DETAIL, BUT...
IT'S A HABIT OF MINE NOW, ISN'T IT? BEING A PUPPET FOR SOMEONE AND HAVING TO LEARN HOW TO CUT THE STRINGS. NABU DID IT TOO...
IT'S LIKE I'M ALWAYS HAVING TO PROVE MYSELF.
BUT YOU KEEP BREAKING FREE, HECTOR.
YOU HAVE BEEN INTERTWINED WITH THE CURSE THAT HAS PLAGUED YOUR FATHER.
YOUR LIFE, AND LIVES, WILL NEVER BE EASY. BUT TOGETHER...
...TOGETHER WE CAN FACE ANYTHING. WE DON'T HAVE TO WORRY. WE DON'T HAVE TO RUN.
NOT ANYMORE, DARLING.

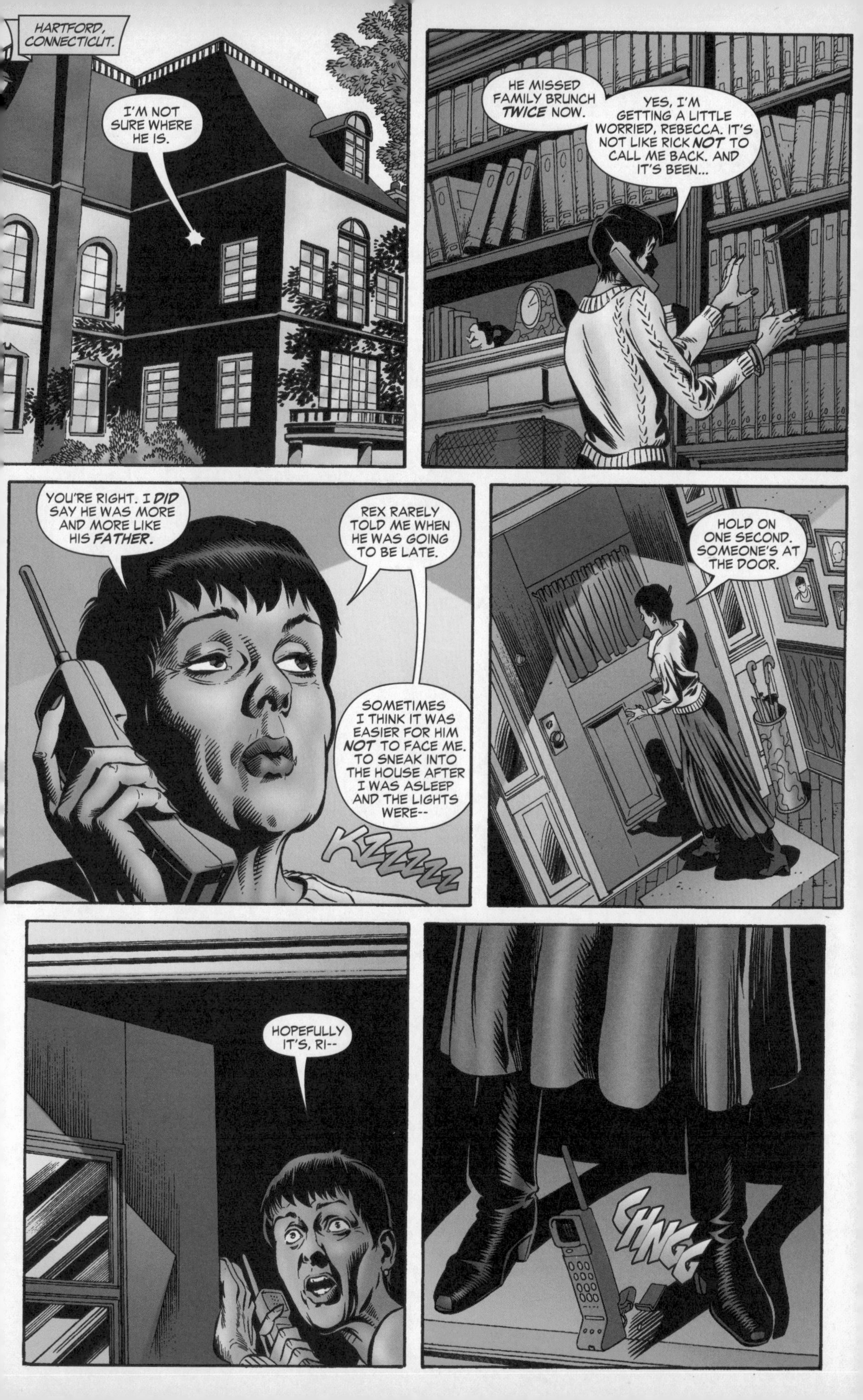
HARTFORD, CONNECTICUT.
I'M NOT SURE WHERE HE IS.
HE MISSED FAMILY BRUNCH TWICE NOW.
YES, I'M GETTING A LITTLE WORRIED, REBECCA. IT'S NOT LIKE RICK NOT TO CALL ME BACK. AND IT'S BEEN...
YOU'RE RIGHT. I DID SAY HE WAS MORE AND MORE LIKE HIS FATHER.
REX RARELY TOLD ME WHEN HE WAS GOING TO BE LATE.
SOMETIMES I THINK IT WAS EASIER FOR HIM NOT TO FACE ME. TO SNEAK INTO THE HOUSE AFTER I WAS ASLEEP AND THE LIGHTS WERE--
KZZZZZ
HOLD ON ONE SECOND. SOMEONE'S AT THE DOOR.
HOPEFULLY IT'S, RI--
CHNGG

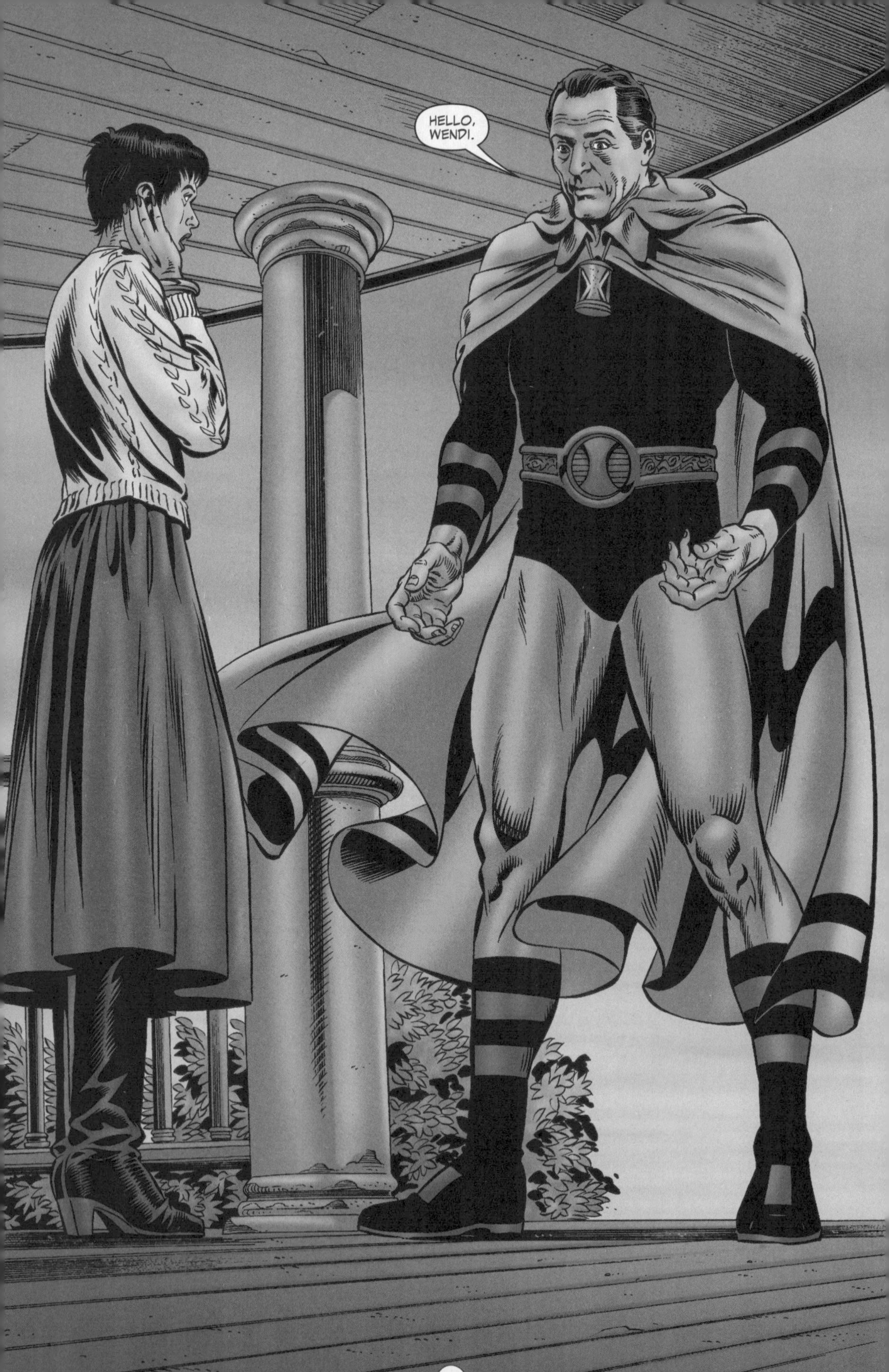
HELLO, WENDI.

JSA

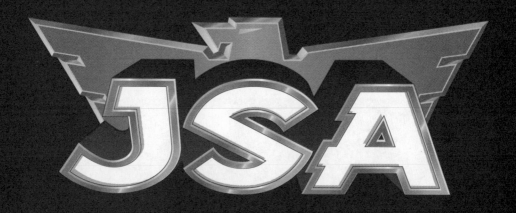

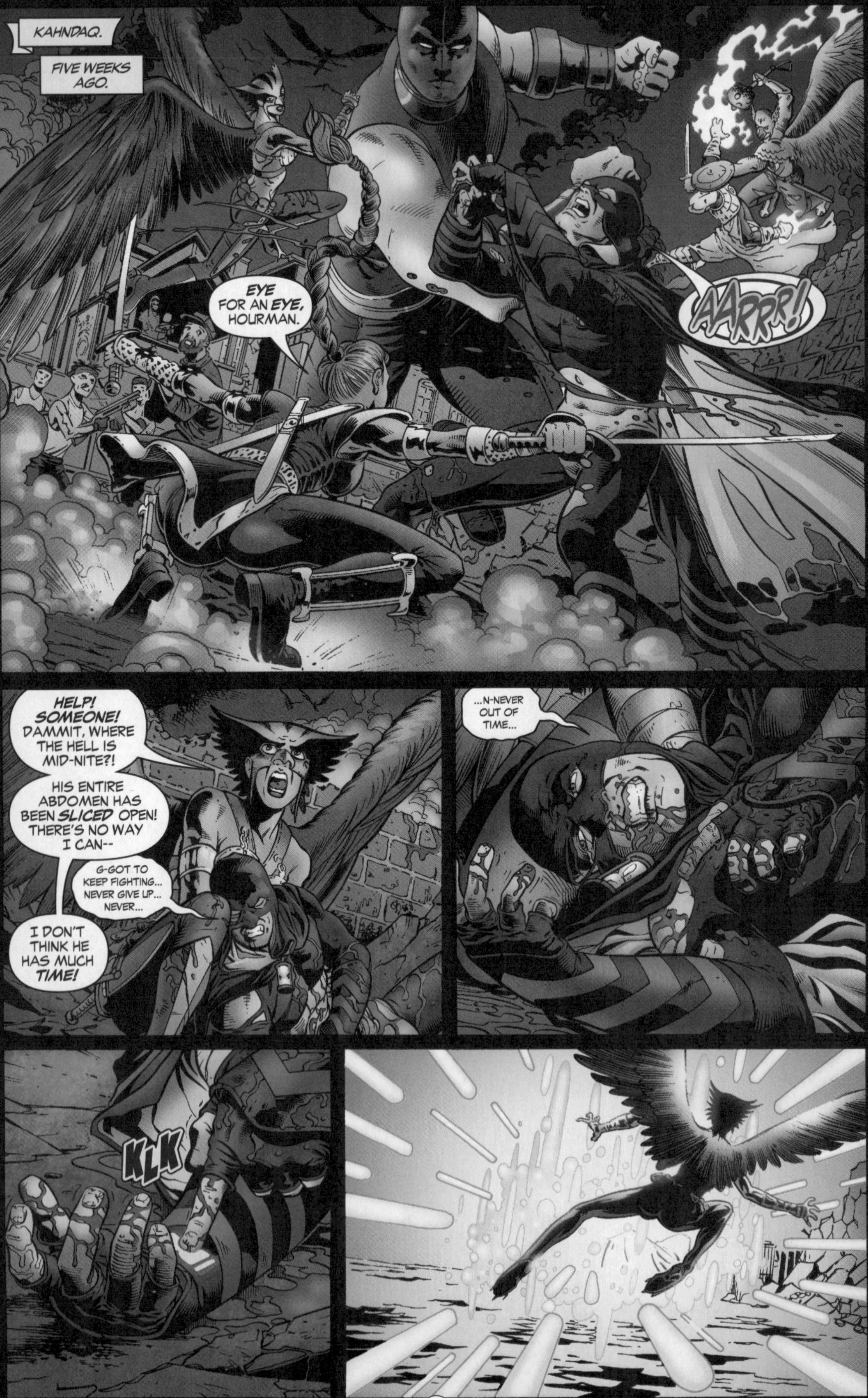
KAHNDAQ.
FIVE WEEKS AGO.
EYE FOR AN EYE, HOURMAN.
AARRR!
HELP! SOMEONE! DAMMIT, WHERE THE HELL IS MID-NITE?!
HIS ENTIRE ABDOMEN HAS BEEN SLICED OPEN! THERE'S NO WAY I CAN--
G-GOT TO KEEP FIGHTING... NEVER GIVE UP... NEVER...
I DON'T THINK HE HAS MUCH TIME!
...N-NEVER OUT OF TIME...
KLK

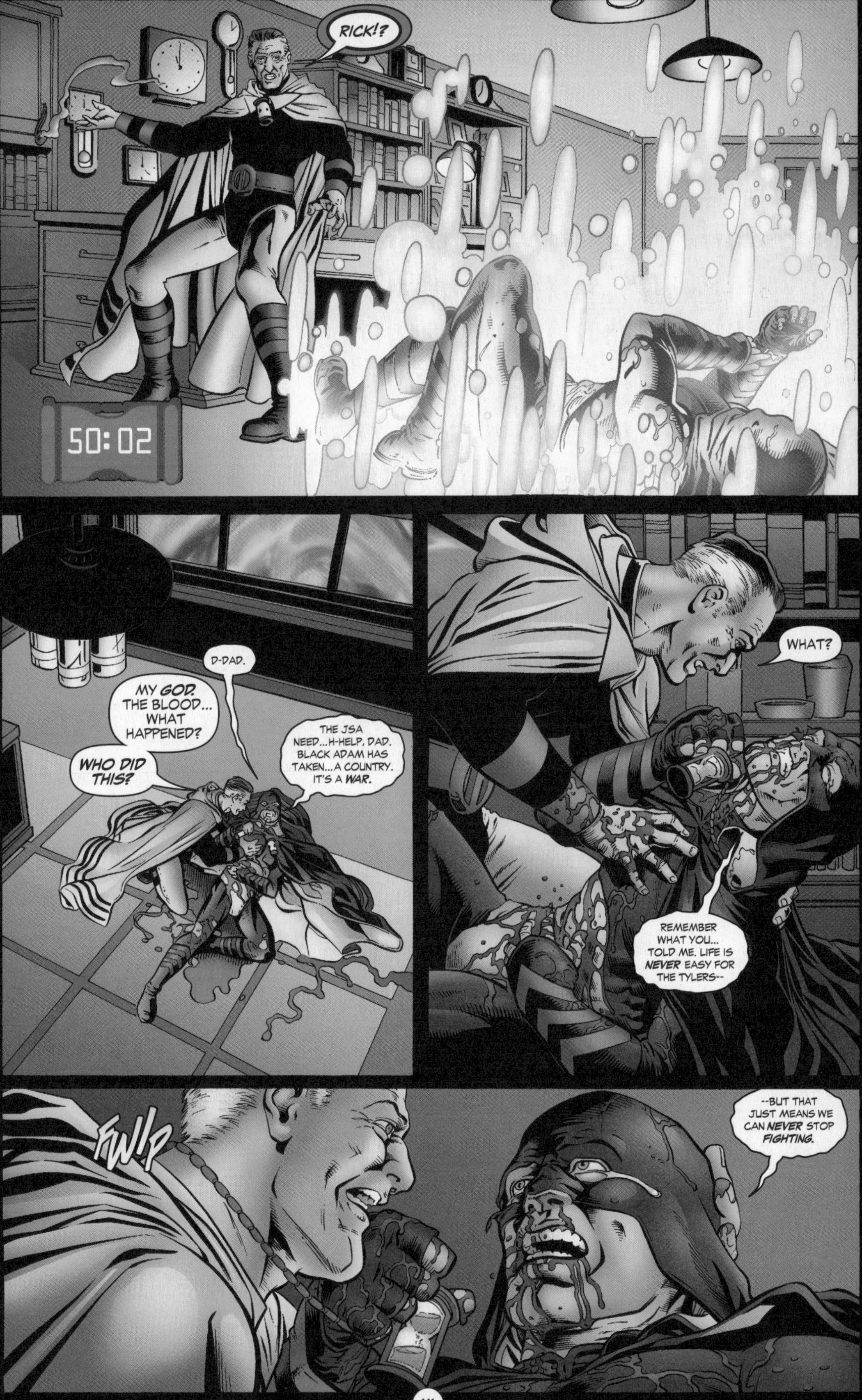
RICK!?
50:02
D-DAD.
MY GOD. THE BLOOD... WHAT HAPPENED?
WHO DID THIS?
THE JSA NEED...H-HELP, DAD. BLACK ADAM HAS TAKEN...A COUNTRY. IT'S A WAR.
WHAT?
REMEMBER WHAT YOU... TOLD ME. LIFE IS NEVER EASY FOR THE TYLERS--
FWIP
--BUT THAT JUST MEANS WE CAN NEVER STOP FIGHTING.

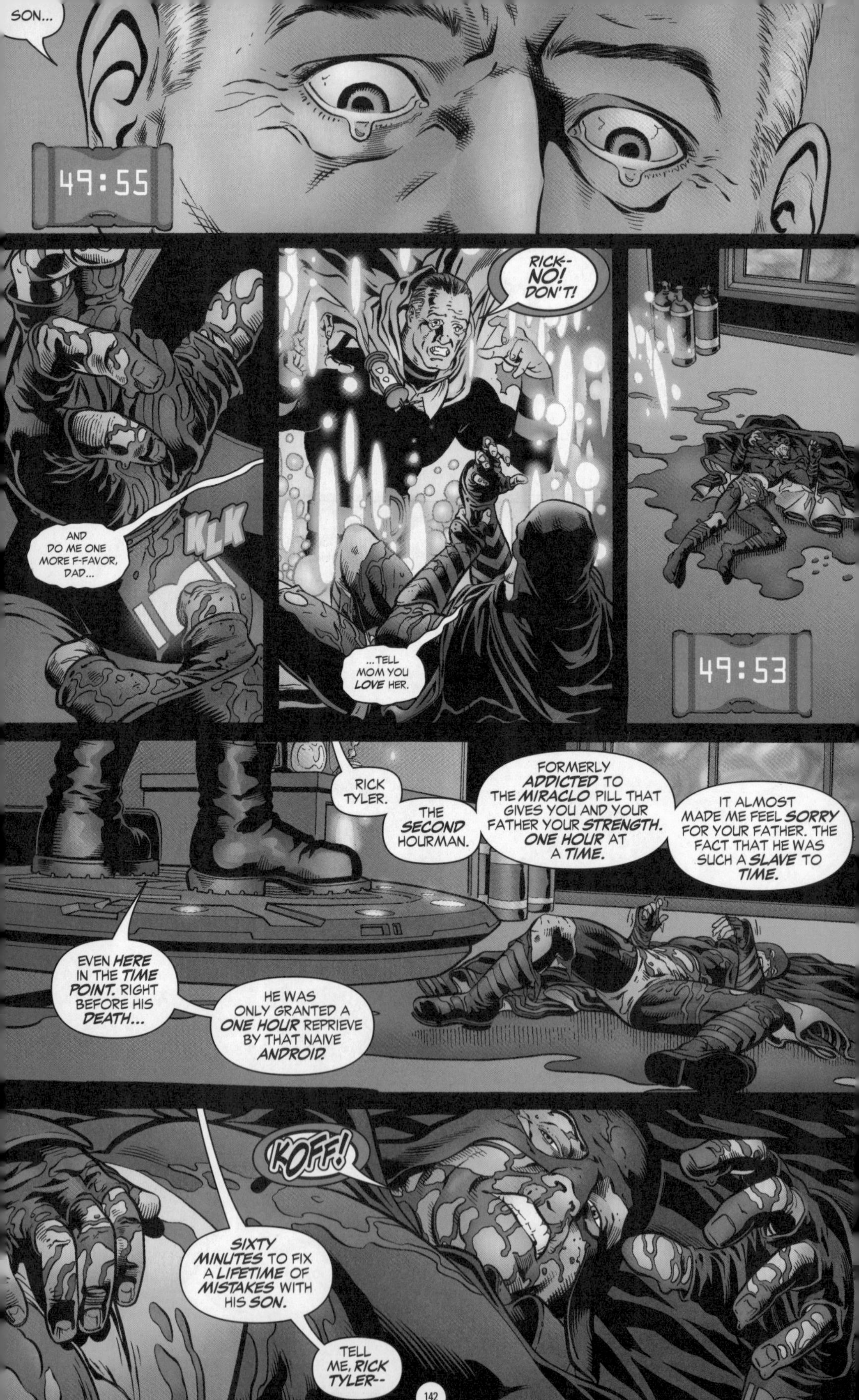
SON...
49:55
KLK
AND DO ME ONE MORE F-FAVOR, DAD...
RICK-NO! DON'T!
...TELL MOM YOU LOVE HER.
49:53
RICK TYLER.
THE SECOND HOURMAN.
FORMERLY ADDICTED TO THE MIRACLO PILL THAT GIVES YOU AND YOUR FATHER YOUR STRENGTH. ONE HOUR AT A TIME.
IT ALMOST MADE ME FEEL SORRY FOR YOUR FATHER. THE FACT THAT HE WAS SUCH A SLAVE TO TIME.
EVEN HERE IN THE TIME POINT. RIGHT BEFORE HIS DEATH...
HE WAS ONLY GRANTED A ONE HOUR REPRIEVE BY THAT NAIVE ANDROID.
KOFF!
SIXTY MINUTES TO FIX A LIFETIME OF MISTAKES WITH HIS SON.
TELL ME, RICK TYLER--

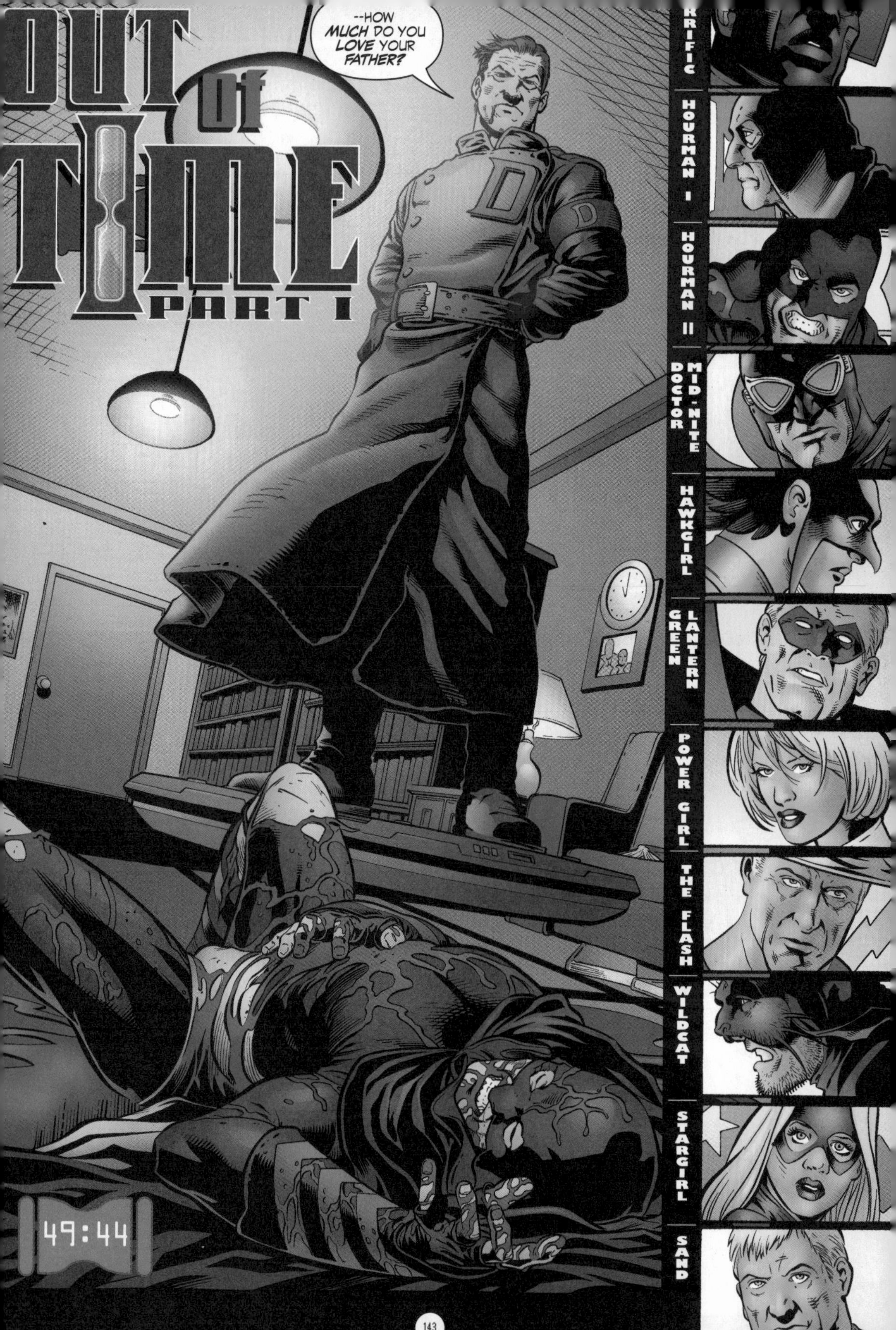

OUT of TIME
PART I
--HOW MUCH DO YOU LOVE YOUR FATHER?
49:44
RRIFIC
HOURMAN I
HOURMAN II
DOCTOR MID-NITE
HAWKGIRL
GREEN LANTERN
POWER GIRL
THE FLASH
WILDCAT
STARGIRL
SAND

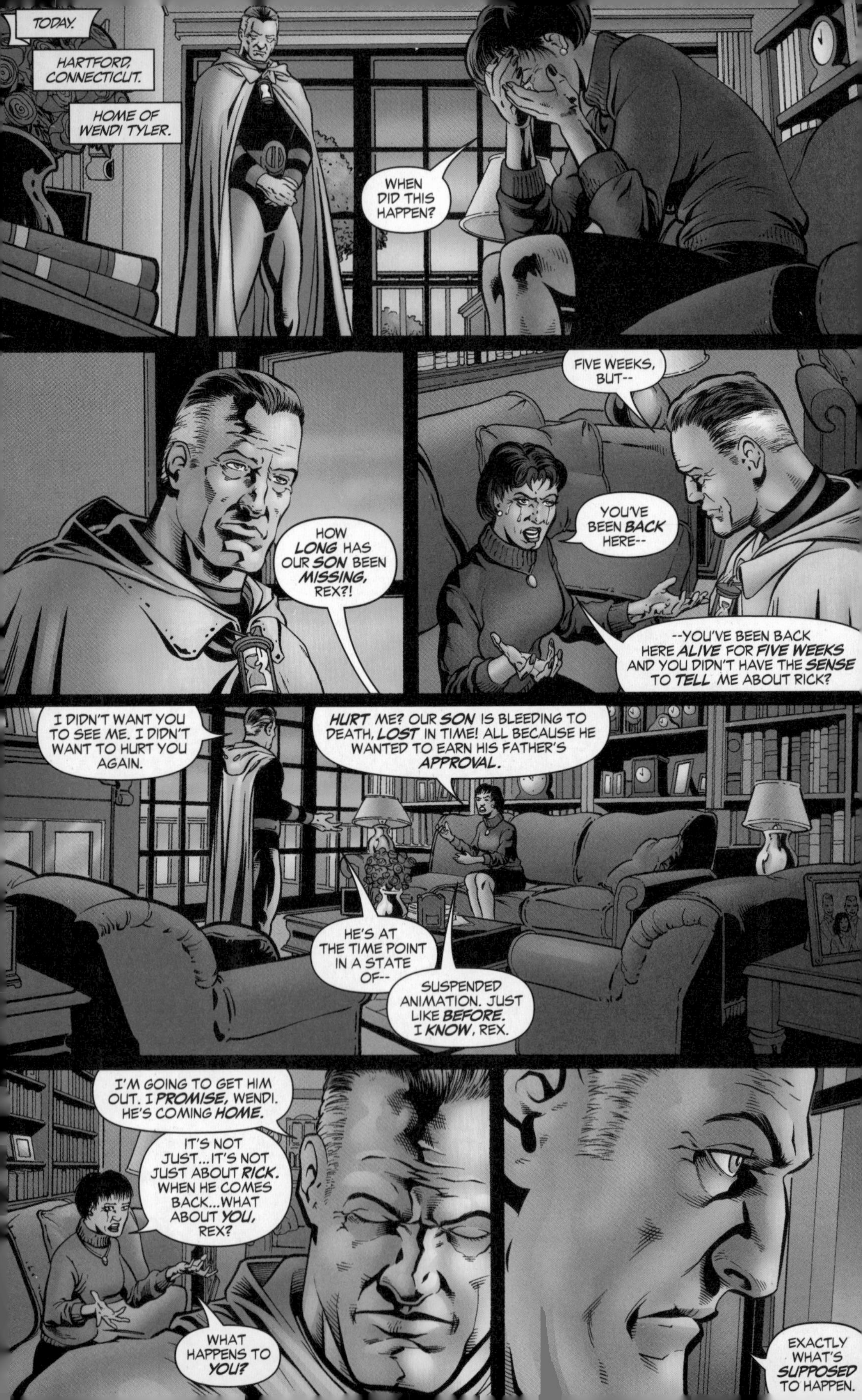
TODAY.
HARTFORD, CONNECTICUT.
HOME OF WENDI TYLER.
WHEN DID THIS HAPPEN?
HOW LONG HAS OUR SON BEEN MISSING, REX?!
FIVE WEEKS, BUT--
YOU'VE BEEN BACK HERE--
--YOU'VE BEEN BACK HERE ALIVE FOR FIVE WEEKS AND YOU DIDN'T HAVE THE SENSE TO TELL ME ABOUT RICK?
I DIDN'T WANT YOU TO SEE ME. I DIDN'T WANT TO HURT YOU AGAIN.
HURT ME? OUR SON IS BLEEDING TO DEATH, LOST IN TIME! ALL BECAUSE HE WANTED TO EARN HIS FATHER'S APPROVAL.
HE'S AT THE TIME POINT IN A STATE OF--
SUSPENDED ANIMATION. JUST LIKE BEFORE. I KNOW, REX.
I'M GOING TO GET HIM OUT. I PROMISE, WENDI. HE'S COMING HOME.
IT'S NOT JUST...IT'S NOT JUST ABOUT RICK. WHEN HE COMES BACK...WHAT ABOUT YOU, REX?
WHAT HAPPENS TO YOU?
EXACTLY WHAT'S SUPPOSED TO HAPPEN.

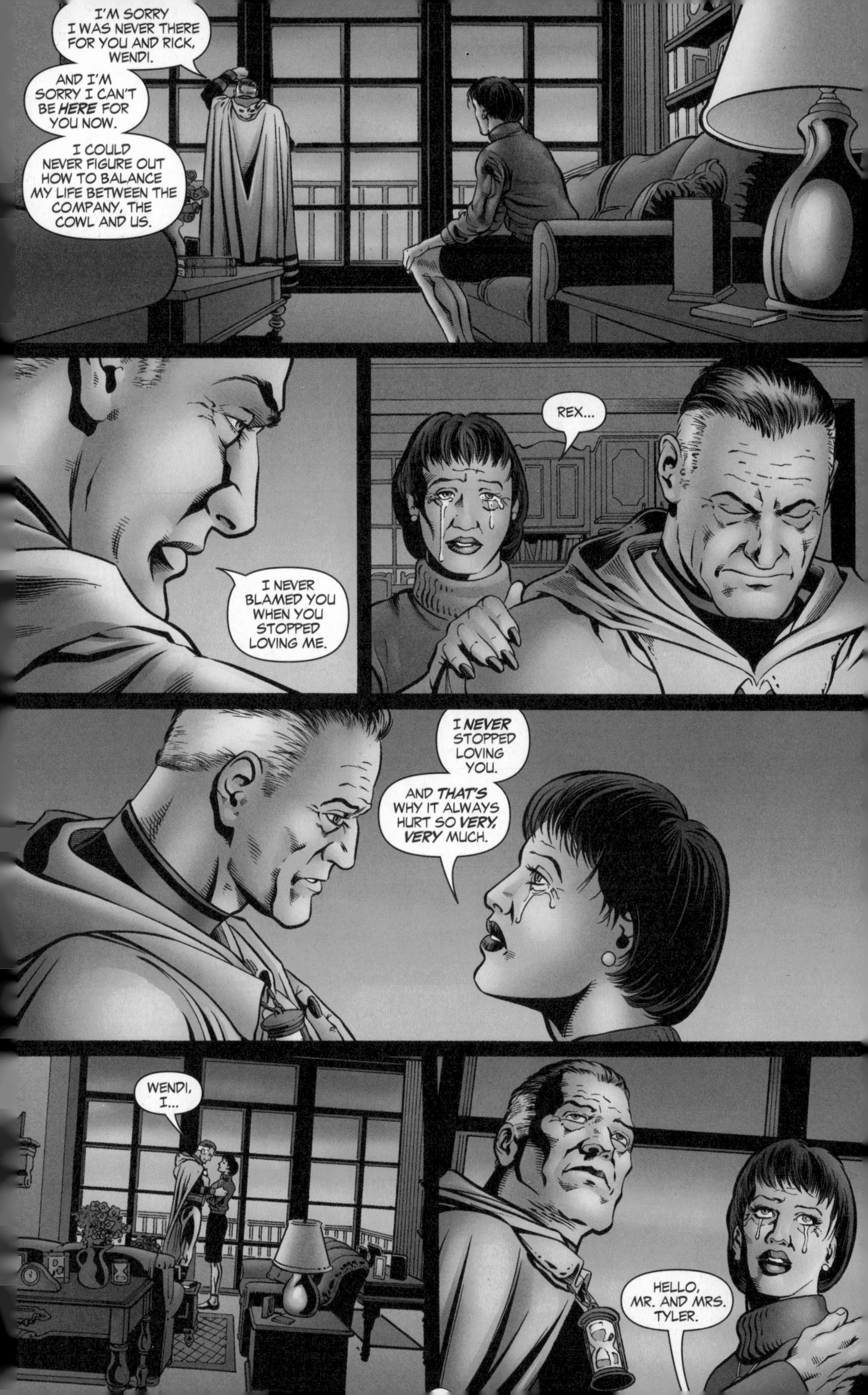
I'M SORRY I WAS NEVER THERE FOR YOU AND RICK, WENDI.
AND I'M SORRY I CAN'T BE **HERE** FOR YOU NOW.
I COULD NEVER FIGURE OUT HOW TO BALANCE MY LIFE BETWEEN THE COMPANY, THE COWL AND US.
I NEVER BLAMED YOU WHEN YOU STOPPED LOVING ME.
REX...
I **NEVER** STOPPED LOVING YOU.
AND **THAT'S** WHY IT ALWAYS HURT SO **VERY, VERY** MUCH.
WENDI, I...
HELLO, MR. AND MRS. TYLER.

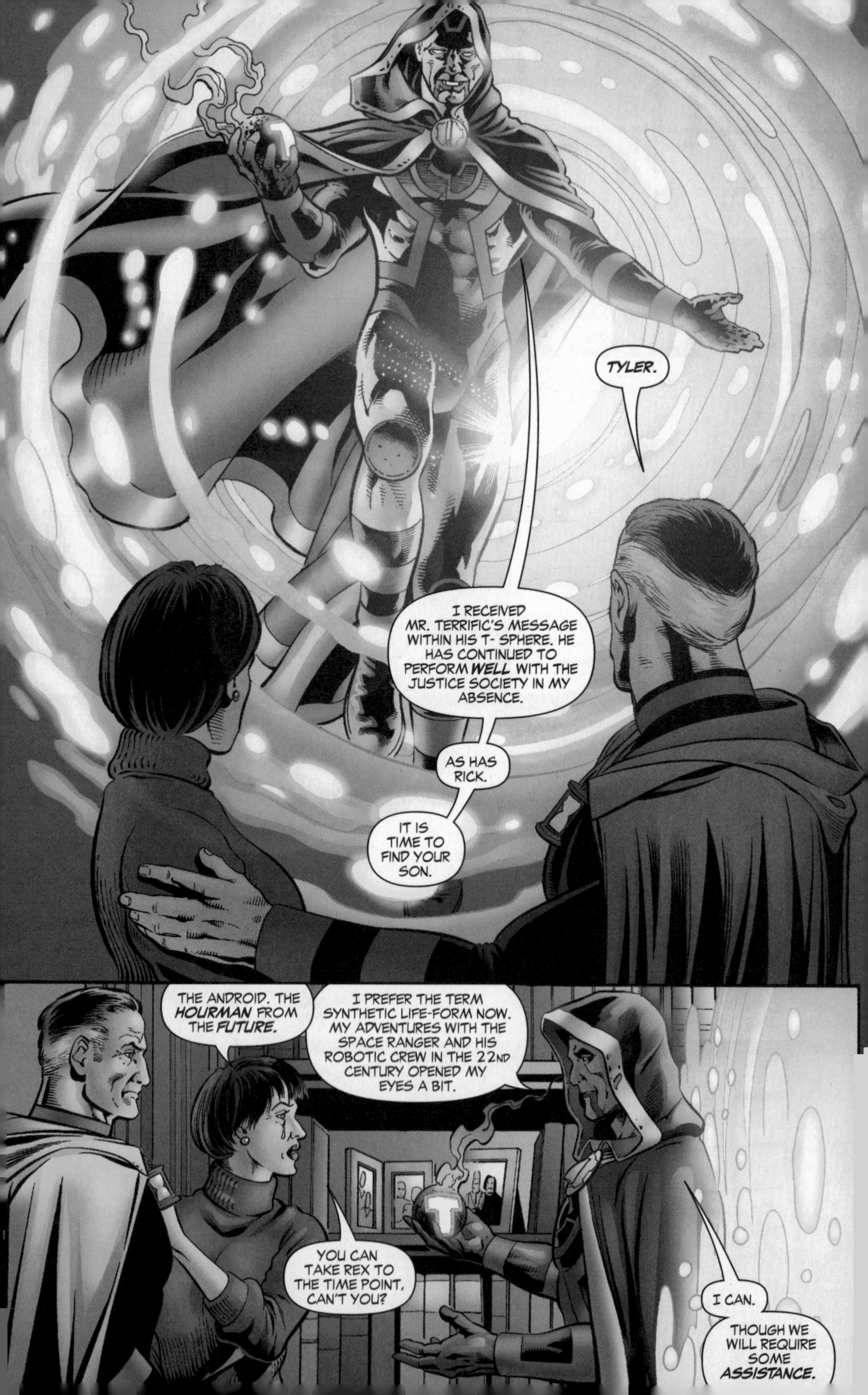
TYLER.
I RECEIVED MR. TERRIFIC'S MESSAGE WITHIN HIS T- SPHERE. HE HAS CONTINUED TO PERFORM WELL WITH THE JUSTICE SOCIETY IN MY ABSENCE.
AS HAS RICK.
IT IS TIME TO FIND YOUR SON.
THE ANDROID. THE HOURMAN FROM THE FUTURE.
I PREFER THE TERM SYNTHETIC LIFE-FORM NOW. MY ADVENTURES WITH THE SPACE RANGER AND HIS ROBOTIC CREW IN THE 22ND CENTURY OPENED MY EYES A BIT.
YOU CAN TAKE REX TO THE TIME POINT, CAN'T YOU?
I CAN.
THOUGH WE WILL REQUIRE SOME ASSISTANCE.

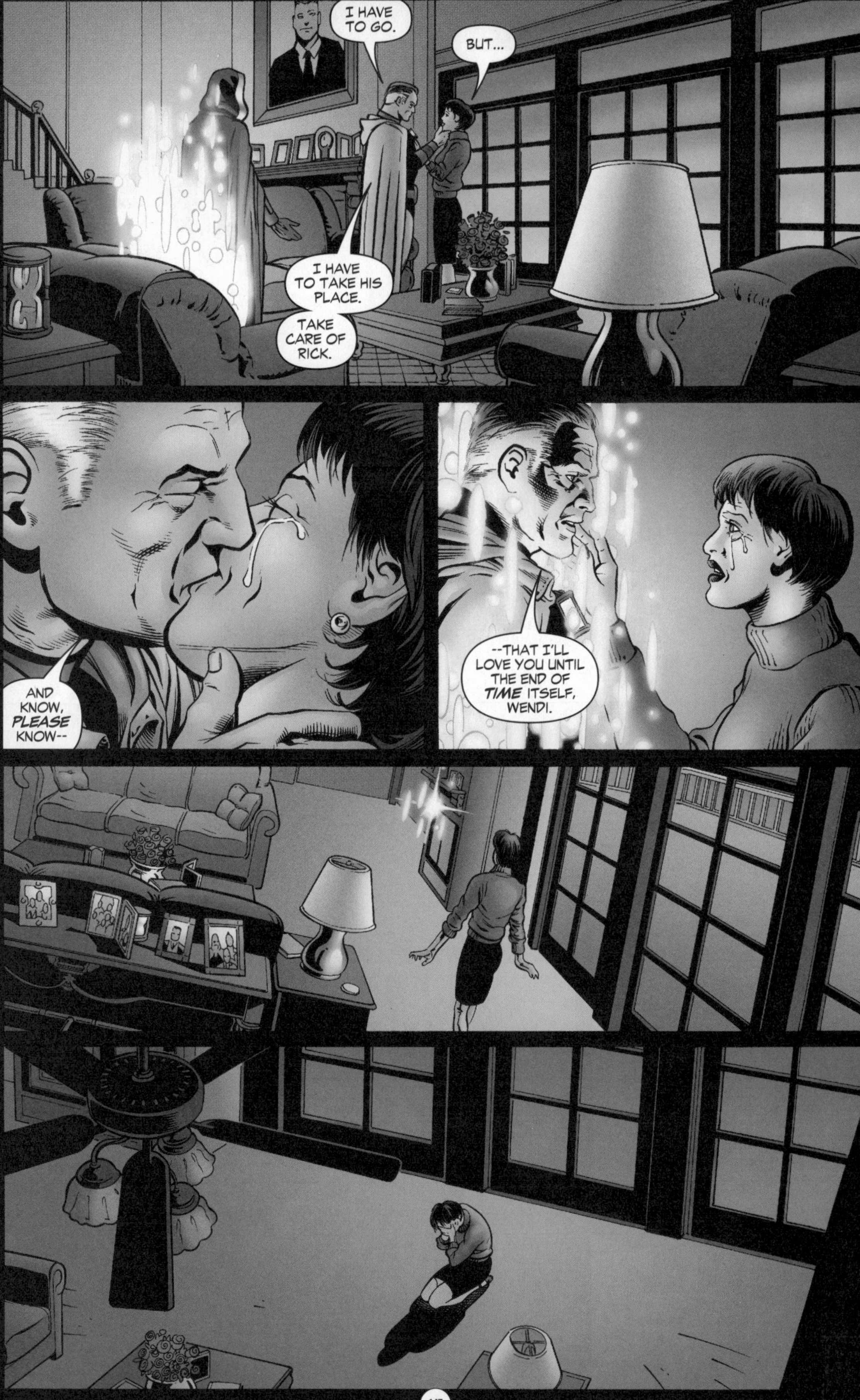
I HAVE TO GO.
BUT...
I HAVE TO TAKE HIS PLACE.
TAKE CARE OF RICK.
AND KNOW, *PLEASE* KNOW--
--THAT I'LL LOVE YOU UNTIL THE END OF *TIME* ITSELF, WENDI.

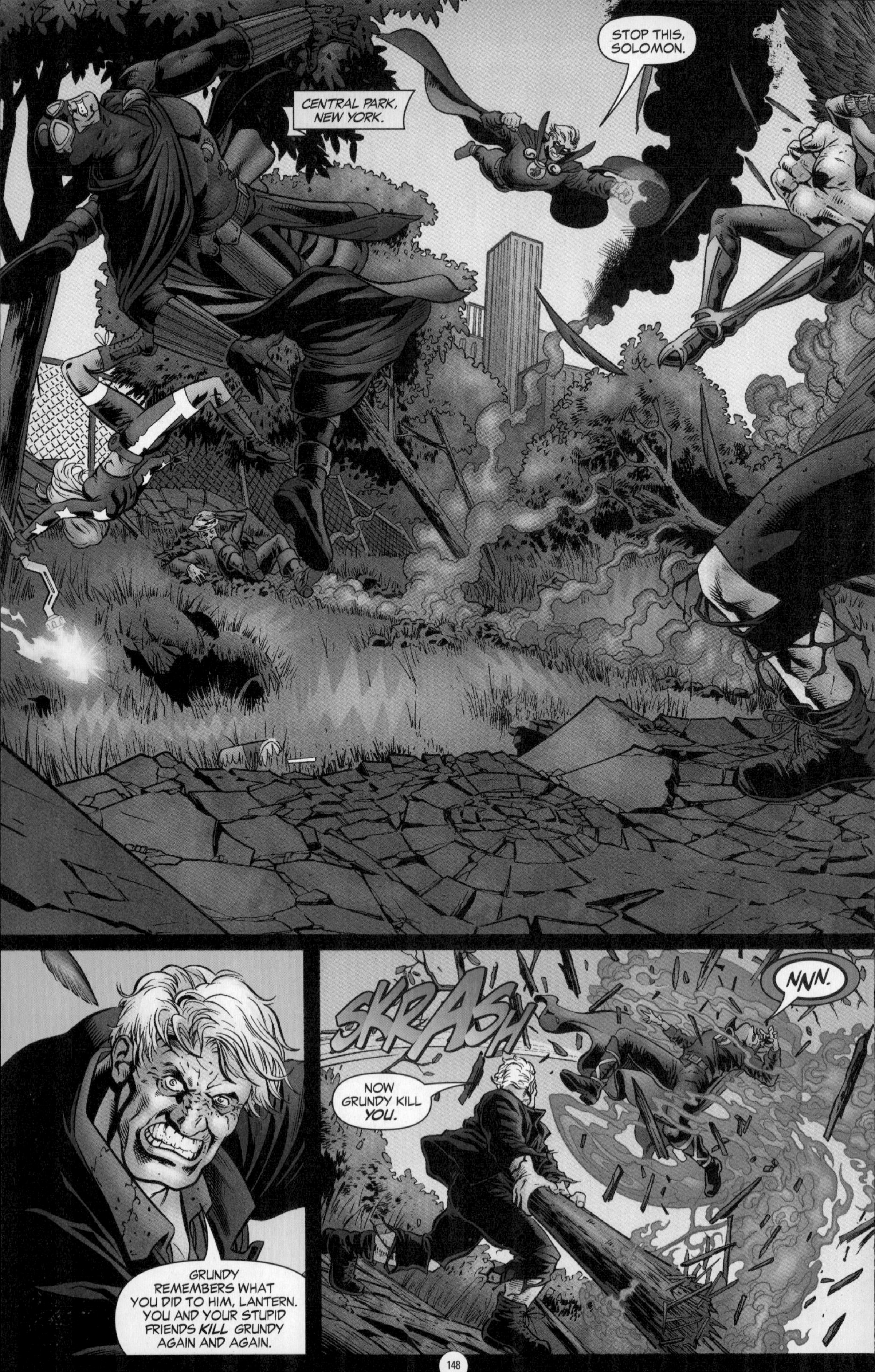

CENTRAL PARK, NEW YORK.
STOP THIS, SOLOMON.
GRUNDY REMEMBERS WHAT YOU DID TO HIM, LANTERN. YOU AND YOUR STUPID FRIENDS KILL GRUNDY AGAIN AND AGAIN.
SKRASH
NOW GRUNDY KILL YOU.
NNN.

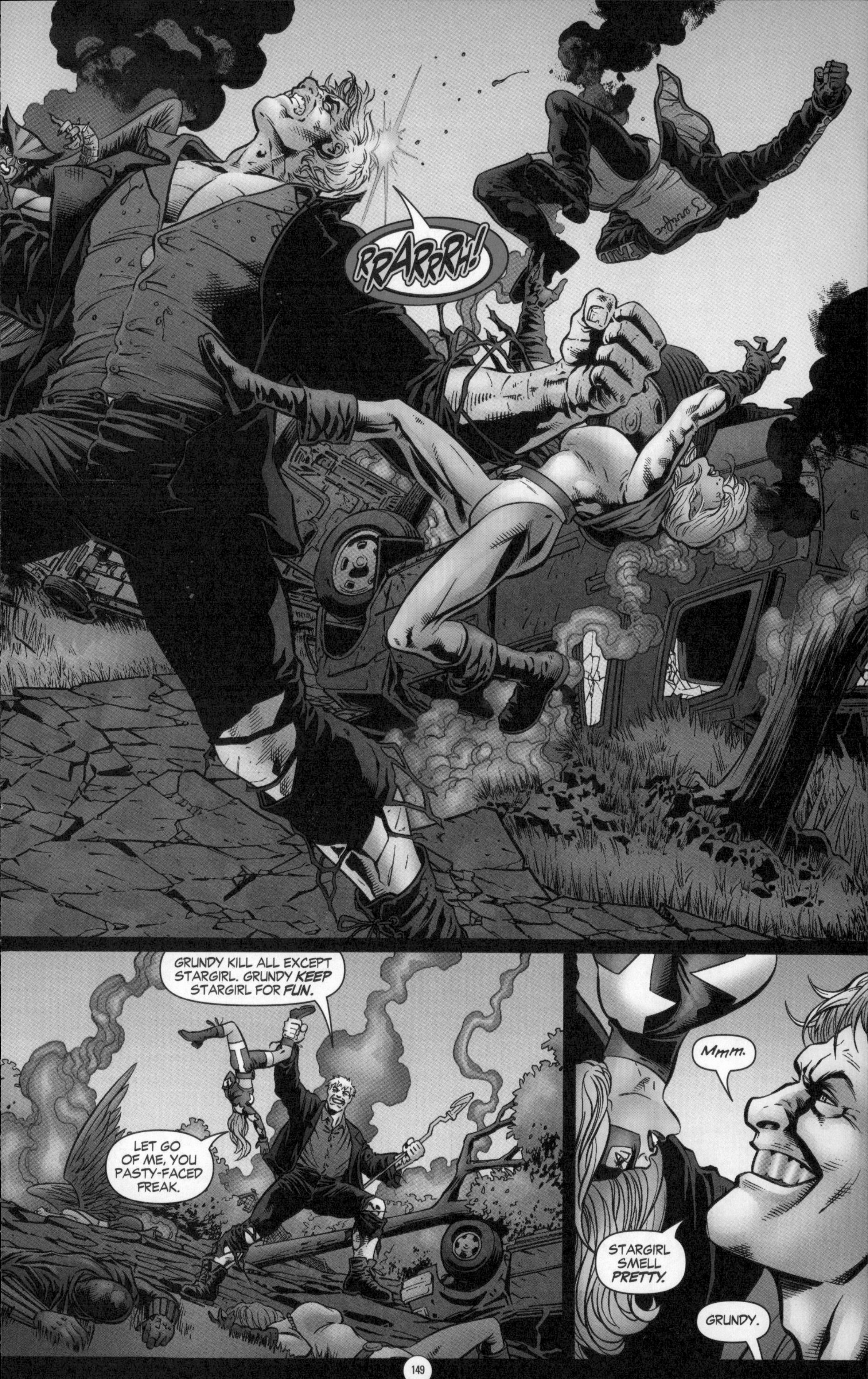
RRARRRH!
GRUNDY KILL ALL EXCEPT STARGIRL. GRUNDY *KEEP* STARGIRL FOR *FUN*.
LET GO OF ME, YOU PASTY-FACED FREAK.
*Mmm.*
STARGIRL SMELL *PRETTY*.
GRUNDY.

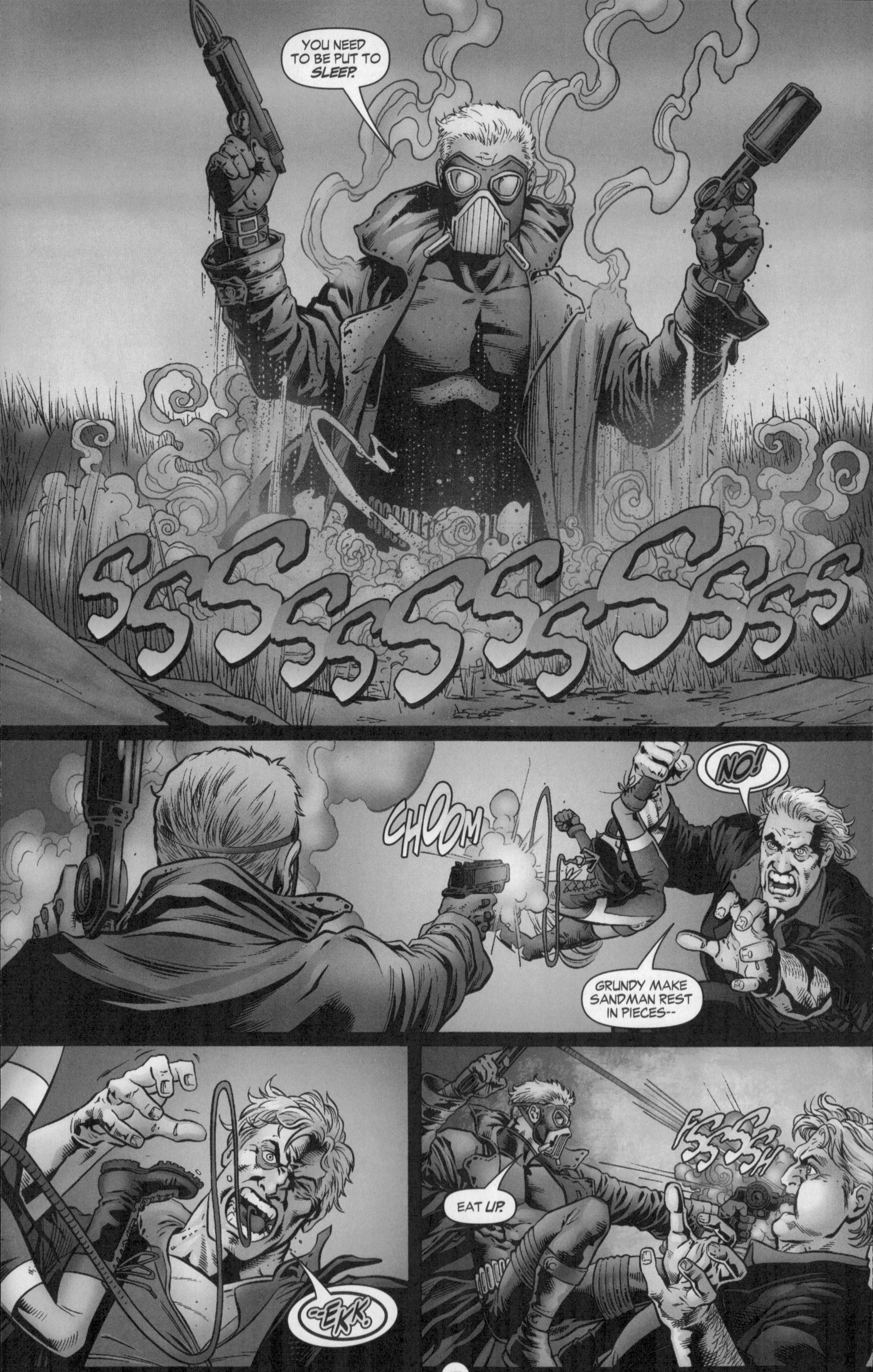
YOU NEED TO BE PUT TO SLEEP.
SSSSSSSSSSSSSSS
CHOOM
NO!
GRUNDY MAKE SANDMAN REST IN PIECES--
--EKK.
EAT UP.
FSSSH

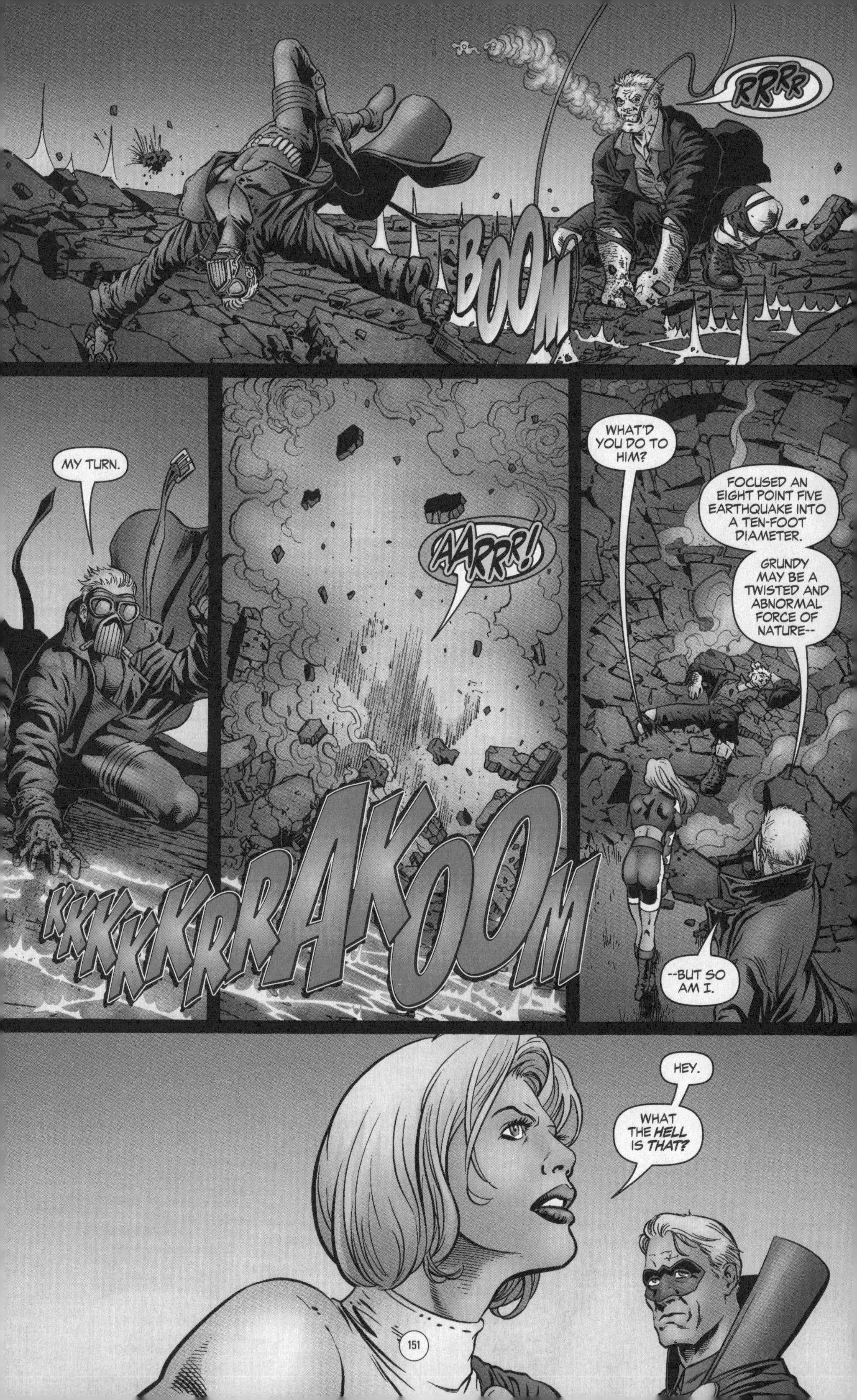
RRRR
BOOM
MY TURN.
AARRR!
KKKKKRRAKOOM
WHAT'D YOU DO TO HIM?
FOCUSED AN EIGHT POINT FIVE EARTHQUAKE INTO A TEN-FOOT DIAMETER.
GRUNDY MAY BE A TWISTED AND ABNORMAL FORCE OF NATURE--
--BUT SO AM I.
HEY.
WHAT THE HELL IS THAT?

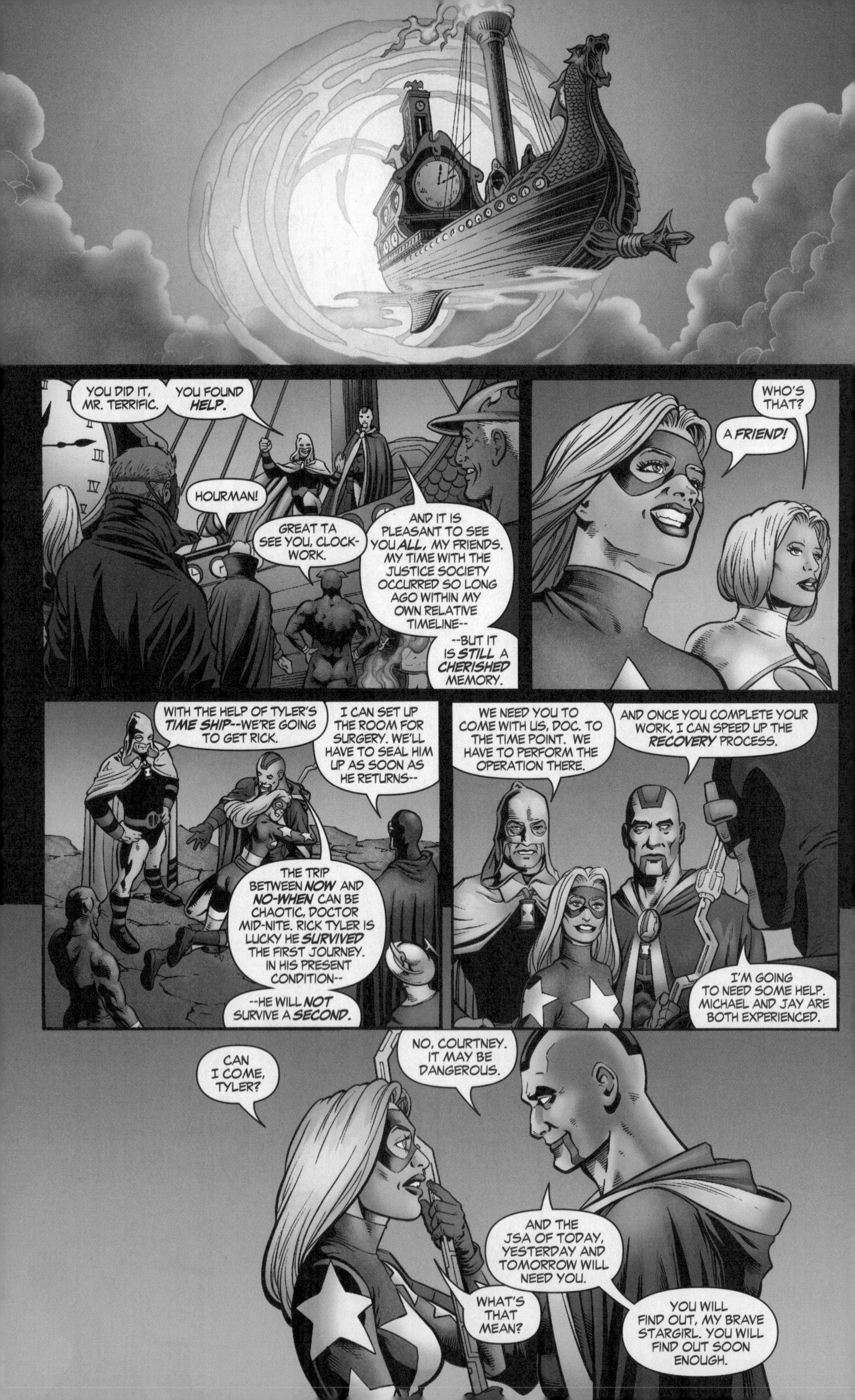
YOU DID IT, MR. TERRIFIC.
YOU FOUND HELP.
HOURMAN!
GREAT TA SEE YOU, CLOCK-WORK.
AND IT IS PLEASANT TO SEE YOU ALL, MY FRIENDS. MY TIME WITH THE JUSTICE SOCIETY OCCURRED SO LONG AGO WITHIN MY OWN RELATIVE TIMELINE--
--BUT IT IS STILL A CHERISHED MEMORY.
WHO'S THAT?
A FRIEND!
WITH THE HELP OF TYLER'S TIME SHIP--WE'RE GOING TO GET RICK.
I CAN SET UP THE ROOM FOR SURGERY. WE'LL HAVE TO SEAL HIM UP AS SOON AS HE RETURNS--
THE TRIP BETWEEN NOW AND NO-WHEN CAN BE CHAOTIC, DOCTOR MID-NITE. RICK TYLER IS LUCKY HE SURVIVED THE FIRST JOURNEY. IN HIS PRESENT CONDITION--
--HE WILL NOT SURVIVE A SECOND.
WE NEED YOU TO COME WITH US, DOC. TO THE TIME POINT. WE HAVE TO PERFORM THE OPERATION THERE.
AND ONCE YOU COMPLETE YOUR WORK, I CAN SPEED UP THE RECOVERY PROCESS.
I'M GOING TO NEED SOME HELP. MICHAEL AND JAY ARE BOTH EXPERIENCED.
CAN I COME, TYLER?
NO, COURTNEY. IT MAY BE DANGEROUS.
AND THE JSA OF TODAY, YESTERDAY AND TOMORROW WILL NEED YOU.
WHAT'S THAT MEAN?
YOU WILL FIND OUT, MY BRAVE STARGIRL. YOU WILL FIND OUT SOON ENOUGH.

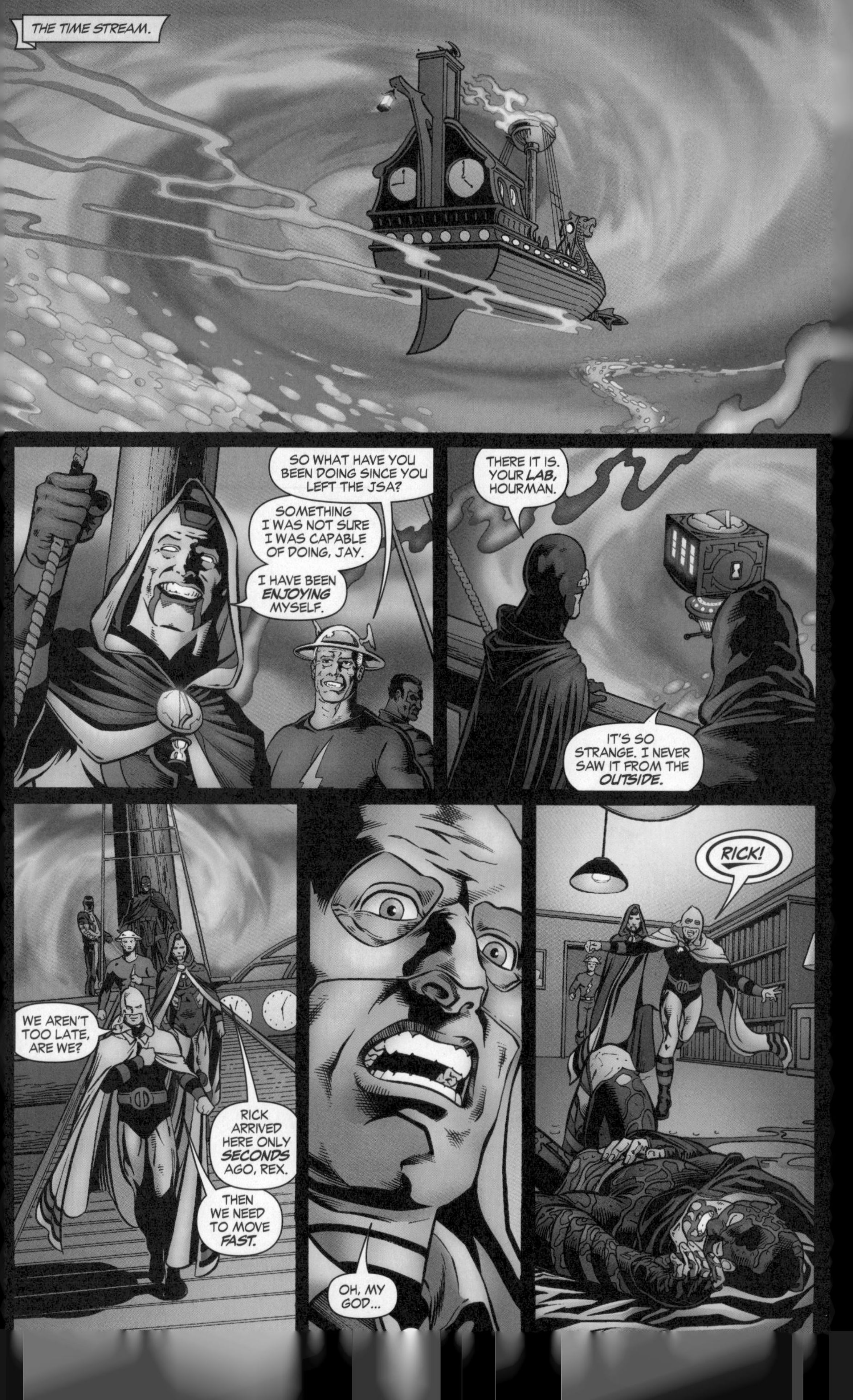
THE TIME STREAM.
SO WHAT HAVE YOU BEEN DOING SINCE YOU LEFT THE JSA?
SOMETHING I WAS NOT SURE I WAS CAPABLE OF DOING, JAY.
I HAVE BEEN ENJOYING MYSELF.
THERE IT IS. YOUR LAB, HOURMAN.
IT'S SO STRANGE. I NEVER SAW IT FROM THE OUTSIDE.
WE AREN'T TOO LATE, ARE WE?
RICK ARRIVED HERE ONLY SECONDS AGO, REX.
THEN WE NEED TO MOVE FAST.
OH, MY GOD...
RICK!

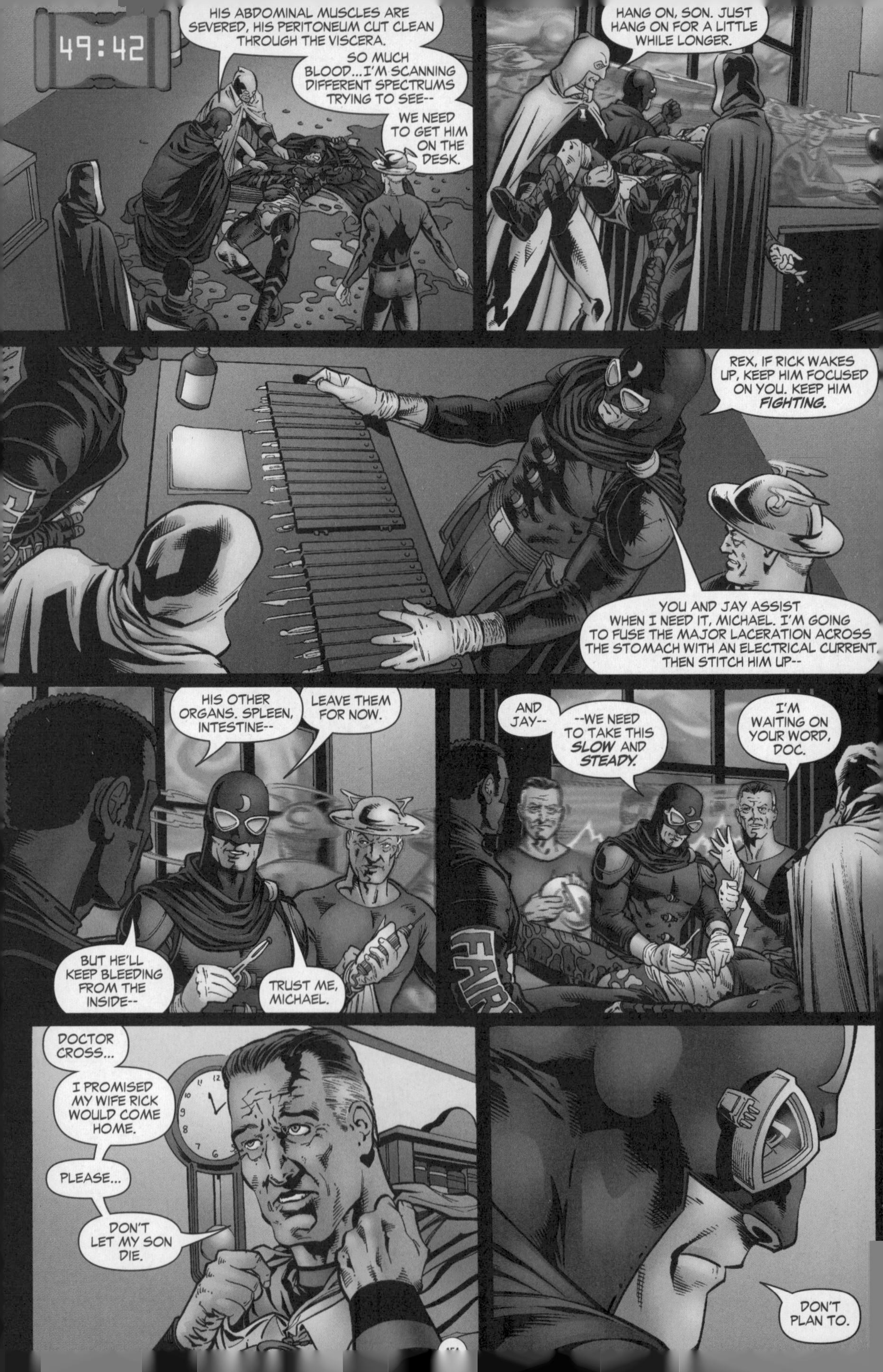
49:42
HIS ABDOMINAL MUSCLES ARE SEVERED, HIS PERITONEUM CUT CLEAN THROUGH THE VISCERA.
SO MUCH BLOOD...I'M SCANNING DIFFERENT SPECTRUMS TRYING TO SEE--
WE NEED TO GET HIM ON THE DESK.
HANG ON, SON. JUST HANG ON FOR A LITTLE WHILE LONGER.
REX, IF RICK WAKES UP, KEEP HIM FOCUSED ON YOU. KEEP HIM FIGHTING.
YOU AND JAY ASSIST WHEN I NEED IT, MICHAEL. I'M GOING TO FUSE THE MAJOR LACERATION ACROSS THE STOMACH WITH AN ELECTRICAL CURRENT, THEN STITCH HIM UP--
HIS OTHER ORGANS. SPLEEN, INTESTINE--
LEAVE THEM FOR NOW.
BUT HE'LL KEEP BLEEDING FROM THE INSIDE--
TRUST ME, MICHAEL.
AND JAY--
--WE NEED TO TAKE THIS SLOW AND STEADY.
I'M WAITING ON YOUR WORD, DOC.
DOCTOR CROSS...
I PROMISED MY WIFE RICK WOULD COME HOME.
PLEASE...
DON'T LET MY SON DIE.
DON'T PLAN TO.

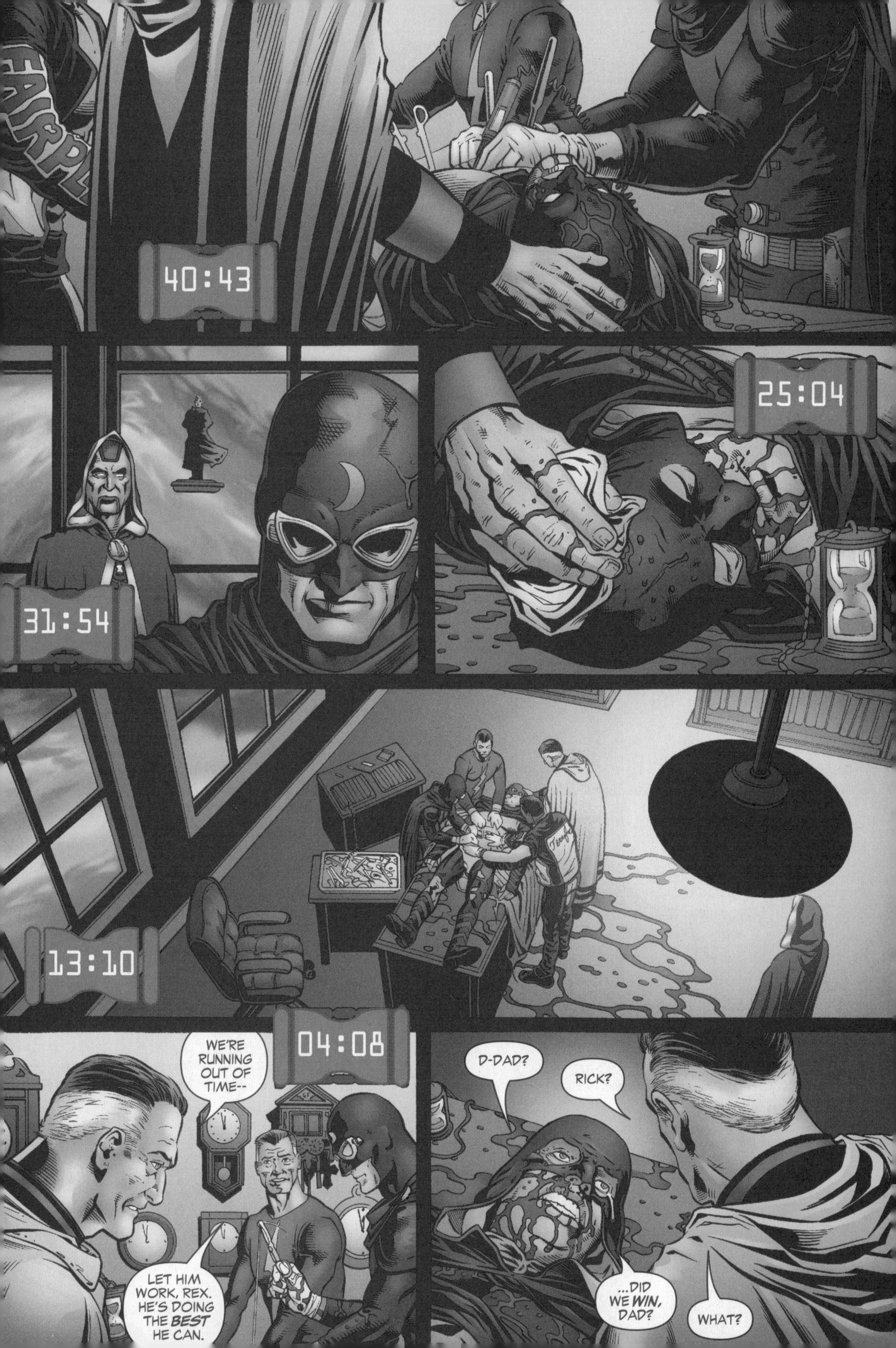
40:43
31:54
25:04
13:10
WE'RE RUNNING OUT OF TIME--
04:08
LET HIM WORK, REX. HE'S DOING THE *BEST* HE CAN.
D-DAD?
RICK?
...DID WE *WIN,* DAD?
WHAT?

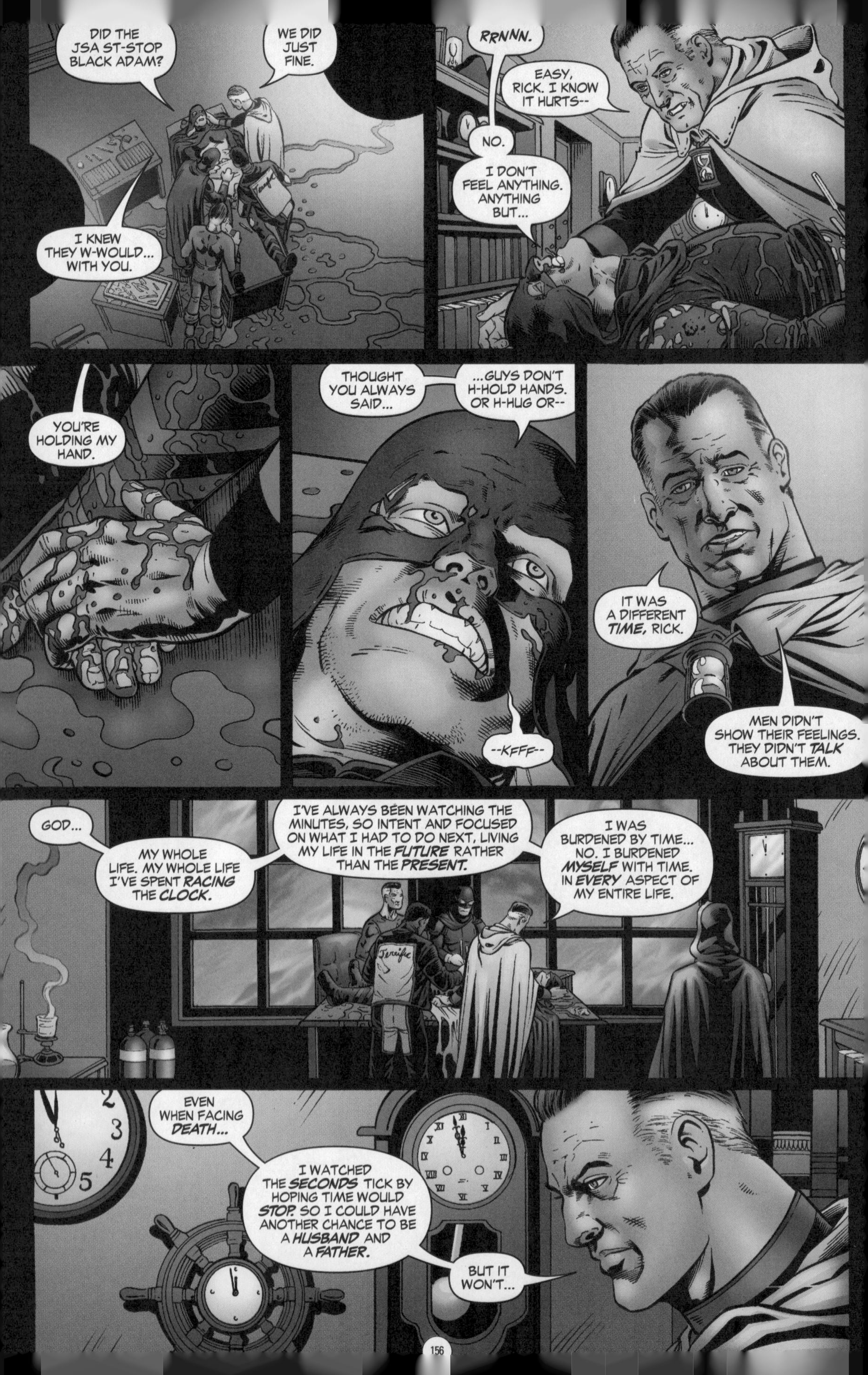
DID THE JSA ST-STOP BLACK ADAM?
WE DID JUST FINE.
I KNEW THEY W-WOULD... WITH YOU.
RRNNN.
EASY, RICK. I KNOW IT HURTS--
NO.
I DON'T FEEL ANYTHING. ANYTHING BUT...
YOU'RE HOLDING MY HAND.
THOUGHT YOU ALWAYS SAID...
...GUYS DON'T H-HOLD HANDS. OR H-HUG OR--
--KFFF--
IT WAS A DIFFERENT TIME, RICK.
MEN DIDN'T SHOW THEIR FEELINGS. THEY DIDN'T TALK ABOUT THEM.
GOD...
MY WHOLE LIFE. MY WHOLE LIFE I'VE SPENT RACING THE CLOCK.
I'VE ALWAYS BEEN WATCHING THE MINUTES, SO INTENT AND FOCUSED ON WHAT I HAD TO DO NEXT, LIVING MY LIFE IN THE FUTURE RATHER THAN THE PRESENT.
I WAS BURDENED BY TIME... NO. I BURDENED MYSELF WITH TIME. IN EVERY ASPECT OF MY ENTIRE LIFE.
EVEN WHEN FACING DEATH...
I WATCHED THE SECONDS TICK BY HOPING TIME WOULD STOP. SO I COULD HAVE ANOTHER CHANCE TO BE A HUSBAND AND A FATHER.
BUT IT WON'T...

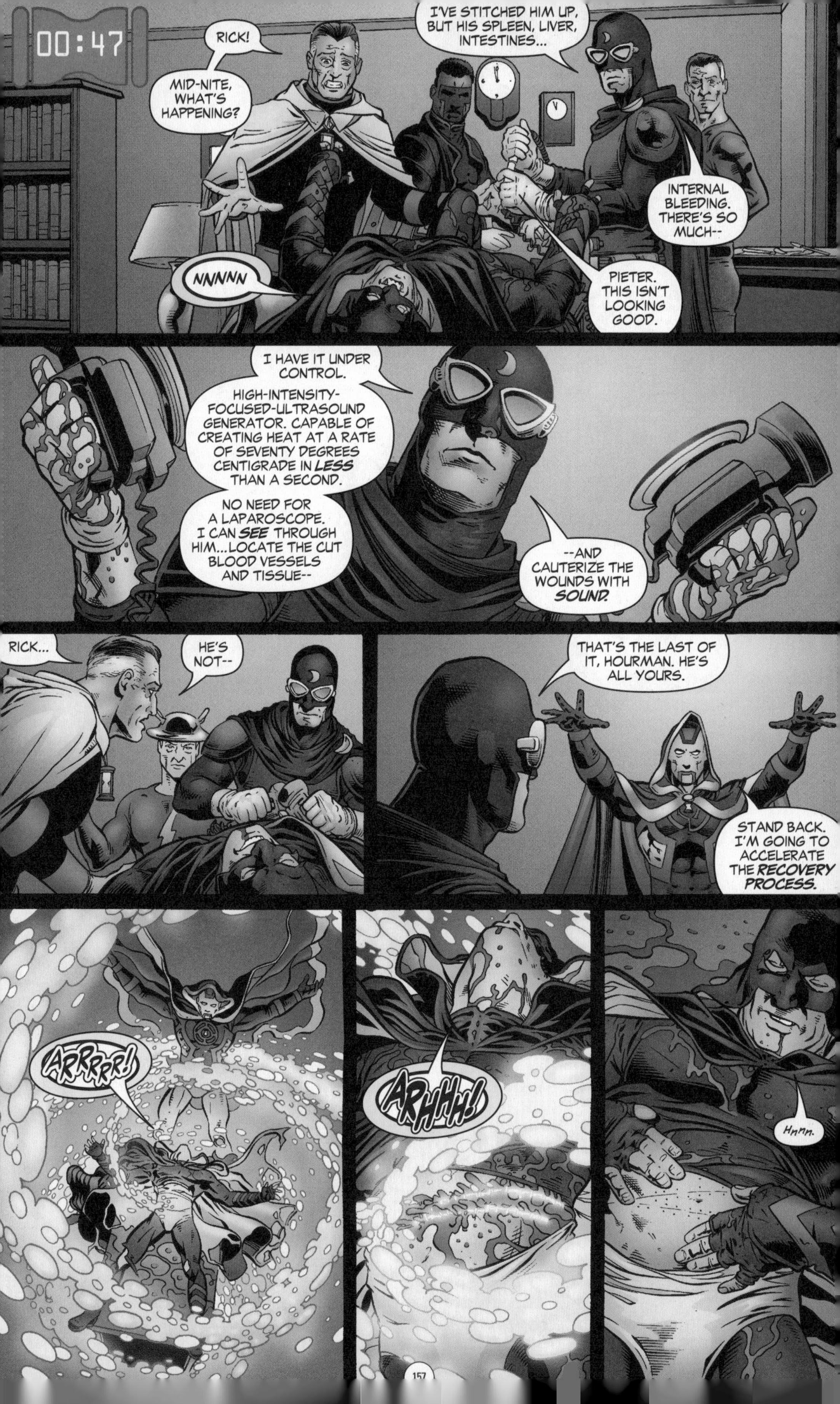

00:47
RICK!
MID-NITE, WHAT'S HAPPENING?
I'VE STITCHED HIM UP, BUT HIS SPLEEN, LIVER, INTESTINES...
INTERNAL BLEEDING. THERE'S SO MUCH--
NNNNN
PIETER. THIS ISN'T LOOKING GOOD.
I HAVE IT UNDER CONTROL.
HIGH-INTENSITY-FOCUSED-ULTRASOUND GENERATOR. CAPABLE OF CREATING HEAT AT A RATE OF SEVENTY DEGREES CENTIGRADE IN LESS THAN A SECOND.
NO NEED FOR A LAPAROSCOPE. I CAN SEE THROUGH HIM...LOCATE THE CUT BLOOD VESSELS AND TISSUE--
--AND CAUTERIZE THE WOUNDS WITH SOUND.
RICK...
HE'S NOT--
THAT'S THE LAST OF IT, HOURMAN. HE'S ALL YOURS.
STAND BACK. I'M GOING TO ACCELERATE THE RECOVERY PROCESS.
ARRRRR!
ARHHH!
Hnnn.

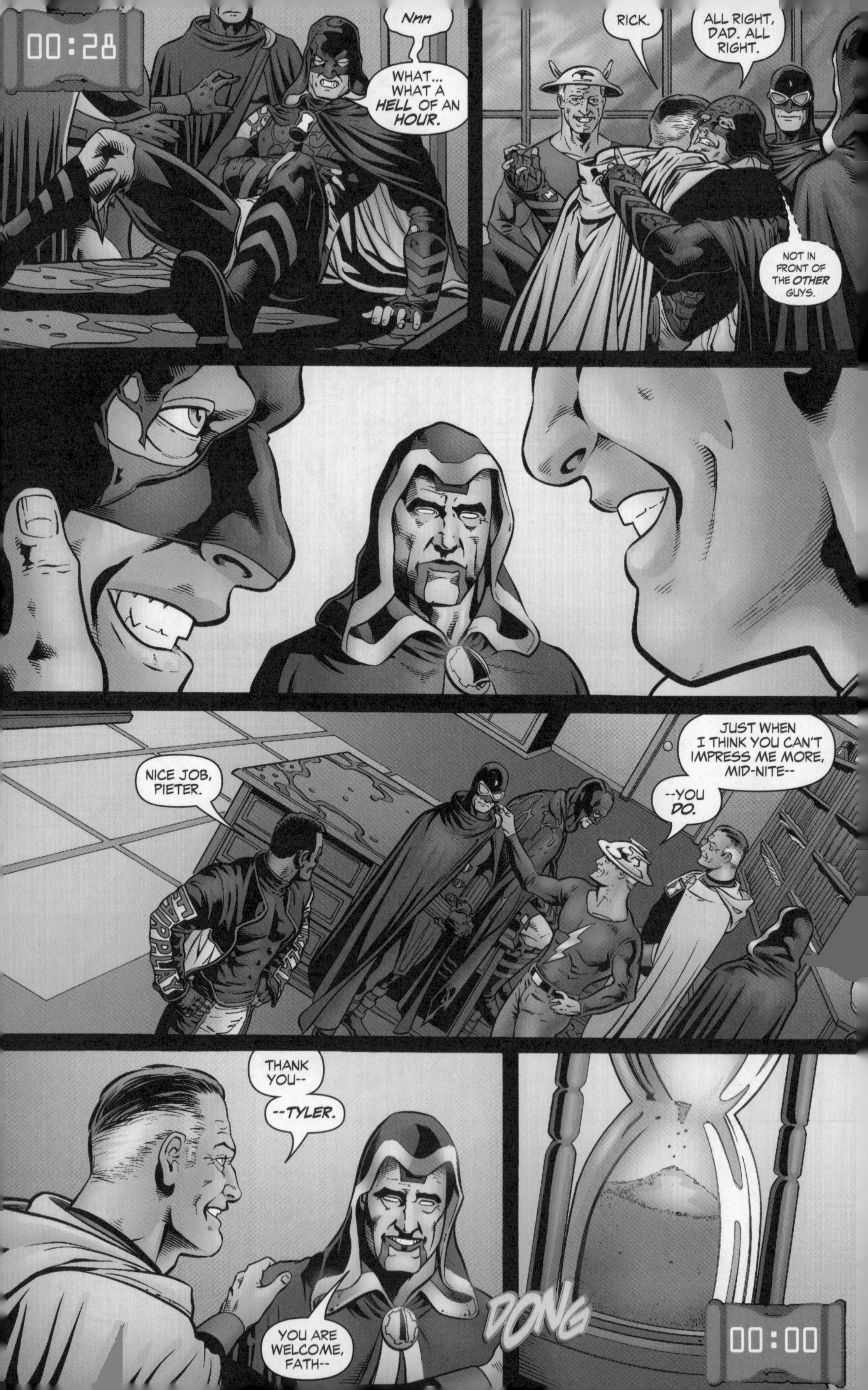
00:28
Nnn
WHAT... WHAT A HELL OF AN HOUR.
RICK.
ALL RIGHT, DAD. ALL RIGHT.
NOT IN FRONT OF THE OTHER GUYS.
NICE JOB, PIETER.
JUST WHEN I THINK YOU CAN'T IMPRESS ME MORE, MID-NITE--
--YOU DO.
THANK YOU--
--TYLER.
YOU ARE WELCOME, FATH--
DONG
00:00

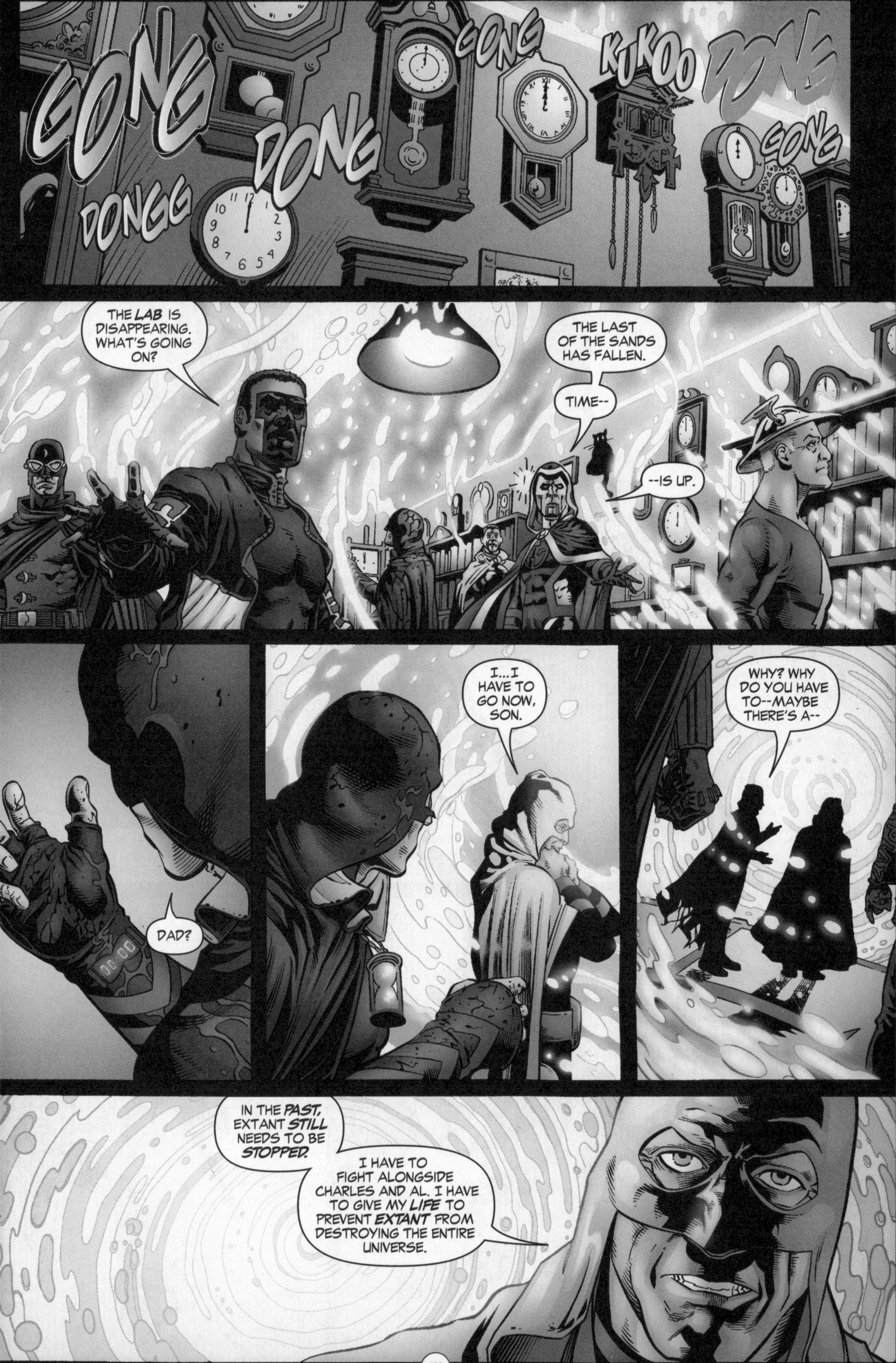

GONG
DONGG
DONG
GONG
KUKOO
DONG
GONG
THE LAB IS DISAPPEARING. WHAT'S GOING ON?
THE LAST OF THE SANDS HAS FALLEN.
TIME--
--IS UP.
DAD?
I...I HAVE TO GO NOW, SON.
WHY? WHY DO YOU HAVE TO--MAYBE THERE'S A--
IN THE PAST, EXTANT STILL NEEDS TO BE STOPPED.
I HAVE TO FIGHT ALONGSIDE CHARLES AND AL. I HAVE TO GIVE MY LIFE TO PREVENT EXTANT FROM DESTROYING THE ENTIRE UNIVERSE.

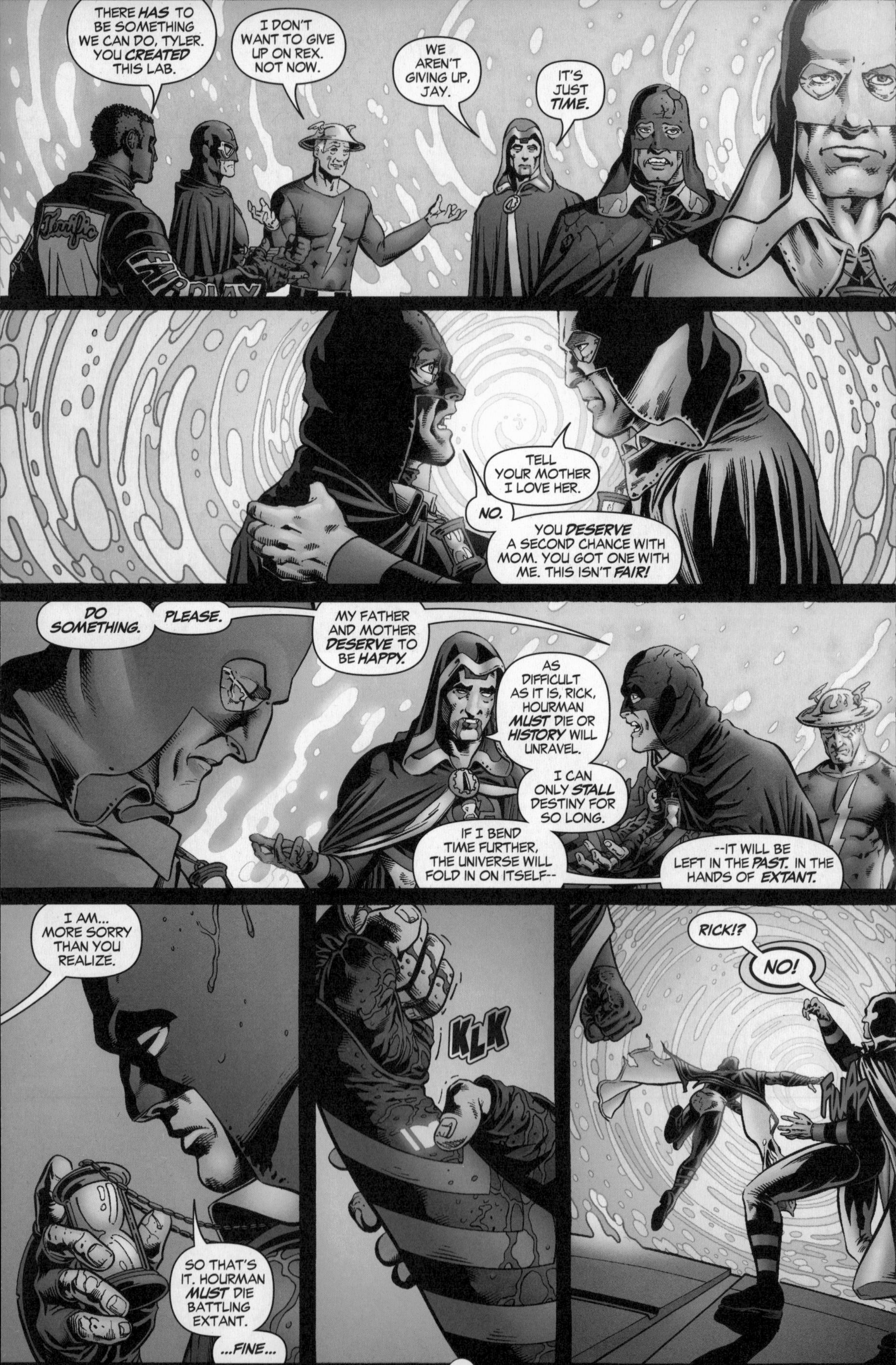
THERE HAS TO BE SOMETHING WE CAN DO, TYLER. YOU CREATED THIS LAB.
I DON'T WANT TO GIVE UP ON REX. NOT NOW.
WE AREN'T GIVING UP, JAY.
IT'S JUST TIME.
Terrific
FAIR PLAY
TELL YOUR MOTHER I LOVE HER.
NO.
YOU DESERVE A SECOND CHANCE WITH MOM. YOU GOT ONE WITH ME. THIS ISN'T FAIR!
DO SOMETHING.
PLEASE.
MY FATHER AND MOTHER DESERVE TO BE HAPPY.
AS DIFFICULT AS IT IS, RICK, HOURMAN MUST DIE OR HISTORY WILL UNRAVEL.
I CAN ONLY STALL DESTINY FOR SO LONG.
IF I BEND TIME FURTHER, THE UNIVERSE WILL FOLD IN ON ITSELF--
--IT WILL BE LEFT IN THE PAST. IN THE HANDS OF EXTANT.
I AM... MORE SORRY THAN YOU REALIZE.
SO THAT'S IT. HOURMAN MUST DIE BATTLING EXTANT.
...FINE...
KLK
RICK!?
NO!
FWAP

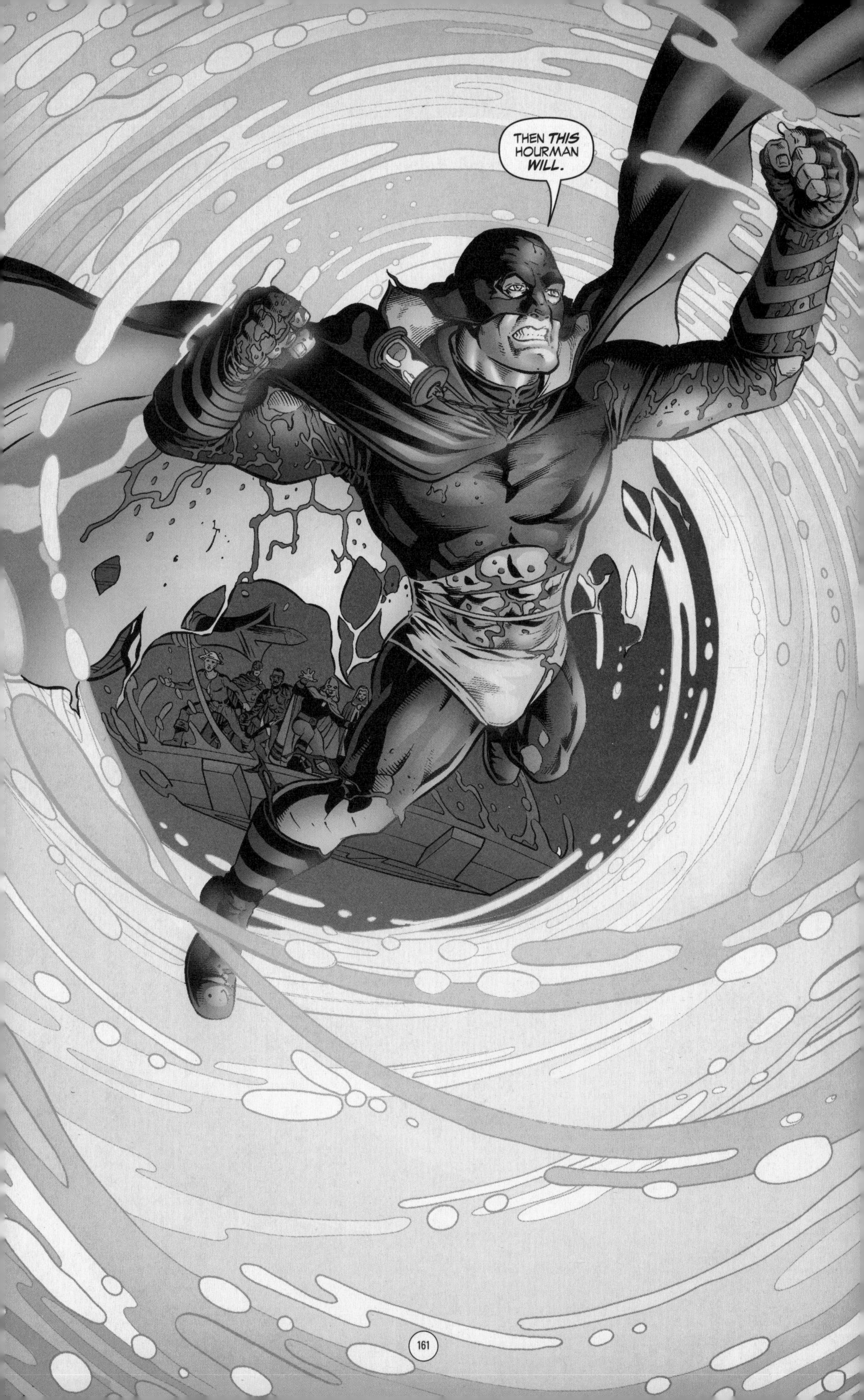
THEN THIS HOURMAN WILL.

JSA

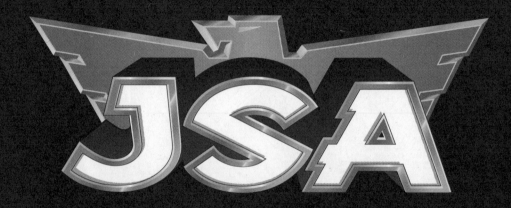

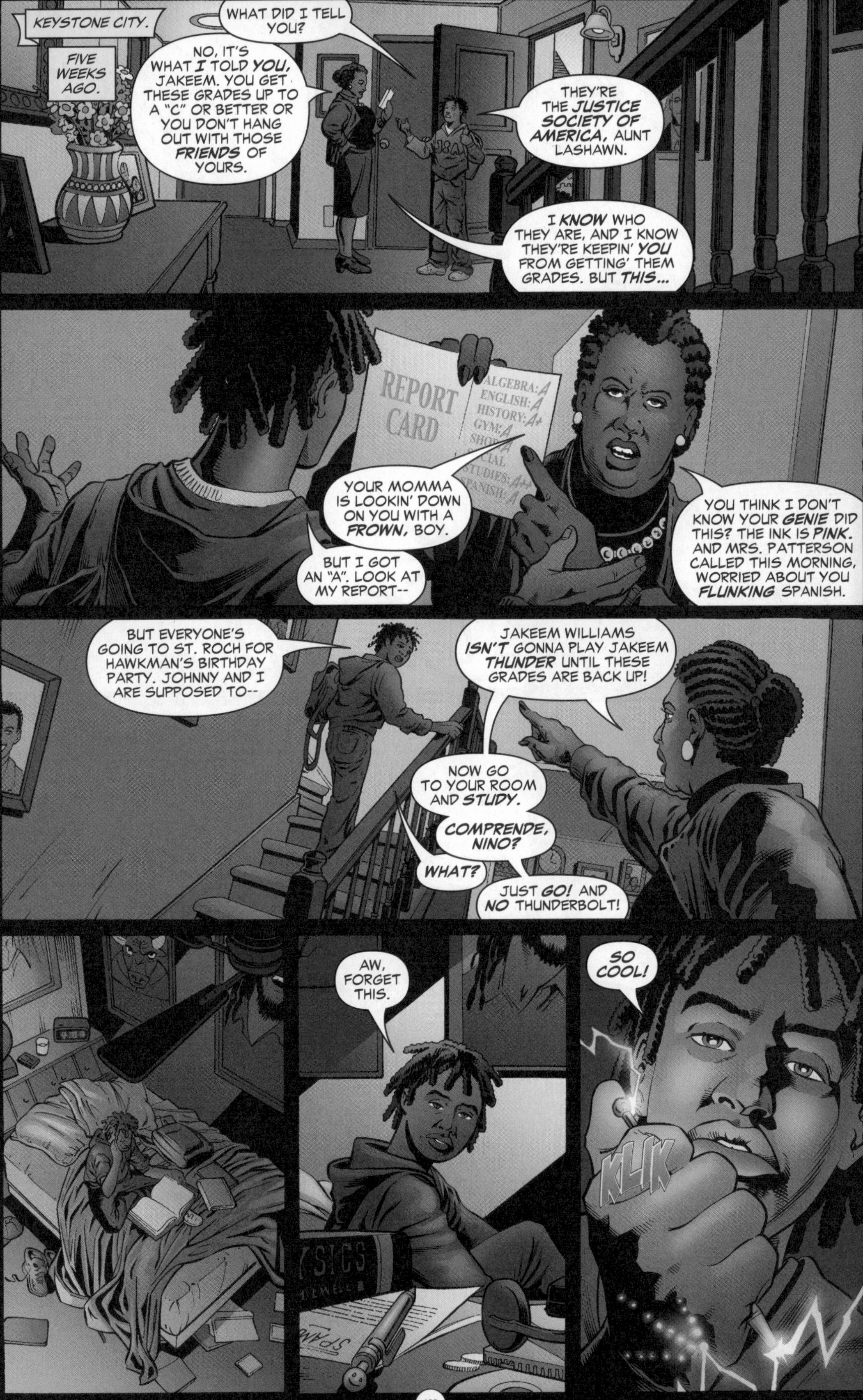

KEYSTONE CITY.
WHAT DID I TELL YOU?
FIVE WEEKS AGO.
NO, IT'S WHAT I TOLD YOU, JAKEEM. YOU GET THESE GRADES UP TO A "C" OR BETTER OR YOU DON'T HANG OUT WITH THOSE FRIENDS OF YOURS.
THEY'RE THE JUSTICE SOCIETY OF AMERICA, AUNT LASHAWN.
I KNOW WHO THEY ARE, AND I KNOW THEY'RE KEEPIN' YOU FROM GETTING' THEM GRADES. BUT THIS...
REPORT CARD
ALGEBRA: A
ENGLISH: A
HISTORY: A+
GYM: A
SHOP: A
SOCIAL STUDIES: A++
SPANISH: A
YOUR MOMMA IS LOOKIN' DOWN ON YOU WITH A FROWN, BOY.
BUT I GOT AN "A". LOOK AT MY REPORT--
YOU THINK I DON'T KNOW YOUR GENIE DID THIS? THE INK IS PINK. AND MRS. PATTERSON CALLED THIS MORNING, WORRIED ABOUT YOU FLUNKING SPANISH.
BUT EVERYONE'S GOING TO ST. ROCH FOR HAWKMAN'S BIRTHDAY PARTY. JOHNNY AND I ARE SUPPOSED TO--
JAKEEM WILLIAMS ISN'T GONNA PLAY JAKEEM THUNDER UNTIL THESE GRADES ARE BACK UP!
NOW GO TO YOUR ROOM AND STUDY.
COMPRENDE, NINO?
WHAT?
JUST GO! AND NO THUNDERBOLT!
AW, FORGET THIS.
SO COOL!
KLIK

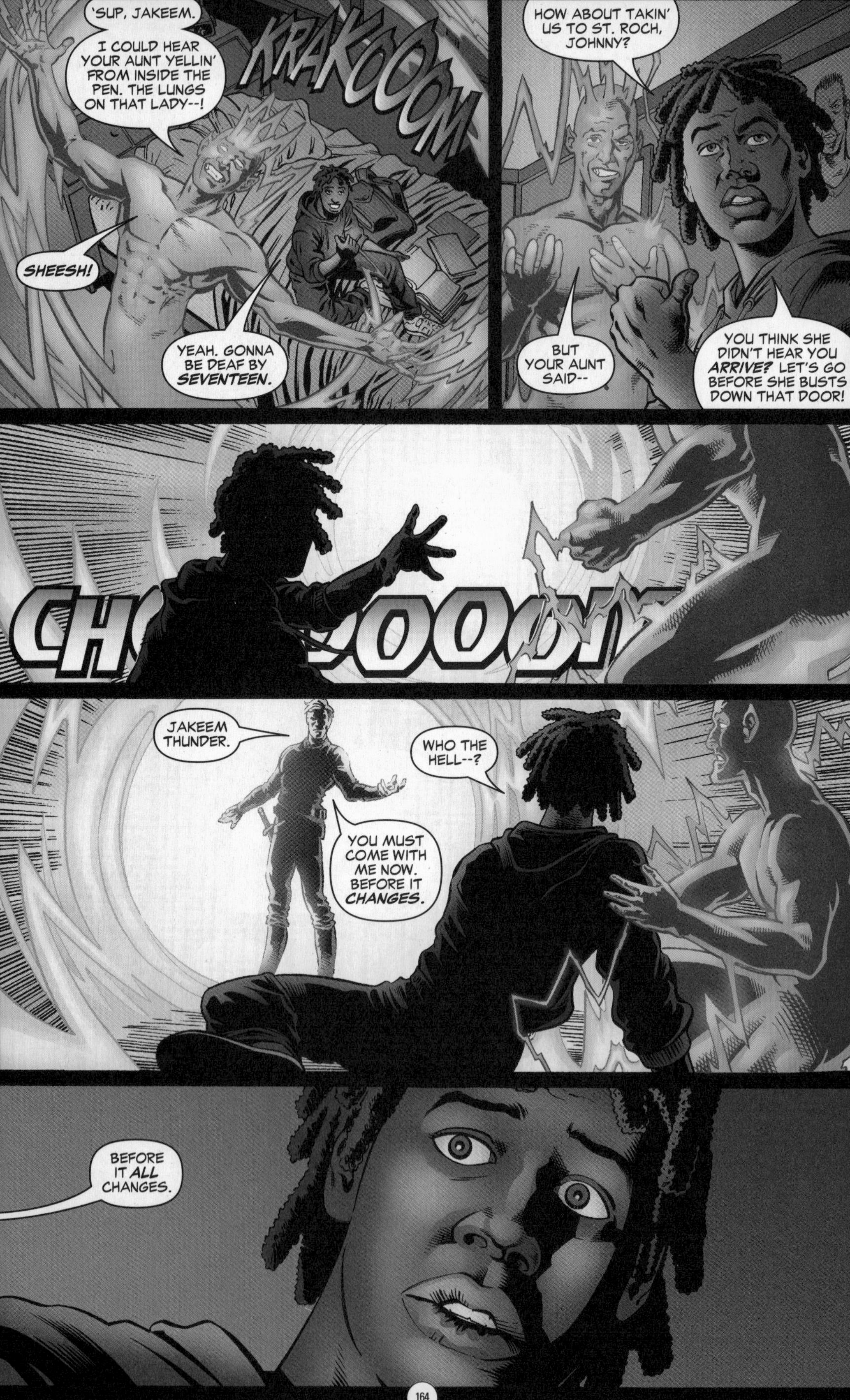
'SUP, JAKEEM.
I COULD HEAR YOUR AUNT YELLIN' FROM INSIDE THE PEN. THE LUNGS ON THAT LADY--!
KRAKOOOM
SHEESH!
YEAH. GONNA BE DEAF BY SEVENTEEN.
HOW ABOUT TAKIN' US TO ST. ROCH, JOHNNY?
BUT YOUR AUNT SAID--
YOU THINK SHE DIDN'T HEAR YOU ARRIVE? LET'S GO BEFORE SHE BUSTS DOWN THAT DOOR!
JAKEEM THUNDER.
WHO THE HELL--?
YOU MUST COME WITH ME NOW. BEFORE IT CHANGES.
BEFORE IT ALL CHANGES.

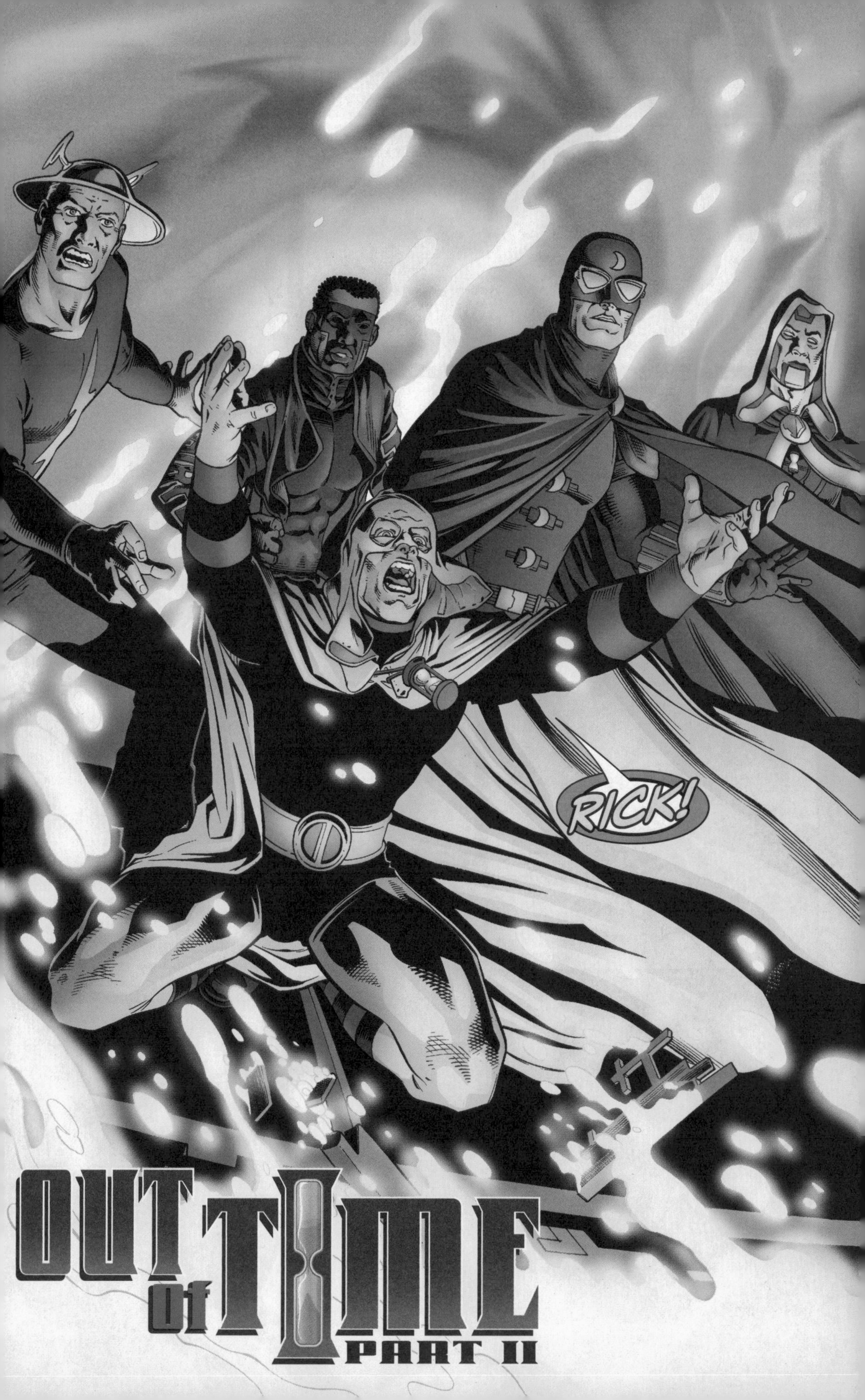
RICK!
OUT of TIME
PART II

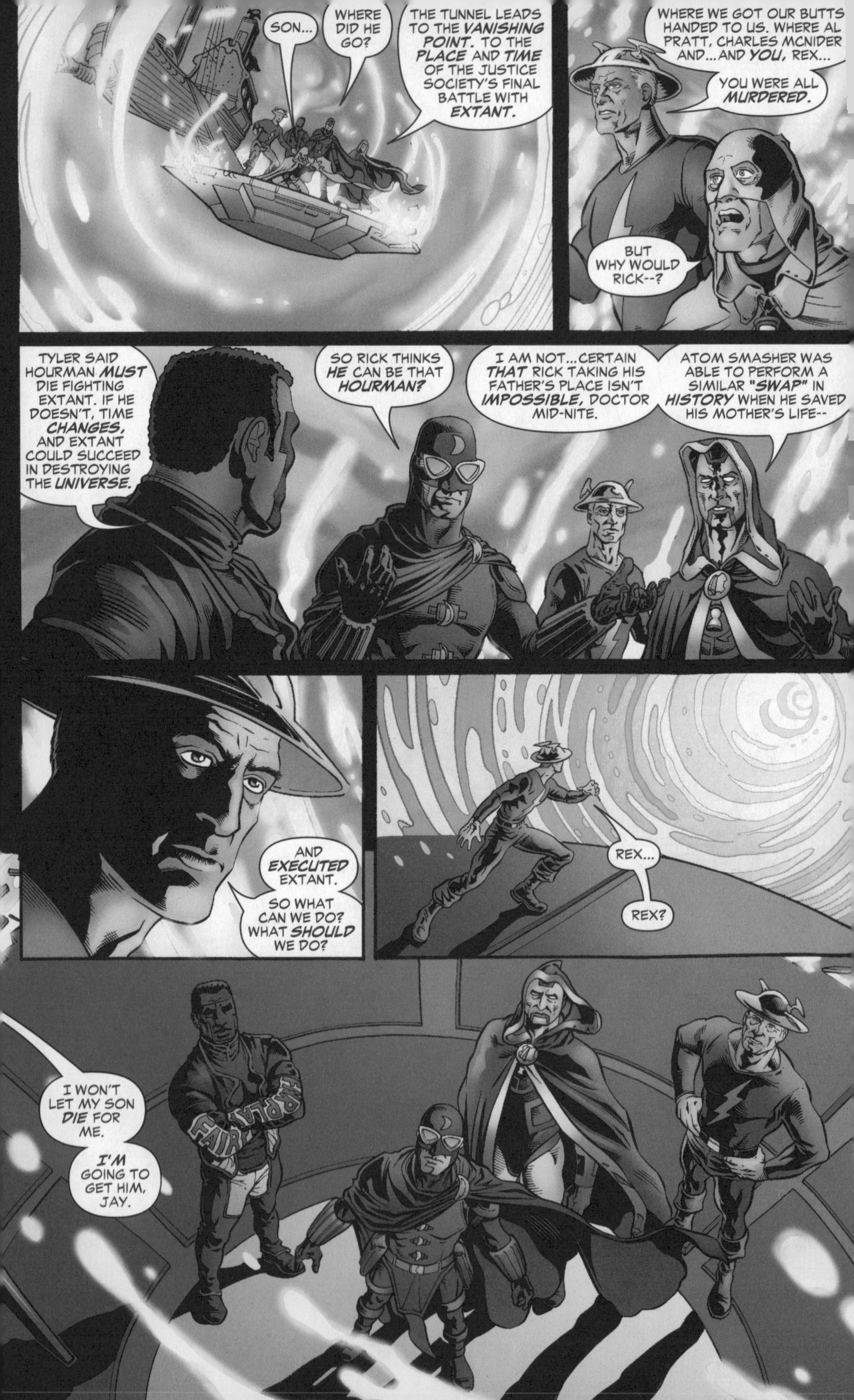
SON...
WHERE DID HE GO?
THE TUNNEL LEADS TO THE VANISHING POINT. TO THE PLACE AND TIME OF THE JUSTICE SOCIETY'S FINAL BATTLE WITH EXTANT.
WHERE WE GOT OUR BUTTS HANDED TO US. WHERE AL PRATT, CHARLES MCNIDER AND...AND YOU, REX...
YOU WERE ALL MURDERED.
BUT WHY WOULD RICK--?
TYLER SAID HOURMAN MUST DIE FIGHTING EXTANT. IF HE DOESN'T, TIME CHANGES, AND EXTANT COULD SUCCEED IN DESTROYING THE UNIVERSE.
SO RICK THINKS HE CAN BE THAT HOURMAN?
I AM NOT...CERTAIN THAT RICK TAKING HIS FATHER'S PLACE ISN'T IMPOSSIBLE, DOCTOR MID-NITE.
ATOM SMASHER WAS ABLE TO PERFORM A SIMILAR "SWAP" IN HISTORY WHEN HE SAVED HIS MOTHER'S LIFE--
AND EXECUTED EXTANT.
SO WHAT CAN WE DO? WHAT SHOULD WE DO?
REX...
REX?
I WON'T LET MY SON DIE FOR ME.
I'M GOING TO GET HIM, JAY.

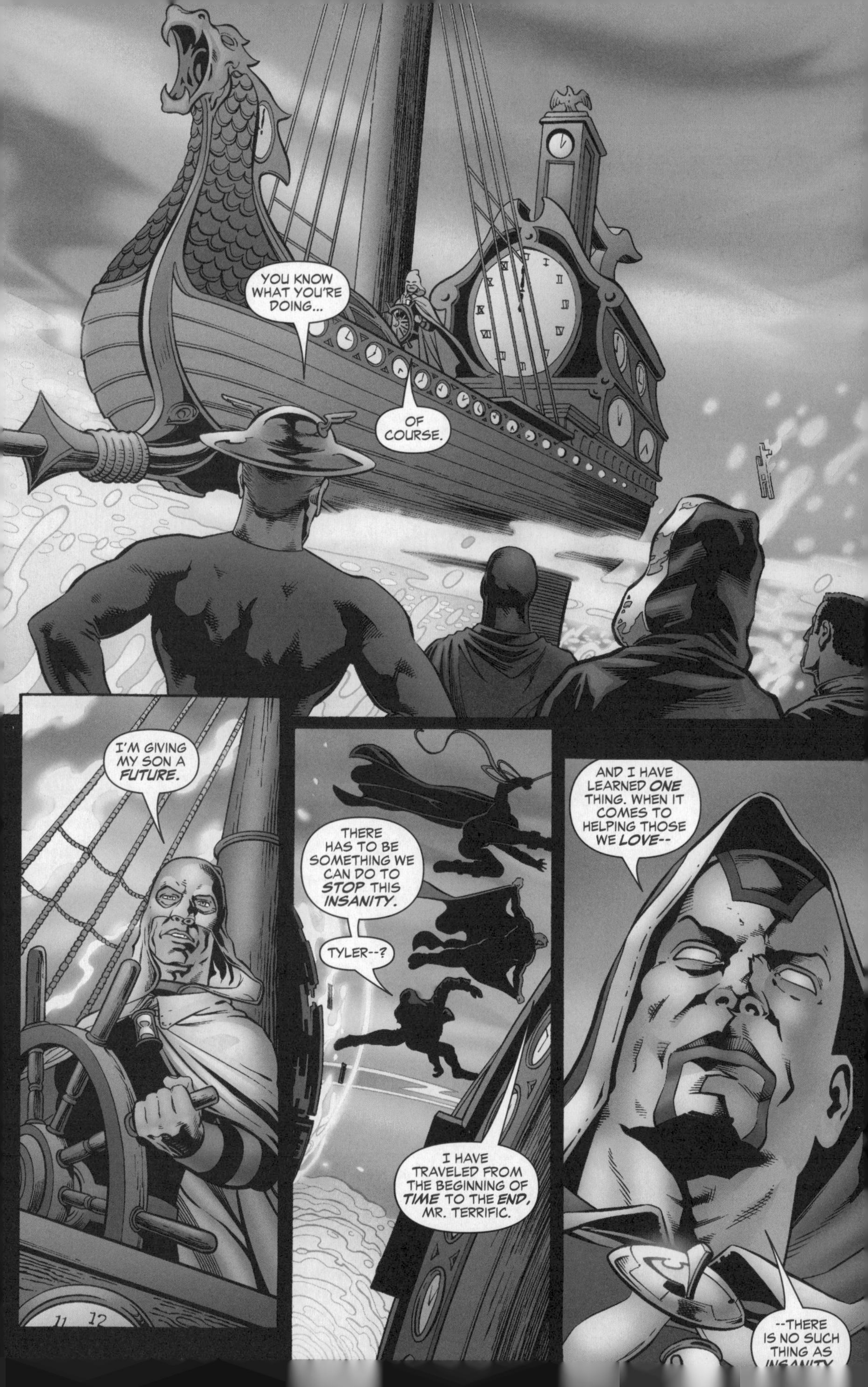
YOU KNOW WHAT YOU'RE DOING...
OF COURSE.
I'M GIVING MY SON A FUTURE.
THERE HAS TO BE SOMETHING WE CAN DO TO STOP THIS INSANITY.
TYLER--?
I HAVE TRAVELED FROM THE BEGINNING OF TIME TO THE END, MR. TERRIFIC.
AND I HAVE LEARNED ONE THING. WHEN IT COMES TO HELPING THOSE WE LOVE--
--THERE IS NO SUCH THING AS

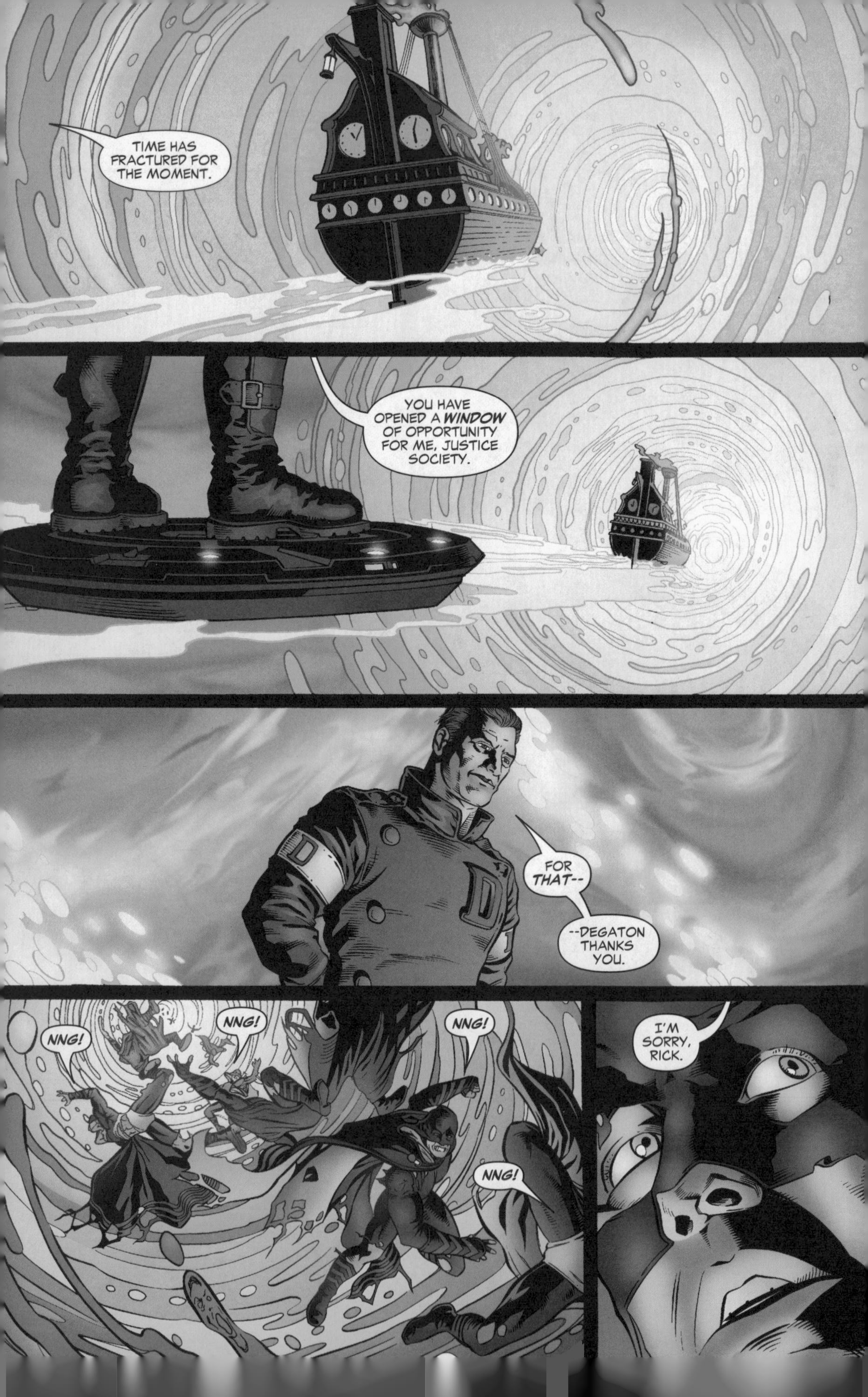

TIME HAS FRACTURED FOR THE MOMENT.
YOU HAVE OPENED A *WINDOW* OF OPPORTUNITY FOR ME, JUSTICE SOCIETY.
FOR *THAT*--
--DEGATON THANKS YOU.
NNG!
NNG!
NNG!
NNG!
I'M SORRY, RICK.

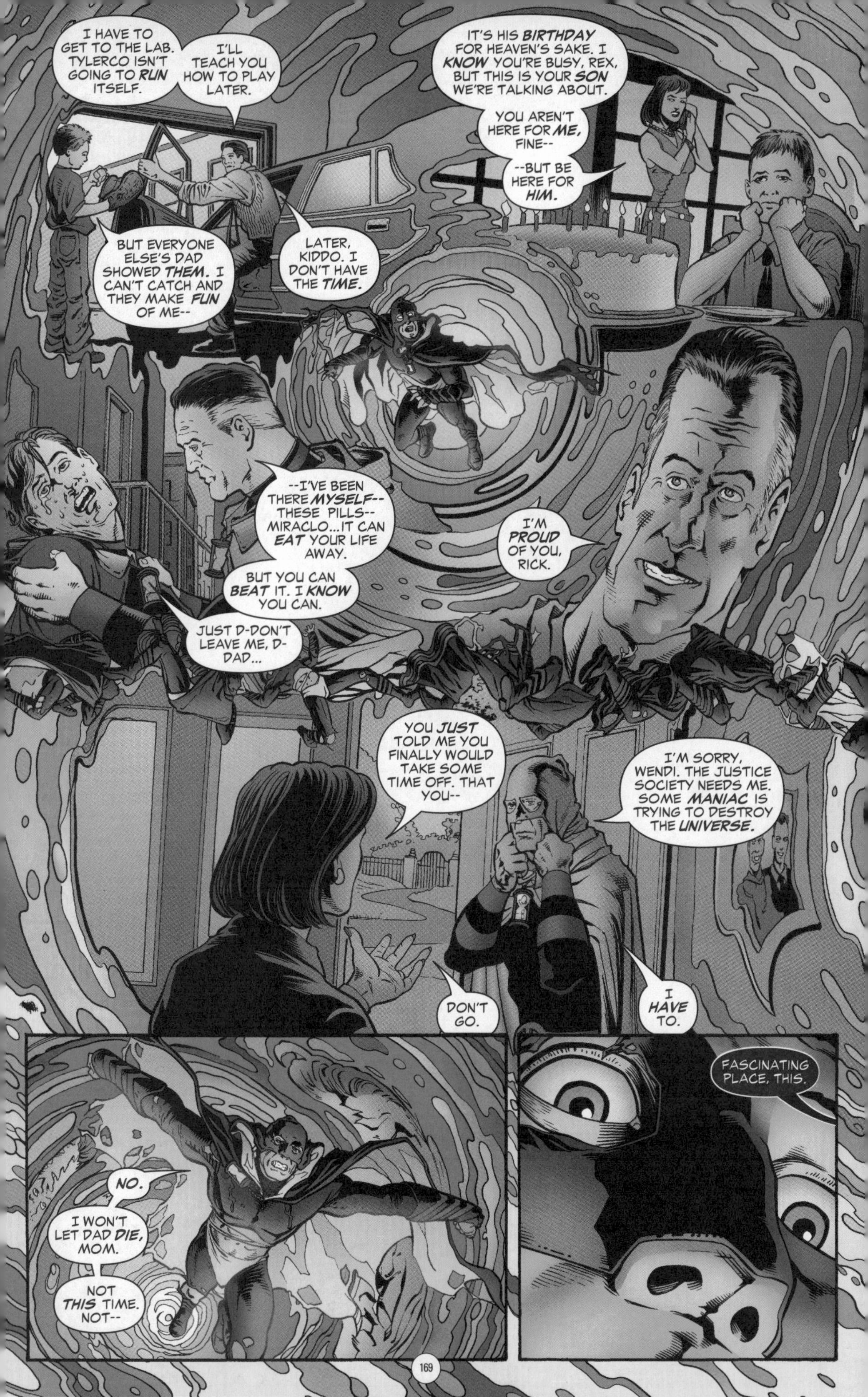
I HAVE TO GET TO THE LAB. TYLERCO ISN'T GOING TO RUN ITSELF.
I'LL TEACH YOU HOW TO PLAY LATER.
BUT EVERYONE ELSE'S DAD SHOWED THEM. I CAN'T CATCH AND THEY MAKE FUN OF ME--
LATER, KIDDO. I DON'T HAVE THE TIME.
IT'S HIS BIRTHDAY FOR HEAVEN'S SAKE. I KNOW YOU'RE BUSY, REX, BUT THIS IS YOUR SON WE'RE TALKING ABOUT.
YOU AREN'T HERE FOR ME, FINE--
--BUT BE HERE FOR HIM.
--I'VE BEEN THERE MYSELF-- THESE PILLS-- MIRACLO...IT CAN EAT YOUR LIFE AWAY.
BUT YOU CAN BEAT IT. I KNOW YOU CAN.
JUST D-DON'T LEAVE ME, D-DAD...
I'M PROUD OF YOU, RICK.
YOU JUST TOLD ME YOU FINALLY WOULD TAKE SOME TIME OFF. THAT YOU--
I'M SORRY, WENDI. THE JUSTICE SOCIETY NEEDS ME. SOME MANIAC IS TRYING TO DESTROY THE UNIVERSE.
DON'T GO.
I HAVE TO.
NO.
I WON'T LET DAD DIE, MOM.
NOT THIS TIME. NOT--
FASCINATING PLACE, THIS.

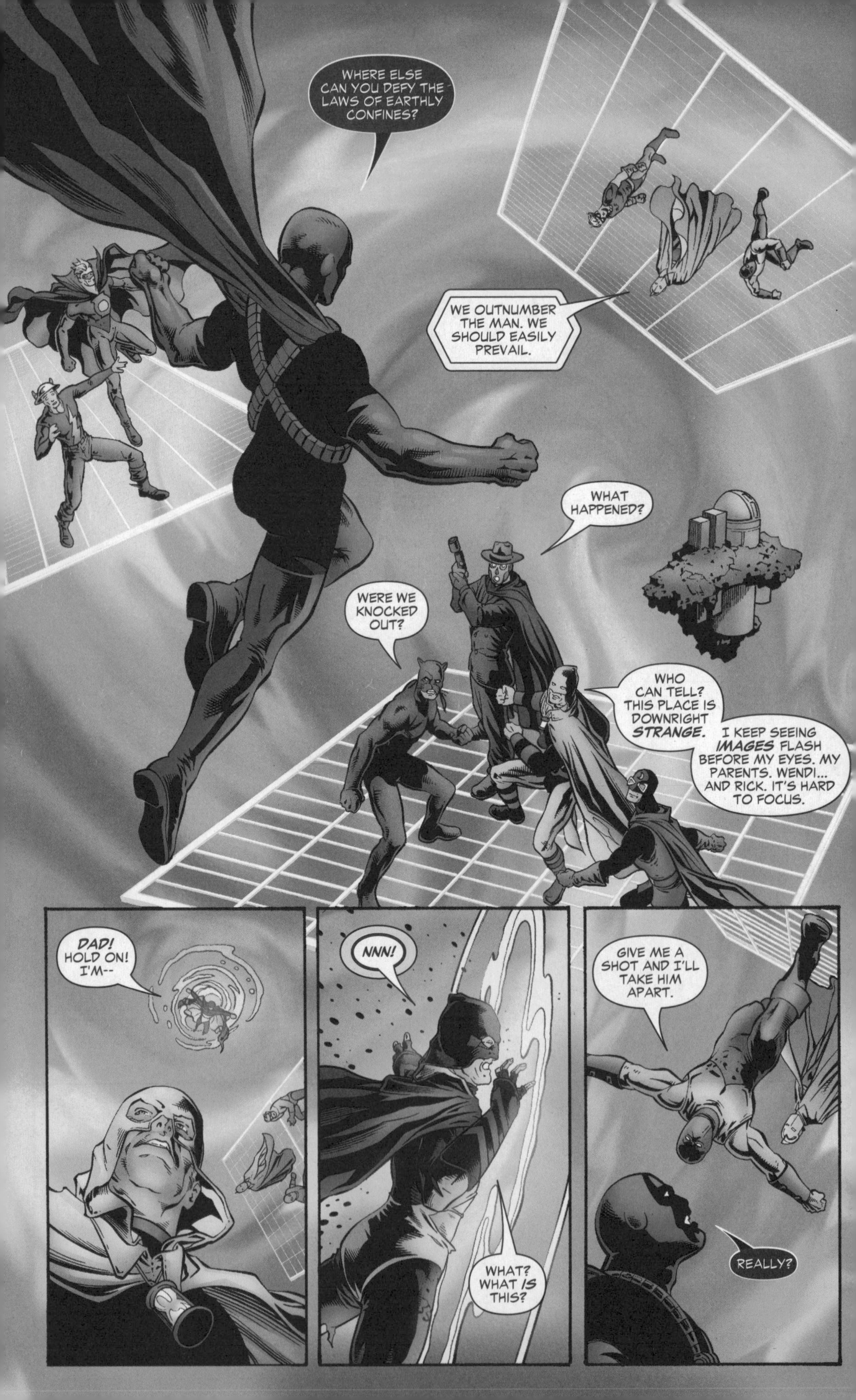

WHERE ELSE CAN YOU DEFY THE LAWS OF EARTHLY CONFINES?
WE OUTNUMBER THE MAN. WE SHOULD EASILY PREVAIL.
WHAT HAPPENED?
WERE WE KNOCKED OUT?
WHO CAN TELL? THIS PLACE IS DOWNRIGHT STRANGE.
I KEEP SEEING IMAGES FLASH BEFORE MY EYES. MY PARENTS. WENDI... AND RICK. IT'S HARD TO FOCUS.
DAD! HOLD ON! I'M--
NNN!
WHAT? WHAT IS THIS?
GIVE ME A SHOT AND I'LL TAKE HIM APART.
REALLY?

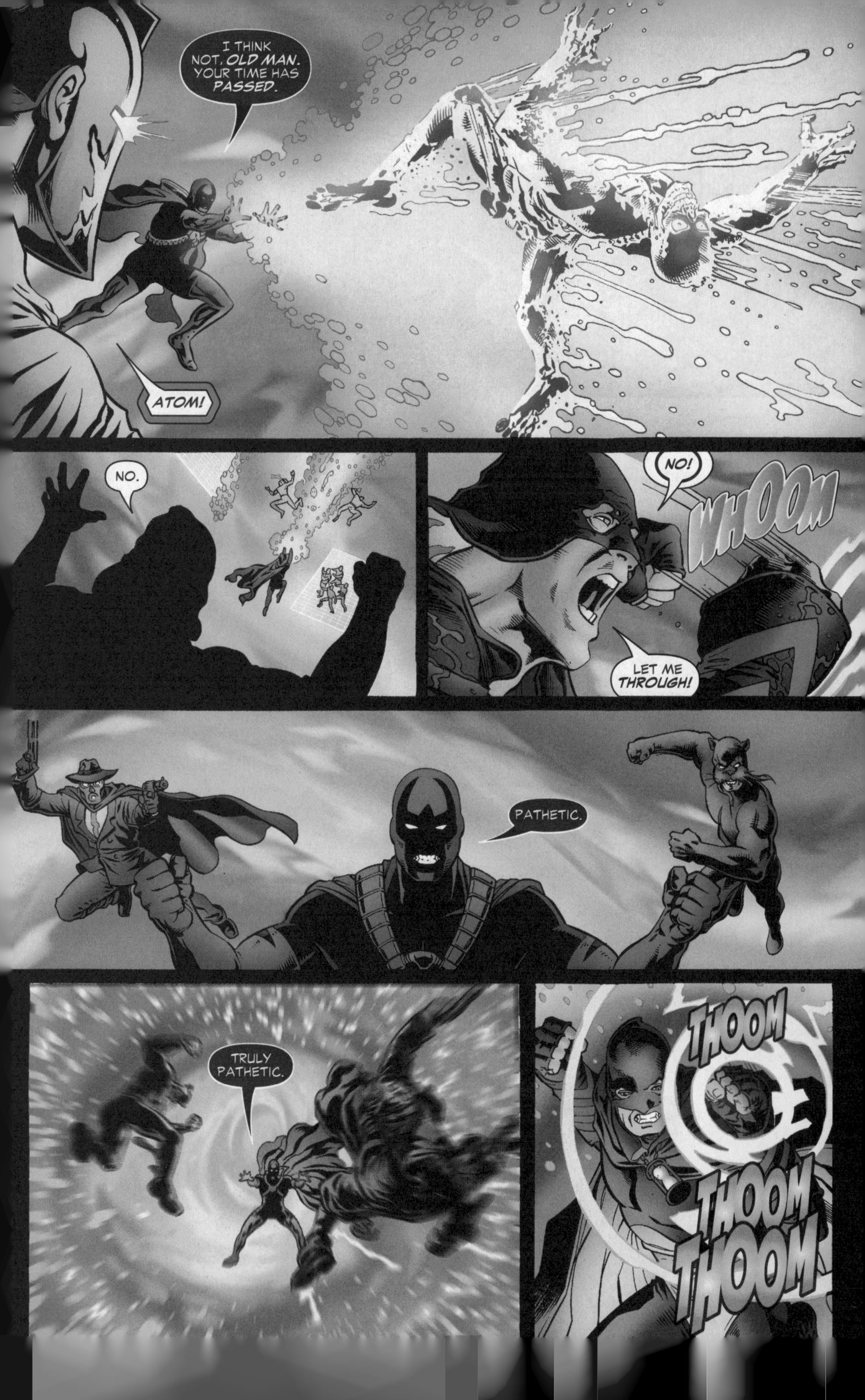
I THINK NOT, OLD MAN. YOUR TIME HAS PASSED.
ATOM!
NO.
NO!
WHOOM
LET ME THROUGH!
PATHETIC.
TRULY PATHETIC.
THOOM
THOOM
THOOM

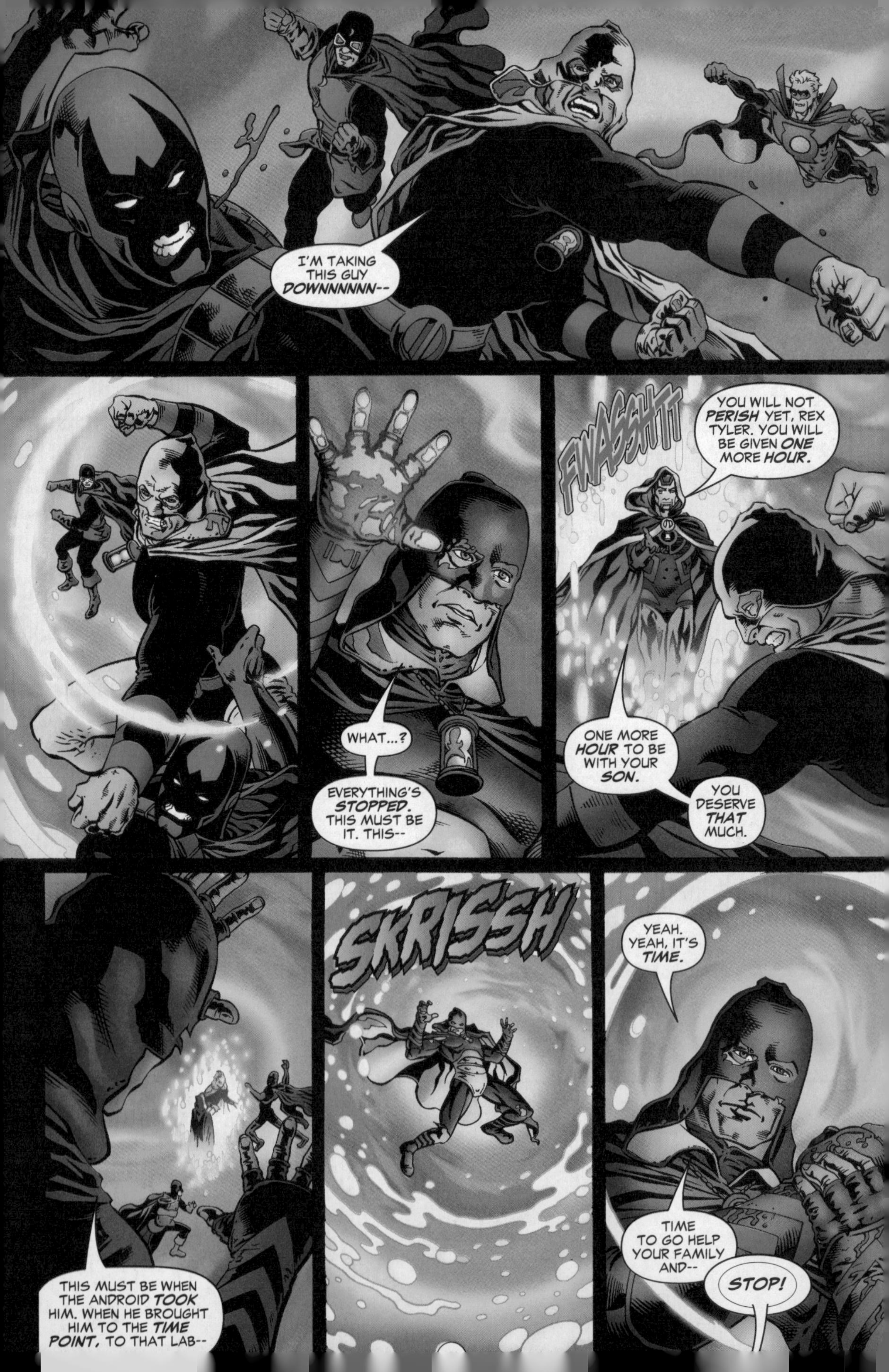
I'M TAKING THIS GUY DOWNNNNNN--
FWASSHTT
YOU WILL NOT PERISH YET, REX TYLER. YOU WILL BE GIVEN ONE MORE HOUR.
WHAT...?
EVERYTHING'S STOPPED. THIS MUST BE IT. THIS--
ONE MORE HOUR TO BE WITH YOUR SON.
YOU DESERVE THAT MUCH.
THIS MUST BE WHEN THE ANDROID TOOK HIM. WHEN HE BROUGHT HIM TO THE TIME POINT, TO THAT LAB--
SKRISSH
YEAH. YEAH, IT'S TIME.
TIME TO GO HELP YOUR FAMILY AND--
STOP!

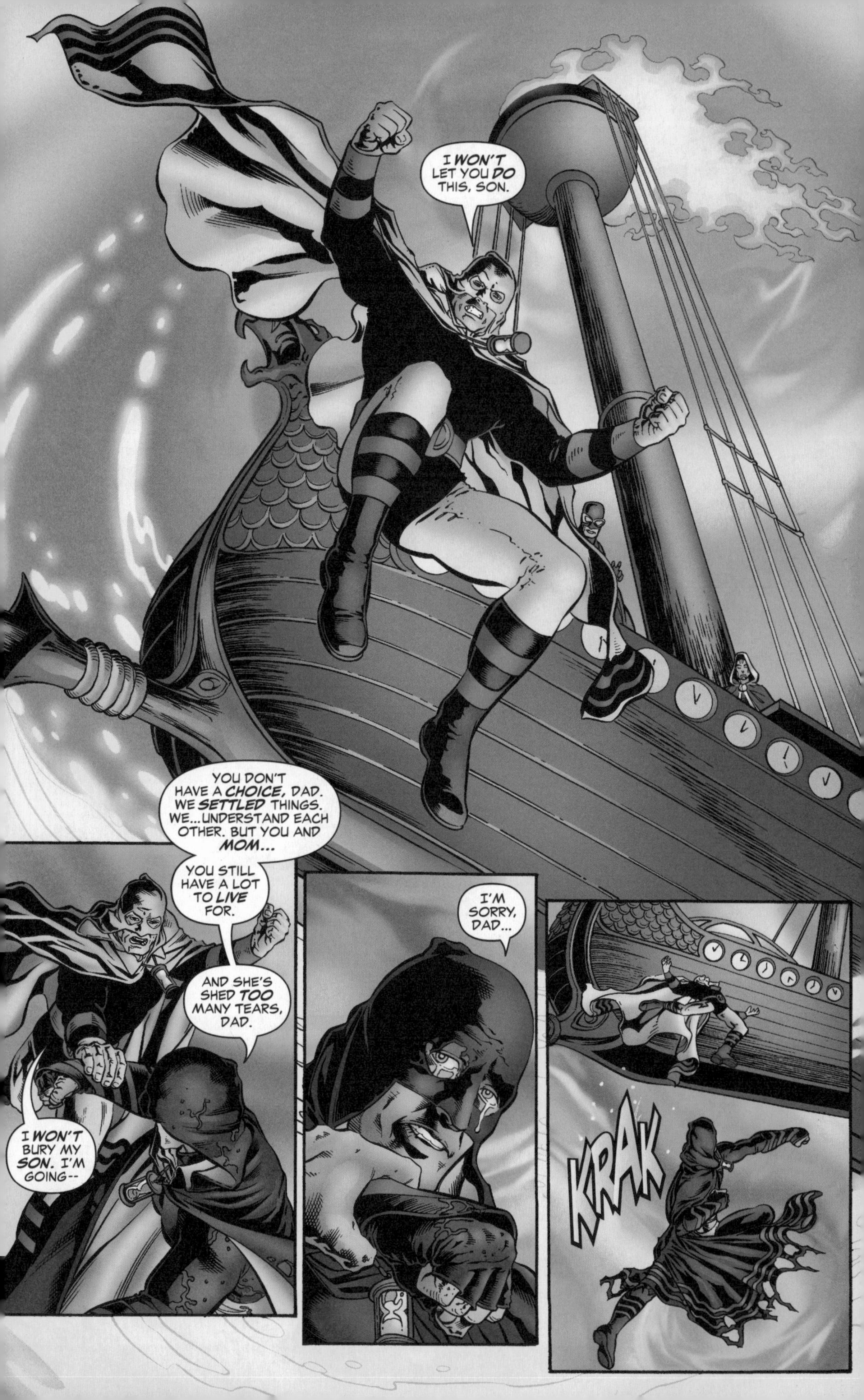
I WON'T LET YOU DO THIS, SON.
YOU DON'T HAVE A CHOICE, DAD. WE SETTLED THINGS. WE...UNDERSTAND EACH OTHER. BUT YOU AND MOM...
YOU STILL HAVE A LOT TO LIVE FOR.
AND SHE'S SHED TOO MANY TEARS, DAD.
I WON'T BURY MY SON. I'M GOING--
I'M SORRY, DAD...
KRAK

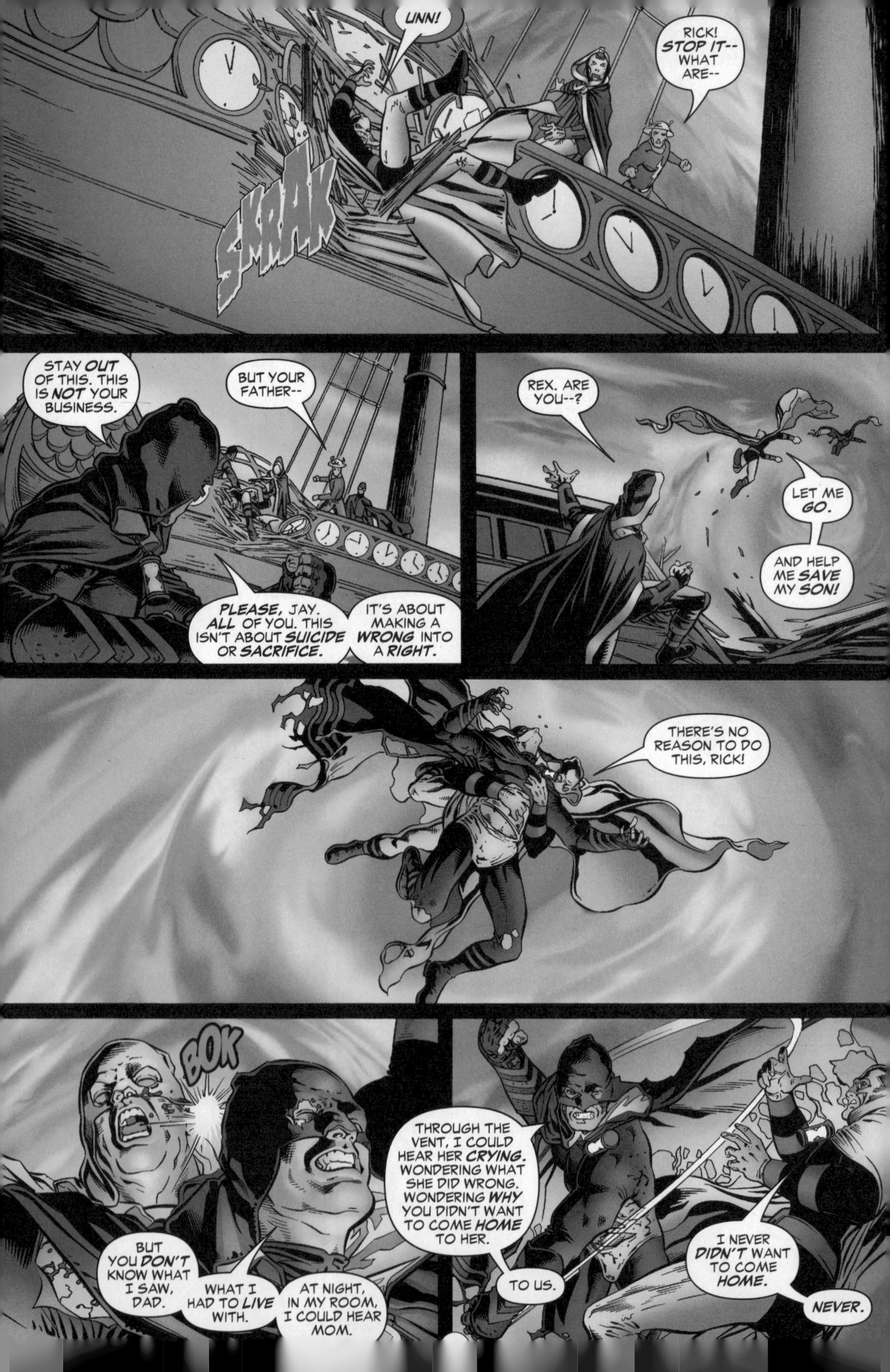
UNN!
RICK! STOP IT-- WHAT ARE--
SKRAK
STAY OUT OF THIS. THIS IS NOT YOUR BUSINESS.
BUT YOUR FATHER--
PLEASE, JAY. ALL OF YOU. THIS ISN'T ABOUT SUICIDE OR SACRIFICE.
IT'S ABOUT MAKING A WRONG INTO A RIGHT.
REX. ARE YOU--?
LET ME GO.
AND HELP ME SAVE MY SON!
THERE'S NO REASON TO DO THIS, RICK!
BOK
BUT YOU DON'T KNOW WHAT I SAW, DAD.
WHAT I HAD TO LIVE WITH.
AT NIGHT, IN MY ROOM, I COULD HEAR MOM.
THROUGH THE VENT, I COULD HEAR HER CRYING. WONDERING WHAT SHE DID WRONG. WONDERING WHY YOU DIDN'T WANT TO COME HOME TO HER.
TO US.
I NEVER DIDN'T WANT TO COME HOME.
NEVER.

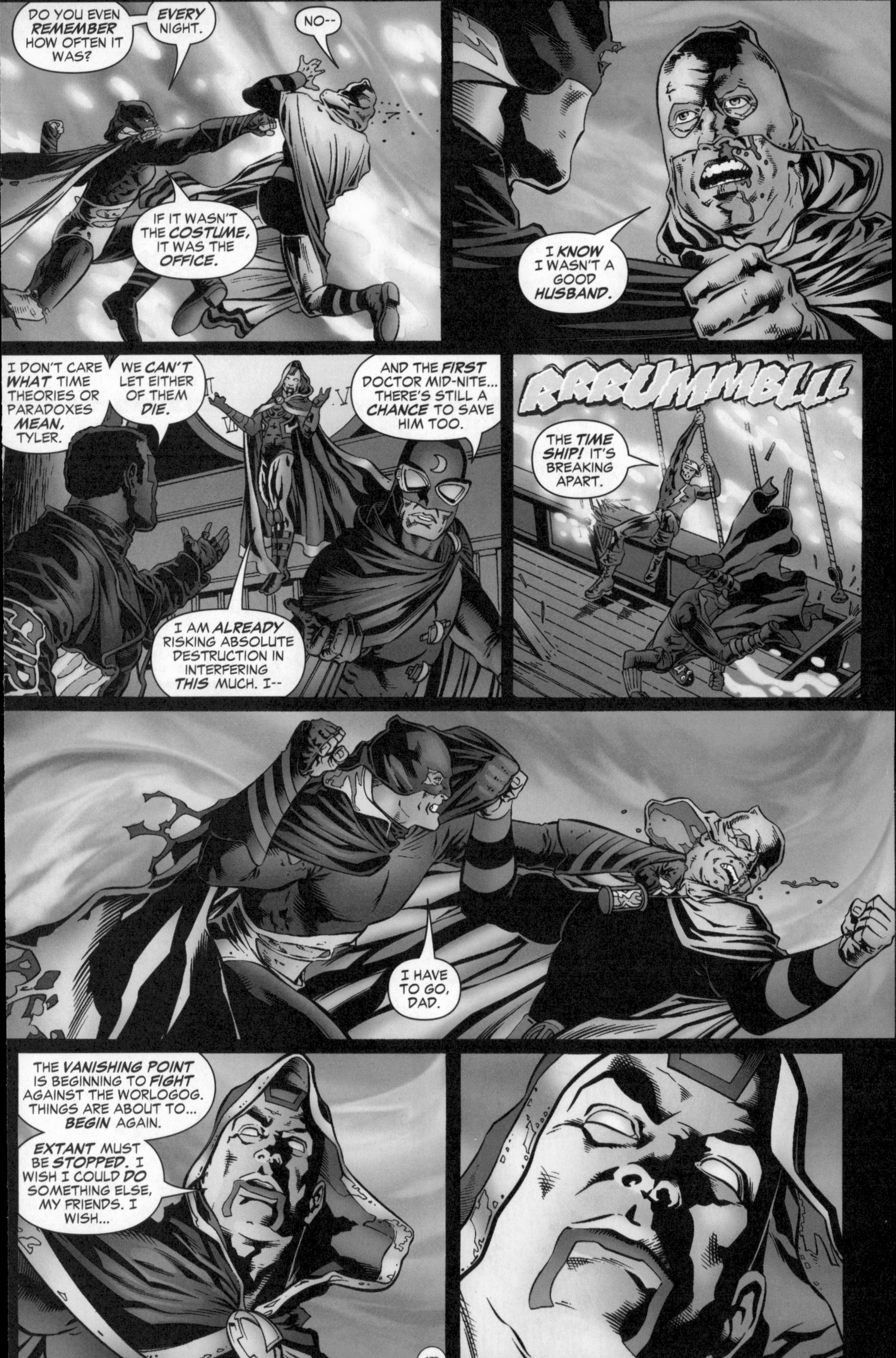
DO YOU EVEN REMEMBER HOW OFTEN IT WAS?
EVERY NIGHT.
NO--
IF IT WASN'T THE COSTUME, IT WAS THE OFFICE.
I KNOW I WASN'T A GOOD HUSBAND.
I DON'T CARE WHAT TIME THEORIES OR PARADOXES MEAN, TYLER.
WE CAN'T LET EITHER OF THEM DIE.
AND THE FIRST DOCTOR MID-NITE... THERE'S STILL A CHANCE TO SAVE HIM TOO.
I AM ALREADY RISKING ABSOLUTE DESTRUCTION IN INTERFERING THIS MUCH. I--
RRRUMMMBLLL
THE TIME SHIP! IT'S BREAKING APART.
I HAVE TO GO, DAD.
THE VANISHING POINT IS BEGINNING TO FIGHT AGAINST THE WORLOGOG. THINGS ARE ABOUT TO... BEGIN AGAIN.
EXTANT MUST BE STOPPED. I WISH I COULD DO SOMETHING ELSE, MY FRIENDS. I WISH...

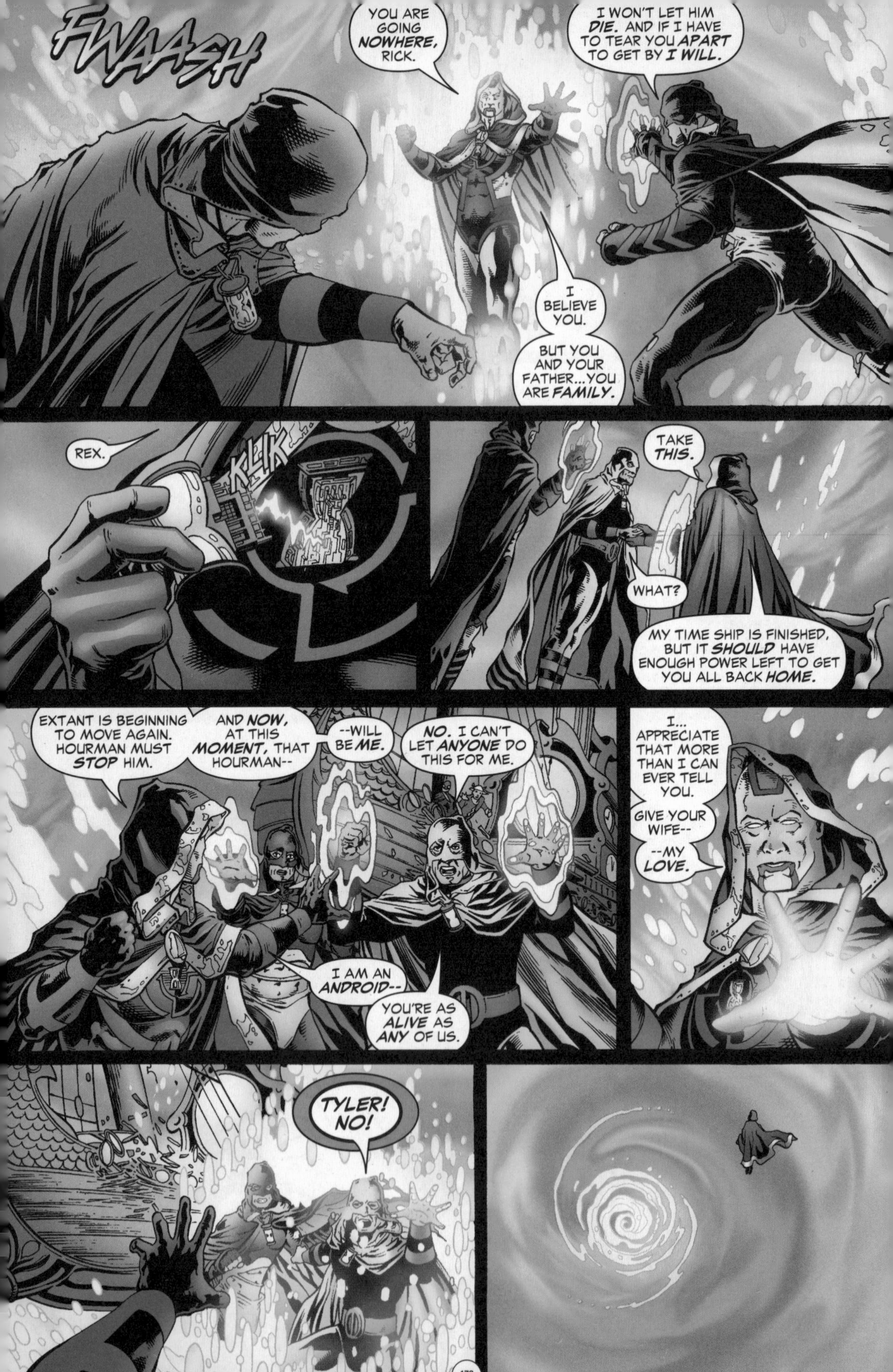
FWAASH
YOU ARE GOING NOWHERE, RICK.
I WON'T LET HIM DIE. AND IF I HAVE TO TEAR YOU APART TO GET BY I WILL.
I BELIEVE YOU.
BUT YOU AND YOUR FATHER...YOU ARE FAMILY.
REX.
KLIK
TAKE THIS.
WHAT?
MY TIME SHIP IS FINISHED, BUT IT SHOULD HAVE ENOUGH POWER LEFT TO GET YOU ALL BACK HOME.
EXTANT IS BEGINNING TO MOVE AGAIN. HOURMAN MUST STOP HIM.
AND NOW, AT THIS MOMENT, THAT HOURMAN--
--WILL BE ME.
NO. I CAN'T LET ANYONE DO THIS FOR ME.
I AM AN ANDROID--
YOU'RE AS ALIVE AS ANY OF US.
I... APPRECIATE THAT MORE THAN I CAN EVER TELL YOU.
GIVE YOUR WIFE--
--MY LOVE.
TYLER! NO!

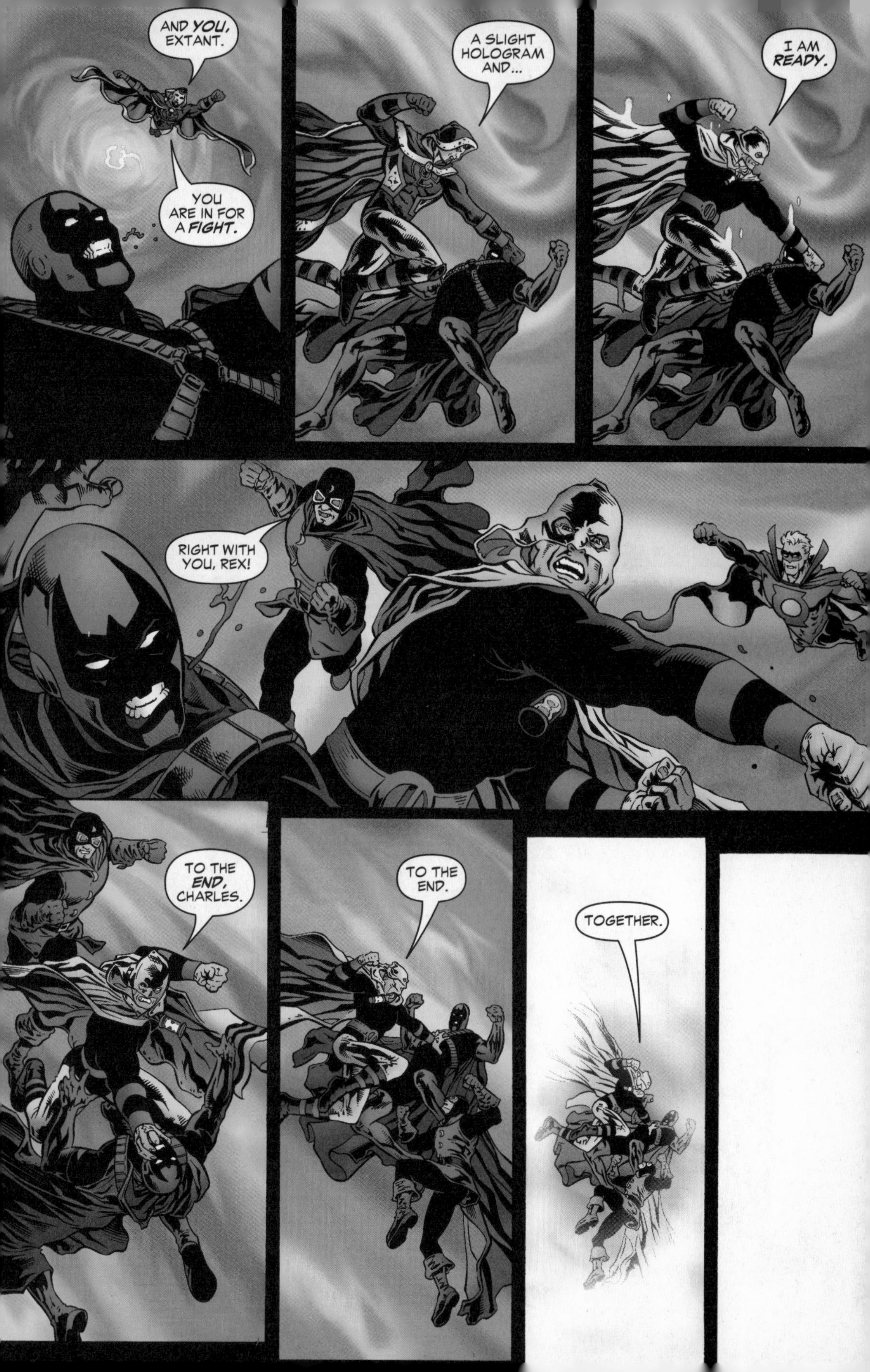
AND YOU, EXTANT.
YOU ARE IN FOR A FIGHT.
A SLIGHT HOLOGRAM AND...
I AM READY.
RIGHT WITH YOU, REX!
TO THE END, CHARLES.
TO THE END.
TOGETHER.

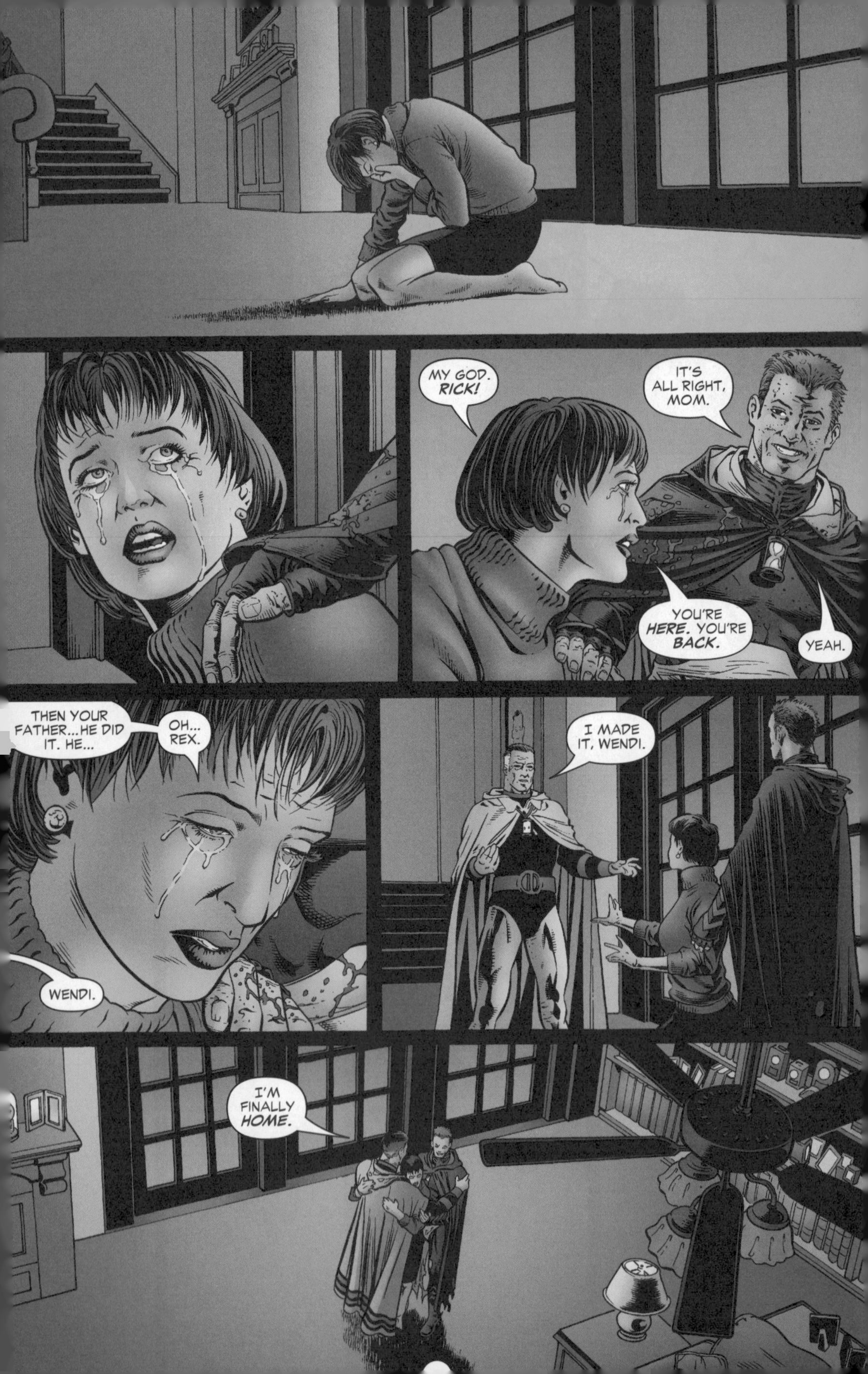
MY GOD. RICK!
IT'S ALL RIGHT, MOM.
YOU'RE HERE. YOU'RE BACK.
YEAH.
THEN YOUR FATHER...HE DID IT. HE...
OH... REX.
WENDI.
I MADE IT, WENDI.
I'M FINALLY HOME.

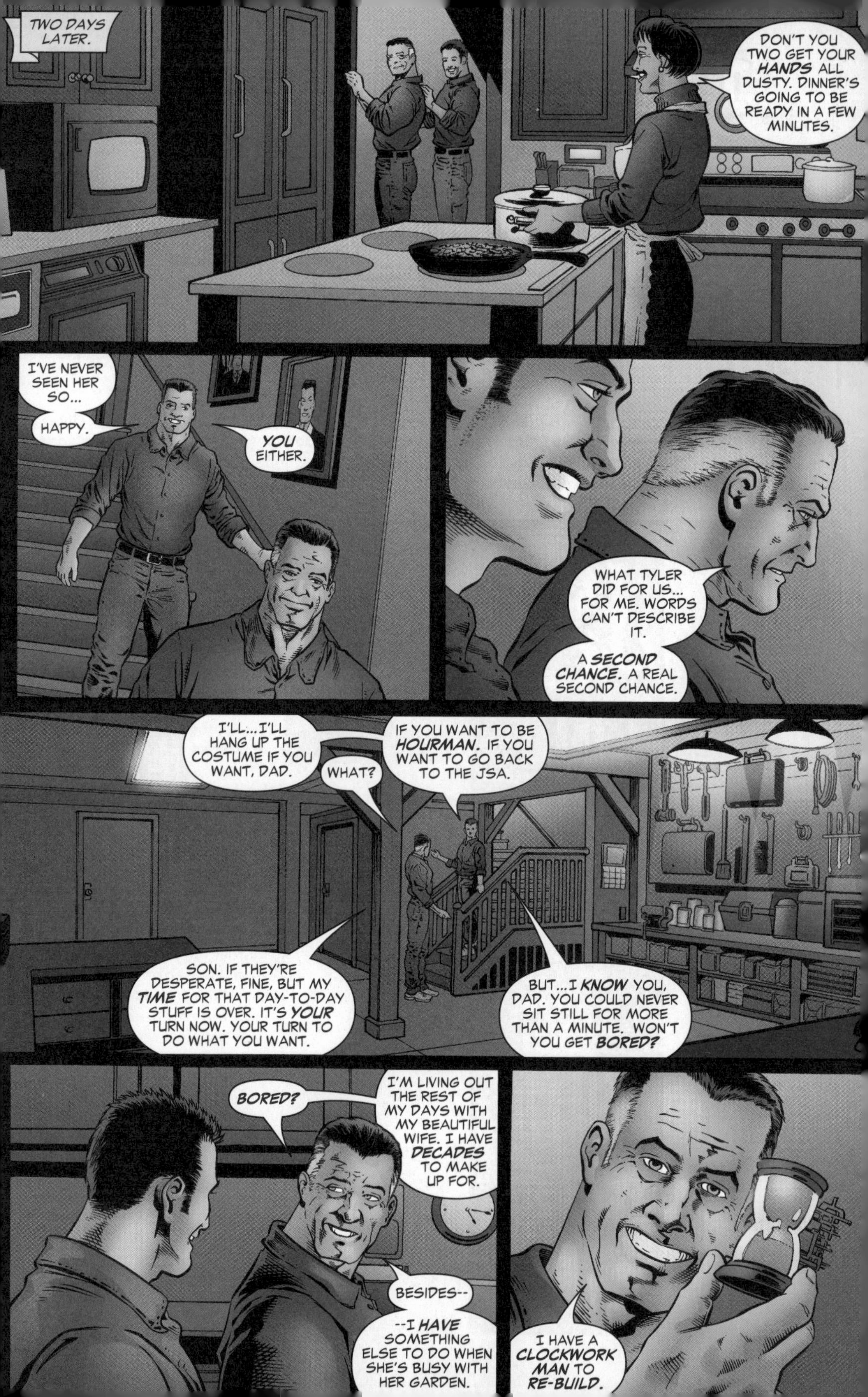
TWO DAYS LATER.
DON'T YOU TWO GET YOUR HANDS ALL DUSTY. DINNER'S GOING TO BE READY IN A FEW MINUTES.
I'VE NEVER SEEN HER SO...
HAPPY.
YOU EITHER.
WHAT TYLER DID FOR US... FOR ME. WORDS CAN'T DESCRIBE IT.
A SECOND CHANCE. A REAL SECOND CHANCE.
I'LL...I'LL HANG UP THE COSTUME IF YOU WANT, DAD.
WHAT?
IF YOU WANT TO BE HOURMAN. IF YOU WANT TO GO BACK TO THE JSA.
SON. IF THEY'RE DESPERATE, FINE, BUT MY TIME FOR THAT DAY-TO-DAY STUFF IS OVER. IT'S YOUR TURN NOW. YOUR TURN TO DO WHAT YOU WANT.
BUT...I KNOW YOU, DAD. YOU COULD NEVER SIT STILL FOR MORE THAN A MINUTE. WON'T YOU GET BORED?
BORED?
I'M LIVING OUT THE REST OF MY DAYS WITH MY BEAUTIFUL WIFE. I HAVE DECADES TO MAKE UP FOR.
BESIDES--
--I HAVE SOMETHING ELSE TO DO WHEN SHE'S BUSY WITH HER GARDEN.
I HAVE A CLOCKWORK MAN TO RE-BUILD.

# IDENTITY CRISIS

The last story in this collection is actually tied to the events of IDENTITY CRISIS, 2004's best-selling miniseries by novelist Brad Meltzer. Brad and JSA writer Geoff Johns were roommates in college, discovering their mutual affection for comics. It's no surprise both wound up writers, first in prose and television respectively, and then comics beckoned.

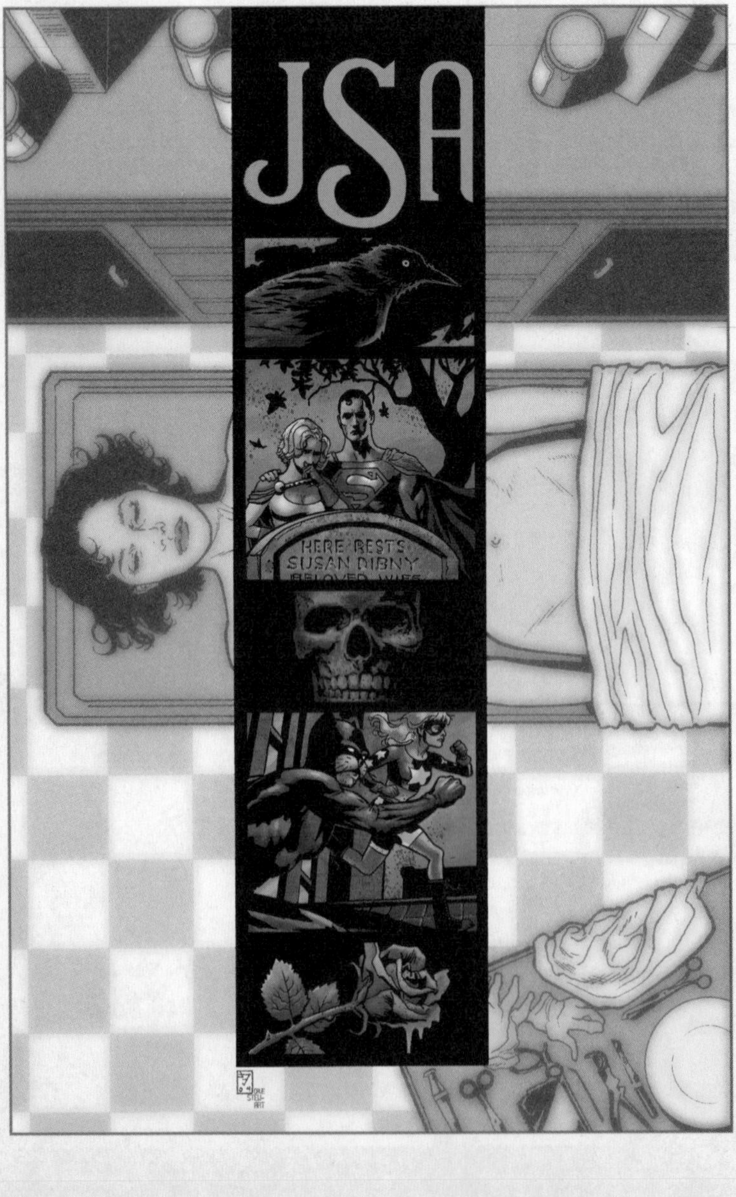
JSA
HERE RESTS
SUSAN DIBNY

IDENTITY CRISIS was an attempt to both humanize the super-heroes and super-villains who populate the DC Universe, but also explore the ramifications of the actions taken by both sides. Geoff explored those themes thoroughly in his own titles, THE FLASH and JSA, maintaining the somber tones from Brad's miniseries.

Being a murder mystery, it was important for all the clues to be there for readers to follow. While those choosing to read only IDENTITY CRISIS missed nothing, this autopsy issue of JSA expanded on the exact nature of Sue Dibny's murder. Earlier in this collection, the bond between Dr. Mid-Nite and Mr. Terrific was established, and the final chapter deepened it as they worked through the procedure.

JSA 67
ART BY JH WILLIAMS III
AND DAVE STEWART

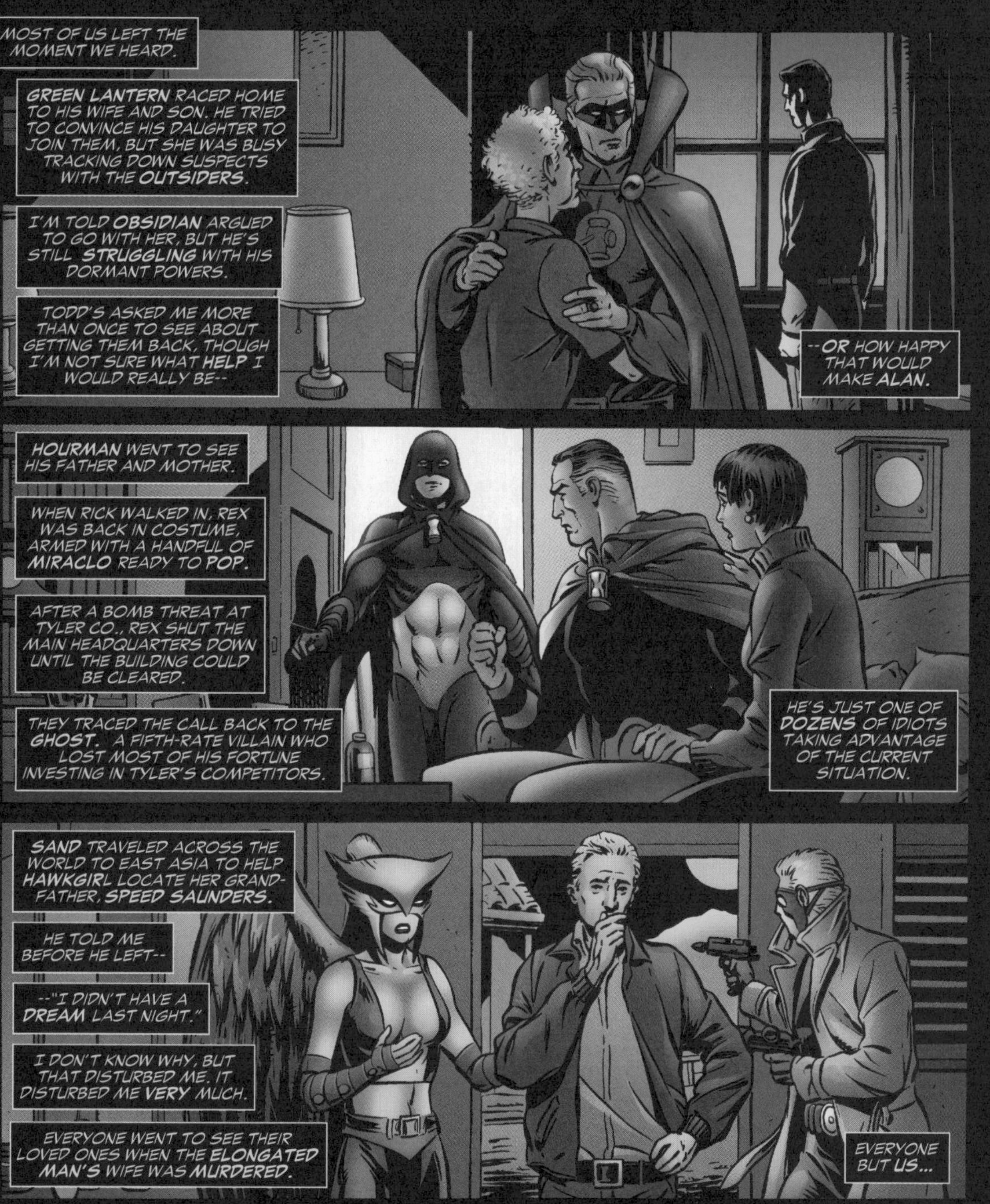
MOST OF US LEFT THE MOMENT WE HEARD.
GREEN LANTERN RACED HOME TO HIS WIFE AND SON. HE TRIED TO CONVINCE HIS DAUGHTER TO JOIN THEM, BUT SHE WAS BUSY TRACKING DOWN SUSPECTS WITH THE OUTSIDERS.
I'M TOLD OBSIDIAN ARGUED TO GO WITH HER, BUT HE'S STILL STRUGGLING WITH HIS DORMANT POWERS.
TODD'S ASKED ME MORE THAN ONCE TO SEE ABOUT GETTING THEM BACK, THOUGH I'M NOT SURE WHAT HELP I WOULD REALLY BE--
--OR HOW HAPPY THAT WOULD MAKE ALAN.
HOURMAN WENT TO SEE HIS FATHER AND MOTHER.
WHEN RICK WALKED IN, REX WAS BACK IN COSTUME, ARMED WITH A HANDFUL OF MIRACLO READY TO POP.
AFTER A BOMB THREAT AT TYLER CO., REX SHUT THE MAIN HEADQUARTERS DOWN UNTIL THE BUILDING COULD BE CLEARED.
THEY TRACED THE CALL BACK TO THE GHOST. A FIFTH-RATE VILLAIN WHO LOST MOST OF HIS FORTUNE INVESTING IN TYLER'S COMPETITORS.
HE'S JUST ONE OF DOZENS OF IDIOTS TAKING ADVANTAGE OF THE CURRENT SITUATION.
SAND TRAVELED ACROSS THE WORLD TO EAST ASIA TO HELP HAWKGIRL LOCATE HER GRAND-FATHER, SPEED SAUNDERS.
HE TOLD ME BEFORE HE LEFT--
--"I DIDN'T HAVE A DREAM LAST NIGHT."
I DON'T KNOW WHY, BUT THAT DISTURBED ME. IT DISTURBED ME VERY MUCH.
EVERYONE WENT TO SEE THEIR LOVED ONES WHEN THE ELONGATED MAN'S WIFE WAS MURDERED.
EVERYONE BUT US...

# THE AUTOPSY

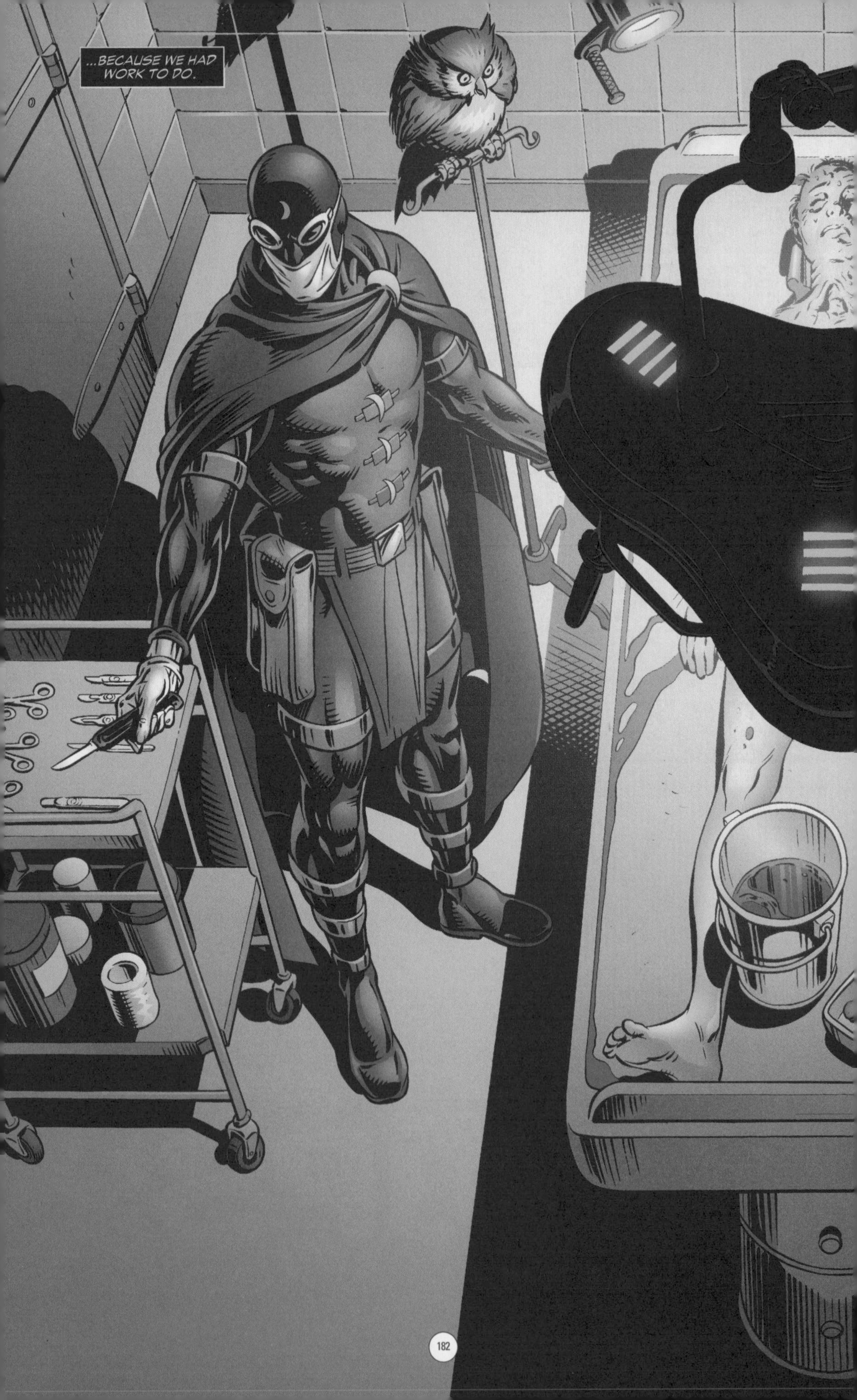
...BECAUSE WE HAD WORK TO DO.

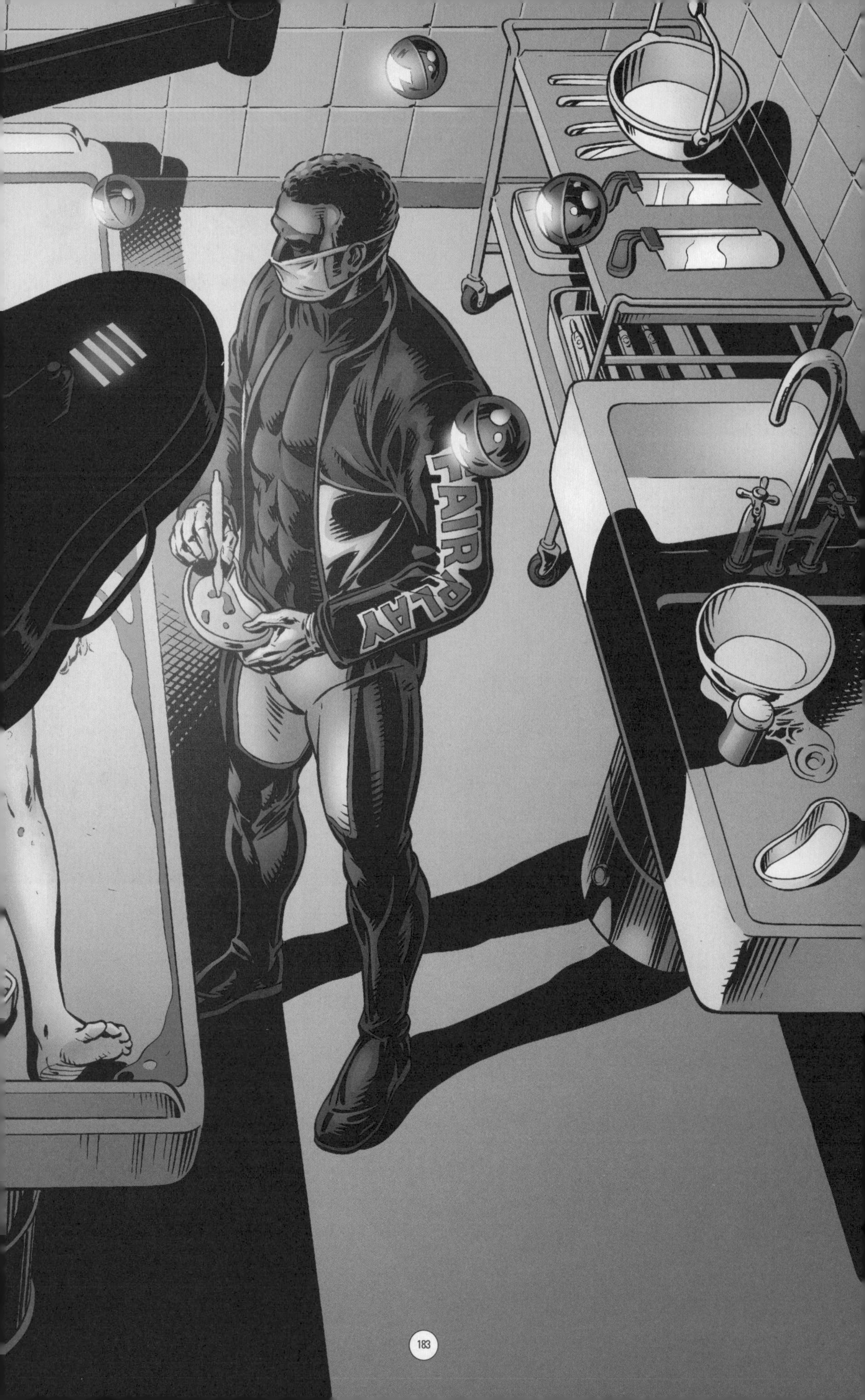
FAIR PLAY

ORIGINALLY, THE D.E.O. WANTED TO SEND ONE OF THEIR PATHOLOGISTS TO EXAMINE SUE DIBNY'S BODY.

BUT NO ONE TRUSTS THE D.E.O.

JAY GARRICK SUGGESTED MYSELF AND MR. TERRIFIC HANDLE THE AUTOPSY.

AND, OF COURSE, EVERYONE TRUSTS JAY GARRICK.

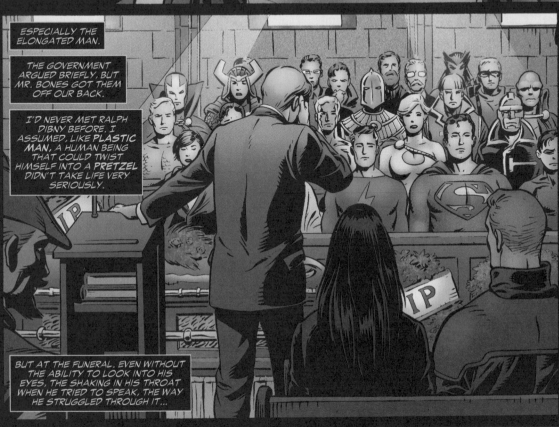

ESPECIALLY THE ELONGATED MAN.

THE GOVERNMENT ARGUED BRIEFLY, BUT MR. BONES GOT THEM OFF OUR BACK.

I'D NEVER MET RALPH DIBNY BEFORE. I ASSUMED, LIKE PLASTIC MAN, A HUMAN BEING THAT COULD TWIST HIMSELF INTO A PRETZEL DIDN'T TAKE LIFE VERY SERIOUSLY.

BUT AT THE FUNERAL. EVEN WITHOUT THE ABILITY TO LOOK INTO HIS EYES, THE SHAKING IN HIS THROAT WHEN HE TRIED TO SPEAK, THE WAY HE STRUGGLED THROUGH IT...

I WEPT.

WHAT CAN SHE TELL YOU, DOCTOR MID-NITE?

MR. TERRIFIC DID NOT.

I DON'T KNOW *HOW* SHE DIED YET, BUT IT *WASN'T* DUE TO *FIRE* OR *SMOKE*. AS I SAID BEFORE--

--HER LUNGS ARE *PINK*. SOMEONE *BURNED* THE BODY TO COVER UP THE *CRIME*.

WE'RE WADING THROUGH THE *DARKNESS* HERE.

AND I'M GOING TO LEAD US *OUT*.

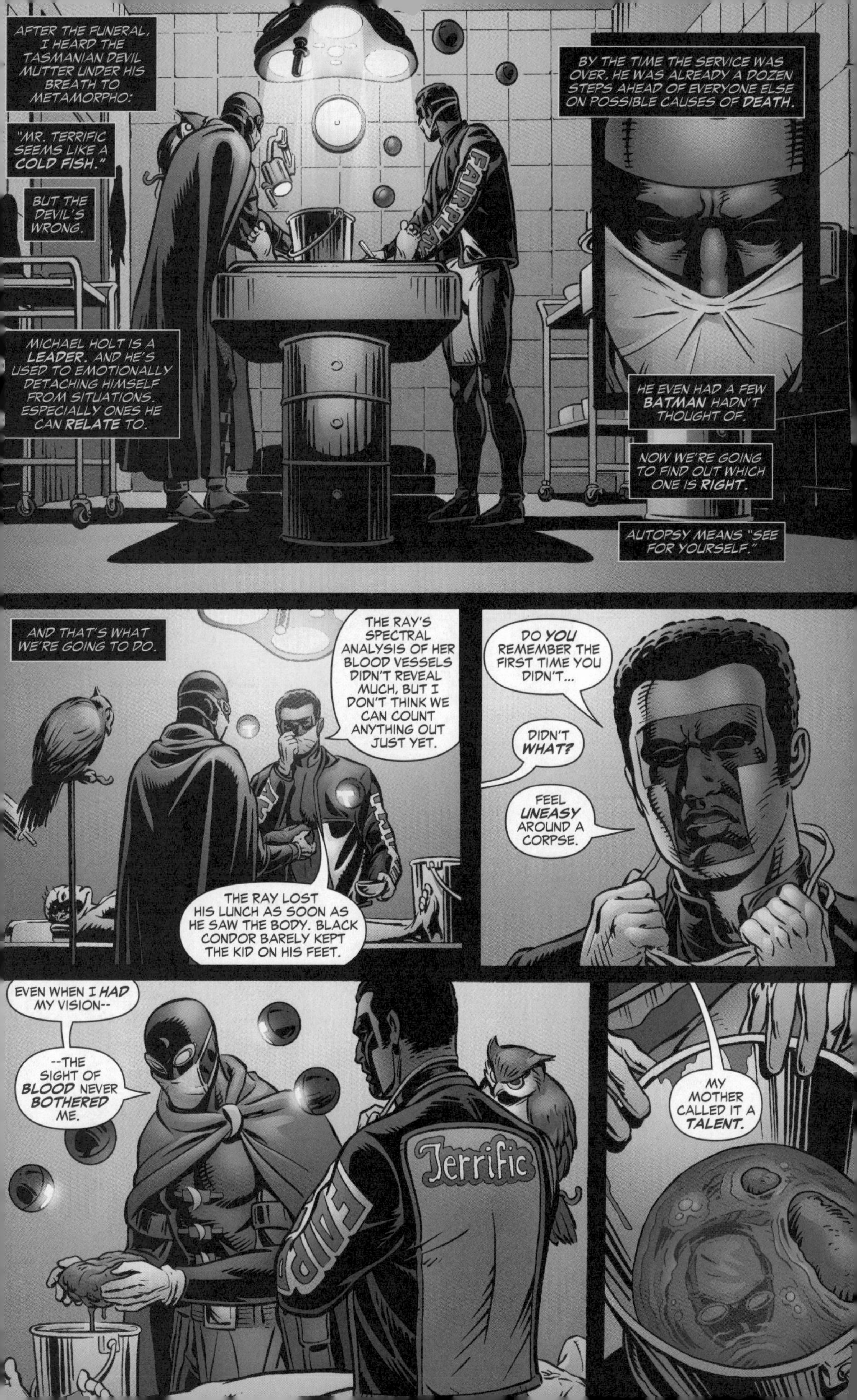
AFTER THE FUNERAL, I HEARD THE TASMANIAN DEVIL MUTTER UNDER HIS BREATH TO METAMORPHO:
"MR. TERRIFIC SEEMS LIKE A COLD FISH."
BUT THE DEVIL'S WRONG.
MICHAEL HOLT IS A LEADER. AND HE'S USED TO EMOTIONALLY DETACHING HIMSELF FROM SITUATIONS. ESPECIALLY ONES HE CAN RELATE TO.
FAIRPLAY
BY THE TIME THE SERVICE WAS OVER, HE WAS ALREADY A DOZEN STEPS AHEAD OF EVERYONE ELSE ON POSSIBLE CAUSES OF DEATH.
HE EVEN HAD A FEW BATMAN HADN'T THOUGHT OF.
NOW WE'RE GOING TO FIND OUT WHICH ONE IS RIGHT.
AUTOPSY MEANS "SEE FOR YOURSELF."
AND THAT'S WHAT WE'RE GOING TO DO.
THE RAY'S SPECTRAL ANALYSIS OF HER BLOOD VESSELS DIDN'T REVEAL MUCH, BUT I DON'T THINK WE CAN COUNT ANYTHING OUT JUST YET.
THE RAY LOST HIS LUNCH AS SOON AS HE SAW THE BODY. BLACK CONDOR BARELY KEPT THE KID ON HIS FEET.
DO YOU REMEMBER THE FIRST TIME YOU DIDN'T...
DIDN'T WHAT?
FEEL UNEASY AROUND A CORPSE.
EVEN WHEN I HAD MY VISION--
--THE SIGHT OF BLOOD NEVER BOTHERED ME.
Terrific
MY MOTHER CALLED IT A TALENT.

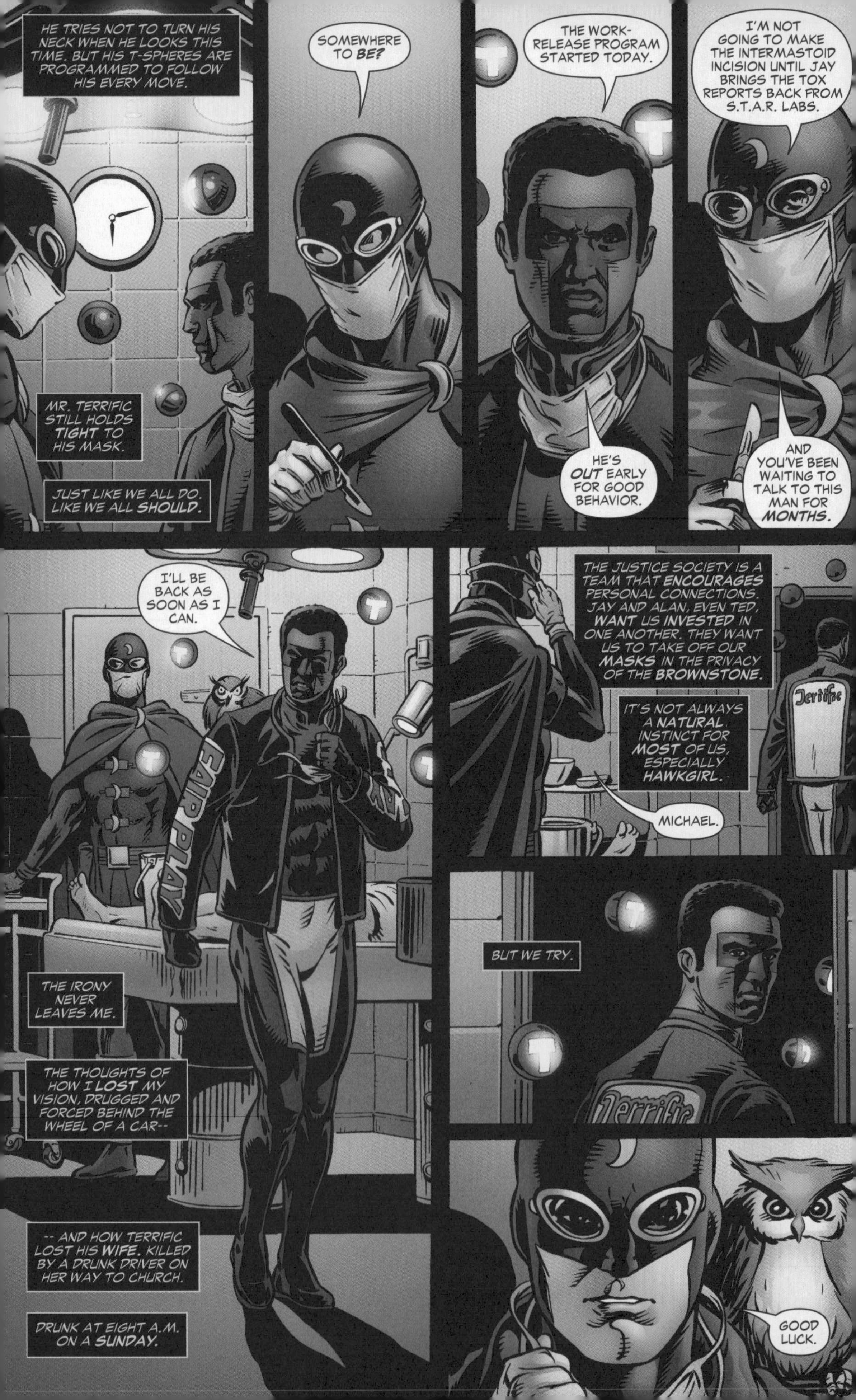

HE TRIES NOT TO TURN HIS NECK WHEN HE LOOKS THIS TIME. BUT HIS T-SPHERES ARE PROGRAMMED TO FOLLOW HIS EVERY MOVE.
MR. TERRIFIC STILL HOLDS TIGHT TO HIS MASK.
JUST LIKE WE ALL DO. LIKE WE ALL SHOULD.
SOMEWHERE TO BE?
THE WORK-RELEASE PROGRAM STARTED TODAY.
HE'S OUT EARLY FOR GOOD BEHAVIOR.
I'M NOT GOING TO MAKE THE INTERMASTOID INCISION UNTIL JAY BRINGS THE TOX REPORTS BACK FROM S.T.A.R. LABS.
AND YOU'VE BEEN WAITING TO TALK TO THIS MAN FOR MONTHS.
I'LL BE BACK AS SOON AS I CAN.
FAIR PLAY
THE IRONY NEVER LEAVES ME.
THE THOUGHTS OF HOW I LOST MY VISION, DRUGGED AND FORCED BEHIND THE WHEEL OF A CAR--
-- AND HOW TERRIFIC LOST HIS WIFE. KILLED BY A DRUNK DRIVER ON HER WAY TO CHURCH.
DRUNK AT EIGHT A.M. ON A SUNDAY.
THE JUSTICE SOCIETY IS A TEAM THAT ENCOURAGES PERSONAL CONNECTIONS. JAY AND ALAN, EVEN TED, WANT US INVESTED IN ONE ANOTHER. THEY WANT US TO TAKE OFF OUR MASKS IN THE PRIVACY OF THE BROWNSTONE.
IT'S NOT ALWAYS A NATURAL INSTINCT FOR MOST OF US, ESPECIALLY HAWKGIRL.
MICHAEL.
Terrific
BUT WE TRY.
Terrific
GOOD LUCK.

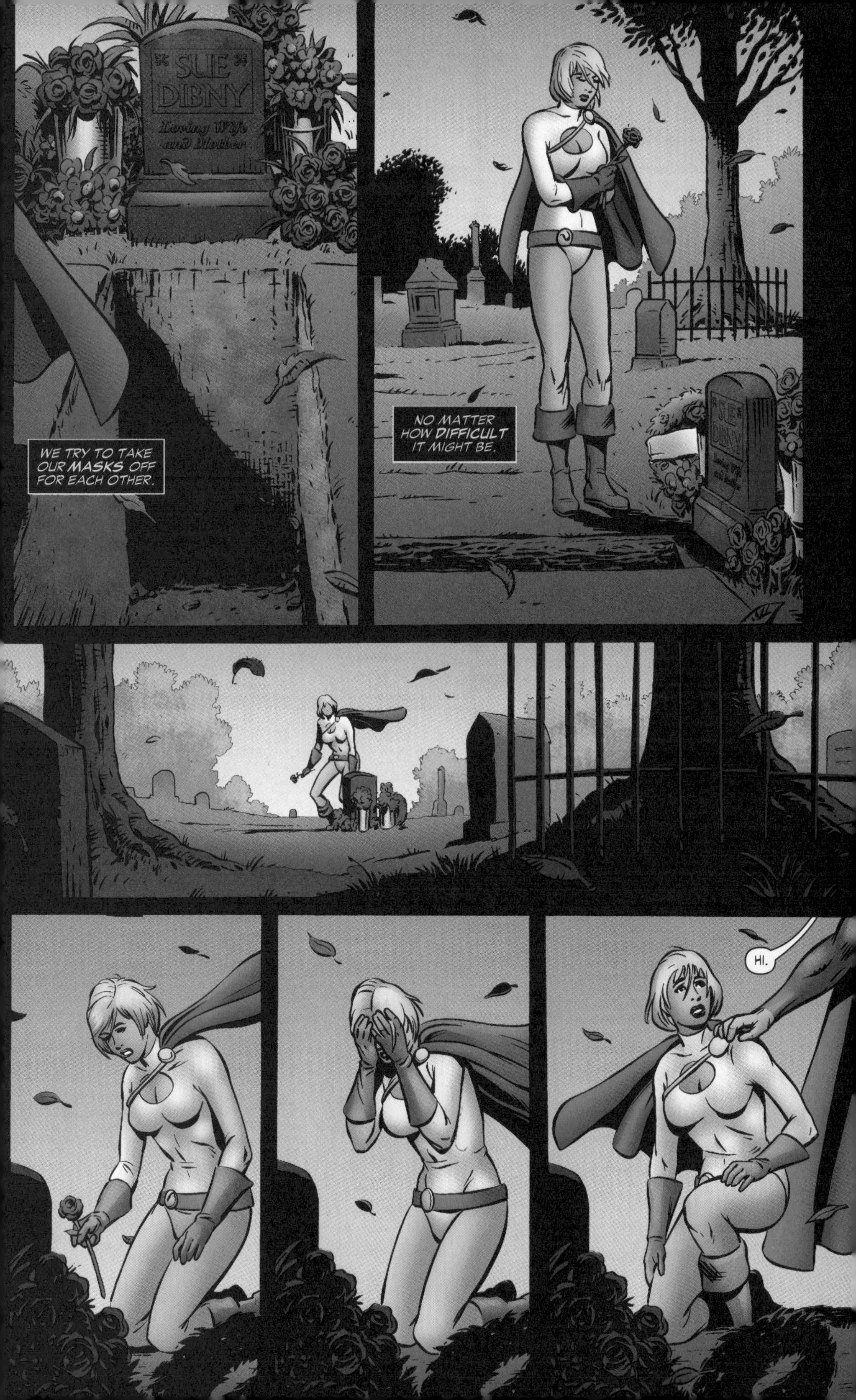
SUE DIBNY
Loving Wife and Mother
WE TRY TO TAKE OUR MASKS OFF FOR EACH OTHER.
NO MATTER HOW DIFFICULT IT MIGHT BE.
HI.

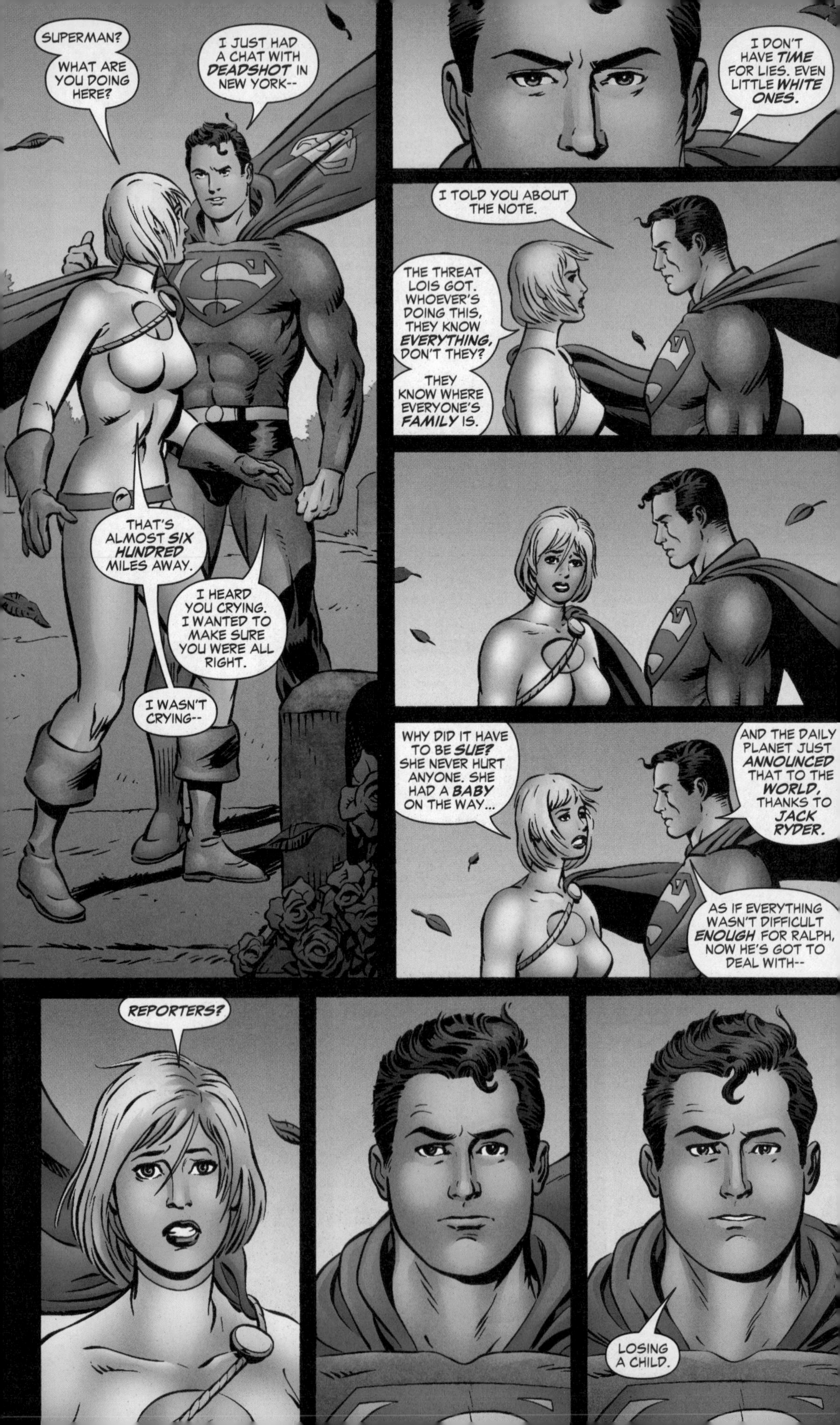
SUPERMAN? WHAT ARE YOU DOING HERE?
I JUST HAD A CHAT WITH DEADSHOT IN NEW YORK--
THAT'S ALMOST SIX HUNDRED MILES AWAY.
I HEARD YOU CRYING. I WANTED TO MAKE SURE YOU WERE ALL RIGHT.
I WASN'T CRYING--
I DON'T HAVE TIME FOR LIES. EVEN LITTLE WHITE ONES.
I TOLD YOU ABOUT THE NOTE.
THE THREAT LOIS GOT. WHOEVER'S DOING THIS, THEY KNOW EVERYTHING, DON'T THEY?
THEY KNOW WHERE EVERYONE'S FAMILY IS.
WHY DID IT HAVE TO BE SUE? SHE NEVER HURT ANYONE. SHE HAD A BABY ON THE WAY...
AND THE DAILY PLANET JUST ANNOUNCED THAT TO THE WORLD, THANKS TO JACK RYDER.
AS IF EVERYTHING WASN'T DIFFICULT ENOUGH FOR RALPH, NOW HE'S GOT TO DEAL WITH--
REPORTERS?
LOSING A CHILD.

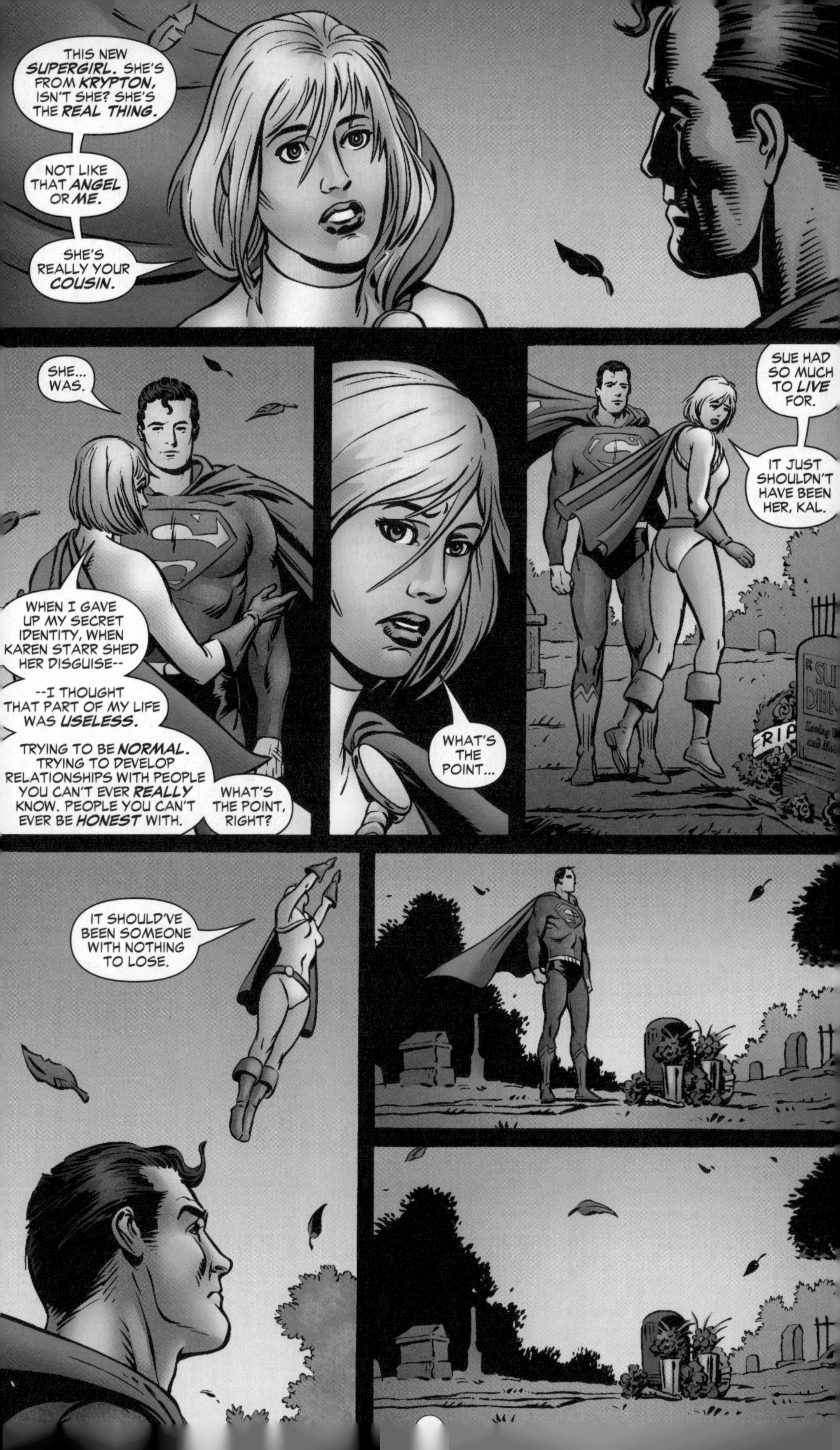

THIS NEW SUPERGIRL. SHE'S FROM KRYPTON, ISN'T SHE? SHE'S THE REAL THING.
NOT LIKE THAT ANGEL OR ME.
SHE'S REALLY YOUR COUSIN.
SHE... WAS.
WHEN I GAVE UP MY SECRET IDENTITY, WHEN KAREN STARR SHED HER DISGUISE--
--I THOUGHT THAT PART OF MY LIFE WAS USELESS.
TRYING TO BE NORMAL. TRYING TO DEVELOP RELATIONSHIPS WITH PEOPLE YOU CAN'T EVER REALLY KNOW. PEOPLE YOU CAN'T EVER BE HONEST WITH.
WHAT'S THE POINT, RIGHT?
WHAT'S THE POINT...
SUE HAD SO MUCH TO LIVE FOR.
IT JUST SHOULDN'T HAVE BEEN HER, KAL.
RIP
IT SHOULD'VE BEEN SOMEONE WITH NOTHING TO LOSE.

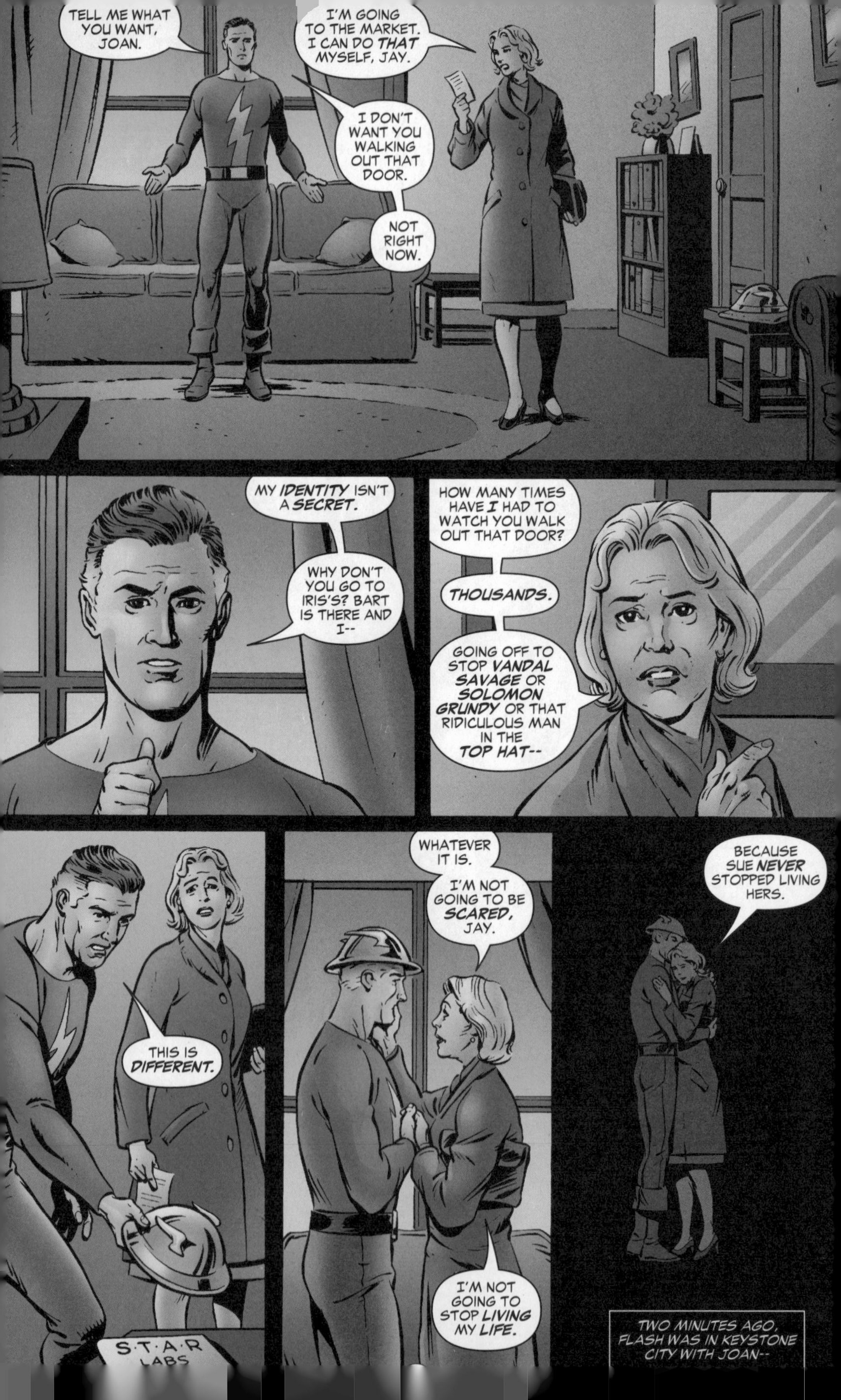
TELL ME WHAT YOU WANT, JOAN.
I'M GOING TO THE MARKET. I CAN DO THAT MYSELF, JAY.
I DON'T WANT YOU WALKING OUT THAT DOOR.
NOT RIGHT NOW.
MY IDENTITY ISN'T A SECRET.
WHY DON'T YOU GO TO IRIS'S? BART IS THERE AND I--
HOW MANY TIMES HAVE I HAD TO WATCH YOU WALK OUT THAT DOOR?
THOUSANDS.
GOING OFF TO STOP VANDAL SAVAGE OR SOLOMON GRUNDY OR THAT RIDICULOUS MAN IN THE TOP HAT--
THIS IS DIFFERENT.
S·T·A·R LABS
WHATEVER IT IS.
I'M NOT GOING TO BE SCARED, JAY.
I'M NOT GOING TO STOP LIVING MY LIFE.
BECAUSE SUE NEVER STOPPED LIVING HERS.
TWO MINUTES AGO, FLASH WAS IN KEYSTONE CITY WITH JOAN--

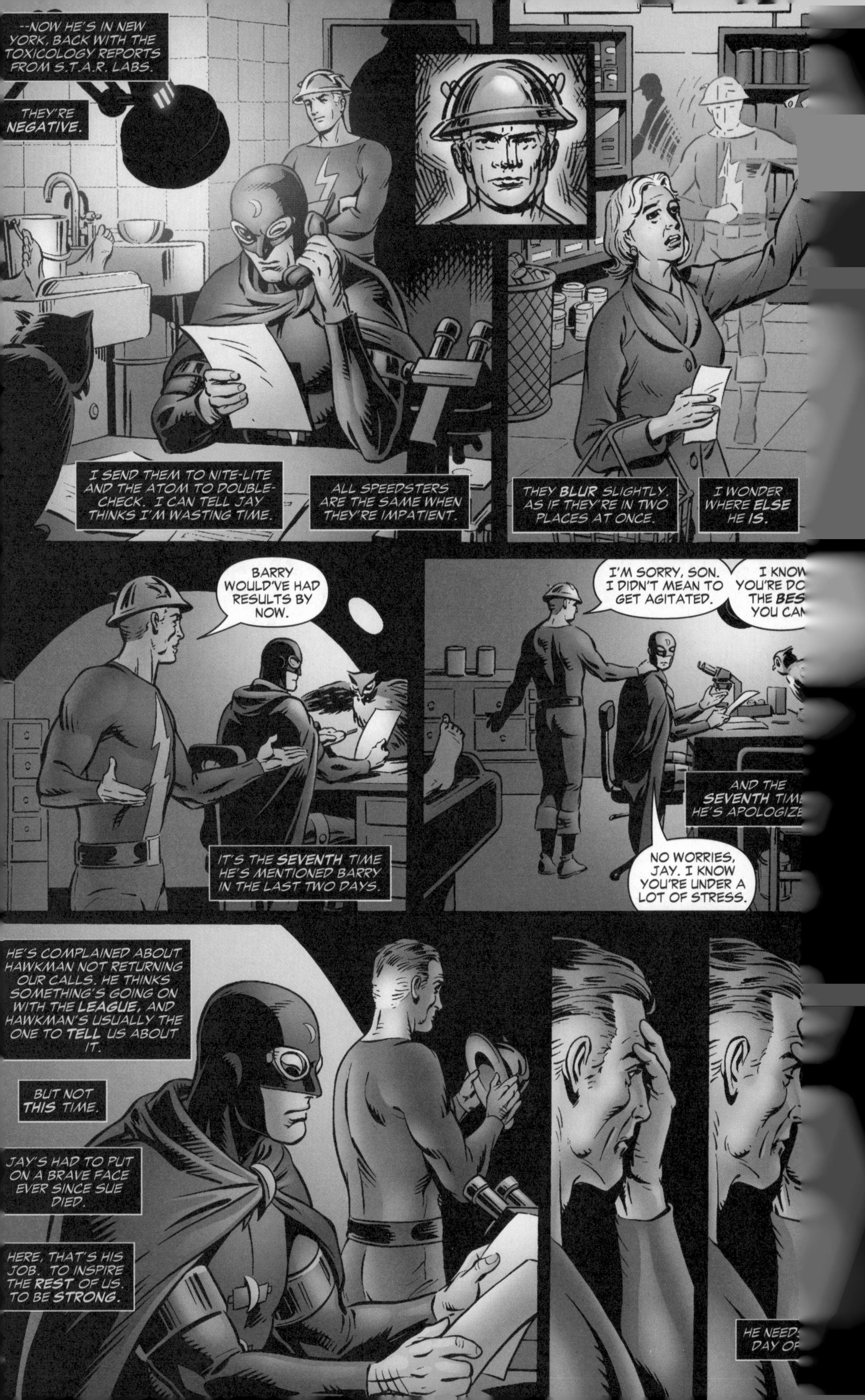

--NOW HE'S IN NEW YORK, BACK WITH THE TOXICOLOGY REPORTS FROM S.T.A.R. LABS.
THEY'RE NEGATIVE.
I SEND THEM TO NITE-LITE AND THE ATOM TO DOUBLE-CHECK. I CAN TELL JAY THINKS I'M WASTING TIME.
ALL SPEEDSTERS ARE THE SAME WHEN THEY'RE IMPATIENT.
THEY BLUR SLIGHTLY. AS IF THEY'RE IN TWO PLACES AT ONCE.
I WONDER WHERE ELSE HE IS.
BARRY WOULD'VE HAD RESULTS BY NOW.
IT'S THE SEVENTH TIME HE'S MENTIONED BARRY IN THE LAST TWO DAYS.
I'M SORRY, SON. I DIDN'T MEAN TO GET AGITATED.
I KNOW YOU'RE DO THE BES YOU CAN
AND THE SEVENTH TIM HE'S APOLOGIZE
NO WORRIES, JAY. I KNOW YOU'RE UNDER A LOT OF STRESS.
HE'S COMPLAINED ABOUT HAWKMAN NOT RETURNING OUR CALLS. HE THINKS SOMETHING'S GOING ON WITH THE LEAGUE, AND HAWKMAN'S USUALLY THE ONE TO TELL US ABOUT IT.
BUT NOT THIS TIME.
JAY'S HAD TO PUT ON A BRAVE FACE EVER SINCE SUE DIED.
HERE, THAT'S HIS JOB. TO INSPIRE THE REST OF US. TO BE STRONG.
HE NEEDS DAY OF

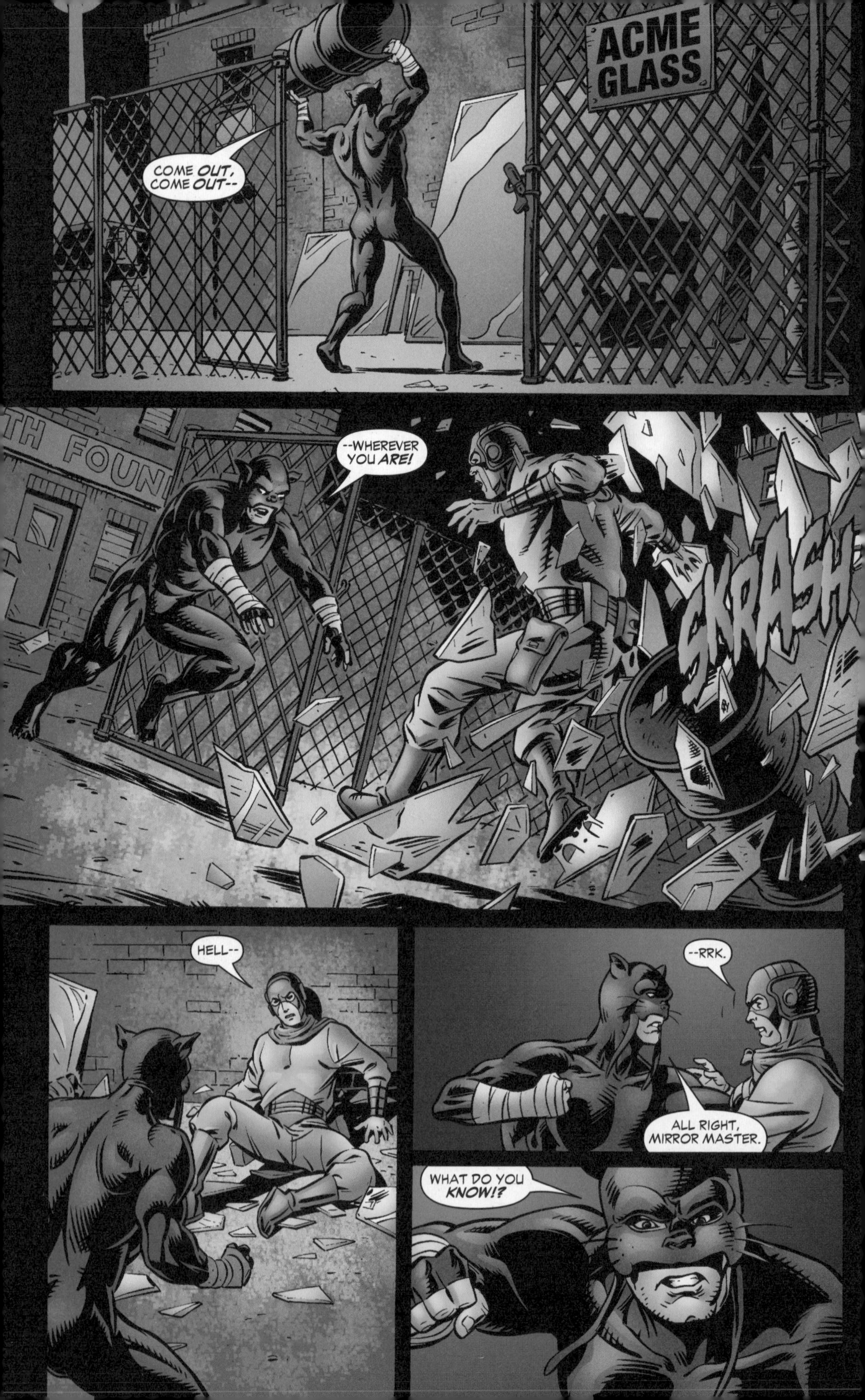
ACME GLASS
COME OUT, COME OUT--
--WHEREVER YOU ARE!
SKRASH
HELL--
--RRK.
ALL RIGHT, MIRROR MASTER.
WHAT DO YOU KNOW!?

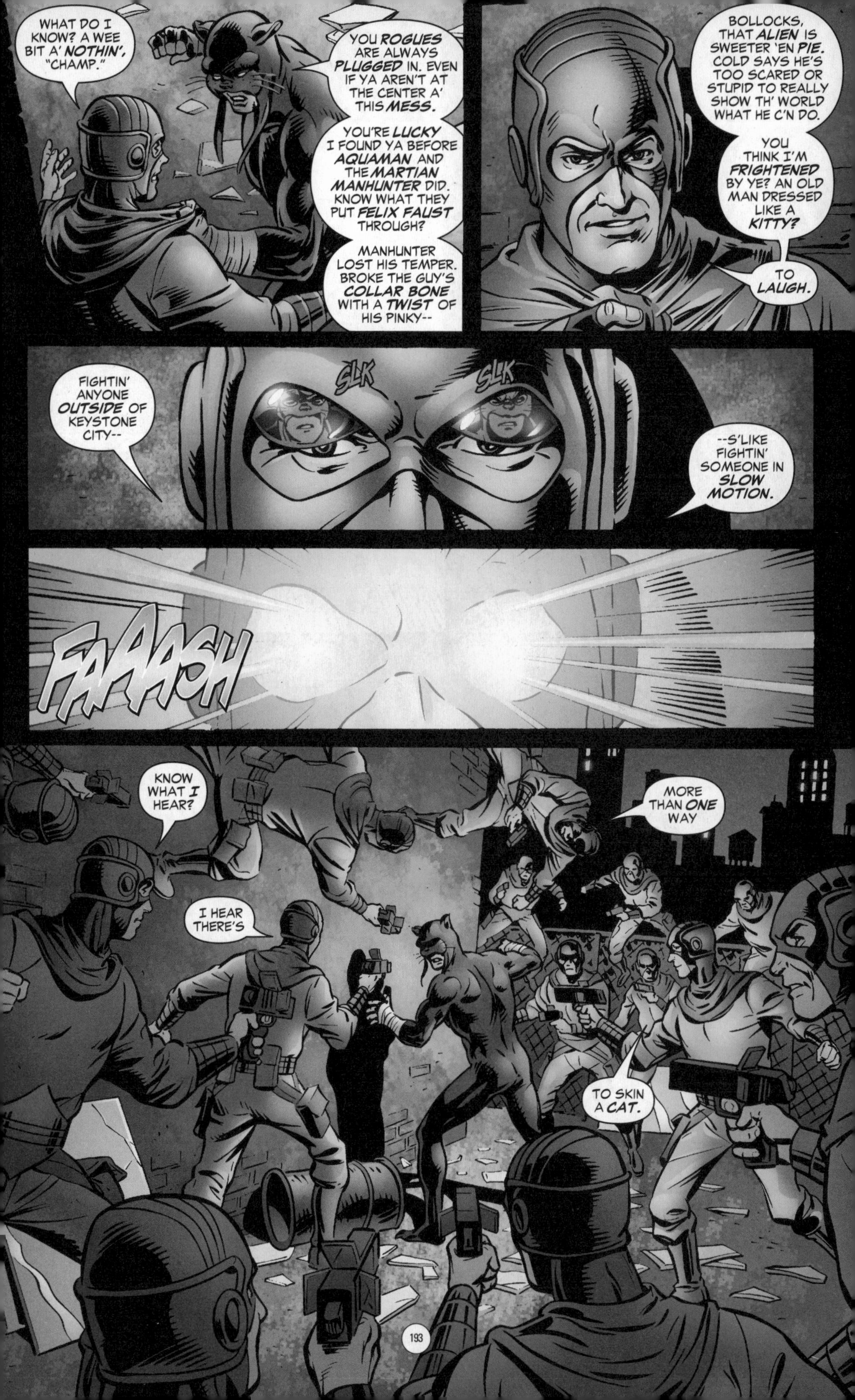
WHAT DO I KNOW? A WEE BIT A' NOTHIN'. "CHAMP."
YOU ROGUES ARE ALWAYS PLUGGED IN. EVEN IF YA AREN'T AT THE CENTER A' THIS MESS.
YOU'RE LUCKY I FOUND YA BEFORE AQUAMAN AND THE MARTIAN MANHUNTER DID. KNOW WHAT THEY PUT FELIX FAUST THROUGH?
MANHUNTER LOST HIS TEMPER. BROKE THE GUY'S COLLAR BONE WITH A TWIST OF HIS PINKY--
BOLLOCKS, THAT ALIEN IS SWEETER 'EN PIE. COLD SAYS HE'S TOO SCARED OR STUPID TO REALLY SHOW TH' WORLD WHAT HE C'N DO.
YOU THINK I'M FRIGHTENED BY YE? AN OLD MAN DRESSED LIKE A KITTY?
TO LAUGH.
SLK
SLK
FIGHTIN' ANYONE OUTSIDE OF KEYSTONE CITY--
--S'LIKE FIGHTIN' SOMEONE IN SLOW MOTION.
FAAASH
KNOW WHAT I HEAR?
I HEAR THERE'S
MORE THAN ONE WAY
TO SKIN A CAT.

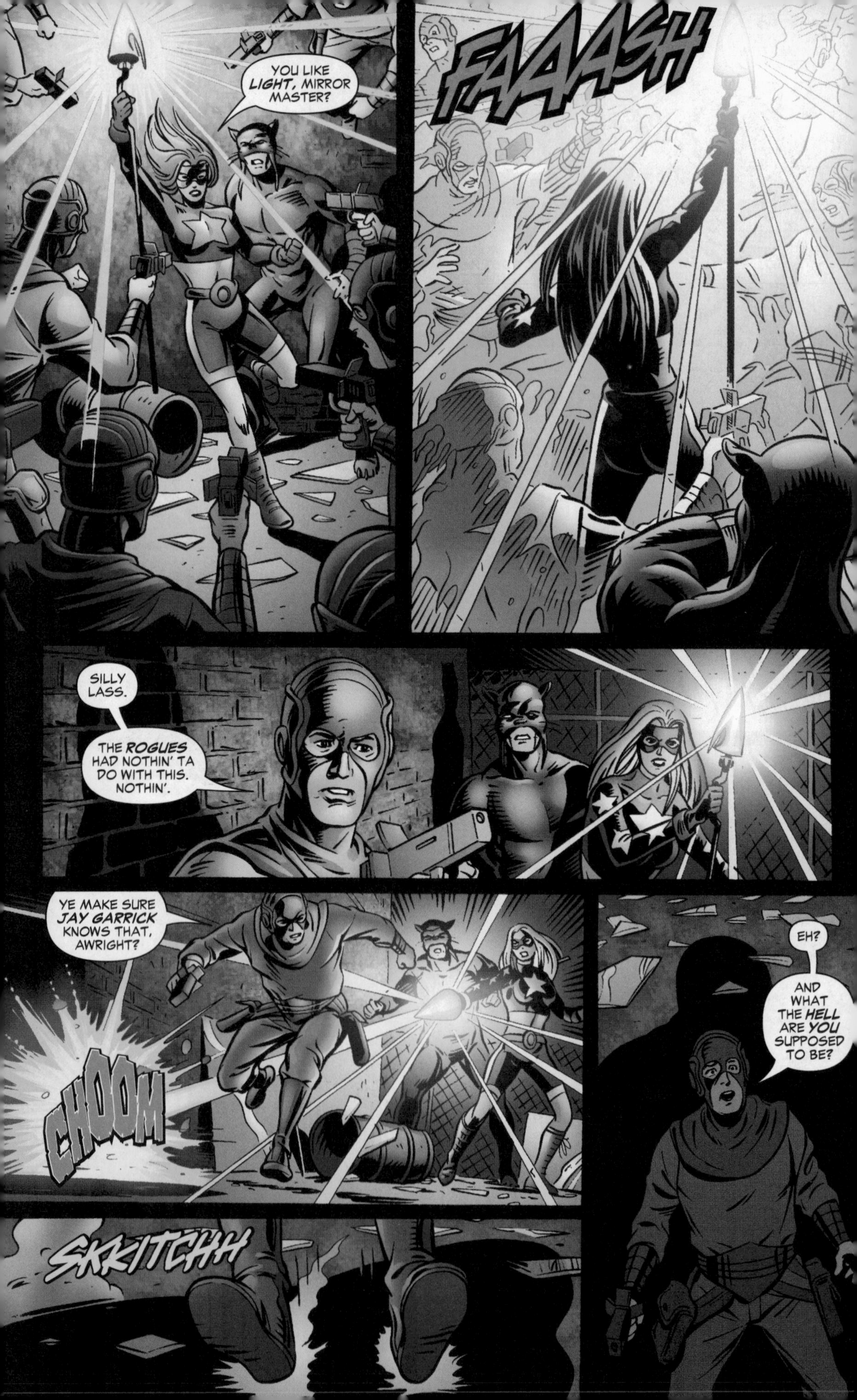
YOU LIKE LIGHT, MIRROR MASTER?
FAAASH
SILLY LASS.
THE ROGUES HAD NOTHIN' TA DO WITH THIS. NOTHIN'.
YE MAKE SURE JAY GARRICK KNOWS THAT, AWRIGHT?
CHOOM
SKRITCHH
EH?
AND WHAT THE HELL ARE YOU SUPPOSED TO BE?

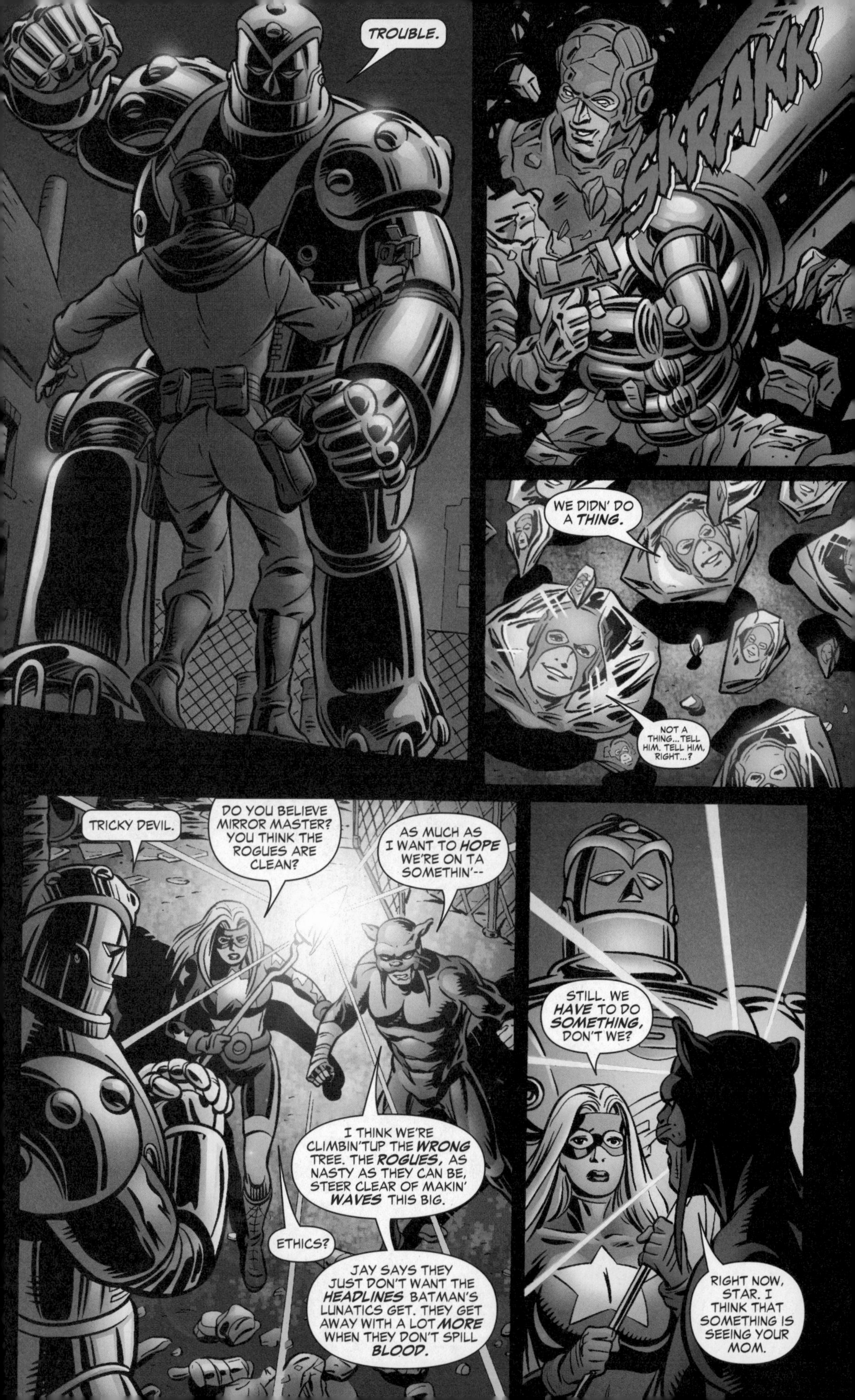
TROUBLE.
SKRAKK
WE DIDN' DO A *THING*.
NOT A THING... TELL HIM. TELL HIM, RIGHT...?
TRICKY DEVIL.
DO YOU BELIEVE MIRROR MASTER? YOU THINK THE ROGUES ARE CLEAN?
AS MUCH AS I WANT TO *HOPE* WE'RE ON TA SOMETHIN'--
I THINK WE'RE CLIMBIN'TUP THE *WRONG* TREE. THE *ROGUES,* AS NASTY AS THEY CAN BE, STEER CLEAR OF MAKIN' *WAVES* THIS BIG.
ETHICS?
JAY SAYS THEY JUST DON'T WANT THE *HEADLINES* BATMAN'S LUNATICS GET. THEY GET AWAY WITH A LOT *MORE* WHEN THEY DON'T SPILL *BLOOD.*
STILL. WE *HAVE* TO DO *SOMETHING,* DON'T WE?
RIGHT NOW, STAR. I THINK THAT SOMETHING IS SEEING YOUR MOM.

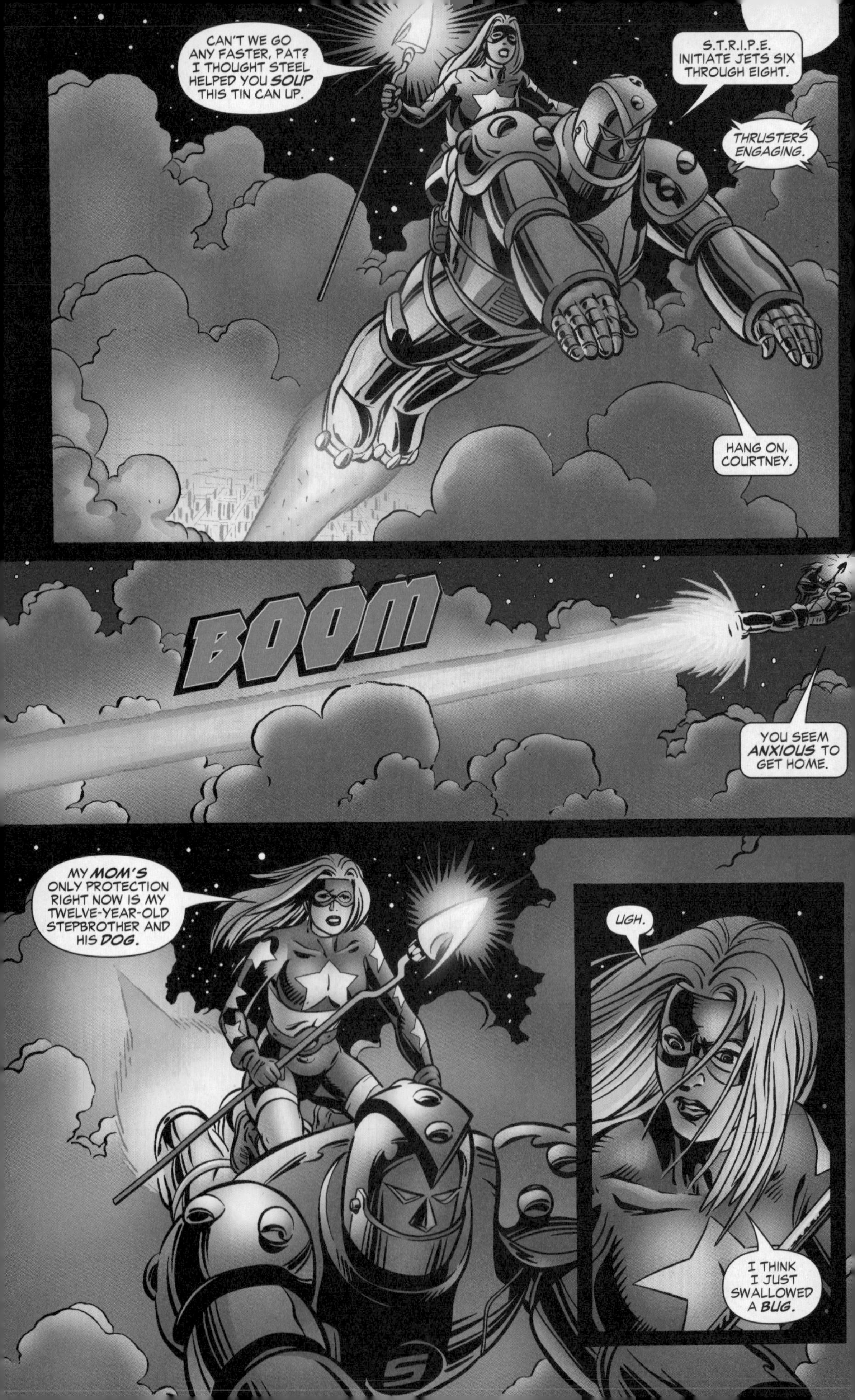
CAN'T WE GO ANY FASTER, PAT? I THOUGHT STEEL HELPED YOU SOUP THIS TIN CAN UP.
S.T.R.I.P.E. INITIATE JETS SIX THROUGH EIGHT.
THRUSTERS ENGAGING.
HANG ON, COURTNEY.
BOOM
YOU SEEM ANXIOUS TO GET HOME.
MY MOM'S ONLY PROTECTION RIGHT NOW IS MY TWELVE-YEAR-OLD STEPBROTHER AND HIS DOG.
UGH.
I THINK I JUST SWALLOWED A BUG.

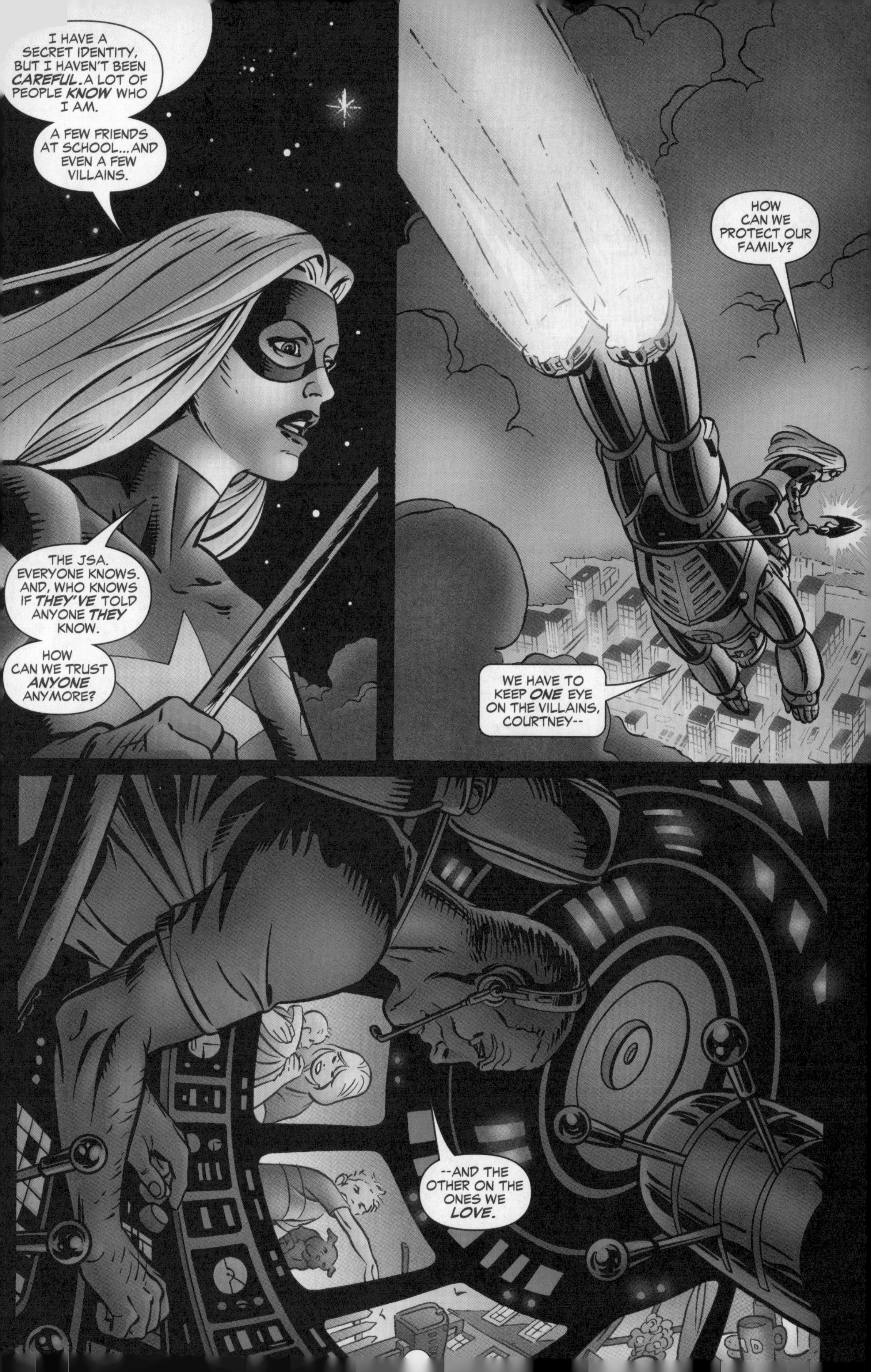
I HAVE A SECRET IDENTITY, BUT I HAVEN'T BEEN CAREFUL. A LOT OF PEOPLE KNOW WHO I AM.
A FEW FRIENDS AT SCHOOL...AND EVEN A FEW VILLAINS.
THE JSA. EVERYONE KNOWS. AND, WHO KNOWS IF THEY'VE TOLD ANYONE THEY KNOW.
HOW CAN WE TRUST ANYONE ANYMORE?
HOW CAN WE PROTECT OUR FAMILY?
WE HAVE TO KEEP ONE EYE ON THE VILLAINS, COURTNEY--
--AND THE OTHER ON THE ONES WE LOVE.

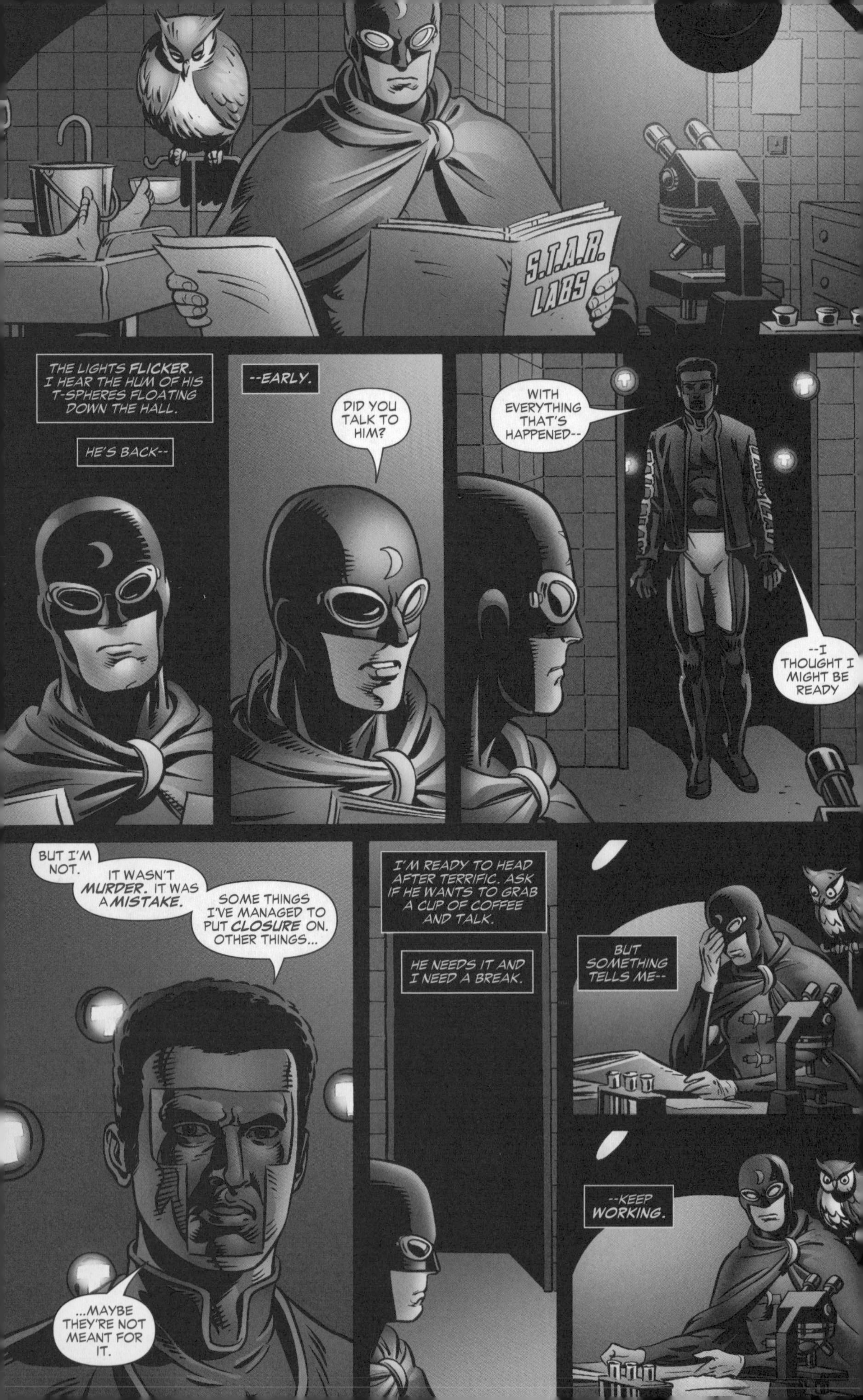
S.T.A.R. LABS
THE LIGHTS FLICKER. I HEAR THE HUM OF HIS T-SPHERES FLOATING DOWN THE HALL.
HE'S BACK--
--EARLY.
DID YOU TALK TO HIM?
WITH EVERYTHING THAT'S HAPPENED--
--I THOUGHT I MIGHT BE READY
BUT I'M NOT.
IT WASN'T MURDER. IT WAS A MISTAKE.
SOME THINGS I'VE MANAGED TO PUT CLOSURE ON. OTHER THINGS...
...MAYBE THEY'RE NOT MEANT FOR IT.
I'M READY TO HEAD AFTER TERRIFIC. ASK IF HE WANTS TO GRAB A CUP OF COFFEE AND TALK.
HE NEEDS IT AND I NEED A BREAK.
BUT SOMETHING TELLS ME--
--KEEP WORKING.

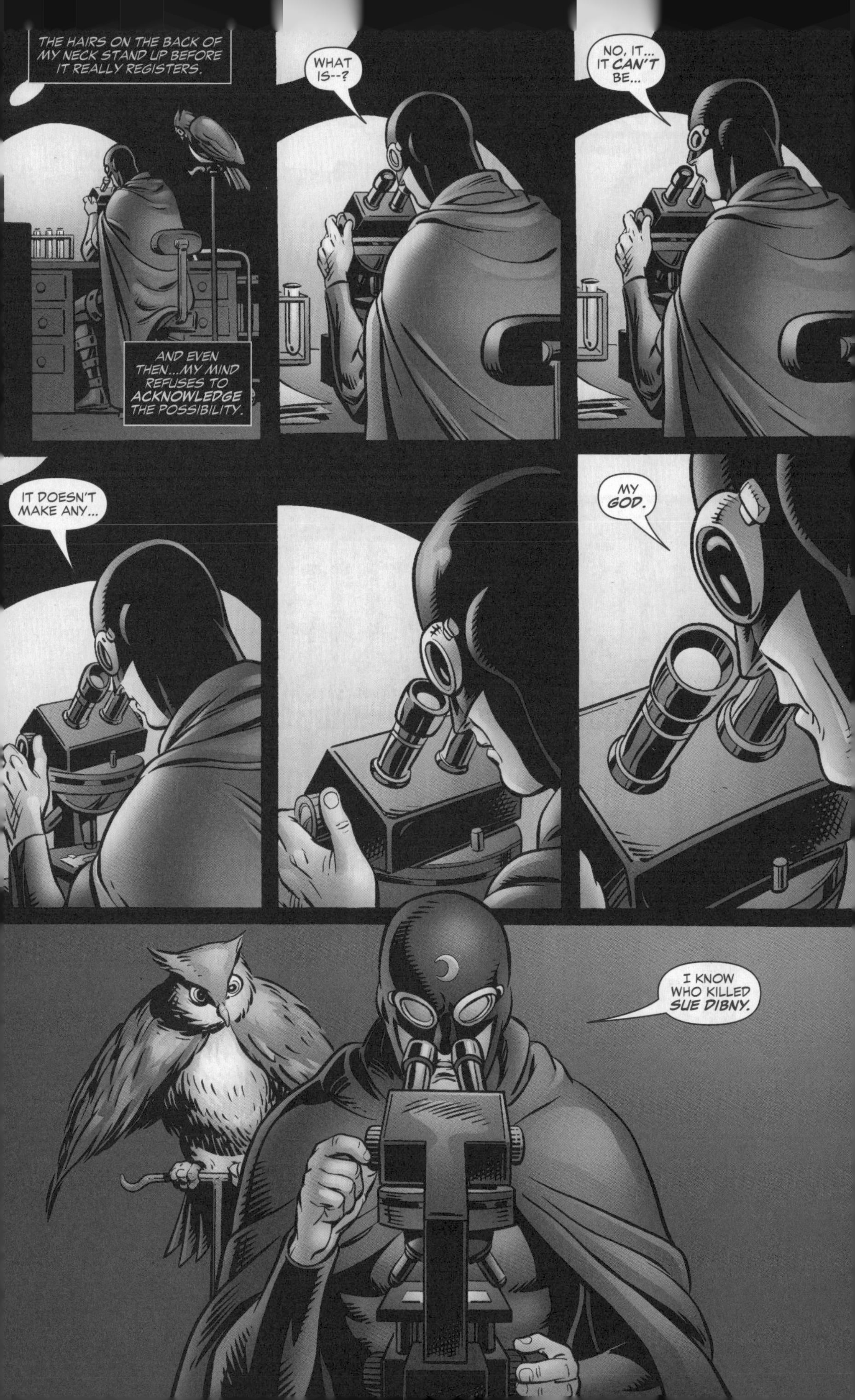
THE HAIRS ON THE BACK OF MY NECK STAND UP BEFORE IT REALLY REGISTERS.
AND EVEN THEN...MY MIND REFUSES TO ACKNOWLEDGE THE POSSIBILITY.
WHAT IS--?
NO, IT... IT CAN'T BE...
IT DOESN'T MAKE ANY...
MY GOD.
I KNOW WHO KILLED SUE DIBNY.

# IDENTITY CRISIS

For fans of just JSA, this volume might end on an odd note. In case you choose not to read the compilation of IDENTITY CRISIS, now in finer bookstores everywhere, we'll spoil the ending right here:

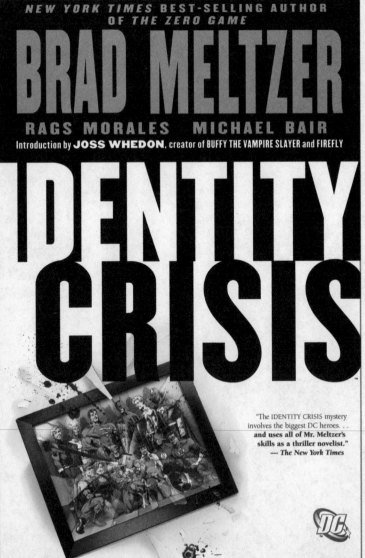

NEW YORK TIMES BEST-SELLING AUTHOR
OF *THE ZERO GAME*

## BRAD MELTZER

**RAGS MORALES    MICHAEL BAIR**

Introduction by **JOSS WHEDON**, creator of *BUFFY THE VAMPIRE SLAYER* and *FIREFLY*

## IDENTITY CRISIS

"The IDENTITY CRISIS mystery involves the biggest DC heroes. . . and uses all of Mr. Meltzer's skills as a thriller novelist."
— *The New York Times*

Jean Loring, the Atom's ex-wife, killed Sue accidentally. Using a spare Atom outfit, complete with size and weight controls, Jean visited her old friend Sue, microscopically entering her brain. The goal was to injure her in her own home, sending a shock wave throughout the super-hero community and reuniting loved ones, including Jean and Ray. Unused to the powers and the biology, Jean caused Sue's brain to hemorrhage. What Dr. Mid-Nite sees in the microscope are tiny footprints – Jean's. Mid-Nite informs J'onn J'onzz who telepathically clues in the rest of the JLA. Jean is subsequently locked away at Arkham Asylum, Gotham City's home for the criminally insane. The Atom, mad with grief, shrinks out of sight and remains out of touch with his comrades. Jean's plan worked, and the various familial and romantic relationships throughout the community deepened.

It also made the villains more aware of the stakes and the lengths to which heroes will go to protect their identities and their loved ones. Those ramifications will be felt throughout the DC Universe, including the JSA.

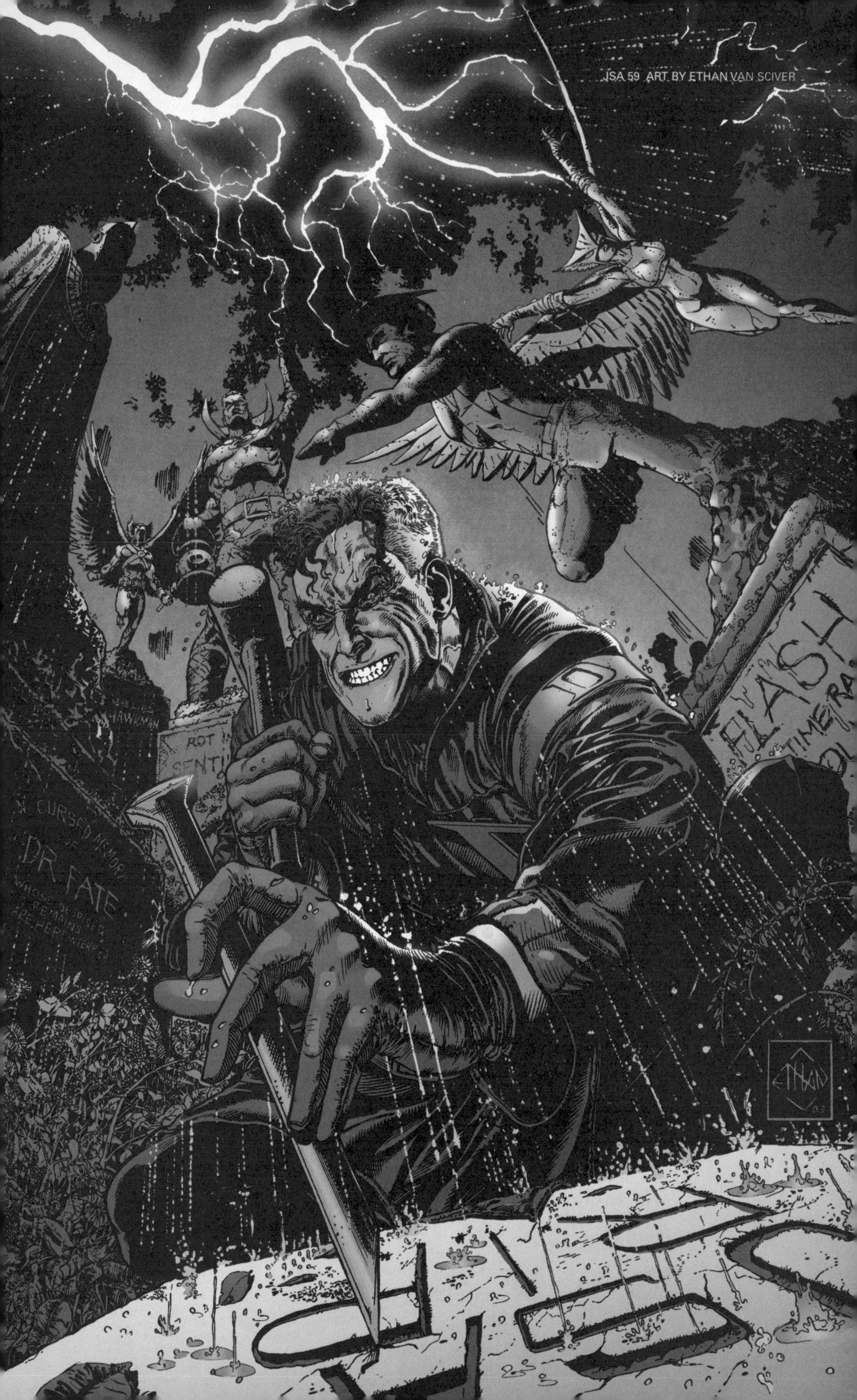

HAWKMAN
DR. FATE
FLASH
ETHAN

JSA 59 ART BY ETHAN VAN SCIVER

JSA 60 ART BY ETHAN VAN SCIVER

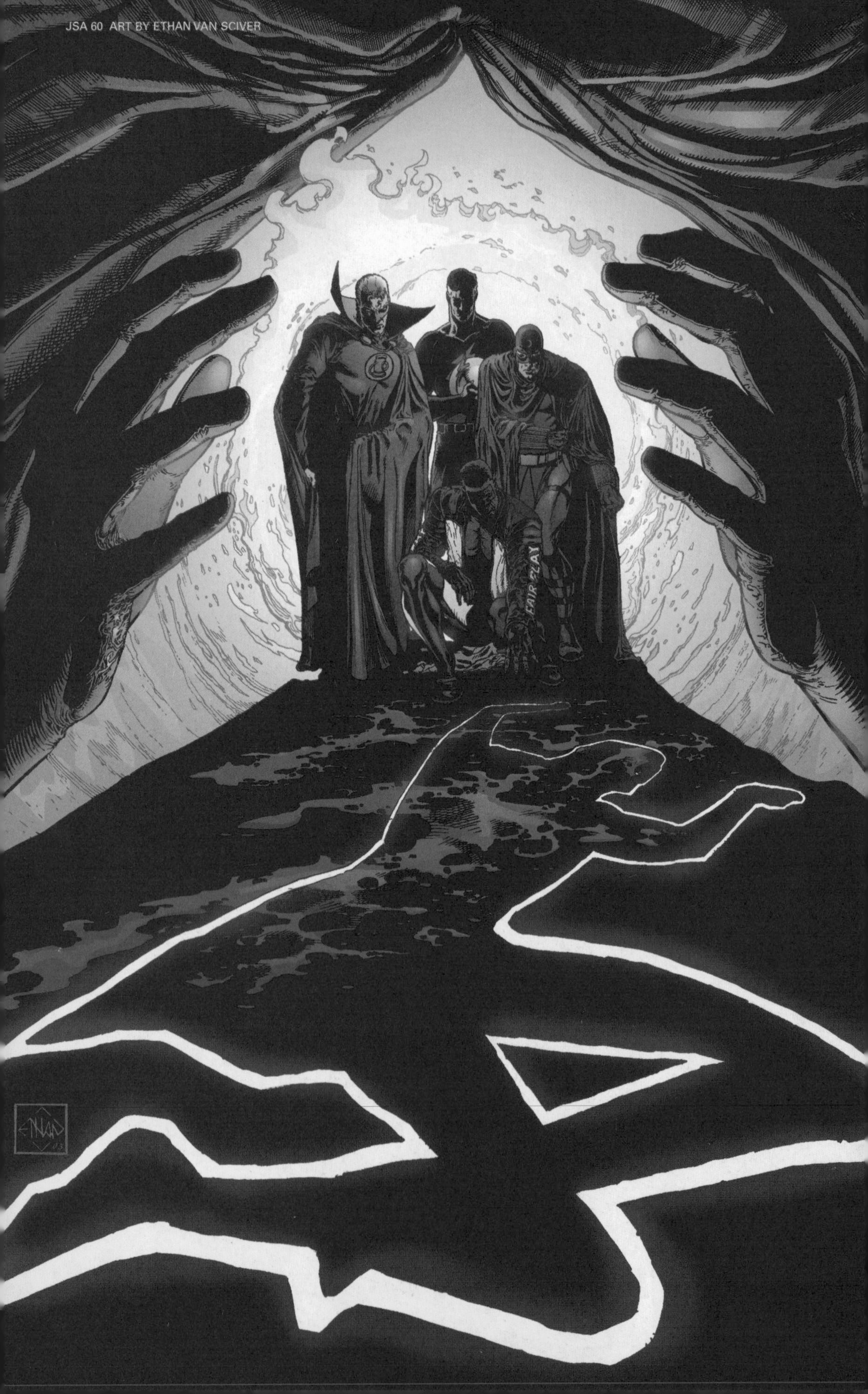
FAIR PLAY

JSA 61  ART BY ETHAN VAN SCIVER

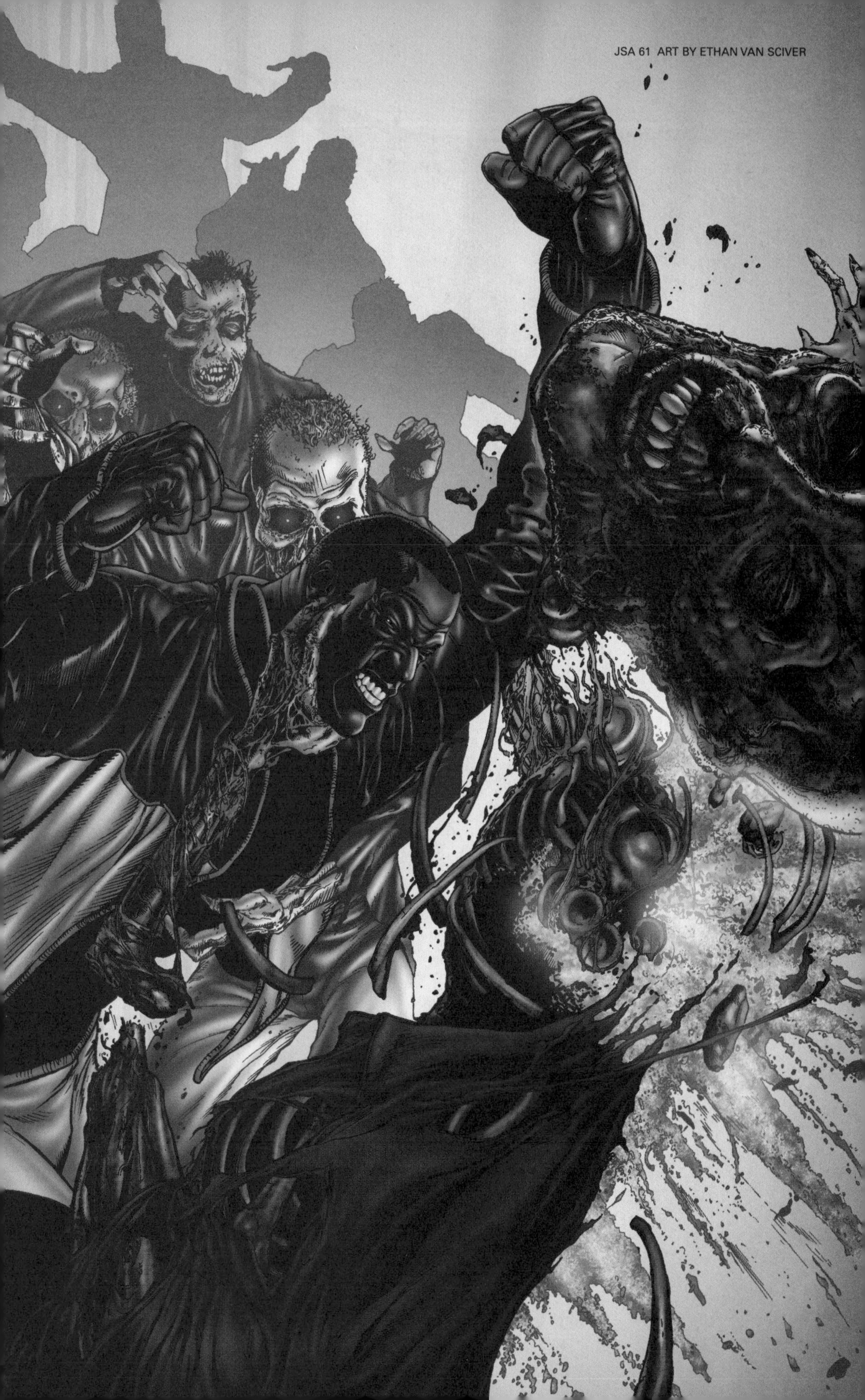

JSA 62 ART BY ETHAN VAN SCIVER

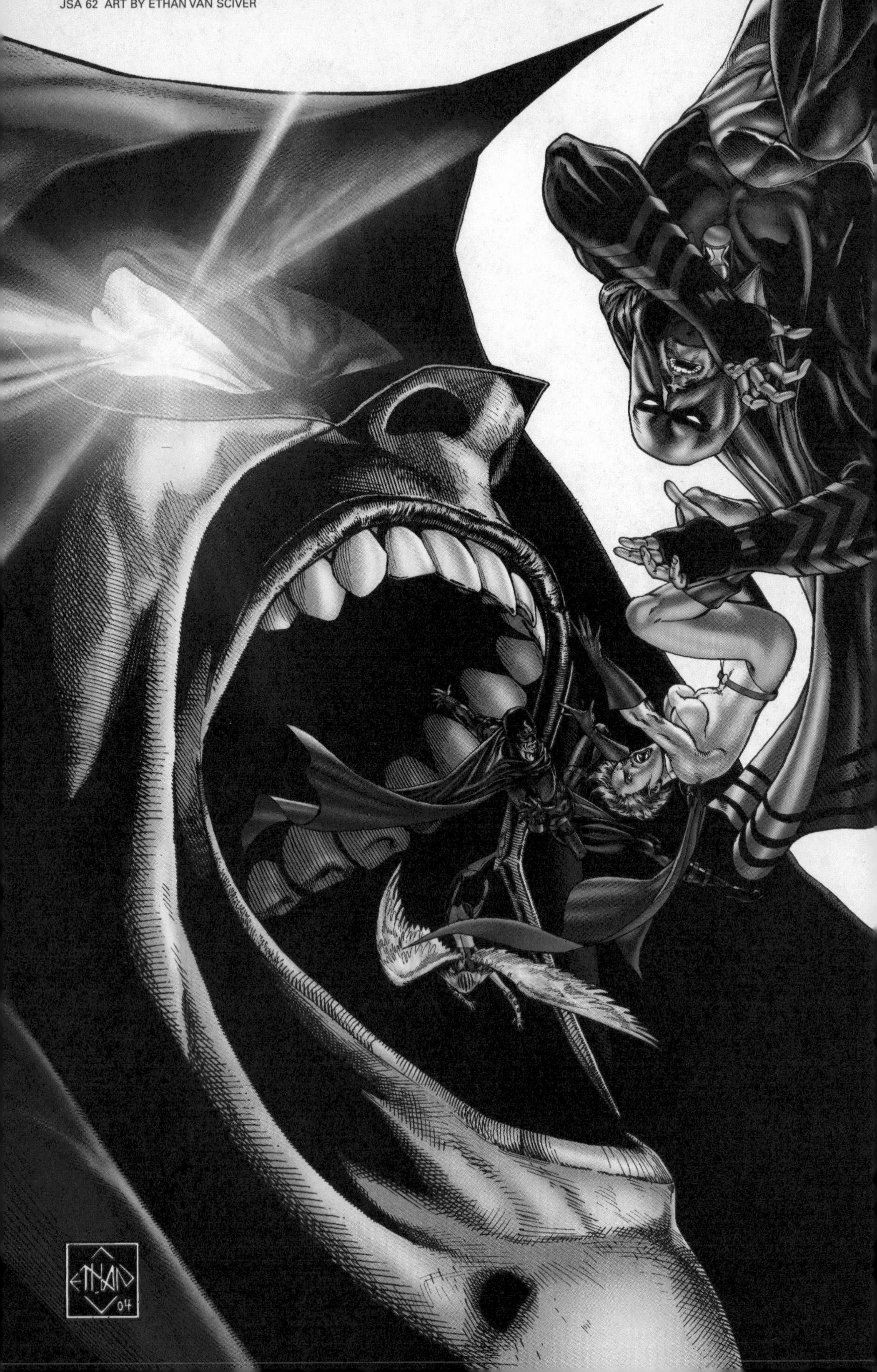

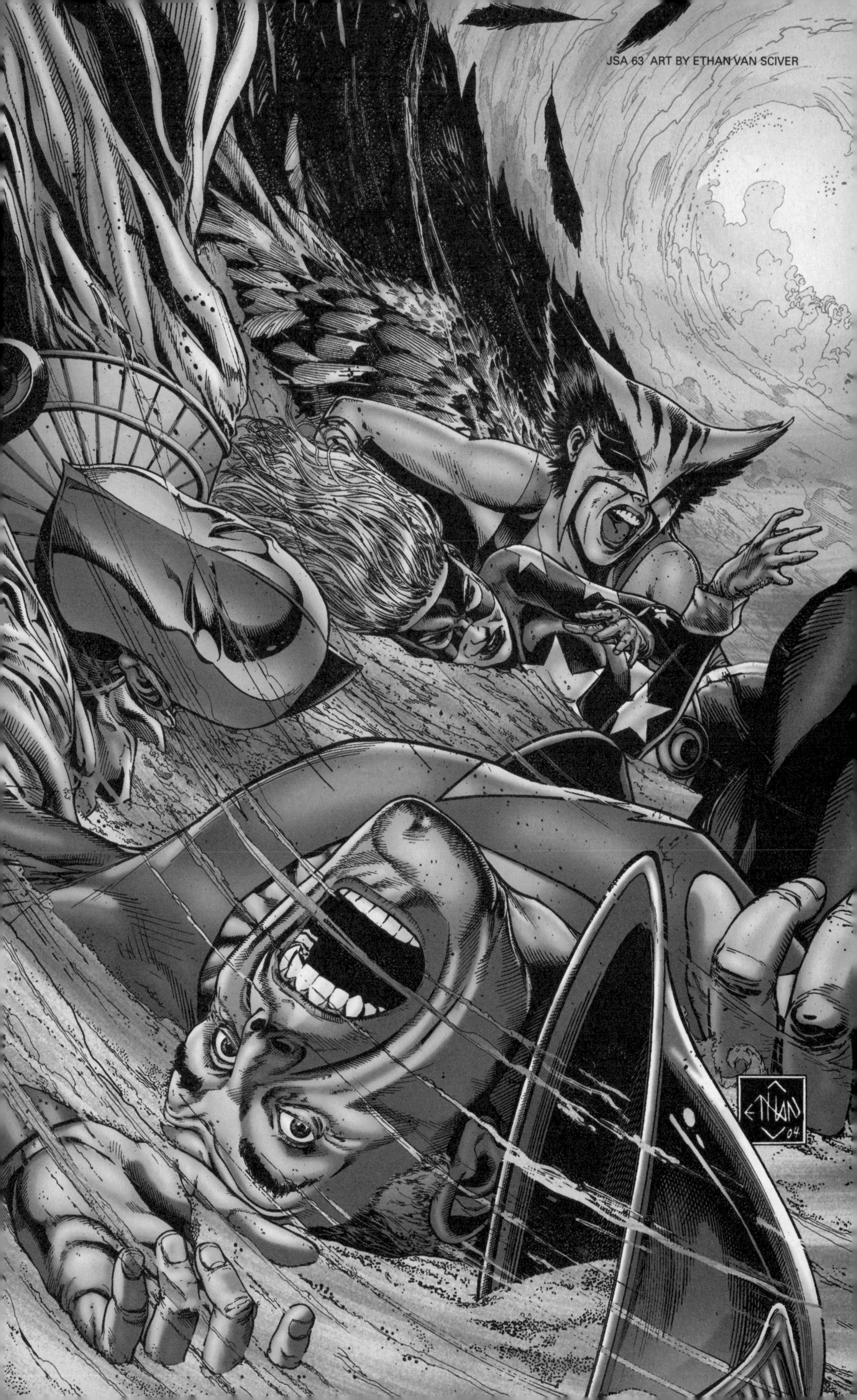

JSA 63 ART BY ETHAN VAN SCIVER

JSA 64 ART BY ETHAN VAN SCIVER

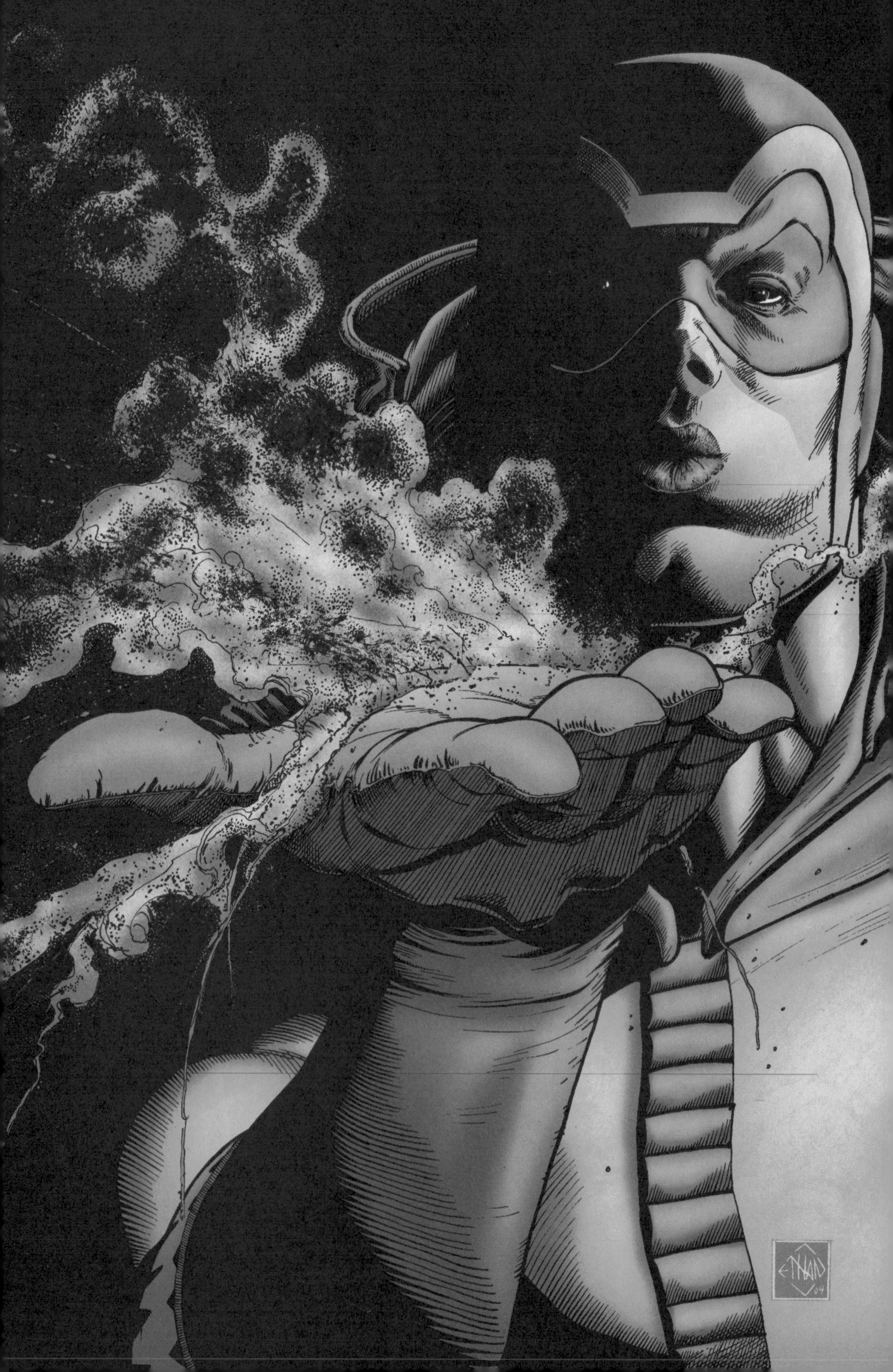

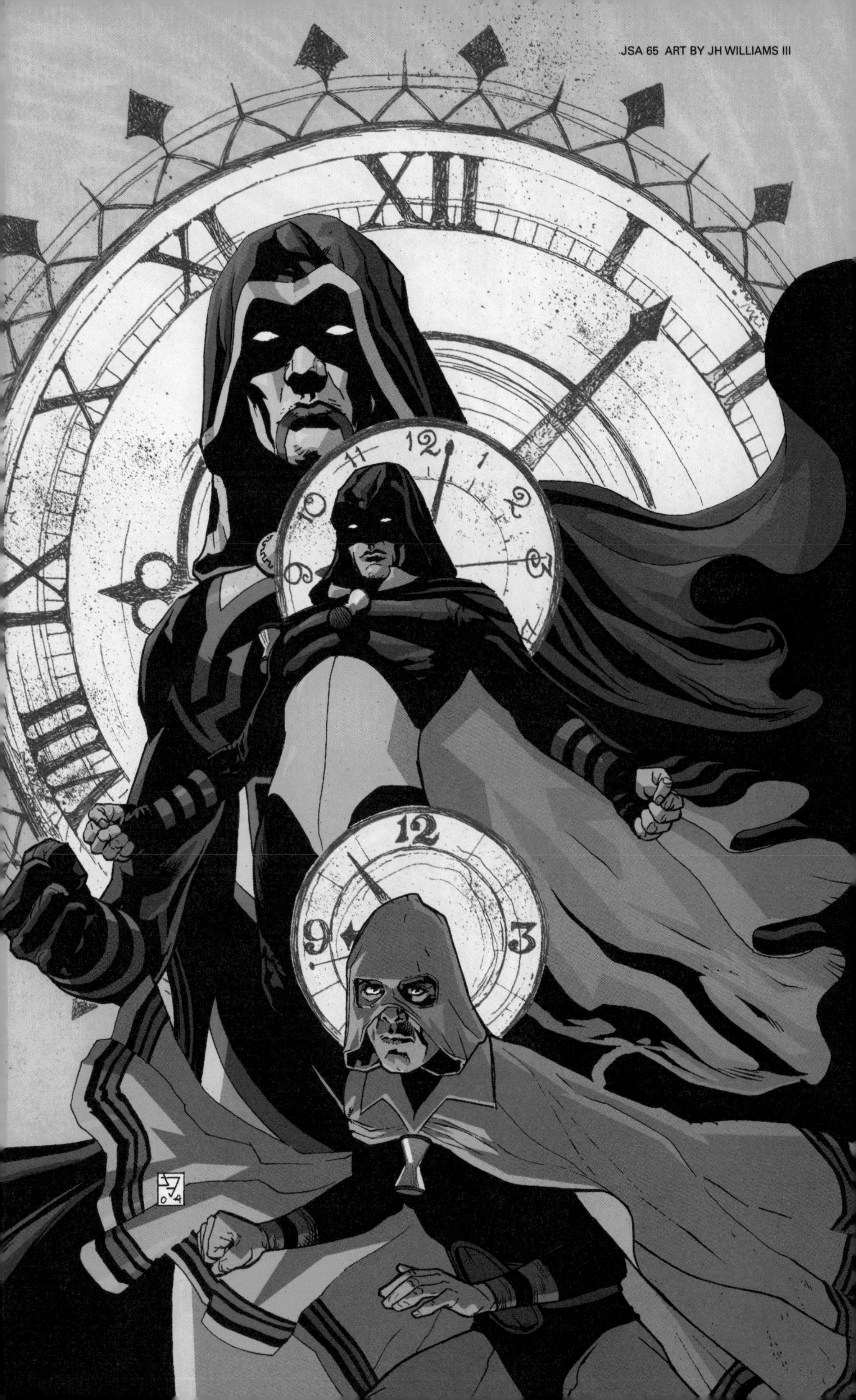

JSA 65 ART BY JH WILLIAMS III

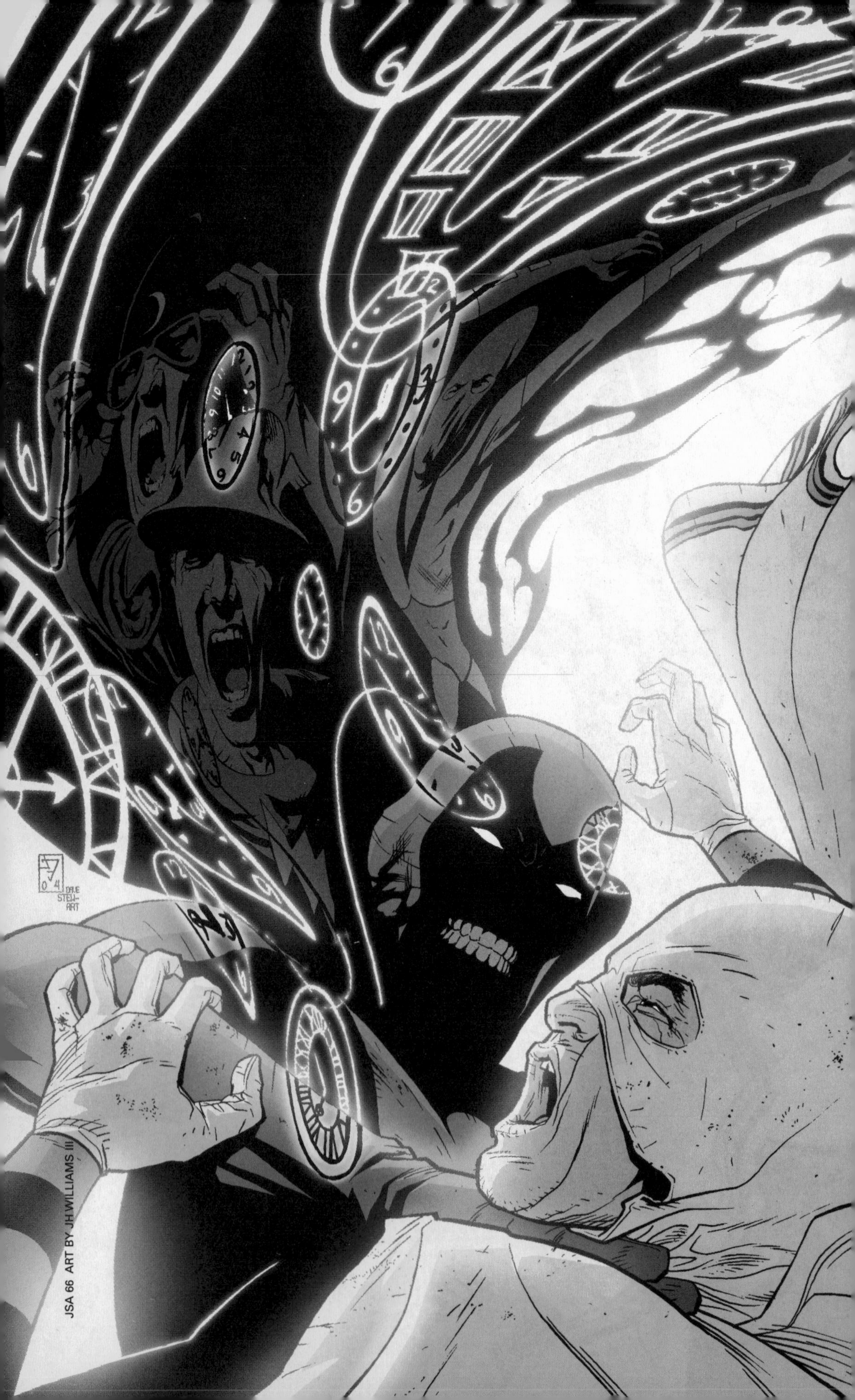
DAVE
STEW-
ART
JSA 66 ART BY JH WILLIAMS III